Train Trips
Exploring
America
by Rail

William G. Scheller

Revised Edition
Includes Canada

The East Woods Press
Charlotte, North Carolina

103569

This book is for Lynne

Copyright 1981, 1984 by William G. Scheller
Second printing

Library of Congress Cataloging in Publication Data

Scheller, William.
   Train trips.

   Includes indexes.
   1. Railroad travel—United States. 2. Railroad travel—Canada. I. Title.
TF23.S28   1984   917.3'04927   83-49037
ISBN 0-88742-000-1

Cover design by Kenn Compton
Photographs courtesy of Amtrak and Via Rail Canada
Typography by Raven Type
Printed in the United States of America

The East Woods Press
Fast & McMillan Publishers, Inc.
429 East Boulevard
Charlotte, NC 28203

Foreword to the Second Edition

The three years that have passed since the appearance of the first edition of *Train Trips* have been important ones for rail travel and rail travelers in North America. Not long after the book was published, talk of proposed federal budget cuts cast a cloud over the future of Amtrak's long-distance route system—but because of public pressure and official recognition of the importance of a healthy passenger rail system, the crisis was averted, sufficient (if not abundant) funds were appropriated, and sails were trimmed in ways that generally did *not* spell out-and-out route cuts. In the succeeding years, Amtrak has not only survived but prevailed. Some trains no longer run, but other routes have come to life for the first time in years. New Superliner cars run on all long-distance routes west of Chicago. The extensive rehabilitation of the "Heritage Fleet" of older coaches, sleepers, and diners is complete. A new generation of single-level, long-distance cars is on the drawing boards. Amtrak has begun running auto-train service from Virginia to Florida, picking up where an unsuccessful private venture left off. Throughout the system, meal service is slowly being restored to pre-austerity levels of quality and graciousness. Americans have decided that their investment in passenger trains is a fair and sound one—after all, highways and airline support services are publicly financed—and that investment is beginning to pay off.

Even while the original *Train Trips* was being written, we were aware that the omission of Canadian routes and cities made necessary by time and other constraints would eventually have to be corrected. We have, thus, included a section on Via Rail Canada in this second edition, covering major destinations along the great Canadian rail pathway from the Atlantic to the Pacific, with directions for connecting services to points north and south.

In addition, this second edition of *Train Trips* includes necessary revisions to the descriptions of U.S. routes and cities. A lot of changes have affected hotels, restaurants, and points of interest between Boston and San Diego, Miami and Seattle, over the past three years; accuracy in a travel guide is a matter of hitting moving targets. If those targets move even more between this writing and the time you read the book, by all means let us know. For now, I hope you enjoy the trains as I do, and that you will find *Train Trips* a useful companion.

Bill Scheller

Amtrak's National R

Legend

Amtrak Train Routes

Connecting Rail Service

○ ○ ○ ○ ○ ○ ○ ○ ○ ○
Dedicated Amtrak Motor Coach Service

★ ★ ★ ★ ★ ★ ★ ★ ★
Seasonal Steamship Service

•••••••••••••••••
Connecting Motor Coach Services

April 29, 1984

Passenger System

Via to Halifax, Sydney and Quebec
Via to Quebec
Via to Ottawa
Via to Winnipeg and Vancouver

Contents

Preface

This book is the result of a year's work, and of more than 34,000 miles of travel on U.S. and Canadian railroads. In a sense, though, it began with hundreds of 17-mile rides on the Erie-Lackawanna Main Line between Paterson and Hoboken, New Jersey, when I was a high school student. That was in the early 1960s, when the E-L still ran passenger service to Binghamton, Scranton, Buffalo, and Chicago. On dark evenings when some after-school activity had cost me my early train connection, I would walk the platforms of the vast Lackawanna terminal in Hoboken, always turning up at the tracks where the *Owl*, the *Phoebe Snow*, and other long-distance trains waited to depart. In the yellow light of the car windows, I could watch stewards and porters getting things underway. With a snap, a fresh tablecloth unfurled; with a push and the turn of a handle, a newly blanketed bed disappeared into a roomette wall. Ahead, a gray diesel throbbed, laying up power against the grades of the Allegheny night. I would walk the length of those trains, out on the platform, and then turn back to the track from which my Paterson local was due to leave. Paterson wasn't very far, but it pleased me to think that the same steel rails that my train traveled went all the way to Chicago, and that the *Phoebe Snow* made the same beautiful, nervous clatter upon those rails as it rode them across the Jersey Meadows. If I had taken the bus to school, this book might never have been written.

So, too, might *Train Trips* have been much more difficult to write had it not been for the assistance of many people, only a few of whom can be acknowledged in the space here. My particular thanks go to John McLeod and Bruce Heard at Amtrak; to Ralph Johansen, Mitch Vlad, Janet Aiton, and the staff of the Canadian Government Office of Tourism in Boston; to Alice Scheller, for her typing of the manuscript and for her stories of life as an Erie clerk in the last days of steam; to Mark Rosenthal and Bill Sullivan; and to the staff members of dozens of convention and visitors' bureaus throughout the United States and Canada, without whom the ferreting out of information about their cities would have been infinitely more time-consuming. Finally, my appreciation must go to all those individuals who, in the darkest days of North American passenger service, refused to let that beautiful, nervous clatter cease.

I. Before You Board

Introduction

"When are you leaving for Chicago?"

"On Sunday. I catch my train at 2:40."

"Train? You mean plane, don't you?"

No, we mean train. But few of us who take them are unfamiliar with exchanges like the one above, or with the querulous stares that frequently follow our insistence that, yes, we are traveling to Chicago—or wherever—on a railroad train. If the rail passenger were to announce that he was going to spend the evening at home looking at the stereopticon, he could hardly expect a more bemused, perplexed, or even patronizingly sympathetic reaction.

And, always, we hear the questions: Why do it? Why not drive, or take a plane? Obviously, trains can't compare with planes if speed is of the essence: when a relative is ill several thousand miles away, when unexpected business travel becomes necessary, when you have a brief vacation and want to spend all of it at your destination. But how often do we fly simply because it's faster—and not because it makes any difference whether we get there sooner? Often, it helps to appreciate the distance between two places, to understand the vastness that separates, say, New York from Los Angeles. People talk about jet lag, but seldom realize that the rapid crossing of time zones and loss of sleep contribute only partly to the feeling of disorientation that often follows air travel. The "lag" syndrome also occurs when your body arrives at Point B while, psychologically, you are still back at Point A. You have no sense of easing into the new environment, of traveling rather than simply taking off and landing. Maybe this explains why all airports look the same; perhaps the sameness of the place they've gotten to and the place they've left is soothing to air passengers.

Rail travel affords a sense of motion, of passage, that can never be a part of jet travel. It gives you an almost simultaneous sense of where you're going, where you are, and where you have been. And, of course, it lets you see the country—not just its beautiful mountains and seacoasts, its lush farmlands and the awesome moonscape of the desert, but the small towns that the interstate highways forgot, the steel mills that gird the underside of Chicago, the dirt farmers' shacks that border southern bayous. Perhaps some of these things are not conventionally pretty, but neither are they conventionally ugly: they are not the strip cities of fast-food outlets and discount stores, not the monotonous acres of plywood, cinder block, and glass that insulate cities from the hinterland. Trains reveal the least homogenized aspects of the American landscape. They have a marvelously abrupt way of entering and departing even the largest of cities—one minute you are downtown, and the next, it seems, you are away in the country.

The advantages of rail over automobile travel are even easier to perceive, and they do not hinge entirely upon the price of gasoline. The car has virtually no edge over the train in speed, especially since the 55-mph speed limit went into effect. Unless drivers took the wheel in shifts and stopped only for gas and food, no car could get from Chicago to Seattle faster than the *Empire Builder*, or from New York to Miami faster than the *Silver Meteor*. And where is the enjoyment in that kind of hell-for-leather driving? The train may not travel much faster than a car, but it moves through the day and night, putting away miles while its passengers sleep, eat, and relax under far less tedious and confining circumstances than those of a car trip—or, for that matter, a journey by bus.

Automobile travel is indispensable for the kind of slow, meandering travel along back roads which allows for unscheduled stops and unplanned layovers. But if you intend to do most of your meandering in an area far from home, why not take the train to a central destination and rent a car once you get there? Some rail package tours even have provisions for discounted car rentals. Or, if you are riding a train with a baggage car, you can bring your bicycle along, and perhaps even pedal to a different station for your return trip. (For details on Amtrak and Via Rail Canada bicycle policies, see the section on baggage in this book.)

But these comparisons of train with other modes of travel and arguments over hasty versus leisurely traveling cannot reveal the true attraction of going by rail. The real delight of a train trip is its peculiar combination of motion and stasis: you know that you are moving, that you are headed somewhere, but you are also living—for however long or short a time—in a separate, self-contained world, in which time may as well have stopped. It is an experience far more different from our daily lives than most vacations afford, and what would seem to be confining is actually quite liberating: you are challenged to use your time as you may never have used it before.

None of this means that train travel is a matter of forced leisure. Quite the opposite: it is possible to get an enormous amount of work done on a train. Business travelers are often quick to dismiss the idea of going anywhere by rail, on the grounds that they just haven't got the time. But many of those extra days in the office before and after a hurried flight to a sales meeting, conference, or trade show might be just as constructively spent on a train, where the traveling businessperson can read reports, draft correspondence and review figures—all without any chance of interruption, particularly from the telephone. It's even possible, in a bedroom or roomette, to work with a portable dictating machine. And all the while, the traveler can mentally prepare for the work at hand at his or her destination.

Of course, even the speed argument fails when the distances are short and covered by frequent corridor trains. While more and more time is pared from train schedules in the Northeast Corridor, air shuttle trips get no shorter, and the traffic between downtown and the airport gets worse. Air passengers must fight their way from midtown Manhattan out to Newark in order to board a plane that will leave them miles outside of Washington; train travelers can board a Metroliner at Penn Station and arrive in the shadow of the Capitol dome.

Those of us who love trains will occasionally point to examples like that of the Metroliner to show that you *can* get there quickly on the railroad, but our hearts aren't really in such arguments. Speed is just a fringe benefit—and more often than not, it is no benefit at all. From time to time the science magazines run stories about a proposed 14,000-mph train that will hurtle through a vacuum tunnel between New York and Los Angeles in just 21 minutes. Twenty-one minutes! No waiter will ask if yours was the pecan pie. No porter will drop a pillow at your seat. No one will amuse the baby while you try to get a picture of a mesa split by sun and shadows. There will be none of the relentless conversation between wheel and rail to lull you to sleep in your berth and, in the morning, none of the cold, heavy pinks and electric blues of a desert sunrise as you crack open your window shade. There will be only 21 minutes aboard a frenetic steel mole.

Well, you won't have to go. By the far-off time that such an extravagant toy is built—if it ever is—New York and Los Angeles will look the same, anyway, and we'll all be able to make conference calls on picture phones. But for now, there are still pots of coffee and cozy roomettes, and decks of cards that say "Amtrak" for sale in the lounge and thousands of miles of the country to see and wonder about—and a chance, perhaps, to come to new terms with yourself as you roll along between here and there. Don't miss it. It's a wonderful way to travel.

One of Amtrak's Superliner coaches. The bi-level cars come in five styles: coaches, baggage-coaches, diners, sleepers and cafe/lounges; they are being phased in on Amtrak's long distance western routes.

A Brief History

In 1929, more than 20,000 passenger trains steamed in and out of American terminals each day. Carrying three-quarters of the nation's intercity passengers, these trains, along with their freight-bearing counterparts, traveled nearly half a million miles of trackage and represented a $26 billion investment. There were 60,000 passenger cars in service. Nor do statistics tell the entire story. The ubiquitousness and romance of the railroad are in the marrow of American popular culture, and in the lore of luxury, only the grand hotel and the ocean liner can equal the magic of the crack limited.

The decline of the private passenger railroads during the 1950s and '60s was swift and precipitous. Although railroads never became irreversibly or necessarily obsolete, like buggywhips, or merely quaint survivors, like kerosene lamps, they were very nearly ignored and mismanaged into an early grave. This and the rash of highway and airport subsidies that accompanied the cheap energy euphoria that ended so abruptly in the early 1970s are a large part of the reason for the passenger train's near disappearance.

It has also been frequently argued (and the argument has some merit) that some of the railroads' troubles were caused by the duplication of services by competing companies running on parallel lines. But the spirit of such rivalries led also to a wide variety of highly touted special services for passengers. No sooner had rail travel passed out of its Spartan adolescence (most pre-Pullman attempts at "sleepers" offered riders anything but a good night's rest) than the industry began fitting out showcase trains with such amenities as baths (and later showers), libraries, barbershops, lounges, and, of course, dining cars. Perhaps no other feature of the crack trains was as dear to railroad company publicists as the diners. Like the proprietors of great restaurants, the roads guarded the secrets of their most renowned dishes. Trains hurtled through the South as their passengers feasted on fried chicken and cornbread, baked on board. The Pennsylvania's *Broadway Limited* had its hot cinnamon buns and demitasse at breakfast, the Southern Pacific its tureens of "Cascade Stew." Sleek transcontinentals made early morning stops high in the Rockies to take on consignments of fresh mountain trout. On the Illinois Central's *Panama Limited*, a dining-car crew of twelve served twenty-two separate entrees.

Innovation followed innovation. Lightweight, streamlined trains appeared, along with glass-domed observation cars and air conditioning. The development of diesel-electric motive power made engine changes unnecessary and eliminated the smoke and cinders long associated with rail travel. As recently as the late 1950s, the larger and more affluent roads continued to order shiny new cars of stainless steel and aluminum for long-distance runs. And the luxuries pioneered on the limited trains of the early 1900s had begun to filter down—by mid-century, nearly anyone who could afford to travel could reasonably picture himself, well-fed and with a comfortable berth waiting, enjoying a drink in a boat-tailed observation lounge as the scenery whipped by at 70 miles an hour.

But even as the streamlined golden age of rail travel began, its eclipse was in the making. Part of the problem had to do with the simple facts of corporate accounting. With the exception of certain premium-priced limited routes, passenger service was not a money-making proposition for the railroads—and even those crack trains represented expenditures in equipment and labor that were not always justified by receipts. Freight service, of course, continued to make money for all but the most poorly managed or superfluous roads. What kept the passenger lines in business was partly the desire for public recognition—the "flagship" principle—and partly the need of people for transportation in an era when private automobile ownership was not as widespread and the highway system not as extensive as they are today and air travel was not yet taken for granted. Also, government legislation began requiring carriers to show cause why certain routes should be dropped from the schedules before such eliminations could be made.

Many observers have charged, of course, that with more aggressive promotion to counter the growing competition from the airlines and the automobile and with elimination of the most undeniably marginal routes, the private roads could have maintained efficient passenger service without sabotaging their freight-supported balance sheets. But the will wasn't there. The decline of the railroads became a self-fulfilling prophecy: as less and less money was spent on upkeep, employee morale diminished, and the companies cut service whenever and wherever the government would allow it. The acquiescence of the Interstate Commerce Commission to some of these route cuts was occasionally sought through somewhat devious means. In their book *All Aboard with E. M. Frimbo: The World's Greatest Railway Buff*, Rogers Whitaker and Anthony Hiss tell the story of one New York State train which carried a sleeping car not listed in the train's timetable. When the company that ran the train applied for permission to discontinue it, they cited as evidence of its unpopularity this sleeper that no one ever used. When asked why the service wasn't listed in the timetable, the company lawyers offered the explanation that a listing was unnecessary, since everyone knew about the service anyway. It was pointed out to the lawyers that the company listed sleepers in the schedules of trains not slated for discontinuance. These revelations proved embarrassing for the railroad, but didn't save the train; it, like so many others, was eventually eliminated.

This loss of enthusiasm for passenger trains on the part of the very firms that ran them was accompanied, in the postwar years, by massive government expenditures for other modes of transportation. These subsidies are often forgotten, particularly by those who argue most vehemently against continued federal underwriting of that portion of Amtrak's operating expenses not covered by passenger revenues. It was government money that built the interstate highway system used not only by private motorists but by the long-distance bus companies, and government money that funds the air traffic control system and helps cover the enormous cost of new air terminals. Passenger rail service is only the most recent, and by far the least lavishly treated, of the major modes of transportation to benefit from government subsidy.

While these changes in attitude and transportation funding were taking place, certain developments were made in rail freight technology that spelled even more trouble for passenger trains. In order to provide freight service more economically, carriers were turning to heavier cars and larger, slower trains. The substantial increase in car weights placed a tremendous amount of stress on the rails, often making them unsafe for passenger trains. Also, the slower speeds that these freights traveled at necessitated the flattening of tracks at curves. No longer banked, those curves could not accommodate speeding passenger trains. Except for brief straightaway runs, the crack expresses that had run at 90 mph and more were frustratingly slowed, victims of an ironic reversal of the usual tendency toward ever-increasing speed in most forms of transportation.

Inevitably, public confidence and interest in the railroads began to fade. The further the companies allowed their equipment and service to deteriorate, the fewer passengers they attracted; the smaller their revenues, the more justified they felt in curtailing service. The prospect of riding dingy coaches over a decaying roadbed at a minimal speed held little attraction when one could take a jet or drive a car that burned gasoline priced at less than 30 cents a gallon. More and more people began to adopt the attitude depicted above—that anyone opting to travel by train must be odd, old-fashioned, out of touch with the modern world.

During this period of our railroads' decline, however, visitors to Europe or Japan found ample evidence that none of these conclusions about train travel had to be true. The railroads in those industrialized nations had never been allowed to deteriorate to the point of being a national disgrace; petroleum and automobile lobbies had never succeeded in squeezing trains out of existence by persuading governments to funnel money into less efficient means of transportation. Instead of getting worse, rail passenger service in those countries got better.

But here in the United States it got worse than worse. Those 20,000 daily trains in 1929 had become only 5,000 by 1950. In 1970, a year which was surely the lowest ebb of American passenger rail service, only 450 trains creaked across the landscape, carrying less than 5 percent of all intercity travelers. One by one, the great "name" trains had been allowed to slip into ignominy and, finally, oblivion—witness the New York Central's famous *Twentieth Century Limited*, limping into Chicago on its last run, in 1967, ten hours late. The American passenger train was about to expire.

The Coming of Amtrak

Fortunately, some individuals both in and out of government realized that a modern industrial nation could not afford to lose one of its principal modes of transportation through neglect. That their voices were heard at all before the time of energy scarcity is cause for amazement; nevertheless, in late 1970 the U.S. Congress passed the Rail Passenger Service Act, which authorized a board of incorporators to set up a corporation which—using public funds—would take over all long-distance and corridor routes that the private roads no longer wished to operate. The entity that they established was the National Railroad Passenger Corporation (NRPC), or Amtrak.

Amtrak took over the trains on May 1, 1971. It was charged with an enormous responsibility, primed for operation with a woefully inadequate sum of money, and equipped with a physical plant—stations, roadbeds, and rolling stock—that would have embarrassed most developing nations. To make matters worse, Amtrak was less than three years old when the first Arab oil embargo made the term *energy crisis* part of our language and sent hundreds of thousands of motorists back to the rails. Tempers frayed as many of these new passengers encountered the antique equipment that the NRPC put into operation to handle this extra load, and exchanges of harrowing Amtrak stories became a feature of social gatherings. However, the crisis and its resulting ridership increase did serve to remind both Amtrak and its federal underwriters that the new corporation had to be more than just a caretaker for a dying industry.

It is worth noting here that Amtrak did not immediately assume responsibility for all of the nation's passenger service; four private firms continued to operate their own long-distance trains. But with the passage of the Southern Railway's *Crescent* into Amtrak's dominion early in 1979, and the Denver and Rio Grande Western *Zephyr*'s incorporation into Amtrak's *California Zephyr* route in 1983, privately operated U.S. long distance service finally became a thing of the past. Of course, local companies and state departments of transportation operate many commuter routes, and there are historic and seasonal excursion trains that run independently. But the vast majority of private carriers were more than eager to turn their passenger service, which had been costing them over $400 million per year, over to Amtrak.

Amtrak began operations in 1971 with fewer than 200 daily trains—exactly one percent of the number that rolled through America just 40 years earlier. Since then, the public company has streamlined schedules by eliminating certain marginal routes, but has revived service in other areas. Virtually every major city in the United States is accessible by train, as are hundreds of smaller towns. There are three east-west routes between Chicago and the West Coast, and as many operating between Chicago and the cities of the Northeast. Trains ply north-south routes on both seaboards and serve the South, Southwest, Intermountain West, and New England.

A similar story might be told about Canadian railroads. By the 1970s, all interprovincial passenger service in Canada was operated by the two giants: Canadian Pacific and Canadian National. Neither the privately owned CP nor the government-backed CN cared very much for the business of running passenger trains, and CP, in particular, was angling to get out of it. But while frequency of service diminished, the major Canadian long-distance trains survived—probably because the population of Canada is largely clustered along its east-west rail routes, and because trains stand up to winter weather better than any other form of transportation. In 1978, a government corporation called Via Rail Canada took over operation of Canadian passenger trains, except for commuter routes and a few private lines such as the Algoma Central, Ontario Northland, and British Columbia Railway. The result is that while some lesser routes have been cut or downgraded to rail diesel car consists, transcontinental service north of the border is alive and well. We'll take a closer look at Via and its routes in Section III of this book.

How Amtrak Operates

The National Railroad Passenger Corporation was not empowered to nationalize the railroads. Freight service remains in the hands of the private carriers, and so do the rights-of-way over which all trains, freight and passenger, must operate. The major exceptions are the Washington-Boston Northeast Corridor, which Amtrak purchased in 1976, and those sections of track maintained by Conrail, a quasi-government firm set up to provide commuter and freight service in the Northeast following the bankruptcy and dissolution of the Penn Central Railroad and several others. Amtrak, then, owns the trains but not most of the track. These trains operate by contract between Amtrak and the private roads. When you look at an Amtrak timetable, you will see a company name in parentheses at the head of the list of station stops for each train. This is the name of the railroad with which Amtrak has contracted to operate that train. In the schedules for trains that cover great distances, you might notice a second and even a third company name. At Denver, Colorado, for instance, the westbound *California Zephyr* leaves Burlington Northern track and enters the right-of-way of the Denver and Rio Grande Western. At such points, train crews also change—because the contractual arrangements call for Amtrak to use the personnel as well as the roadbed of the private companies. The term *train crew* refers to the engineer and fireman, as well as the conductor and his assistants. It does not include dining-car personnel, sleeping-car porters, and other attendants concerned only with passenger services, all of whom are Amtrak employees and remain with the train regardless of which company's right-of-way is being traveled.

American rail passenger service, then, remains a cooperative venture between Amtrak and the private roads. An Amtrak train can only go as fast as a company's roadbed will allow it to and can hold to its timetable only if it meets with no unscheduled interference from freights operating along the same right-of-way. This cooperation is generally undertaken in the proper spirit, and private carriers usually keep such delays to a minimum. Amtrak's suing of Southern Pacific over persistent freight-related delays in the late 1970s is an example of the friction that can develop within this hybridized system of meeting passenger traffic needs, but the Southern Pacific case is much more the exception that the rule. Amtrak's on-time performance record has increased substantially.

One of the most extensive of Amtrak's attempts to upgrade passenger service was the rehabilitation of track in the Northeast Corridor. Corridor trains, which stop at Washington, Philadelphia, New York, New Haven, Providence, Boston, and points in between, serve more passengers that those in any other part of the country. The roadbed along this main artery of the East Coast had long suffered from time and heavy use, with speed, punctuality, and comfort all adversely affected. Now, mile by mile, the old trackage has been replaced with concrete ties (and some new wooden ones), continuous welded rail, and cleaned, newly tamped ballast. Improvements such as these necessarily take time—trains must continue to run while the work progresses—but once completed, they allow substantial amounts of time to be shaved from schedules. Metroliner trains, for instance, can now travel between

New York and Washington in two hours and 49 minutes, which is 40 minutes faster than a few years ago. When the Northeast Corridor is electrified north of New Haven, the trip will be even shorter.

Rolling Stock

Roadbed may affect speed and comfort, but the passenger's primary impressions of any railroad are based on its rolling stock—the coaches, lounges, diners, and sleepers that make up the "consist" of a train.

When Amtrak took on the job of providing rail passenger service, it purchased the equipment that the private roads had been using. Federal funding allotments did provide for the purchase of new cars and locomotives, but neither the company nor its public could wait for the delivery of an entire new generation of rolling stock. The old cars had to suffice. With but few exceptions, this equipment dated from the 1930s, 1940s, and early 1950s, and had hardly received the best of maintenance during the years of declining private passenger service. Frayed upholstery and dirty windows were only the more visible parts of the problem. Older passenger cars were heated—and sometimes even air-conditioned—by steam piped from the locomotive. Individual electric generators and batteries served each car. Failures of these components were commonplace. As a result, passengers often rode in discomfort, and on-time performance became little more than an admirable goal. It was clear that if Amtrak was to attract and keep the patrons it needed to stay in business, its passenger car fleet had to be rehabilitated, as well as supplemented by new stock.

Fortunately, a railroad car is a durable piece of equipment; despite its age and infirmities, it can often be restored to serviceability for less than the cost of replacement. Typically, rehabilitation of an older car costs approximately $300,000, compared to the $1 million price tag for a comparable piece of new equipment.

At facilities such as Amtrak's Beech Grove, Indiana, shops, older cars underwent "head-end" conversion. On a train with head-end power, electricity generated in the locomotive—the "head-end" of the train—powers all functions such as lighting, air-conditioning, and heating. This eliminates the need for failure-prone steam equipment and individual generators and makes repairs, when necessary, much easier. To the passenger this simply means that everything works—that the knobs and switches in the roomettes are not just decorative and that he is not going to be held up outside of Ashtabula while someone checks a steam coupling. Today, all of the older equipment has been rehabilitated, and operates reliably in conjunction with Amtrak's new cars. By the end of the 1980s, though, this "Heritage Fleet" of restored rolling stock is scheduled to be retired in favor of new equipment.

Coaches

Amtrak's new rolling stock has come on line in stages. Since the mid-1970s not a year has gone by without the order or delivery of some of this new generation of cars. Between 1975 and 1977 the Amfleet coaches, now the standard equipment on short and medium-distance eastern and midwestern runs, were put into service.

The distinguishing feature of the lightweight, stainless-steel Amfleet cars is their slope-shouldered aerodynamic profile, reminiscent more of an airplane fuselage than of the tall, boxy coaches of the past. Inside, the carpeted floors, ceilings, and lower walls combine with insulation and air suspension to provide a quiet and comfortable ride. Reclining seats, each equipped with a folding tray table, are more than ample. Although window-seat passengers must duck slightly when taking their seats to avoid the overhead luggage rack, and the top-to-bottom dimensions of the shatterproof Lexan windows are relatively narrow, these are minor drawbacks.

For short-haul routes, the basic Amfleet coach seats 84. The seats, which do not have leg rests, are placed two on either side of the aisle. Rest rooms with washbasin, outlets for razors, and chemical flush toilets are paired at one end of each car, and each train carries a coach equipped with an oversized rest room for handicapped passengers. Long-distance Amfleet coaches differ in that they seat only 60 passengers, and the extra space allows for folding, cushioned leg rests at each seat. These make a big difference during overnight travel. During the early 1980s, these cars were joined by the new Amfleet II 59-seat coaches and lounges. All of the Amfleet II cars have leg rests, and boast larger windows than were used in the original Amfleet design. They point the way towards the single-level sleepers and dining cars which will eventually replace the "Heritage Fleet" in the east.

This new fleet is rounded out by the Amclub cars, which offer somewhat more luxurious seating at a higher fare. Amclub sections (sometimes taking up only one end of a car, sometimes both, but always divided by a central food-service station) feature an off-center aisle separating a row of single from a row of double seats. Club passengers, who must buy tickets in advance, are served meals and beverages at their seats.

Another premium service, provided by Amtrak on the New York-Washington segment of the Northeast Corridor, is the Metroliner. The Penn Central introduced self-propelled electric cars, and they became Amtrak equipment with the PC's demise and the founding of the public company. The Metroliners, now locomotive-pulled coach, snack bar-coach, and Metroclub (single seat on one side of aisle) configurations, can traverse the Corridor's well-maintained right-of-way at speeds of up to 120 miles per hour, thus shaving a half hour or more from regular New York-Washington running time.

A limited number of Amtrak's Turboliner train sets operate in New York State's Empire Corridor. These represent an attempt to apply aerodynamic design and turbine propulsion to rail transportation. Readily identifiable by the sleek, bulletlike snouts of their locomotives, the Turboliners are products of French technology, although a slightly modified second generation has been built in the United States. Their interiors are similar to those found on the Amfleet.

Before 1980, a generation had passed since the last order and delivery of a whole fleet of long-distance railroad passenger cars in North America. But now Amtrak's Pullman-built Superliners have arrived, offering a new era of train travel in the western United States. Although height restrictions will prevent these new cars from seeing service east of Chicago (except for a few short-distance runs in southern Michigan), they now make up the consists of all long-distance western trains.

The Superliners are double-level cars, each a full 16 feet in height. They were built in full-coach, baggage coach, diner, sleeper, and cafe-lounge versions. The coach cars are designed to accommodate passengers traveling longer distances, and have seats on both levels—62 above, 15 below. The upper-level seats are ideal for viewing the western countryside, although the cars do not offer the forward visibility of the old dome coaches. The interior design is also pleasing to the eye; soft beiges, browns, and rust tones, along with subdued shades of blue, have been used for the upholstery and the carpeting on floors and walls. If color schemes seem unimportant, remember that a passenger coach can be your home for up to two days and that it's better to be soothed rather than assaulted by your surroundings.

The seats on the Superliner coach cars are equipped with footrests, leg rests, attendant call buttons, individual reading lamps, and heavy, ample window drapes. A fold-down table, like those on the Amfleet cars, is handy for reading or snacks. Single suitcases may be stored overhead. We might wish for two improvements, though—the seats should have been designed to recline further, and the leg rests ought to lock rather than tighten into position. As it is, they are inclined to slowly settle towards the floor.

The baggage-coach Superliner's lower level contains storage areas for both checked and unchecked baggage, rest rooms and entry vestibule.

The full-coach and baggage-coach Superliner cars have four private rest rooms on their lower levels; fold-down tables for changing infants are a useful feature in these. Also, each car has a women's lounge with private toilet. The cars are entered through the lower-level vestibule, from which a carpeted staircase ascends to the upper-level seating area. Passage from car to car is on upper levels only.

The Superliner cars are equipped with hydraulic suspension that enables them to smooth out uneven sections of track. They are designed to travel in excess of 100 miles per hour, although current operating conditions restrict them to lower speeds.

Amtrak, of course, continues to depend upon the refurbished equipment of its "Heritage Fleet" to make up the consists of many of its trains. Although three manufacturers—Budd, Pullman-Standard, and American Car and Foundry—built the vast majority of this rolling stock, sharp eyes can discern any number of different car configurations on American rails, even beneath the standard "platinum mist" Amtrak color scheme and interior reupholstering. Unlike the new Amfleet coaches, most of the older units feature small smoking lounges adjacent to the men's and women's rest rooms at either end. On the Santa Fe's old "hi-level" coaches, now Amtrak property, these facilities are located along with carry-on baggage space on the lower of two levels, with the upper reserved exclusively for coach seats. In recent years, these cars could frequently be found on the *Southwest Limited* between Los Angeles and Chicago and on the Los Angeles-New Orleans *Sunset Limited*. Fortunately, the hi-levels are compatible with Superliner equipment. They have been converted to head-end power and will be used for years to come.

Dome cars are an endangered species. These were originally ordered by those railroads whose routes traversed areas of spectacular western scenery, and, prior to the arrival of the Superliners, were kept in service by Amtrak on those runs. They feature a glassed-in observation level accessible by a short flight of steps and furnished with day-use seats without leg rests. The new Superliner lounge-cafes, however, serve a comparable function. According to present plans, those dome cars that survive will probably go into service on the Alaska Railroad between Anchorage and Fairbanks. A few also are used on long distance trains in the eastern United States. Some have recently been assigned to the *Auto Train*, to the Washington-Chicago *Capitol Limited* and to the *City of New Orleans* from and to Chicago.

Dining Cars

Snacks, drinks, and light meals aboard Amfleet trains are provided in the Amcafe and Amdinette cars, built to the same specifications as the all-coach units but equipped with central service counters. These are not full-service dining cars like those coupled into the transcontinental trains; they usually offer only sandwiches, hamburgers, and beverages. (Beer, wine, and liquor are served on all Amtrak trains.) Attendants can use microwave ovens for preparing hot items. On the Amcafe cars, passengers bring their purchases back to their seats; Amdinette cars are furnished with booths and a slightly more extensive selection of hot foods—for instance, short ribs of beef or spaghetti and meatballs. On cars of both types, coach seats (usually designated for smoking) take up the remainder of the space.

Like the rest of the newest generation of rolling stock, the 39 Superliner dining cars are built on two levels—kitchens below, seating above. Dumbwaiters convey food to and from the upper-level service area. With this arrangement, the entire upper length of the car is available for dining; 72 diners can be comfortably seated, and it is no longer necessary to stand in the narrow corridor alongside the galley while waiting for a table. (On the "Heritage Fleet" diners, the galley occupies about one-third of the car's length, and 12 four-person tables take up the remainder. Reservations for seatings are often used to prevent the need for stand-up waiting, although corridor "traffic jams" can still occur in busy seasons.)

Many a restaurant would do well to emulate the simple, elegant atmosphere of the Superliner diner. The simple lines and harmonious, earth-toned color schemes of the other cars are continued here. Amtrak has even had new high-impact ceramic tableware—off-white with brown trim—supplied to match the upholstery and linens in these new diners.

Downstairs, the kitchen is equipped with both microwave and convection ovens, as well as grills, warming tables, refrigerators, and dishwashers, all run by electricity. Not long after these cars first started rolling, the new austerity program caused a shift to all-microwave cooking. But on-board meal preparation has been making a limited comeback, and it looks as if the fine galley equipment on the Superliners will see service after all.

Sleeping Cars

In its single-level "Heritage Fleet" sleeping cars, Amtrak offers three basic types of accommodations—roomette, slumbercoach, and bedroom, with bedroom suites available on a limited number of sleepers. Don't look for the old upper and lower fold-down, green-curtained Pullman berths, famous in movie comedy scenes and still found on some lines outside the United States. Amtrak did not continue any of these cars in service.

Each roomette is a marvel of efficiency. It seems impossible that a space less than seven feet long and not much more than a yard wide can contain so many useful features. Yet it does—and without creating a sense of claustrophobia. The two ample mirrors, adequate lighting, high ceiling, and large window in each compartment no doubt help to minimize any cramped feeling.

Made up for day use, a roomette contains an upholstered chair with fold-down armrests. Opposite the chair is a toilet, the cushioned cover of which makes a comfortable footrest or second seat. At night, a turn of a handle on the wall behind the chair brings down a bed which takes up the full length of the room. When folded down into place, the bed covers not

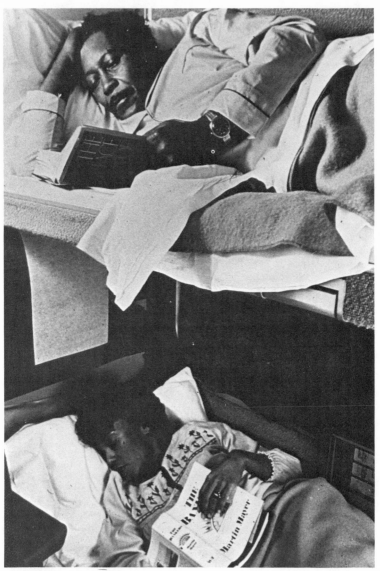

An Amtrak bedroom.

only the chair but the toilet as well. To use the toilet during the night, the bed has to come up; there is no way around it. On some cars, the bed has a small cutaway at one corner which allows you to lift or lower the bed without opening the door. If this feature is not present, the bed takes up nearly the whole space and you must back out into the hall when rearranging the bed. Modest passengers can take comfort, however; an outer curtain as well as a sliding door separates each roomette from the corridor. This whole process, by the way, is not nearly as irritating and time consuming as it no doubt sounds.

In addition to the bed, chair, and toilet, each roomette contains a fold-down sink with hot and cold running water, an ice-water tap and cup dispenser, a shelf for towels and personal effects, a full-length closet that can accommodate two mens' suits, an outlet for razors and hair dryers, individual heat and air conditioning controls, a fan, overhead and mirror lights, a combination reading lamp-night light, a button with which to call the porter, a little hanging caddy for eyeglasses, and something called a shoe locker, which is accessible not only by a door within the compartment but by one opening onto the corridor. (If you have a particularly attentive porter—or if you have asked to have your shoes shined—be sure not to forget the requisite and well-deserved tip.) There are, doubtless, roomette features that have been overlooked here. One of the high points of a long-distance train trip is to settle into bed after having used every one of them at least once. (If you need help, don't hesitate to call the porter.) The sleeping-car beds are comfortable, and are supplied with fresh linens, two blankets, and two pillows. Passengers can have themselves awakened by the porter at a specified hour (with free coffee or tea, if desired), but the best way to wake up early on a train is to leave the window shade open a crack and let morning sunlight over unfamiliar terrain do the job.

A Slumbercoach berth is essentially a smaller version of the standard roomette, although some sleep two in upper and lower berths. It's easy to spot a Slumbercoach by its staggered rows of windows, which reveal the alternating upper and lower arrangement of the compartments. Although somewhat more Spartan than other sleeping accommodations, these are less expensive and are ideal when the entire trip takes place between late evening and early morning. They also have private toilets and washbasins. They are not in service on all long-distance trains, as their numbers are limited—travelers should check schedules or ask ticket agents about Slumbercoach service on specific routes. All now operate in the Eastern part of the United States.

Bedrooms are designed for two people. Each has a separate, walk-in toilet compartment. Berths are upper and lower; the upper berth must be opened by a train attendant. Two basic room designs prevail. In one, passengers sit by day in two separate chairs. In the other, a long sofa is provided. The back of this sofa folds down to become the lower berth.

Larger accommodations on older Amtrak cars are the bedroom suites which can be created by folding back a panel separating two regular bedrooms.

Although a few all-bedroom cars remain in service, especially on Amtrak's *Auto Train*, by far the most common arrangement is the ten-roomette, six-bedroom sleeper. A central corridor separates the roomettes and then turns to one side to allow access to the bedrooms.

The double-level sleepers built as part of the new Superliner fleet represent a major departure from previous designs. Some new luxuries have been added, and, surprisingly, some have been taken away, at least in the economy accommodations.

Each Superliner sleeper has 21 separate rooms—14 economy (10 upper, 4 lower), 5 deluxe, 1 economy family and 1 for handicapped passengers. Unlike the roomettes on older cars, the new economy rooms sleep two people in upper and lower beds. The upper bed folds down from the ceiling (this can be done without the assistance of a porter) and is reached via two carpeted steps. The lower bed is formed by sliding the seats of the room's two cushioned armchairs toward each other and covering them with the mattress pad, sheets and blanket which are stored in the upper berth.

This extra accommodation, however, has been provided at the expense of the private toilet and washbasin—occupants of economy bedrooms must use one of the five rest rooms located on the lower level of Superliner sleeping cars. The absence of these facilities has been the only serious cause of complaints among users of the new cars. However, Amtrak is also installing an upper-level restroom, amont other improvements, on all of its Superliner sleeping cars.

The five deluxe bedrooms, all of which are located on the upper level, can sleep three people comfortably. Seating consists of a long sofa and a swivel armchair. At night, the sofa folds out to become a three-quarter-size bed, and an upper berth folds down from above. There is a sink and a three-way mirror, and also a private toilet. The small room that contains the toilet is also equipped with a hand-held spray shower.

The economy family room, which sleeps five, and the handicapped room, which sleeps two (handicapped person and companion), are located at opposite ends of the lower level of each Superliner sleeper and occupy the full width of each car. This is possible because car-to-car passage is by the upper levels only; as in the Superliner coaches, there is a central stairway and a lower-level entry vestibule.

Seating in the economy family bedroom includes a long sofa, a reclining armchair, and a smaller chair opposite the recliner. As in the deluxe bedroom, the sofa folds out into a double berth, and a single full-length berth folds down from the upper part of the wall. Two smaller berths are provided for children. The economy family room has no private bath, although it is located on the floor with the public facilities.

The handicapped passenger's room has been designed so that a wheelchair may enter through the door and make a complete turn once inside. The lower berth is formed by sliding together two chairs, as in the economy bedroom, and another berth folds down from above. The private bath is complete with toilet, sink, mirror, grab handles, and curtained window. The room's electrical outlet can power a portable respirator. Attendants provide meals for handicapped passengers, since they are confined by the stairwells to the lower level.

Certain features are common to all Superliner bedrooms. There are speakers for a public-address system ("Our estimated time of arrival in Seattle . . ."), also designed to play music when the passenger wishes; a folding tray table, which makes eating or writing much less of an adventure than it was in the old roomettes; and high-intensity lamps that allow one occupant to read while the other sleeps.

Lounges

Of all the "Heritage Fleet," Amtrak's lounge cars are most likely to reflect their original owners' idiosyncrasies. These cars have been carpeted and reupholstered, but their floor plans and seat layouts continue to vary. Some have movable chairs, some only fixed benches and banquettes, but all now have booth seating for light meals. Fortunately, most have round cutouts in their tables to hold cups and glasses secure as the train sways. Each lounge has a buffet counter, bar, and attendant. Superliner trains, of course, carry Superliner lounges. On the upper level is a small service bar, ample seating on banquettes and swivel chairs, and windows that curve up into the ceiling to offer the best railroad view since the days of the dome cars. The lower level includes booth and lounge seating and a service area for light meals.

Motive Power

With the exception of dyed-in-the-wool rail buffs, most passengers do not give much thought to the "head end" of their trains—the locomotive. Everyone knows that roughly between 1945 and 1960, the dirty and wonderful steam engines went off to wherever it is that machines go when they have finished their lives, and that they were replaced by sleek, snub-nosed diesels. On all but the electrified sections of Amtrak right-of-way and the routes given over to the turbo trains discussed earlier, these diesels and their successors are the system's mainstay for motive power.

The term *diesel* is something of a misnomer; the accurate term is *diesel-electric*. These machines do burn diesel fuel, but the similarity between them and the trucks and automobiles that share that appetite ends there. In a diesel truck or car, the explosions that move the pistons turn a crankshaft, which transfers motion through a differential to the drive wheels. In a diesel-electric locomotive, this translation of energy into motion is less direct. Each of these units is actually an electric power plant on wheels: the diesel engine turns a generator, which creates electricity. This electricity runs the powerful electric motors that drive the wheels of the locomotive. A smooth, even application of power to the job at hand is thus assured, with less likelihood of strain being placed on the engine. A multi-speed, automobile-type transmission is unnecessary. When the situation requires—for long trains or the negotiation of steep grades—two or more diesel-electric locomotives can be coupled together to provide the needed horsepower.

At its inception, Amtrak acquired locomotives in the same way that it acquired its other rolling stock—by purchasing or leasing from the private railroads. The motive power available then consisted primarily of engines in the old F and E series, identifiable by a more rounded profile at the cab end. As these represented the first generation of diesel-electrics that took over from steam, it was apparent that purchases of new equipment would have to be made. The engines that have come into service on Amtrak routes during the past ten years, most of which are capable of developing about 3,000 horsepower, have been designed with the requirements of contemporary passenger service in mind—most specifically, the need for an on-board electric generator to provide the head-end power for lighting, heating, and air-conditioning in new and converted cars. A squarish, angular front profile distinguishes these units, most of which belong to the F40PH class—although a handful of P30CH locomotives operates in the Southwest.

All-electric motive power has slowly changed with the maturing of Amtrak. On the electrified right-of-way that reaches from New Haven, Connecticut, to Washington, D.C., all Amtrak trains are electrically powered. On these, pantagraphs draw the current used for propulsion from overhead wires. For nearly half a century, the workhorse of the Northeast Corridor was the massive, slope-shouldered GG1, designed by Raymond Loewy for the Pennsylvania Railroad in 1934. The last of the GG1s was built in 1943; incredibly, these half-million-pound machines provided reliable power for Amtrak trains until the early 1980s. Their replacements are the 6,000-horsepower General Electric E60CP, and the remarkably efficient new General Motors AEM-7. Providing 10,000 horsepower and capable of pulling express trains such as the Metroliner at 125 mph, the AEM-7 has been nicknamed "Mighty Mouse" by its crews.

Stations and Ticketing

Working with—and replacing—the aging rolling stock left over from the last years of private passenger service was only one of Amtrak's initial problems. Many of the stations that the new corporation inherited were virtual ruins, fit only for pigeons and derelicts. Station service was frequently erratic or nonexistent. A turnaround has been made possible by increased ridership and by a program of refurbishment and, when necessary, replacement, often with the cooperation of local governments and transportation authorities.

In the late nineteenth and early twentieth centuries, railroad transportation was so important that the stations built in American towns and cities were often among the largest and most impressive public buildings. In those days, of course, traffic and revenues supported such palaces. But when train travel became unpopular, the very size and expense of the old stations worked to their disadvantage. The growth patterns of our cities also contributed to the problem. As communities expanded outwards, the downtown neighborhoods where railroad terminals were usually located fell into decay. Thus, shabby stations gave passengers an entrée into the shabbier parts of the cities that they served, making railroad travel even less attractive.

Many of the old stations were simply torn down as part of urban renewal projects. Ask a cab driver today why a station is located on the outskirts, and he's likely to tell you about the one that "used to be right downtown." Now that the movement toward downtown revitalization and architectural preservation has come into favor, many venerable stations have been "recycled" to accommodate new functions. Unfortunately, these do not usually include train service, which instead is relegated to new stations on the outskirts.

Because of the expense of maintenance, other old stations, though still standing, have been closed and replaced by smaller new structures built alongside or within their grandiose predecessors. Omaha and Pittsburgh are two cities in which this has taken place. Coming into either city and encountering the cheerful little prefabricated depot and the darkened hulk alongside it, one has the sense of coming upon both a bygone civilization and its successor. Not all new stations are insubstantial; many have been built which incorporate most of the conveniences of the traditional facilities (not including bars and restaurants) without the colossal investment in marble and terrazzo.

Amtrak has made a commitment to provide certain basic services in all of its stations, old and new. Passengers will find stations open at hours when

A busy Friday afternoon at Union Station, Washington, D.C.

trains are arriving and departing. Cleanliness of waiting areas and rest rooms has improved; however, the extent of this improvement can vary. There are always storage lockers, although sometimes not enough (if all station lockers are filled, try a bus depot, if one is nearby). Best of all, it is nearly always possible to purchase tickets, make reservations, and obtain information at station ticket counters; only at small, remote facilities and larger terminals during late evening and early morning hours does this continue to be a problem. Stations served by late trains will usually keep at least one ticket window open until traffic has cleared the station; if not, tickets may be bought on the train. (If an on-board ticket purchase is made during hours when service is available at the station, a three dollar surcharge is added. Also, conductors are not authorized to sell special round-trip excursion tickets when these are available at stations.) If you need tickets or specific information and are not certain whether ticket windows will be open when the train that you wish to take leaves, you should visit the station ahead of time during working hours.

Amtrak also maintains a toll-free telephone number, (800) USA-RAIL, for information and reservations (local numbers for major cities are included as an appendix to this book), but interest in rail travel has grown so rapidly that operators and lines are sometimes unavailable, especially during peak travel months. Amtrak is aware of this problem and has made improvements, but in the meantime you may find your call put "on hold."

Whether your inquiry is made in person or by phone, you'll find that reservations are less of a problem than they were in what was otherwise the golden age of rail travel. When Amtrak took over passenger service, there was no nationwide reservation service. Now, using video display computer terminals, a ticket agent or telephone information operator can give you an immediate report on the availability of accommodations for the time and route that you are requesting. Reservations are required for all sleeper and club-car bookings and for coach travel on trains described in the Amtrak timetable as "all-reserved." When you make reservations, you will be informed of the deadline for actual ticket purchase; after that time, the reservations are automatically canceled. Cancellations on the part of the passenger should be made as soon as plans change. A service charge is levied on cancellations not made or made within thirty minutes of departure.

The failure of some passengers to make cancellations sufficiently in advance, or to make them at all, does have its positive side. On many trains—particularly the Florida routes in winter or the western routes in summer—sleeping accommodations must be made far in advance. If you discover when making your reservation that all sleeping facilities are booked, you can still check with an agent before departure for any last-minute cancellations. Even after you have boarded the train, it's a good idea to ask the conductor if anyone has failed to show up for a reserved bedroom, roomette, or slumbercoach berth. If any are available, you can pay the extra fare and secure your sleeper accommodation. This is not recommended as standard practice—it's always best to reserve well in advance—but if you should suddenly rebel at the idea of a night spent in coach, it doesn't hurt to ask.

Ticketing can be more than a simple matter of buying passage from point A to point B. While sales of the USA Railpass were discontinued some time ago in the United States—the pass may only be purchased abroad, by foreign travelers—round-trip excursion fares are available between most points, along with an enormous variety of special package tours, which can include hotel accommodations and admissions to sporting and cultural facilities as well as rail travel. Tour offerings change from season to season; any travel agent handling Amtrak bookings will be able to provide brochures outlining the latest packages.

The round-trip excursion fares generally apply to specific times: for instance, in the Northeast Corridor between New York and Boston, travel on excursion-rate tickets is not allowed after 11 A.M. on Fridays or Sundays. This doesn't mean that you'll be barred from the train during those hours, but you will have to make up the difference between the excursion and one way rates. Most excursion-rate round-trip tickets also restrict passengers from making stopovers during a trip. Payment of regular one-way fares entitles the ticket holder to stop anywhere along the route for as long as he or she wishes as long as the trip is completed before the expiration date on the ticket. (This does not apply to Metroliner routes in the Northeast.) However, passengers traveling in all-reserved coaches or on sleepers must make specific reservations in advance. For instance, if you are going from Chicago to Los Angeles on the *Southwest Limited* and wish to stop off in Kansas City and Albuquerque, you will pay only the basic one-way rate between your point of departure and final destination—*but* you will have to let the ticket agent know how long each of your layovers will be and exactly what sort of accommodations you will require for each leg of the trip. Charges for sleeper bookings are calculated separately from the base fare and added on, regardless of whether there will be stopovers along the way. Amtrak's brochure, "All About Amtrak Fares," available from travel agents or from Amtrak Distribution Center, P.O. Box 7717, Itasca, IL 60143, explains the regulations governing off-peak, 30-day, and 40-day excursion rates.

Amtrak has been offering special "All Aboard America" fares. In this program, the United States is divided into three zones—east, central, and west. Passengers may travel within any single zone for a set price, for 30 days, with one stopover permitted in each direction, in addition to the destination. Additional fees entitle the traveler to cover two zones or even the entire country. Consult Amtrak or one of its travel agents for latest details.

The Amtrak system is designed to interconnect with other rail and bus services for travel to places not directly served by Amtrak. Amtrak ticket agents are generally authorized to book a traveler's complete itinerary over such interconnecting routes, charging whatever rates have been set by the cooperating carrier.

Planning Routes and Making Connections

While today's railroad traveler is not faced with the enormous selection of routes and schedules offered by private carriers 40 years ago, the choice is sufficient to make advance planning worthwhile. Before purchasing tickets for a trip, stop at a travel agency or Amtrak station and pick up a copy of the National Train Timetables. This free 64-page booklet includes schedules for all Amtrak trains, information on connecting carriers, station addresses, sample fares, and a system map. The timetables are issued several times each year, so be sure that you are consulting the latest edition. While schedule changes are usually minor (unless new routes have been introduced), connections can sometimes be affected. If you plan in advance of the publication of the timetable that will apply when you make your trip, leave room for possible adjustments.

Amtrak ticket agents will book travel over whatever route and with whatever stopovers you wish, but quoted fares apply only to direct routes, or to the most direct combination of connecting routes if through service is not available. For instance, if you wish to travel from Chicago to New Orleans, the standard fare applies to a seat on the *City of New Orleans*, the most direct route between the two cities. But if you want to visit a friend in San Antonio along the way, you'll be riding the *Eagle* into Texas and making a connection on the *Sunset Limited* for New Orleans. This is a more circuitous route, and it will cost a bit extra. Of course, you can specify the *City of New Orleans* for your return trip to Chicago, thus saving both time and money and avoiding a repeat of the scenery you saw on the way south. (As of this writing, there's a twist to this particular connection: the *Sunset Limited* runs only three times a week, which could influence the date of your arrival or the length of your stay in San Antonio.)

Scenery can also be an important consideration in choosing between alternate routes. If you're going from Chicago to Los Angeles, you can use this book and an Amtrak map to decide between the northern route of the *California Zephyr*—the plains, Rockies, Sierra Nevada, and Bay area, followed by a trip south on the *Coast Starlight*—and the more direct route of the *Southwest Limited*, with its views of the New Mexico and Arizona deserts.

Timing can also affect your enjoyment of scenery. The most sublime vista in the world may as well be the refineries in New Jersey if it's pitch black out and you're asleep. Amtrak's long-distance trains operate on once-daily schedules (the *Sunset* and the *Eagle* are thrice-weekly trains), so there is unfortunately no way to avoid darkness along certain scenic stretches. The *Pioneer*, which runs between Seattle and Salt Lake city, rumbles through Idaho in the wee hours, and there's nothing to be done about it. But when alternate routes are available, you may wish to weigh the daytime scenery of one against that of the other.

There is one instance in the Amtrak system of a choice of day or night services on parallel routes between two cities. These cities are New York and Montreal, and the routes are the *Adirondack* and the *Montrealer*. The *Adirondack* is the day train, and the scenery it offers is just what the name implies, along with some fine views of Lake Champlain. The *Montrealer* is a good way to traverse the distance between the two cities overnight, but travelers enchanted with the idea of a train ride through Vermont should count on seeing little more of that state than its celebrated moonlight.

On shorter, heavily traveled routes, trains are often scheduled at intervals throughout the day. Examples include the Northeast Corridor and the corridors between Los Angeles and San Diego and Chicago and Detroit. Such schedules not only assure the option of daylight travel for sightseers, but give business travelers the opportunity of arriving at their destinations at the beginning of a work day, rather than getting there the night before and taking a hotel room.

Amtrak's on-time performance record is respectable, but unforeseen difficulties can still cause a train to run late. You will avoid disappointments if you arrange your itinerary to include as few "cliffhangers" as possible. In fact, Amtrak agents will not write tickets for connections involving a long-distance train arrival and a layover at Chicago's Union Station of less than one hour unless specifically requested to do so by the passenger—in which case, no responsibility for the connection is assumed by the company. Decide for yourself which arrangements are most comfortable. If you are traveling from Los Angeles to Chicago on the *Southwest Limited*, for example, and plan to head on to New York, weigh the *Southwest*'s Chicago arrival time of 3 P.M. against the 4:50 P.M. departure of the *Broadway Limited* and the 6:20 P.M. departure of the *Lake Shore Limited*. The *Lake Shore* is the better bet if you want a little more time in Chicago—maybe for a quick visit to the Art Institute or a stop at the Berghoff for bratwurst. (All times quoted are per winter 1983–84 timetables.) In cases where the timetable indicates a *guaranteed connection*, Amtrak is obligated to reimburse passengers for accommodations should the connection be missed.

As noted above, Amtrak provides information in its timetables for some interconnecting bus and rail lines. If the connection you have in mind is not listed, check with a travel agent or with an agent of the company providing the service regarding schedules. It's always better to plan for layovers in advance.

Having worked out all of your routing and scheduling details and confirmed them through Amtrak's computer reservation system, you may find it useful to prepare an itinerary showing places and times of departure and arrival of each of the trains that you will take. This itinerary will serve as a useful reference during your travels, and you can keep track of your progress.

The accompanying chart on the following page is one example of such an itinerary.

Baggage

Most stations served by long-distance trains are equipped to handle checked baggage. Not all baggage need be checked. Coach passengers are allowed to carry on two pieces of personal baggage, so long as an excessive amount of space is not required. For sleeping-car patrons, the limits are obviously set by what will fit into the compartment. One medium-sized and one small bag is usually plenty—remember that you have to get in there yourself.

Up to three pieces of baggage may be checked without charge on long-distance trains offering this service. Each piece should not exceed 75 pounds, nor the whole consignment 150 pounds; otherwise, shipping charges can be assessed. If you have items to be checked, you should be at the station at least a half hour before the train's departure time. Baggage handlers will not accommodate last-minute arrivals.

Bicycles may be brought on board as part of an Amtrak passenger's baggage allowance. Each bike counts as one of the three pieces of baggage allowed per person. This policy extends only to trains in which there is a baggage car and to stations at which baggage is handled. In other words, even if your bike is accepted as baggage on a long-distance train, you must plan to get off at a stop at which personnel are available to remove baggage. Timetables list those points at which baggage is not handled. Amtrak also has rules regarding the packing of bicycles—handlebars must be parallel to the frame, and pedals removed; also, all bikes must be properly boxed. Inquire ahead as to whether boxes are available at the baggage department of your local depot (there is a small charge); otherwise, you will probably be able to find a suitable box at a bike shop. VIA Rail Canada has a similar bicycle policy, although they do not require that bikes be boxed or partially dismantled.

Because of the limits on carry-on baggage, and because rummaging through several weeks' supply of clothing and paraphernalia is no fun when you're standing in a coach aisle and reaching into a luggage rack, it makes sense to pack the things you'll need while on the train in a small, separate bag or in an easily accessible corner of your suitcase. This will require only a few minutes' thought before you leave and can save a lot of aggravation during the trip.

Sample Itinerary

Train	From	To	Date	Leave	Arrive
Lake Shore Limited	Boston	Chicago	5/4	5:15 P.	12:51P.5/5
California Zephyr	Chicago	Denver	5/11	2:10 P.	7:00A.5/12
California Zephyr	Denver	Reno	5/17	7:30 A.	7:50A.5/18
California Zephyr	Reno	Oakland	5/19	7:50 A.	2:50 P.
Coast Starlight	Oakland	Los Angeles	5/25	8:30 A.	6:55 P.
Southwest Limited	Los Angeles	Kansas City	5/31	7:45 P.	6:40A.6/2
Southwest Limited	Kansas City	Chicago	6/6	6:55 A.	3:00 P.
Lake Shore Limited	Chicago	New York	6/6	6:20 P.	1:30P.6/7
Colonial	New York	Boston	6/7	3:13 P.	7:41 P.

Note: the scheduling information in the above itinerary is given only as a sample. While it corresponds to Amtrak timetables in effect at the time of this writing, readers should remember that these timetables are subject to change.

Time on the Train

A transcontinental journey on the rails takes roughly three days, not counting stopovers along the way. For most people, any trip of more than a few hours' duration is likely to raise the question: How do I spend all that time?

It isn't the business of guidebooks to suggest ways of filling every minute of a traveler's day—but because time spent on trains is so different, so completely free of outside demands, a few suggestions might be of help to all but the most passively contemplative passengers.

The first thing that occurs to most of us is reading. The train is a wonderful place for reading. But unless you are bent on getting one particularly engrossing book finished, or are poring over work- or study-related material, it's a good idea to plan ahead so that you will have a varied reading list and can switch books to suit your moods. Don't go overboard—there's no room on the train for half your library. One good plan is to think about the books that you've been wanting to read and bring along two or three that represent clear differences in content and style. You might want a serious history or biography for morning and a light novel for the drowsy afternoon stretches. Magazines and books of short stories are good for when you want to read something from beginning to end over a short time. A book about the place you're headed for—or passing through—might be a welcome choice. Select whatever appeals to you, but be realistic: if *The Origin of Species* or *Silas Marner* has sat unread on your shelf at home for years, don't sequester yourself on the train with the same volumes, thinking you'll have a change of heart. Pack along the Darwin or Eliot, but include some alternatives that you're more likely to read.

The train is also a good place for doing a little writing of your own. You might consider beginning or continuing a personal journal. The grist for your mill is all around you: you are traveling through places that you perhaps have never seen before (and actually seeing them, not just cloud formations or the exit signs on an interstate highway), meeting new people, and enjoying a leisure that is impossible in the world of responsibilities, telephones, and failure-prone possessions. Start simply by describing things and making notes on conversations; after a while, your sense of your surroundings—the train, its passengers, and the entire trip—will grow more acute, and your journal will begin to contain more complex and subtle observations. You can also get quite a bit of letter writing done on the train, providing that your correspondents can forgive the lapses in your penmanship caused by occasional rough stretches of roadbed.

The simplest train activity is, of course, looking out the window. Some travelers are content to watch whatever passing scene the trip affords, and some like to anticipate the sights by following their routes on a map. Most paperback atlases nowadays are prepared with the motorist in mind, and rail routes are not likely to be indicated. If you do find a map or atlas that shows where the tracks run, remember that each route will be designated according to the company that owns the right-of-way—in other words, the lines will not be marked "Amtrak." To find the route your train is taking, check the Amtrak timetables or this guide to see which company's track your train is traveling over. Then locate that company's main line from city to city along your route. If your map does not show railroads, you can get a rough idea of the course you're following by finding your station stops and playing "connect the dots." Many main-line rail routes follow major highways—or rather, the highways follow the tracks, which were laid first. The *Lake Shore Limited*, for instance, parallels the New York State Thruway to Buffalo, US 20 in Ohio, and I-80 to Chicago. The *California Zephyr* roughly follows I-80 to Denver, US 6 to Salt Lake City, and then I-80 again to Oakland.

If you want to look inside rather than out, several "car-spotting" guides are available to help you. They are usually available in the bookstores at larger stations. By looking up a car's number in these guides, you can learn when and for which railroad company the car was built. (Numbers are printed on the doors and sides of cars and should not be confused with the changeable numbers assigned when each train's consist is made up.) Of course, this information varies only with the pre-Amfleet and pre-Superliner rolling stock that Amtrak purchased from its predecessors. Occasionally, you may run into a traveling rail buff who can color in a good deal more of the history and variety of Amtrak's older equipment.

However you spend your time on the train, the days will pass most pleasantly if you vary your activities. One of the distinct advantages of railroad travel is that you are not bound to your seat for the duration of the trip; on longer routes, you can leave your coach or sleeping compartment and walk to the diner or lounge. As the day begins, you might wish to make a rough, informal plan of how to pass the hours—so much time reading; a break to write a letter or an entry in your journal; coffee and conversation in the lounge; lunch; then a few pages of a different book or a look at your maps and travel guides. The best part of such an impromptu schedule is that there is absolutely no need to follow it if something else comes along. You may meet another passenger with whom you would like to talk, become mesmerized by the mountains, coast, or desert, or simply fall asleep. A word of caution on naps, however. One of the easiest things in the world is to sleep on a train during the day. It may be the rocking motion; it may be the sense of complete suspension in a world of schedules and responsibilities. Whatever the reason, it's certainly pleasant. But the problem, on long trips, is that a day given to sporadic naps can lead to a restless night—particularly if you are sleeping in a coach seat. It helps to be tired when you settle in for an evening's rest on a train. So if you find yourself tempted to nod off frequently while riding the train, resist—if only for the sake of a good night's rest.

Meals

On trips of more than a few hours, meals become a consideration. You have two alternatives. You can buy your food on the train, or you can pack it along. Bringing your own food is easy enough if only one or two meals are called for—something simple, such as sandwiches and some fruit, is all you'll need. Beverages are available in the lounge or cafe. But if economy dictates that you pack your own food for a longer trip, a bit more planning is in order. First of all, you will have to bring things that do not need refrigeration and that do not take up too much room. (For easy access, keep all of your food in a small day pack or in a plastic bag in one corner of your luggage.) This list should give you some idea of foods that fit these requirements.

—Cheese, preferably hard, aged varieties.

—Smoked, seasoned luncheon sausages, such as Thuringer, Cervelat, Landjaeger, or summer sausage. Go to a delicatessen or butcher shop dealing in German specialties—the clerk should be able to recommend meats that need little or no refrigeration.

—Dense rye or whole-grain breads, preferably unsliced. These pack well, take very little space, can be sliced as desired, and are quite filling. Bring along a pocketknife and, if you have some room in your knapsack or suitcase, a thin board—in case you ride in a car without folding trays at each seat. If you do use one of the trays, be careful not to damage it with your knife.

—Carrots. These will stay fresh if kept in a plastic bag.

—Apples and oranges. Anything softer, such as plums or ripe pears, can get messy. Fruit is a bulky item, so bring only as much as you think you'll need. Nearly all Amtrak cafe cars sell apples and oranges, so you may want to spend a few extra cents and save the trouble of carrying them aboard.

—Chocolate bars. If for no other reason than that you deserve a small reward for economizing so thoroughly. In warmer weather, select the no-melt, "tropical" bars available at camping-supply stores.

The alternative is to purchase your meals on the train. There are three basic types of Amtrak food service. The least elaborate, found on short-haul corridor trains, consists of snacks, sandwiches, and beverages sold at a central counter in one car of the train and carried back to the seating areas by passengers. These facilities are microwave oven-equipped for hamburgers and hot dogs; for health food fans they usually stock yogurt and dried fruit and nuts. Coffee, tea, milk, soft drinks, beer, wine, and cocktails are available.

The next step up is the "Amcafe" service on medium-distance trains, such as the *Montrealer*. Amcafe cars have booth service in addition to the take-out counter. There are usually a couple of hot entrees available at dinnertime, microwave-prepared airline style. Breakfast and lunch offerings are basic. (The club car service on Metroliner and other Northeast Corridor trains is in a separate class, with continental breakfasts and Amcafe-type lunch and dinner entrees served at the passengers' seats.)

Full-service dining cars are employed on long-distance trains. No aspect of the golden age of railroad travel has been praised more lavishly than the sumptuous diners, but these had nearly all faded into memory by the time Amtrak took over. The new management knew they belonged to an era which could not be brought back. Instead of trying, Amtrak ran a simple, but quite satisfactory, operation in which galley crews prepared meals to order—no microwaves—for reasonable prices. Tables were graced with linen, stainless flatware, china, and fresh carnations.

The budget cuts of 1981 hit Amtrak passengers right in the stomach. Almost overnight, the niceties disappeared. They were replaced by meals that could have dropped straight out of a 747, served all-courses-at-once on plastic trays. Linen and stainless gave way to paper and more plastic. The pretty blue china coffeepots also vanished.

That was the bad news. The good news was that passengers did not accept these changes without complaint, and that Amtrak's new president, W. Graham Claytor, is a member of the old school which holds that it should be possible to get something decent to eat on a long-distance train. Little by little, things have improved. Breakfasts on the longer routes are cooked to order once again. Prime rib made a comeback in 1982, along with 10-ounce

Passengers enjoy the scenery from the Superliner lounge/cafe which operates on Amtrak's long-distance western trains. (Amtrak Photo)

New York strip steaks that are grilled to the passenger's specifications. Other entrees, though still not made on board from scratch, are at least starting to show more variety—roast boneless loin of pork, vegetable lasagna, regional seafood, and shrimp Louis at lunch. Best of all, courses are now served separately and in sequence, rather than crowded onto a single tray all at once. There are insulated carafes of coffee at each table, and the stainless flatware is back. Prices are still within reason—the steak, as of January 1984, sells for $10.25. The price includes vegetable and potato. There still may be some need for progress, but the dark days of '81 are behind us.

Traveling With Children

Rail passengers who are apprehensive about bringing along small children should remember that the main cause of squirming and tempermentalness on airplane, bus, and automobile trips is simple immobility. The same freedom of movement that makes long-distance passenger train travel appealing to adults assures a more comfortable and relaxing experience for youngsters as well. This is not to say that children should be given the run of the train and allowed to rove endlessly up and down the aisles, since few things are as annoying to other passengers. Besides, unguarded toddlers can fall easily if the train rocks. But trips to the lounge or diner help break travel monotony for children, and can be spaced, along with naps and other activities, throughout a day on the train.

If the child is old enough to read—and if he or she likes to read—a book or two is the best activity. Games should be confined to those which do not require boards (although small magnetic checker sets are handy) or a large number of small pieces. Card games are a good choice. The same rules of compactness and simplicity should apply to toys, since elaborate playthings wind up hogging luggage space and spilling over into the aisles.

One way to help children pass their time on the train enjoyably is to tell them whatever you can about the cities and terrain outside the window. A little narration, coupled with the ever-changing scenery, can keep young riders' interest up. You don't have to play tour guide or know everything there is to know—just point things out, and ask the children to do the same. Make a game out of looking for elk in the Cascades, or ask them how they think tumbleweeds got their name. The possibilities are as endless as the array of things you'll see from the train.

The lounges adjacent to rest rooms on older, restored Amtrak coaches are convenient for parents of infants and children still in diapers, as are the Superliner rest rooms with their fold-down changing tables. The women's lounges on both Superliner and conventional coaches and the dressing rooms on long-distance Amfleet cars are well-suited for the needs of nursing mothers.

Amtrak's policy on children's fares varies according to the age of the child. One child less than 2 years old may travel free for each person over 12 years old in a party, providing the baby does not take up a separate seat. Other children under 2 (if their number exceeds that of the over-12 members of the party) are charged the regular children's rate, which is one-half the adult fare. (The discount for children is only 25% on Auto Train.) All passengers over 12 pay full fare. Information on family excursion rates is available from Amtrak ticket agents or by dialing the applicable toll-free information number for your area.

With approval from Amtrak in advance, children between the ages of 8 and 11 may travel unaccompanied by an adult. Full adult fares are charged for children traveling alone.

Handicapped Travelers

Recent efforts have been made to make all modes of transportation more accessible and comfortable for handicapped passengers. Amtrak has been doing its best to accomplish this goal. We noted the inclusion of handicapped accommodations on all Superliner sleeping cars; in addition, Superliner coaches have one lower-level handicapped passenger seat. These extra-wide seats, which swivel and recline, are equipped with fixed armrests that allow transfer from wheelchair to seat. Aisles alongside handicapped seating are sufficiently wide for wheelchair passage. As on the sleepers, passage to other cars is restricted by stairways. Since this makes visits to the diner or lounge impossible, meals will be served to handicapped passengers by train attendants. A special rest room is located a short distance from the handicapped seat on each coach. (Long-distance Amfleet coaches also feature restrooms ample enough to accommodate passengers in wheelchairs.)

Many of the older, refurbished "Heritage Fleet" sleeping cars have been fitted with special bedrooms for handicapped passengers.

Needless to say, it would be impossible for Amtrak to provide enough of these special coach seats and bedrooms to make specific reservations unnecessary. Anyone requiring these facilities should make reservations early and should be sure to make clear the nature of his or her disability and the services required. The same applies to special diets, which can usually be accommodated by dining-car personnel if advance notice is given.

Using This Book

This guide is intended to provide practical information on all U.S. rail routes and the principal cities along them, along with major Canadian routes and cities. It is not expected that it will thus replace longer, more detailed works dealing exclusively with individual cities or regions, but it should serve to orient the rail traveler to places that are accessible by train, in a way geared particularly to his or her arrival at the stations—not at airports or via interstate highways. If, however, you wish to travel light and carry as few guidebooks as possible, these pages will present enough information to help you plan a brief stay in any of these rail cities.

Since a train route is a series of destinations along a line, cities are presented here in the sequence in which they occur on those routes. Each chapter heading is the name of a route or of a parallel system of routes. The practical information for the cities is prefaced by a discussion of whatever circumstances might be peculiar to that route, and—where applicable—of the history and lore of passenger railroading along the right-of-way followed by present-day trains. Similarly, passages describing topographical features, railroadiana, and points of interest along the route separate the city information sections within each chapter.

As an example, the section on the *California Zephyr* contains information on Omaha, Denver, Reno, Sacramento, and San Francisco, with notes on what lies between these major points along the route. Chicago, the eastern end of the *Zephyr* run, is covered at the end of the section on the *Lake Shore Limited*. A cross-reference in the *Zephyr* section directs the reader there for information on that city. This practice is followed wherever such "overlapping" of cities occurs.

Since this is a rail travelers' guide, the main emphasis in each city section is upon those accommodations, restaurants, and points of interest that are most easily accessible to the train station. Wherever possible, the object is to allow the traveler to do as much of his or her sight-seeing as possible on foot, or via simple bus or rapid-transit trips. Each city section also contains telephone information numbers for municipal transit systems and addresses and phone numbers of visitors' bureaus, at which transit maps are often available. These maps may be used to help the traveler determine public transportation connections to major points of interest.

Since ease of access to rail terminals has largely determined which establishments are included in the guide, readers will find that hotels make up the major portion of listings of lodging places for each city. People accustomed to traveling by car have no doubt observed that most downtown hotels are more expensive than highway motels; however, the convenience of access afforded by staying in a central location goes a long way toward offsetting the extra expense. If you arrive in a city by train and then economize by taking a motel room on the outskirts, you will likely exhaust most of your savings in taxi fares or car rentals. At the very least, your sight-seeing time will be wasted and your patience tried by long waits for buses, which usually run less frequently in the suburbs (when they are available at all) than they do in town. Also, it's nice to know that you have a nearby retreat if you get tired during the day.

A word on lodging rates: although this guide can give readers some idea of relative expense, inflation has made it futile to fix price categories. Besides, tariffs in many hotels range so widely that a certain amount of overlapping is inevitable. In most guidebooks, for instance, it is common to find establishments listed under "moderate" whose rooms cost more than the less expensive accommodations listed in the "deluxe" category. For this reason, this guide lists lodgings in each city section in a rough ascending order according to average price for a double room. If you are looking for relatively inexpensive accommodations, check the beginning of the list. If higher-priced rooms are within your budget, scan the entries further down the page. Approximate dollar figures representing the lower end of the scale for that city and some idea of its upper limits, preface each list. Remember, though, that these figures are necessarily those that apply at the time of this writing—winter, 1983–84.

Youth hostels, where they are available, have been placed at the top of the lists, as they nearly always offer the least expensive lodging. For more detailed information on hostels and hosteling, consult *Hosteling U.S.A.: The Official American Youth Hostels Handbook*, published by East Woods Press in association with American Youth Hostels, Inc.

A similar practice has been followed with regard to restaurants. As with hotels, of course, the inclusion of particular restaurants in these listings does not imply an endorsement, although outstanding quality or value are recognized. Unless they are unusually good, eating places at the lower end of the price spectrum have not been listed, since their number is legion and their locations apparent to anyone who walks the streets of large American cities. As with hotels, the object is to give a representative cross section, with emphasis upon accessibility to people touring cities on foot or by public transportation.

In order to avoid clutter in the listings for points of interest, hotels, and restaurants, specific remarks concerning holiday closures have not been made. It is generally correct to assume that most museums, historical sites, and other attractions will be closed on major holidays such as Christmas, Thanksgiving, and New Year's Day. There are also many restaurants that close on holidays; Sundays and Mondays are also common "off days" for eating places in all price brackets. Your best bet, should a major holiday occur during your trip, is simply to call ahead to see if the place you want to visit, or dine at, is open. And—whether it's a holiday or not—it's always a good idea to phone for restaurant reservations. This particularly applies to the places mentioned toward the end of each set of restaurant listings in this book.

Certain assumptions have also been made regarding hotel amenities. Except in certain older, lower-priced establishments, you may expect to find a television—usually color—and a telephone in your room. These features are therefore not mentioned in the hotel listings, except for less expensive hotels where they are the exception rather than the rule.

One final word on hotels: you will notice that two telephone numbers are given for many of the establishments listed. If you are calling from out of town, dial the "800" number to avoid paying tolls.

II. Routes and Cities: Amtrak

A Heritage Fleet cafeteria-lounge car is a true fun car where passengers can read, meet people, snack and otherwise enjoy themselves.   (Amtrak Photo)

1. The *Lake Shore Limited* and the *Broadway Limited*

The two New York-Chicago Amtrak limiteds, the *Lake Shore* and the *Broadway*, have honorable forebears. The *Broadway Limited* was the name of the Pennsylvania's premier train, which followed the same route as its modern descendant down through Philadelphia and across the Alleghenies toward the Midwest. The *Lake Shore Limited*, though, does not retain the name of its predecessor. That name has been respectfully retired; there can never be another *Twentieth Century Limited*.

The *Lake Shore Limited*

The westbound *Lake Shore* actually has two points of origin, Boston and New York. Trains leave Boston in late afternoon and New York in early evening, and head for a meeting at Albany-Rensselaer station, after which the *Lake Shore* is complete for the remainder of its trip to Chicago. The consist is drawn from Amtrak's "Heritage Fleet" of rebuilt, all-electric cars and from Amfleet equipment. Sleepers are attached to both sections. However, hungry passengers boarding in Boston must content themselves with a cafeteria-lounge car until they reach Albany, since only the New York section carries a full-service diner. There is a last seating for dinner as the train leaves Albany.

(Similarly, the eastbound *Lake Shore* serves both eastern terminals. During the mid-morning stop in Albany, the train is divided into two sections.)

Boston

Boston trades heavily upon its past. It is not a static place—although that charge could once be leveled with some justification—but one that regards its history as an important possession, just as some cities value their topography, architecture, or style. For Boston, this means a disassociation of yesterday's memories from the vital processes of today. Young towns like Omaha, Kansas City, or even Chicago can sense that their contemporary lives are continuations of beginnings made scarcely more than a century ago; but for a city 350 years old, this can hardly be true.

Boston has progressed through many stages: from rude market town, to bustling colonial port, to financial center, to what local politicians now like to call a "world city." Just what this often-bandied-about phrase means is not quite clear, but it appears to involve the construction of a lot of expensive hotels and convention centers and the attraction of international visitors. While this spate of boosterism, with its mania for Centers, Places, Complexes, and Malls, may someday cost the city the charm that it enjoyed as a mere provincial capital, Boston still retains a great deal of variety and plenty of tangible evidence of the many eras through which it has passed.

Most cities grow by building outward, like the chambered nautilus, and (until recently) by neglecting their oldest and most central districts. This was not so with Boston, however, whose peninsular location dictated an entirely different sort of urban expansion. Faced with a shortage of land, Boston leveled its hills and dumped fill along its shoreline. And since this was a slow process, those neighborhoods that already existed were used and reused: this nautilus lived in all its chambers at once.

The "made land," as the filled-in areas were first called, by now occupies easily as much of Boston as the original peninsula. South Station, Amtrak's Boston facility on Atlantic Avenue near the Fort Point Channel, itself stands on a spot over which tea might have floated on the night of the famous party. The only parts of central Boston that were not originally under water are the North End, Beacon Hill, and parts of the downtown shopping and financial district.

This style of development has led to sharp distinctions among neighborhoods, even in this small, compact, and easily walkable city. Within a few blocks of South Station lies Chinatown, bordered closely by the business and commercial streets. These thoroughfares may be lined with tall buildings now, but they still follow the paths of the rutted lanes of the seventeenth century. In other words, prepare not only to get lost on these streets but to be unable to find anyone who can make sense of them.

The North End is the nub of Boston's peninsula. Here is where most of the earliest Bostonians resided and did business, and where, since about 1900, the city's Italians have congregated. To visit it today is to combine Paul Revere with prosciutto. The North End is separated from the rest of the city by the Fitzgerald Expressway, but also by Quincy Market, the prototype for all urban recycling projects geared toward turning old, workaday structures into fantasies of restaurants, bars, and boutiques.

Downtown's other flank is bordered by Boston Common and the more formal Public Garden. Across the Common, the gold-domed Massachusetts State House stands atop a hill where colonists once placed a signal beacon—hence the name of both the hill and the street that begins here. No other city can boast a residential district as beautiful as Beacon Hill at its core; walk down Mt. Vernon or Chestnut Street to enjoy a fine sampling of Federalist architecture.

Past Arlington Street, between Boylston Street and the Charles River, lies the most famous made land in Boston, the Back Bay. These streets were designed along the line of the Parisian boulevards of the 1850s, and they are lined with brick and brownstone row houses eclectic in inspiration but remarkably compatible in appearance. Most are apartments and condominiums now.

Prudential Center and Copley Place—an extravagant new development incorporating shops, restaurants, and two high-rise hotels, which many critics feel intrudes upon the scale of the neighborhood—separate the Back Bay from the South End, another filled-in neighborhood that enjoyed a brief nineteenth-century vogue before entering a century of obscurity as a rooming-house slum. Today, it enjoys a revival, and is well worth an hour's walk. The feeling here is English, rather than French, with narrow bow-fronted houses facing tree-lined streets and squares.

A city of parts, yes, but also one which enjoys a single unifying influence—that of its dozens of colleges and universities. Boston's population is youthful, its cultural institutions strong, and its entertainment lively and diverse, largely because the city and its environs are one enormous campus. For an appreciation of this aspect of Boston's personality, head over to Cambridge, and follow Massachusetts Avenue from M.I.T. to Harvard Square. It isn't what it was in 1968, but within an hour's time you can still buy handmade sandals and an old school tie, browse through arcane bookshops, and choose your lunch from among the cuisines of a score of nations.

Boston has divested itself of as many traditions as it has retained, despite what it might have you believe. But in one way its great age still sets it apart: like an old house, it has accumulated a lot of fascinating paraphernalia in its nooks and corners.

Points of Interest

Boston's Freedom Trail links together the city's principal colonial and revolutionary sites. The Trail starts at Boston Common. From there, follow red pavement markings to the new (1795) **State House, Park Street Church, Old Granary Burying Ground, King's Chapel, Old Corner Book Store, Old South Church, Old State House, Boston Massacre site, Faneuil Hall, Paul Revere House,** and **Old North Church.** For details on the stops along the Trail, visit the Information Center on the Tremont Street side of Boston Common or the Boston National Historical Park office and visitors' center at 15 State Street, downtown (617-242-5642).

Museum of Fine Arts. 465 Huntington Avenue. 617-267-9377. All periods and media; extensive collections of Greek, Roman, and Egyptian jewelry and small artifacts; American painters; furnishings; silver. The museum's striking new West Wing is the locus for traveling exhibitions and a permanent collection of modern art. Open Wednesday through Sunday, 10 A.M.–5 P.M.; Tuesday 10 A.M.–9:00 P.M. Closed Monday.

Museum of Science. Science Park, on Charles River. 617-723-2500. A pioneer in the creation of "please touch" exhibits. Displays cover natural history, technology, animals, and man. Also **Hayden Planetarium.** Open Monday through Thursday, 9 A.M.–4 P.M.; Friday, 9 A.M.–10 P.M.; Saturday, 9 A.M.–5 P.M.; Sunday, 10 A.M.–5 P.M.

Children's Musuem. Museum Wharf, downtown. 617-426-8855. Plenty of "do-it-yourself" exhibits—an "attic" full of dress-up clothes; a TV camera and monitor; play-store area with nutritional information; displays focusing on other countries. Open Tuesday through Sunday, 10 A.M.–5 P.M.; Exhibit Center open Friday until 9 P.M. Closed Monday.

Isabella Stewart Gardner Museum. 280 Fenway. 617-734-1359. The Italian-style palazzo built by Boston arts patron "Mrs. Jack" Gardner, containing her personal collection. Much of it was acquired with the help of famed connoisseur Bernard Berenson. Concerts in courtyard, summers. Open Wednesday through Sunday, 1 P.M.–5:30 P.M.; Tuesday until 9:30 P.M. Closed Monday.

John F. Kennedy Library. Columbia Point, Dorchester. 617-929-4500 This stunningly beautiful structure faces the late president's beloved Atlantic and houses papers from his administration as well as personal belongings, including his White House desk. Tapes and films. Open every day, 9 A.M.–5 P.M.

Harvard University, Cambridge, is worth visiting both for a look at its renowned Yard and a tour of its museums. These include:

—**Peabody Museum.** 11 Divinity Avenue. 617-495-2248. Ancient history; famous glass flowers. Open Monday through Saturday, 10 A.M.–4:30 P.M.; Sunday, 1–4:30 P.M.

—**Fogg Art Museum.** 32 Quincy Street. 617-495-2387. All periods; Revere silver. Open Monday through Friday, 9 A.M.–5 P.M. (Thursday until 9 P.M.); Saturday, 10 A.M.–5 P.M.; Sunday, 2–5 P.M.

—**Busch-Reisinger Museum.** 29 Kirkland Street. 617-495-2338. German and Central European Art. Open Monday through Saturday, 9 A.M.–4:45 P.M.

Boston has two lofty observatories—the **John Hancock Building,** Copley Square, 617-247-1977; open every day, 9 A.M.–10:15 P.M. and Sunday, 1–10:15 P.M.; and the **Prudential Skydeck,** Prudential Center, 617-236-3318; open weekdays, 9 A.M.–11 P.M.; Friday and Saturday until midnight; Sunday, 10 A.M.–11 P.M.

The Greater Boston Convention and Visitors' Bureau has a reception center at 15 State Street, 617-367-9275 (367-9278 for foreign visitors). There is also a kiosk dispensing Freedom Trail maps and brochures on local points of interest on Tremont Street at Boston Common.

Public Transportation

Boston has subways and light-rail surface lines extending throughout the city and its nearer suburbs. Lines are coded red, blue, orange, and green. There are also extensive bus routes. The system is run by the Massachusetts Bay Transit Authority (MBTA). For schedule and fare information, call 617-722-3200 weekdays; 722-5000 nights and weekends. The MBTA also runs trains to the northern suburbs from North Station.

Lodging

Boston has plenty of downtown hotel rooms, and more are under construction. The trouble, however, is that most of the new establishments are at the upper end of the price scale. Cambridge and the area west of Back Bay, toward Brookline, have more reasonable accommodations; these are easily reached by public transit. Rates will vary from $50 to $130.

Fenway Howard Johnson's. 1271 Boylston Street. 617-267-8300. A short trolley ride from Back Bay and downtown; about 2 miles from South Station. Pool. Restaurant, bar.

Holiday Inn. 1651 Massachusetts Avenue, Cambridge. 617-491-1000. A short walk from Harvard Square and subway to Boston. Pool. Restaurant, bar.

Sheraton-Commander 16 Garden Street. 617-547-4800. A large, quiet, comfortable hotel facing Cambridge Common, just off Harvard Square. Coffee shop and lounge; also Dertad's, a highly regarded restaurant.

Lenox. 710 Boylston Street. 617-536-5300 or 800-225-7676. Located near the Prudential Center in the heart of Back Bay, 1½ miles from the station, this small hotel offers many of the same conveniences that its fancier neighbors feature, but at a more moderate price. Restaurant and bar, the latter known for its piano singalongs.

Copley Plaza. 138 St. James Avenue, Copley Square. 617-267-5300. 1 mile from station. Big and classy in the old-fashioned sense, with the lobby ambience of an elegant ocean liner. Spacious rooms. Fine restaurants, several opulent lounges and bars. One of Boston's best.

Ritz-Carlton. Arlington and Newbury streets. 617-536-5700. 1 mile from station. The discreet, postage-stamp-sized lobby is deceptive; this is one of the most luxurious hotels anywhere. Some of the suites have working fireplaces; some rooms face the Public Garden. Excellent service, a fine cafe and bar, and a sumptuous first-quality restaurant.

Restaurants

Do not come to Boston looking for beans. They were never a restaurant specialty, just a Saturday-night economy dish at home. You will find plenty of seafood, most notably lobster and scrod. There is no such fish as scrod; it's actually a thick cut of young cod or haddock. Boston has many fine Italian restaurants and several noteworthy haute cuisine establishments as well as a generous supply of *nouvelle cuisine* spots. Bucking this trend is a fine new New York-style steak house, Grill 23, at 161 Berkeley Street in the Back Bay (617-543-2255).

Regina's. 11½ Thatcher Street. 617-227-0765. Pizza so good it has been flown thousands of miles. No fancy additions, but you can pile on the basics and even order extra cheese and oil. Wash it down with a beer glass full of Chianti.

Jacob Wirth's. 31 Stuart Street. 617-338-8586. An ancient saloon with an ornate back bar, bentwood chairs, and bare wooden floor, where you can eat herring in sour cream, brisket, and piles of bratwurst and kraut. Raise a mug of the house dark beer to old Jake, whose portrait hangs over the bar.

The Romagnolis' Table. North Market Building, Quincy Market. 617-367-9114. The Romagnolis, of public television fame, operate this fine Italian restaurant. Fresh, homemade pasta is featured—try tortellini or fettuccini in a creamy walnut and prosciutto sauce.

Durgin-Park. North Market Buildings, Quincy Market. 617-227-2038. This venerable establishment dates back to long before the modern "recycling" of the Market and has been updated by the addition of a cozy oyster bar at street level. Upstairs, it's business as usual with preposterously large servings of roast beef set before diners at long tables.

L'Espalier. 30 Gloucester Street. 617-262-3023. Owner-chef Moncef Meddeb has built one of the best culinary reputations in Boston with his refined yet highly individualistic approach to the classic and *nouvelle* repertory. New items appear on the menu daily; all are built on the freshest of seasonal ingredients. Several respected critics feel this is Boston's best restaurant.

New York City

In his book *Civilisation*, Kenneth Clark imagines "an immensely speeded up movie of Manhattan Island during the last hundred years." It would look, Clark writes, "less like a work of man than like some tremendous natural upheaval." Clark is right; the City of New York as we know it has largely been the creation of the twentieth century, the result of labor so willful, energetic, and swift that it is impossible to envision it as having ever been anything other than the maddening and beautiful metropolis that we know today.

Few people stop to reflect that New York is older than Boston, for unlike its ancient rival in baseball and finance it prefers to identify the present—at least the present century—as its true Golden Age. It has jackhammered that present out of solid Manhattan schist and is as proud of it as other cities are of their most venerable relics.

Aside from this sense of dynamism, the immediate impressions of a first-time visitor to New York are liable to center on the collective personality of New Yorkers. These perceptions are largely the result of advance publicity that has created certain time-honored notions about what a New Yorker is like. Such stereotypes do perhaps have some basis in fact, but it's a mistake to interpret the legendary New York crustiness and sharpness of tongue to mean indifference or even outright antipathy to outsiders. While it isn't hearty and forthright like that of Midwesterners or effusive and solicitous like that of Southern Californians, New York's spirit contains a great deal of warmth. Convolutions of sarcasm—of irony, really—are second nature to the New Yorker, and for that matter to people from North Jersey as well. It's a way of dealing with a fast-moving, heads-up environment, and it doesn't necessarily imply hard-heartedness or ill will toward non-natives. Don't feel bad—New Yorkers talk this way to their best friends.

Many first-time visitors also despair of ever coming to terms with the city's size and diversity. Awed, and somewhat resigned, they settle for a bus tour through Midtown, a hansom cab in Central Park, a ride to the top of the Empire State Building, and a Broadway show. There's nothing wrong with any of these things; in fact, deliberately concentrating on the highlights is one way to screen out the city's confusion. It is possible, though, to divide and conquer New York, given a little time, a subway map, and a good pair of shoes.

The first round of division has already been done for you. There are five boroughs: Manhattan, Brooklyn, Queens, the Bronx, and Staten Island. The latter four have plenty to see and do, but the simple fact is that Manhattan has more. If time is short (all time in New York is short, really), Manhattan should be first on your agenda.

One of the best places to begin a tour of Manhattan is where the city itself began three and half centuries ago—at the island's southern extreme. Although Amtrak's two New York terminals—Grand Central and Pennsylvania stations—appear on a map to be below the center of Manhattan, they are both located in the area known as "Midtown"; the term "Lower Manhattan" properly applies only to the neighborhoods that lie to the south of the numbered cross streets, beyond Greenwich Village, Soho, Chinatown, and the Lower East Side.

Lower Manhattan is the civic and financial heart of the city, but it isn't as dull as that makes it sound. Even though all physical evidence of Dutch Fort Amsterdam and the earliest settlements has long since been paved under, a walk through this area will reveal a lot more of the history and character of New York than many of the tourist "musts" farther north. Within this, the most compact section of the entire city, you will find the World Trade Center, Trinity Church, the New York Stock Exchange, St. Paul's Chapel, the Woolworth building, City Hall, Fraunces Tavern, and the Brooklyn Bridge. Just south of the great bridge's Manhattan footings is the South Street Seaport, which preserves not only a historic stretch of waterfront but also a collection of sailing vessels. If you continue south past the Seaport streets, you will soon reach the Battery. This park occupies the extreme tip of Manhattan, which is where the original Dutch encampment was. Here are Castle Clinton, an 1812 fort, and the Old Customs House, with its Daniel Chester French sculptures facing Bowling Green.

Now that you are anchored both in Manhattan's history and in its topography, move up-island the way the city itself did. Either on foot or through a series of short subway rides, you can make your way through Chinatown and Little Italy, the restored loft neighborhood of Soho (for *south of Houston* Street), and Greenwich Village. The streets beyond here were a favorite area for residential construction during the middle years of the nineteenth century. But commerce was always close behind, and today you must go a good deal further north to find anything like the fashionable neighborhoods that developers once sought to establish here.

Times Square may not be an altogether savory sight these days, but it serves as a convenient point of reference for Midtown visitors. This is where the terms "East Side" and "West Side" begin to become really useful; west is toward the Hudson River, and east is toward the East River. The cross streets are labeled accordingly, with Fifth Avenue the dividing line. From Times Square you would head east on Forty-second Street to reach the Public Library, Grand Central Station, and the United Nations. North, along Broadway, would lead you to the theater district, Columbus Circle (at the southwest corner of Central Park), and Lincoln Center. From this point in Midtown Manhattan, Fifth Avenue (2 blocks east of Times Square) is generally the favored north-south thoroughfare for visitors. The Empire State Building is south of Forty-second Street, at Fifth Avenue and Thirty-fourth Street. North of Forty-second Street, Fifth Avenue becomes the shopping street of legend, passing Rockefeller Center and culminating in Grand Army Plaza at the Hotel Plaza and the entrance to Frederick Law Olmsted's landscaping masterpiece, Central Park. A word about the Park: while it is heavily used and generally quite safe during the day, its after-dark reputation is not just hyperbole or cliché.

With the Park on its left, Fifth Avenue becomes a residential street—that is, a place where people do not merely live, but reside. There are many architectural jewels along upper Fifth Avenue and on the East Side cross streets that meet it at the Park, but the grandest, and the most important to visitors to New York, is the Metropolitan Museum of Art at Fifth Avenue and Eighty-second Street. Another landmark institution, the Museum of Natural History, is located almost directly across the Park at Seventy-ninth Street and Central Park West. The West Side, north of Lincoln Center, is also largely residential, although without (except for the area nearest the Park) the reputation for chic exclusiveness cultivated on the East Side. The principal point of interest north of the Park on the West Side is Columbia University, the campus of which extends along Broadway above 100th Street.

Harlem, long the cultural capital of black America, occupies the blocks that reach beyond the northern limits of Central Park. Contrary to conventional understanding, this area is not entirely a slum. It has its streets of tidy row houses as well as its tenements. As for population density, Harlem is actually losing inhabitants. Many black residents fear upper-middle-class-white encroachment, or "gentrification," in this enclave, which after all is a symbol of identity as well as one of oppression.

Between Harlem and Manhattan's northern tip lie the modest residential neighborhoods of Washington Heights and Inwood. Fort Tryon Park, just north of the George Washington Bridge, is the site of the Cloisters, an imposing abbeylike structure housing the Metropolitan Museum's medieval collections.

Around New York: The Other Boroughs

Although a week or less in New York will almost surely call for an exclusive focus upon Manhattan, the four other boroughs are accessible enough by public transportation, and their attractions sufficiently varied, to provide a welcome change of pace during even a short visit to the city.

Brooklyn

Perhaps the easiest way to take time off from Manhattan is to walk across the Brooklyn Bridge to Brooklyn, New York's most heavily populated borough. Of course, you could take a subway, but a foot crossing of John Augustus Roebling's peerless span will reward you with fine views of Lower Manhattan, especially at dusk. On the Brooklyn side of the bridge is the borough's oldest neighborhood, Brooklyn Heights. The Heights was the first of the many Brooklyn neighborhoods that have been restored and revitalized during the past twenty years, and there is a good deal of splendid early nineteenth-century architecture to be seen here. Another attractive district is Park Slope, which borders on Prospect Park, home of the Brooklyn Museum and Brooklyn Botanic Garden.

If you are in need of more open space than Prospect Park can offer, take the Rockaway subway from Manhattan out to the Jamaica Bay Wildlife Refuge, part of the Gateway National Recreation Area. This is only one unit of the twenty-six-thousand-acre Gateway; others are on Staten Island and along the New Jersey shore.

The Bronx

Nearly everyone has heard of the Bronx Zoo and Botanical Gardens. These great institutions are located in the smallest of three huge parks that spread across successive ridges on New York's only mainland borough: Van Cortlandt Park, site of the historic Van Cortlandt Mansion; Bronx Park (zoo and gardens); and Pelham Bay Park, which has two wildlife preserves, nature trails, and a broad sweep of beach along Long Island Sound. Clearly, there is more here than Yankee Stadium and the perennially maligned South Bronx.

Staten and Some Smaller Islands

Manhattan's Battery is the point of departure for the fabled Staten Island Ferry. The borough that lies across Lower New York Bay is completely different from the other four; parts of it are nearly rural, parts resemble small towns, and parts are indistinguishable from Long Island's most sterile suburbs. St. George, where the Staten Island Ferry docks, is a quiet brick village looking north across the bay to its sister settlement on Manhattan, for which fate had other things in store.

A ferry from the Battery also takes passengers to Liberty Island, where the Statue of Liberty stands, and to Ellis Island, where millions of European immigrants first set foot on American soil. Restoration of both the Statue of Liberty and the Ellis Island buildings is under way as of this writing; during parts of 1984 and 1985, visitors may find the Statue closed because of these long overdue repairs.

Points of Interest

Federal Hall National Memorial. Wall and Broad streets. 212-264-8711. A

Greek Revival successor to the building where George Washington was inaugurated. Mementoes of Washington; other historical displays, including Bill of Rights room. Open every day from 9 A.M. to 4:30 P.M.

New York Stock Exchange. 20 Broad Street. 212-623-5167. Visitors' Center, at which questions about stocks and finance are answered by pushbutton recordings; also gallery overlooking the trading floor. It can get exciting toward closing. Open Monday through Friday from 10 A.M. to 4 P.M.

Statue of Liberty. Liberty Island. 212-732-1236/1286. France's gift to the United States, this 152-foot Frédéric Bartholdi statue is made of copper, with a stairway ascending to Liberty's crown. Below is the **Museum of Immigration.** Open every day from 9 A.M. to 6 P.M. Accessible by boats from the Battery; they leave on the hour beginning at 9:15 A.M. (Last boat 5 P.M. Memorial Day–Labor Day.) Note above remarks regarding the closing of the Statue for repairs and restoration.

Ellis Island. 212-732-1236/1286. Chances are your relatives passed this way. The processing center was closed in 1954, but is now open for guided tours. Boats leave the Battery four times daily; phone for schedules. Expect restoration work to be proceeding during 1984 and 1985.

World Trade Center. Vesey Street, foot of W. Broadway. 212-466-7377. Two 110-story towers; take elevator to observatory atop 2 World Trade Center for expansive views of the city, its harbor, and New Jersey. Open every day from 9:30 A.M. to 9:30 P.M.

Empire State Building. Fifth Avenue and Thirty-fourth Street. 212-736-3100. No longer the world's tallest, but still a masterpiece of the art deco era. Two observation levels—on 86th and 102nd floors—afford fine Midtown views. Open every day from 9:30 A.M. to midnight; phone for special holiday hours.

United Nations. First Avenue (along East River) from Forty-second to Forty-eighth streets. 212-754-7713 (754-7765 weekends). The UN General Assembly meets here beginning in late September of each year; tickets to the visitors' gallery are available on a first-come, first-served basis. Delegates' dining room open to public. Guided tours (reservations required) given throughout each day from 9 A.M. to 4:45 P.M.

Metropolitan Museum of Art. Fifth Avenue at Eighty-second Street. 212-535-7710. One of the half-dozen greatest art museums in the world. Allow at least a full day if you are serious; you'll probably need even more time. The Temple of Dendur and the American Wing are important recent additions. Open Tuesday through Saturday, 10 A.M.–4:45 P.M. (closes 8:45 P.M. on Tuesday); Sunday and holidays, 11 A.M. Closed Monday. The **Cloisters** (212-923-3700) is the Met's medieval art museum in Manhattan's Fort Tryon Park (see above). Open Tuesday through Saturday, 10 A.M.–4:45 P.M.; Sunday and holidays from noon in summer and 1 P.M. other seasons.

Museum of Modern Art. 11 W. Fifty-third Street. 212-956-6100. American and European art movements of the late nineteenth and twentieth centuries are represented; design forms an important part of the collection. Still photography; film screenings. Sculpture garden. Major expansion underway. Open Friday through Tuesday, 11 A.M.–6 P.M.; Thursday, to 9 P.M. Closed Wednesday.

Whitney Museum of American Art. Madison Avenue and E. Seventy-fifth Street. 212-794-0600. An outgrowth of the Whitney Studio Club, this important museum has focused on modern and contemporary American artists for over fifty years. Open Tuesday, 11 A.M.–9 P.M.; Wednesday through Saturday, 11 A.M.–6 P.M.; Sunday, Noon–6 P.M. Closed Monday.

Frick Collection. Fifth Avenue and Seventieth Street. 212-288-0700. The collection of steel baron Henry Frick, a Carnegie associate, arranged in his home—furniture, decorative objects, sculpture, painting, graphics. Renaissance through nineteenth century. Hours vary with season; call for schedule information.

Guggenheim Museum. Fifth Avenue between Eighty-eighth and Eighty-ninth streets. 212-860-1313. One of Frank Lloyd Wright's last buildings, and still controversial. Modern paintings and sculpture displayed along spiral ramp. Open Wednesday through Sunday, 11 A.M.–5 P.M.; Tuesday, to 8 P.M. Closed Monday.

Museum of the City of New York. Fifth Avenue between 103rd and 104th streets. 212-534-1672. More than 350 years of Gotham's history are packed into this excellent museum. Don't miss the Fort Amsterdam reconstruction. Open Tuesday through Saturday, 10 A.M.–5 P.M.; Sunday, 1–5 P.M. Closed Monday.

American Museum of Natural History. Central Park West and Seventy-ninth Street. 212-873-4225. Generations of children have gaped at the dinosaur skeletons here, but there's lots more; halls of reptiles and amphibians; habitat groups showing man and animals in a multitude of environments. Set aside at least one day. Open daily, 10 A.M.–4:45 P.M.; to 8 P.M. Wednesday. Nearby is the **Hayden Planetarium,** one of the nation's best. Call 212-873-8828 for show and exhibit schedules.

New York Zoological Park. Bronx Park. 212-220-5100. The famous Bronx Zoo. Animals occupy replicas of their natural habitats as much as possible. New Asian Section with monorail. Aviary; children's zoo; special facility for nocturnal creatures. Hours vary with season; call for schedule information.

New York Botanical Garden. Bronx Park. 212-220-8777. Indoor and outdoor plantings, both native and exotic. Pleasant woods pathways. Grounds are open every day, 10 A.M. until an hour before dusk; hours vary with season for special exhibits. Call for schedule information.

Brooklyn Museum. 188 Eastern Parkway (at Washington Avenue). 212-638-5000. Art from all periods, all parts of the world, but especially strong in decorative arts. There are thirty furnished period rooms and a collection of architectural odds-and-ends scavenged from New York buildings that are no more. Open Wednesday through Saturday, 10 A.M.–5 P.M.; Sunday from noon.

As befits the city's size, there are several locations in New York where visitors can obtain information. The New York Convention and Visitors' Bureau is at 2 Columbus Circle; call 212-397-8222 for information. The Times Square Information Center is at the corner of Broadway and 42nd Street; call 212-221-9869.

Public Transportation

The New York City subway system (a consolidation of the IRT, IND, and BMT lines) is one of the wonders of the world, despite the graffiti that defaces most cars. It serves Manhattan, Brooklyn, the Bronx, and Queens; Staten Island has elevated trains. The Metropolitan Transit Authority runs the subways, as well as bus network. For information on fares and schedules, call

212-330-1234. The Visitors' Bureau (see above) carries subway maps. New Jersey (Conrail commuter trains at Hoboken) may be reached by bus from the Port Authority terminal at Eighth Avenue and Forty-first Street, or by PATH subway from Penn Station or the World Trade Center. Call 201-434-6100 for information. Trains to Long Island and the Westchester suburbs leave from Grand Central Station. Call 212-739-4200 for Long Island information; 212-736-6000 for Conrail's Harlem and Hudson division (Westchester).

Lodging

There are plenty of hotels in New York, and they are expensive. Well, not all of them—but "cheap" here often means "fleabag." Few acceptable accommodations for two are available for less than $60; the upper limit can easily exceed $200. The hotels listed below are all in Midtown, within 2 miles or so of Grand Central and Pennsylvania stations and always easily accessible by cab, bus, or subway.

Picadilly. 227 W. Forty-fifth Street. 212-246-6600/800-223-6600. Recently renovated theater-district hotel, opposite Shubert Alley. Nicely kept; one of the city's true bargains. Lounge, coffee house, Cafe Ziegfeld restaurant on premises.

George Washington. Lexington Avenue at Twenty-third Street. 212-475-1920/800-261-9328 (212-757-2981 collect in New York State). Older hotel; not fancy but quite reasonable. Gramercy Park location—convenient to Greenwich Village as well as Midtown. Coffee shop, lounge.

Algonquin. 59 W. Forty-fourth Street. 212-840-6800. This small, innlike hotel was the gathering place of the famous Algonquin "round table" in the 1930s. Most rooms have brass beds. Lounges, three good restaurants, late supper buffet. Reasonable, considering location and quality.

Penta. Seventh Avenue and 56th Street. 212-736-5000. Formerly the New York Sheraton, the Penta is directly across from Penn Station. It's just been restored and couldn't be more convenient for the train traveler. Note the phone number—remember the song? (Hint: this used to be the Hotel Pennsylvania.)

Tuscany. 120 E. Thirty-ninth Street. 212-686-1600. This Midtown hotel prides itself on its in-room features: FM radio, adjustable beds with vibrators, bathroom phones, butler's pantries, Barca-Lounger chairs. Restaurant, lounge, entertainment. Near Grand Central Station.

Grand Hyatt New York. Park Avenue and 42nd Street. 212-883-1234. Right next to Grand Central Station, where the old Commodore used to be, this is the Hyatt chain's flashy New York flagship. Features Trumpet's, a *nouvelle cuisine* restaurant; many amenities.

St. Regis—Sheraton. 2 E. Fifty-fifth Street. 212-753-4500/800-325-3535. At the heart of the Fifth Avenue shopping district. Beautifully decorated rooms, with high ceilings. Lounges and restaurants, including the famous Old King Cole Room with its Maxfield Parrish mural. Weekend rates available.

Plaza. Fifth Avenue at Fifty-ninth Street. 212-759-3000/800-228-3000. Few hotels anywhere are as famous as the Plaza, with its Central Park location, historic landmark status, and sumptuous rooms—some even with marble fireplaces. Several restaurants and lounges, including the Oak and Edwardian rooms, Palm Court, and Oyster Bar.

Restaurants

The main thing to remember about New York restaurants is not that there are so many of them or that some are fabulously expensive, but that there is an exhaustive selection in every price range. It is possible for two people to spend $100 per night on meals for two months, and never eat at the same place twice; it is also possible to make that same $100 last a week, and still come away satisfied.

Dozens of national cuisines are represented in New York—more, perhaps, than in any other city. What follows is a highly arbitrary list, including some very expensive places. Unless otherwise noted, all restaurants listed are in Manhattan.

The Oyster Bar. Grand Central Station lower level. 212-599-1000. This highly active place has the widest assortment of fresh oysters in the city, and an extensive selection of other seafood as well. Try the oyster pan roast.

Hershey's. 167 W. Twenty-ninth Street. 212-LA4-5389. The Jewish dairy restaurant is a New York tradition. Blintzes, pirogen, noodle soups, egg dishes, gefilte fish, and more. Always plenty of buttermilk, sour cream, seltzer, and matzos. Closed weekends.

Kleine Konditorei. 234 E. Eighty-sixth Street. 212-737-7130. This was once a predominantly German neighborhood, of which the Kleine Konditorei ("Little Confectionery") is a reminder. Walk past glass counters filled with *torten* to the seating area. The menu includes sauerbraten, the familiar wursts, and Kasseler rippchen (smoked pork chops).

Grotto Azzurra. 387 Broome Street (corner of Mulberry). 212-226-9283/925-8775. A tiny basement restaurant in Little Italy—but the lines that spill up the stairs and onto the street should tell you something. Shellfish fra diavolo; spedini alla Romana; chicken cacciatore and dozens of other a la carte specialties. Wine served in pitchers with apple slices.

Angelo's. 146 Mulberry Street. 212-966-1277/226-8527. Also in Little Italy. A somewhat larger establishment than the Grotto, but nearly as good. Veal dishes recommended. In season, you can get a huge fresh pear with provolone for dessert; also homemade pastries.

Gage and Tollner. 372 Fulton Street, Brooklyn. 212-875-5181. A Brooklyn institution; over 100 years old with a decor to match. Specializes in steak, chops, and seafood—the broiled soft clam bellies are justly famous. Homemade pastries.

The Coach House. 110 Waverly Place. 212-777-0303/777-0349. This respected West Village restaurant serves excellent beef and lamb dishes, including a lamb stew that seems to have been made with chops rather than shoulder. Good desserts.

Windows on the World. 1 World Trade Center, North Tower. 212-938-1111. This 107th-floor aerie is three restaurants in one: The Restaurant (rack of lamb, trout en croûte, Sunday buffet); the Cellar in the Sky (fixed price, seven entrees, five wines—very intimate); and the Hors d'Oeuverie (drinks, hors d'oeuvres, and dessert). The views are superb. Remember that Windows on the World is a "club" restaurant at lunchtime—but for $7.50 per person, they'll waive the membership requirement.

Lutece. 249 E. Fiftieth Street. 212-752-2225. It has been called the finest restaurant in New York. One thing is certain—it is a bastion of the old French haute cuisine, in which butter and cream are no sin. Veal medallions aux morilles; salmon; and a penchant (carried out splendidly) for en croûte preparations. Excellent cellar; dine indoors or in garden.

Boston to Albany/New York to Albany

Leaving Boston, the *Lake Shore* follows Conrail track into the city's western suburbs. In summer, it's still light out long after Worcester and Springfield have been left behind, and travelers may enjoy a fine sampling of Berkshire scenery. After Springfield the tracks leave the coastal plain for higher ground; Washington Summit, at 1489 feet, is the highest spot along the route from Boston to Chicago. Five miles east of Pittsfield, to the north (right) of the tracks, are huge paper mills where the blank stock for U.S. currency is produced. Pittsfield itself is both an industrial center and the focus for the summer arts scene in the Berkshires. Herman Melville lived here when he wrote *Moby Dick*; he and Nathaniel Hawthorne were part of a wave of "summer people" that has never stopped. Soon after leaving Pittsfield, the *Lake Shore* crosses into New York State, traverses the Taconic Range in darkness, and comes within view of the skyline of Albany at about 10 P.M. At Albany, the Boston and New York sections of the train meet and unite.

The name of the majestic river that the *Lake Shore*'s New York section follows as it speeds north was also the designation of a whole class of steam locomotives that were built to pull the *Twentieth Century Limited* to Chicago and back. Commodore Cornelius Vanderbilt had laid the backbone of his railroad empire, the New York Central System, along the river as far as Albany, and then along the route of the old Erie Canal. Since the tracks thus lay at or near sea level, the Central's main line became known as the "water-level route." Different types of terrain called for different steam engines, and for the water-level route the swift, light Hudson was ideal. This was a 4-6-4 design; that is, it rode on two pairs of small front wheels, three pairs of drivers, and two pairs of smaller trailing wheels. In its great days, the *Century*'s Hudsons wore a streamlined sheathing that was pure art deco.

Leaving New York, then as now, required electrically powered engines, since the city has allowed no other motive power within its limits since the beginning of this century. The switch from electric to steam was made at Croton-Harmon, which is today where the *Lake Shore* takes on its diesel engine for the trip to Albany and beyond.

The *Lake Shore* is not the only train serving the cities of Upstate New York. The *Niagara Rainbow* and *Empire State Express* run daily between New York City and Niagara Falls. Several shorter-distance trains, some of them Turboliners, serve points in between.

Albany

Amtrak's Albany station is a new building across the Hudson in Rensselaer, a town named for one of the Dutch landholding families whose history was deeply intertwined with that of the Hudson River Valley, both before and after the Netherlands lost its holdings here. Albany, which stands at the head of that valley, is perhaps the oldest continuous settlement in the original 13 colonies. Henry Hudson arrived here in 1609; in 1614, Dutch traders built Fort Nassau, and ten years later Fort Orange occupied the site of the town which the British renamed Albany. Nevertheless, it has remained small and somewhat provincial in spite of the fact that it has long been the capital of New York State.

Albany is a city of remarkably contrasting architecture, thanks to ambitious government building programs set a century apart. The two older treasures are Henry Hobson Richardson's City Hall, a masterpiece of the Romanesque

Revival rich in polychrome stonework and topped by a massive campanile, and the State House, a French Renaissance extravaganza that consumed the attention of three other architects as well as the peerless Richardson, who designed its "Million Dollar" grand staircase.

New York has always had a penchant for spending big money; multiply the cost of Richardson's staircase by a thousand and you have the tab for the Empire State Plaza, a phalanx of monolithic marble office towers set into an expanse of brick and shrubbery and accented by an egg-shaped theater that looks as though it bore the first visitors from the Crab Nebula. It sits right in the middle of downtown, and you will either love it or hate it.

Albany is strategically located for train travelers who want to disembark, engage a rental car or bus, and visit such spots as Saratoga (also accessible by train), Howe Caverns, and the southern Adirondacks.

Points of Interest

Albany Institute of History and Art. 125 Washington Avenue. 518-463-4478. Regional art and history; paintings, artifacts, and documents relating to early Dutch settlements, British colonial period, nineteenth and twentieth centuries. Open Tuesday through Saturday from 10 A.M. to 4:45 P.M.; Sunday 2–5 P.M. Closed Monday.

Ten Broeck Mansion. 9 Ten Broeck Place. 518-436-9826. Home of General Abraham Ten Broeck, a local political figure of the colonial and early federal period. Authentic furnishings. Open Tuesday through Sunday from 2–4 PM. Closed Monday.

Cherry Hill. 523½ South Pearl Street. 518-434-4791. The prominent Van Rensselaer family lived here for two hundred years. Priceless furnishings, chinaware, paintings. Open Tuesday through Saturday from 10 A.M.–4P.M.; Sunday from 1 PM–4 P.M. Closed Monday.

State Capitol. Top of State Street Hill. 518-474-2418. Tours of architectural landmark. Phone for schedules.

Empire State Plaza. Eagle Street and Madison Avenue. 518-474-2418. There are a number of things to see at the Plaza, among them the **Forty-second-Floor Observation Deck** (weekdays, 9 A.M.–5 P.M.); and **State Museum** (518-474-5843, weekdays 9 A.M.–5 P.M.). Tours of the entire Plaza are given three times daily. Phone for schedule.

The Albany County Convention and Visitors' Bureau is located at 600 Broadway. Call 518-434-1217 for information.

Public Transportation

The Capital District Transportation Authority provides bus service in and around Albany. Call 518-482-8822 for schedule and fare information.

Lodging

Albany is in need of a few more downtown hotels. Most establishments are out along the highways or near the airport. Even downtown accommodations, though, are not convenient to the Amtrak station in Rensselaer. Rates vary from $35 to $70 and up.

Wellington. 136 State Street. 518-434-4141. Plain and simple, but right downtown within walking distance of State House and Empire State Plaza. Restaurant, lounge.

Best Western Inn Towne. 300 Broadway. 518-434-4111/800-528-1234. A modern downtown hotel, completely renovated within the past few years. Some suites available. Pool. Restaurant, lounge with entertainment.

Restaurants

Steaks, seafood, and Italian traditional sums up most of what Albany has to offer the diner. Clams are also popular here. Some of the bars are open until 4 A.M.; listen close for political scoops.

Daddy O's. 124 Washington Avenue. 518-465-8806. Downstairs, quick-service burgers, sandwiches, and chef's salad; upstairs, a roof garden featuring steamed clams and steak.

La Bella Napoli. 97 Beaver Street. 518-463-9771. All the southern Italian basics—veal scallopini, calamari, steak alla pizzaiola. A local favorite for many years.

Ogden's. Howard at Lodge. 518-463-6605. Near the Empire Plaza, in a renovated stone-and-brick building. Good, hearty lunches. Fancier at dinner—sole véronique, veal normandie, shrimp steamed in beer. Always a daily fish special. Extensive wine list. Homemade desserts.

Albany to Rochester

The *Lake Shore*'s westward run follows what was once the commercial lifeline of upstate New York, the Erie Canal. This 363-mile waterway, parts of which are still visible to rail travelers on the eastbound, daylight run between Syracuse and Utica, was completed in 1825. But only six years later, the Mohawk and Hudson, a railway company later incorporated into the New York Central System, launched its *De Witt Clinton* on the tracks between Albany and Schenectady. This spelled eventual obsolescence for the Erie Canal and opened the way for rapid development of the cities of the Mohawk Valley.

The westbound *Lake Shore* traces the canal's route in darkness, stopping at Schenectady, Utica, Syracuse, and, in the smallest hours, at Rochester. (If, however, you are on one of the "Empire Service" day trains, the best of the Mohawk Valley scenery extends for nearly 100 miles from Schenectady to Rome.)

Rochester

Three things, over the years, have worked to Rochester's advantage: its natural setting, at the point where the Genesee River empties into Lake Ontario; its location on the path of the Erie Canal; and, finally—and perhaps most important—its connection with George Eastman, who chose the city as the place in which to manufacture his cameras and film. The city still touches the lakefront (the downtown area is 6 miles south of the water), and one of the Erie Canal aqueducts can still be seen beneath the Broad Street Bridge, but is undoubtedly the third of these three factors that has given the greatest impetus to Rochester's growth.

Rochester is a company town. This description is not meant in the negative sense; however, it is hard to avoid the words *Eastman* and *Kodak* as you travel around the city.

Rochester is also—for whatever reason—a clean, well-mannered town, which is why it has long suffered under the "nowhere" reputation that accrues to such places. Its political apparatus is highly regarded for its integrity and efficiency. Its services, particularly the bus system, are reliable. And it has visual interest: the fine old mansions that line East Avenue; the restored City Hall, with its glass-roofed Renaissance atrium; the Times Square Building, surmounted by art deco wings. In May, head out to Highland Park for the Lilac Festival; you'll see hundreds and hundreds of bushes in bloom. All in all, not a bad place for a *Lake Shore* layover.

Now, if only the train didn't arrive in the middle of the night . . .

Points of Interest

International Museum of Photography at George Eastman House. 900 East Avenue. 716-271-3361. A vast trove of photographs from all periods in the medium's history; also collection of cameras, displays explaining photographic processes, and exhibits of contemporary camera work. It's all housed in the mansion of George Eastman, inventor of the Kodak. Open Tuesday through Sunday, 10 A.M.–4:30 P.M. Closed Monday and Christmas.

Kodak plant tours. Manufacture of film, paper, and chemicals can be observed at Kodak Park; at the company's Elmgrove Plant, see cameras and other equipment made. Phone for tour schedules: 716-458-1000, extension 72487 (Kodak Park); 716-325-2000, extension 63426 (Elmgrove).

Rochester Museum and Science Center. 657 East Avenue. 716-271-4320. Anthropology and the natural sciences, as well as American history. Extensive collection of Iroquois Indian artifacts. Period rooms; optical science exhibits. Open Monday through Saturday, 9 A.M.–5 P.M.; Sunday and holidays (except Christmas), 1 P.M.–5 P.M.

Margaret Woodbury Strong Museum. One Manhattan Square (corner Chestnut Street and Manhattan Drive). 716-263-2700. Based primarily on one woman's lifetime collection, the Strong Museum documents American culture and popular taste from 1820 to 1930 through painting, sculpture, household furnishings and equipment, toys, and crafts. Open Tuesday through Saturday, 10 A.M.–5 P.M.; Sunday, 1–5 P.M. Closed Monday.

Memorial Art Gallery. University of Rochester, 490 University Avenue. 716-275-3081. Ancient Egyptian to contemporary art in permanent collection; also traveling exhibitions. Open Wednesday through Saturday, 10 A.M.–5 P.M.; Tuesday, 2–9 P.M.; Sunday, 1–5 P.M. Closed Monday.

Susan B. Anthony House. 17 Madison Street. 716-235-0816. Former residence of famous feminist, containing many of her furnishings and personal effects. Open Wednesday through Saturday, 11A.M.–4 P.M.; other times by appointment only.

The Rochester Convention and Visitors' Bureau is situated adjacent to the Holiday Inn on E. Main Street, between St. Paul and S. Water Street. Call 716-546-3070 for information.

Public Transportation

Rochester's buses are run by the Regional Transit Service. For fare and schedule information, call 716-288-1700. No fare is charged within a designated downtown loop between 10 A.M. and 2 P.M.

Lodging

The Amtrak station is just north of the loop that surrounds the downtown area, but because many Rochester visitors are business travelers, most hotels and motels are on the outskirts, near major highways. There are, however, a handful of downtown establishments. Prices range from about $35 to $90 or more at the top hotels.

Travelodge Downtown. 390 South Avenue. 716-454-3550. 12 blocks from station. Just south of downtown, near Inner Loop highway (US 15). Clean and inexpensive. Free coffee in rooms.

One Eleven East Avenue Hotel. 111 East Avenue. 716-232-1700. 9 blocks from station. The most central downtown location available. Outdoor pool, sauna, whirlpool. Restaurant, lounge.

Rochester Plaza. 70 State Street. 716-546-3450. Larger modern hotel; downtown location. Pool. Recently remodeled; excellent restaurant. Part of Stouffer chain.

The Strathallen. 550 East Avenue. 716-461-5010. A prestige hotel in the East Avenue Preservation District. Our Rochester advisor says it's where oil sheiks stay when they come to town. Hattie's Lounge, on the top floor, is a comfortable spot with fireplaces and superb views.

Restaurants

Dining in Rochester has improved a good deal over the past few years, largely through the efforts of downtown hotels. Some might argue, though, that the city's complement of small neighborhood eateries is its real treasure.

Oswald's Hof Brau Haus. 406 Lyell Avenue. 716-254-9660. Inexpensive German restaurant, also featuring some American dishes. For sausage, kraut, and beer, you can hardly go wrong here.

Budapest. 253 Alexander Street. 716-325-3700. Hungarian cuisine, as you might well imagine. Also American selections. Live entertainment.

Edward's. 13 South Fitzhugh Street. 716-423-0140. Perhaps the city's best, say those who should know; American and continental specialties served in a restored, historic downtown building. A good value within its price bracket.

There are also some good dining spots along "Restaurant Row," Alexander Street just off East Avenue. Some names: **Chez Jean Pierre; Lloyd's; Rio Bamba. Rooney's,** at 90 Henrietta Street, has an imaginative and well-executed *nouvelle* menu.

Rochester to Cleveland

Leaving Buffalo, a little less than an hour past Rochester, the *Lake Shore* finally begins to earn its name as it parallels the margin of Lake Erie. This is a land of vineyards and cherry orchards, and one which boasts a peculiar product—goat's milk fudge.

Lake Shore was also the name of a favorite car on the post-World War II *Twentieth Century.* In service until 1958, this segment of the *Century's* streamlined consist carried a bar, "Century Club" lounge, and shower bath, and its passengers could avail themselves of the services of a secretary and a barber. They were also treated to the morning newspapers of the city toward which they were headed and to the latest stock prices. Such luxury was de rigueur on a train that traveled in such a hurry that its steam locomotive used to take on water from troughs placed between the rails, without ever stopping. Sixteen hours, New York to Chicago. It lasted from 1902 to 1967.

The lakeside approach to Cleveland is made through the lands of the Western Reserve, a parcel of land once claimed by Connecticut as a sort of colony's colony. Not until several decades after independence did Connecticut relinquish its Ohio holdings, and it is often said that the small towns here have a New England look about them. Cleveland, however, does not resemble Hartford or New Haven.

Cleveland

Cleveland, into whose lakeside station the westbound *Lake Shore Limited* rolls early each morning, went for the same bumpy economic ride as a lot of northeastern industrial cities in the 1970s and early 1980s, but got the worst of the publicity associated with the decline of the smokestack towns because of its technical fiscal default. As civic officials somewhat testily point out, this really shouldn't be the way people think of Cleveland. Things have picked up here, as we should have expected they would: "post industrial" prophecies aside, cities this size do not simply shrivel up and die, even though there are bound to be some hard times as the economic base shifts. New construction—$750 million of it—has put a new face on downtown, and the promotion of a venture capital pool and high technology research promises to improve the local employment picture.

Cleveland dates back to 1796, when it was founded by General Moses Cleaveland and his party of surveyors who had come to map out Connecticut's Western Reserve. Its early prosperity was derived from the production of iron and steel, and from shipping on Lake Erie. By the 1860s, it was the largest city in the vicinity of the new western Pennsylvania oil fields and a hub of small-time petroleum distilling activity. In 1863, the year in which rail access to the fields was completed, a twenty-four-year-old commission merchant named John Davison Rockefeller organized a distilling firm that was soon to swallow all the others and emerge as the Standard Oil Company. Rockefeller ran his business for years from Cleveland before moving to New York (his office building still stands on Superior Avenue near W. Ninth Street), and he is buried in Lake View Cemetery here.

Travelers overly accustomed to Cleveland's bad press of the past few years are in for as much of a surprise as those who think that Lake Erie is barren of fish and sailboats. Both Cleveland and the inland sea it faces are on the rebound; for evidence of the city's survival, just walk uphill from the station to the Hanna Fountain Mall, a summer haven for lunching office workers and live outdoor music. From here you can begin the exploration of a downtown and city that are still very much in business.

Points of Interest

University Circle. East Boulevard and Euclid Avenue. Located at the Case Western Reserve University campus on Cleveland's east side, this is the home of many Cleveland cultural institutions. The **Cleveland Museum of Art** is at 11150 East Boulevard (216-421-7340); open Tuesday, Thursday, and Friday, 10 A.M.–6 P.M., Wednesday 10 A.M.–10 P.M., Saturday, 9 A.M.–5 P.M.; Sunday, 1–6 P.M.; closed Monday. The **Crawford Auto-Aviation Museum,** housing over two hundred historic vehicles, is at 10825 East Boulevard (216-721-5722); open Tuesday through Saturday, 10 A.M.–5 P.M.; Sunday, Noon–5 P.M.; closed Monday. Also on University Circle is **Severance Hall,** where the Cleveland Orchestra performs.

Cleveland Museum of Natural History. Wade Oval, University Circle. 216-231-4600. Fine exhibits document living and extinct life forms, including the fossil remains of "Lucy," the most complete early hominid found to date. Planetarium, observatory. Open Monday through Saturday 10 A.M.–5 P.M.; Sunday 1–5 P.M.

The Arcade. 401 Euclid Avenue, opposite E. Fourth Street. 216-621-8500. This is one of the first enclosed, multitiered shopping malls ever built (1890). Meticulously restored and tenanted with attractive shops, it makes for a very beautiful and useful indoor space. There is a good sandwich shop with balcony tables and a fine new and used bookshop called Keisogloff's.

Terminal Tower. Public Square. Cleveland's landmark building has a top-floor observatory, which is open Saturday and Sunday, noon–5 P.M. Note the barrel-vaulted and coffered ceiling as you go into the lobby. Outside, in the southeast quadrant of Public Square, stands the **Soldiers and Sailors Monument** (212-621-3710). This high-Victorian structure is dedicated to Cleveland's Civil War dead and features (on the inside) impressive bronze relief sculptures of Lincoln, his generals, and advisers. Open every day, 9 A.M.–5 P.M.

Howard Dittrick Museum of Historical Medicine. 11000 Euclid Avenue. 216-368-3648. See recreations of nineteenth-century pharmacy and doctor's office, primitive fetishes, Chinese medicine dolls, early microscopes. Open Monday through Friday, 10 A.M.–5 P.M.; Sunday, 1–5 P.M. (open Saturday instead of Sunday in June, July, August).

Public Transportation

The Greater Cleveland Regional Transit Authority operates the city's buses, as well as the rapid-transit trains that run along the green, blue, and red lines to the suburbs. For schedule and fare information call 216-621-9500.

Lodging

The convenient location of Cleveland's Amtrak station gives travelers easy access to many downtown motels and hotels. Those first two blocks, however, are long ones. Expect to pay anywhere from $35 to $90.

Holiday Inn Lakeside. 1111 Lakeside Avenue. 216-241-5100. Two blocks from station. This is the one that you see on the bluff as you get off the train—it's probably the closest hotel for the rail traveler. Pool, sauna, health club. Restaurant, lounge.

Hollenden House. 610 Superior Avenue. 216-621-0700. A comfortable, mid-sized downtown hotel. Lounge, restaurant, indoor pool. Suites available.

Restaurants

Cleveland's old-line specialties belong to the heavy, hearty central European traditions, although "continental" cuisine is making its inroads, for better or worse. Lake Erie whitefish used to be a local delicacy, but the lake hasn't recovered sufficiently to provide a substantial harvest.

The Whole Grain. Illuminating Building, 55 Public Square. 216-861-0997. Wholesome soups, salads, and sandwiches served cafeteria style. Breakfast.

Captain Frank's. E. Ninth Street Pier. 216-771-4900. Seafood dishes, steaks, chops. The location, just across the road from the Amtrak station, makes this a good spot to kill time while waiting for the late-night, eastbound *Lake Shore*—and there's a TV in the bar.

Ohio City Tavern. 2801 Bridge Avenue. 216-687-0505. The Tavern started out as a stagecoach stop; today, it retains an "old Cleveland" ambience (with surprising touches like a stained glass ceiling). Try the chicken in provolone cheese sauce; also steaks, seafood.

Cleveland to Detroit and Chicago

The *Lake Shore* continues west out of Cleveland, stopping at Elyria and Sandusky, where connections can be made for ferries to the Lake Erie islands. Along with the trains, huge lake steamers were once a favored means of travel between Cleveland and Detroit; now, Amtrak has made a rail connection between the two cities possible once again. Detroit-bound passengers change at Toledo for the *Lake Cities*, which heads north toward the motor capital, then cuts westward across Michigan (Ann Arbor, Jackson, Battle Creek, Kalamazoo) on its way to Chicago. Schedules are designed both for this westbound connection and for the convenience of eastbound *Lake Cities* passengers wishing to continue on toward New York or Boston. (The *Lake Cities* is not the only Chicago-Michigan train. The *Twilight Limited* and *Wolverine* serve Detroit daily, and the *International* connects Chicago with Toronto by way of Port Huron.

Detroit

Amtrak's Detroit station, on Vernor Highway near Michigan Avenue, is in a gritty, nondescript neighborhood that all too accurately fits the public notion about this town. Turn east on Michigan Avenue, and you'll approach a typical mid-century American skyline—gray, step-backed office towers, the cityscape of hotel big-band broadcasts, black telephones, and fireside chats. Detroit, it appears, must surely wear a slouch hat, its felt worn thin and a little shiny.

In the middle of the picture, though, stands an incongruous aspiration of blue glass, the half-billion-dollar Renaissance Center—"an architectural precursor," one promoter insists, "of the twenty-first century." The "Ren Cen," as it has come to be called, is bright, clean, and dynamic—slender, elegant crystals of blue quartz dropped from space. But Detroiters must surely wonder whether they still want it to be considered a precursor of the future: however striking Ren Cen may be, it has not been an economic success.

As for the city that stands behind it, forecasters are now a little more sanguine than they were when the first edition of *Train Trips* was written—the U.S. auto industry has shown itself capable of snapping out of what many had considered its terminal slump, and of course Detroit answers to the carmakers' ups and downs. But even during the '60s boom years, Detroit suffered from ills that have become the textbook phenomena of urban America: erosion of its tax base, middle-class flight to the suburbs, downtown blight. The terrible race riots of 1967 were the culmination of these and many other problems. Renaissance Center—and, more importantly, the combination of private funding and municipal cooperation that made it and other revitalization efforts possible—is regarded by Detroit's boosters as evidence that the city can make a comeback. Needless to say, the jury is still out. Many people feel that it was a mistake to lavish money on a shiny symbol when less visible corners of the city still struggle for their economic life; others are sure that a centerpiece is necessary, and that downtown is the place to start.

Regardless of your feelings about the politics of Renaissance Center, you'll probably have fun getting lost amidst its shops and will no doubt enjoy the top-story views of Detroit and across the river to Canada. But explore the 313-225-1701. Coins of the past twenty-five hundred years; unusual curren-

rest of downtown as well; head out Woodward Avenue to visit the institutions clustered in Detroit's Cultural Center; go see the assembly lines in action at the automobile factories. Decide for yourself if this city is really on the upswing—if those Ozlike towers harbor wizards dealing in results, or only in appearance.

Points of Interest

Greenfield Village and Henry Ford Museum. Off US 12 near Southfield Road, Dearborn. 313-271-1620. Henry Ford's 260-acre Greenfield Village is two things: a monument to the industrial revolution and a memorial to the world it made obsolete. Here are Edison's laboratories, the Wright brothers' bicycle shop, and the birthplace of Luther Burbank; also buildings transported from the Cotswolds, a courthouse where Lincoln practiced law, and dozens of other historic structures and working crafts and industrial exhibits. All are authentic, and the landscaping is beautiful. The Henry Ford Museum, adjacent to the village, houses Ford memorabilia, including his first engine, first car, and first Model T; also decorative arts and extensive technology exhibits. Open 9 A.M–5 P.M. daily; closed only on Thanksgiving, Christmas, and New Year's Day.

Detroit Zoological Park. 8450 W. Ten Mile Road, at Woodward Avenue. 313-398-0900. One of the nation's better zoos; 40 natural habitat exhibits; also animal shows; miniature railroad, tractor trains. Open mid-May through mid-September, Monday through Saturday, 10 A.M.–5 P.M.; Sunday and holidays, 9 A.M.–6 P.M. Rest of year, open Wednesday through Sunday, 10 A.M.–4 P.M.

Belle Isle. This is an island park in the Detroit River, accessible via the MacArthur Bridge. In addition to its 1,000 acres of greenery, the park features the **Whitcomb Conservatory,** with greenhouses and outdoor flower gardens, open every day from 9 A.M.–6 P.M.; the oldest aquarium in the Western Hemisphere, and the **Dossin Great Lakes Museum.** Here you can see a reconstructed salon from the passenger steamer *City of Detroit III* and many other paintings, models, and artifacts dating back to the days of sail on the lakes. Open from Wednesday to Sunday from 10 A.M.–5:45 P.M. While you're on the island, visit the Belle Isle Aquarium (313-398-0903). Opened in 1904, this is the nation's oldest fresh water aquarium, and houses over 5,000 fish. Open daily 10 A.M.–5:30 P.M. Belle Isle also has a small zoo (313-398-0903), open daily 10 A.M.–5 P.M., and a Nature Interpretive Center (313-267-7157) open Wednesday through Sunday 10 A.M.–4 P.M.

Detroit Institute of Arts. 5200 Woodward Avenue. 313-833-7900. Art from every major culture and historical period. Extensive African collections. Don't miss the Diego Rivera mural, capturing the blue-collar sinew of Detroit. Open Tuesday through Sunday from 9:30 A.M.–5:30 P.M. Closed Monday.

Children's Museum. 67 E. Kirby Avenue, near Woodward Avenue. 313-494-1210. American history miniatures; toy workshop, bird and mammal exhibits, ethnic heritage displays. Planetarium shows on Saturday. Open Monday through Friday from 1–4 P.M.; also Saturday from 9 A.M. October through May.

International Institute. 111 E. Kirby Avenue. 313-871-8600. "Gallery of Nations" in which arts and crafts of 43 nations are displayed. Also luncheons featuring foreign cuisines. Open Monday through Friday from 9 A.M.–5 P.M.

cies; bank notes and paper money. Open Monday through Thursday from 8:30 A.M.–8:30 P.M.; Friday 8:30 A.M.–5 P.M.

General Motors Exhibit. 3044 W. Grand Boulevard. 313-556-4444/3056. General Motors tour and exhibits focus on the company's current products. Open 9 A.M.–6 P.M. Monday–Friday; closed weekends and holidays.

The Metropolitan Detroit Convention and Visitors' Bureau is located in 100 Renaissance Center, Suite 1950. There is also a visitors' information center on Jefferson Avenue at the foot of Woodward. Call 313-963-0879 for information.

Public Transportation

Two public transportation agencies serve Detroit. Downtown and the nearer environs are the province of the Department of Transportation. For information, call 313-933-1300. Buses from downtown to the outer suburbs and a commuter rail service are run by the Southeast Michigan Transportation Authority (SEMTA). The SEMTA number for fare and schedule information is 313-962-5515. In addition, open-sided trolley cars shunt back and forth between Grand Circus Park and the Renaissance Center.

Lodging

Before Detroit's urban revitalization program began, its downtown was short on quality hotels. The gap has been filled, although primarily by the very expensive Westin Hotel in Renaissance Center. All downtown lodgings are about 2 miles from the Amtrak station. Rates will vary from $40 to $125 and up.

Youth Hostels. YMCA. 2020 Witherell Street. 313-962-6126. 1 block from Grand Circus Park. Also **YWCA.** 2230 Witherell Street. 313-961-9220.

Balmar Motel. 3250 E. Jefferson. 313-568-2000. Probably the best bargain in downtown Detroit. Near Renaissance Center. Pool, saunas, cabana. Restaurant.

Mariner Hotel. 231 Michigan Avenue (corner Washington Boulevard) 313-965-1050/800-654-2000. Conveniently located on the trolley line, between Grand Circus Plaza and the Renaissance Center. Some suites available. Rooftop pool, sauna. Restaurant, lounge.

Hotel Pontchartrain. 2 Washington Boulevard 313-965-0200/800-323-7500. A twenty-five-story modern hotel opposite Renaissance Center and overlooking the Detroit River. Heated pool. Rooftop restaurant, several lounges.

Westin Renaissance Center Detroit. Renaissance Center. 313-568-8000/800-228-3000. This Western International extravaganza stands at the core of Renaissance Center and, at seventy-three stories, is the world's tallest hotel. Superlative views, especially from the revolving rooftop restaurant lounge. Twenty-four-hour room service, along with 13 different restaurants and lounges and "cocktail pods" in the atrium. Year-round pool, health club. The whole effect is pure futurama.

Restaurants

According to Detroit's promotional literature, James Beard has ranked the city among America's three top restaurant towns (the other two must be New York and San Francisco). A number of good places survived downtown's lean **Money Museum.** National Bank of Detroit. 200 Renaissance Center.

years; also, turn to a neighborhood called Greektown (vicinity of Beaubien Street and Monroe Avenue) for good, inexpensive ethnic cooking.

New Hellas Cafe. 583 Monroe Avenue. 313-961-5544. Since 1901. An excellent, inexpensive moussaka; also pastitsio, stuffed grape leaves, shish kebab, lamb dishes. Flaming kasseri cheese is a specialty. Baklava recommended. Other favorite Monroe Street spots are the **Grecian Gardens** and **Old Parthenon.**

The Bull Market. 135 W. Lafayette Avenue. 313-963-8010. Convenient downtown location, though only open until 8 P.M. (bar until 9). Lamb chops à la greque; fresh whitefish. Good desserts.

Pontchartrain Wine Cellars. 234 W. Larned Street. 313-963-1785. Intimate bistro atmosphere. Cooking mostly provincial French—lamb, ratatouille, skewered shrimp—along with classics such as veal Cordon Bleu.

Travelers opting to remain on the *Lake Shore* instead of changing for Detroit continue due west into the flatlands of northern Indiana. Leaving Toledo, the train enters onto a 67½-mile stretch of track which is the third longest straightaway in the United States. Between Bryan, Ohio, and Elkhart, Indiana, the tracks ascend to their highest point—995 feet—on the New York-Chicago route. A lesser height of land, just beyond South Bend, Indiana (home of Notre Dame University), marks the division of the St. Lawrence and Mississippi watersheds. Unfortunately, the route offers no view of the famous Indiana Dunes, along the south shore of Lake Michigan, although parts of these are visible to *Lake Cities* passengers heading out of Chicago. The *Lake Shore* instead makes its entry into the metropolis by way of the steel towns of Gary and Hammond, whose furnace flames light the lakeside horizon on dreary days.

Somewhere amidst these factories and freight yards, the *Lake Shore*, like the old *Twentieth Century*, rolls across the border between Indiana and Illinois, into the South Side of America's second largest city.

Chicago

Chicago is the great rail terminus of America, the place from which tracks radiate in every direction of the compass. "Player with railroads," Sandburg called it, but the railroads made Chicago as much as Chicago made the railroads. The founding of the small lakeside settlement which grew to become America's second city did predate the laying of track from the East, but the town's central location in relation to established and developing trade routes assured its future prominence. In 1848 no railroads entered Chicago; six years later, it was the rail capital of the Midwest.

In his book *Chicago*, Norman Mark quotes Henry B. Fuller as having said, "Chicago is the only great city in the world to which all its citizens have come for the avowed purpose of making money." This statement grants too much altruism to the settlers of other metropolises; but there can be no doubt that fewer emigrant-entrepreneurs set about their business with greater dispatch than the founders of Chicago.

A canal link to the Mississippi River was begun in 1827, and two years later the first meat-packing plant opened. In 1832, when the streets were initially laid out, the population of Chicago stood at 100. By 1837, when the town was organized as a city, this figure had grown to nearly 4200. Numbers can only tell so much about a place, and their recital gets wearisome—but one set of statistics speaks volumes about the sheer dynamism of Chicago's growth: in 1838, 38 bags of wheat were shipped east from the fledgling town; in 1842, 587,000 bushels left Chicago for the markets of the Atlantic Seaboard. The total in 1858 was 20 million bushels of assorted grains; the pattern of growth was set. Had the trade in beaver pelts never been replaced by the lucrative business of transporting the bounty of the newly broken prairie farmlands, neither Chicago nor its railroads could have grown at such a pace. In 1857, New York Central tracks reached Chicago, and by the end of that decade the city that had grown up around old Fort Dearborn was the rail center not only of its region but of the nation as well.

Like all Amtrak service originating and terminating at Chicago, the *Lake Shore* makes use of Union Station, the only remaining downtown depot served by long-distance trains. Union Station is neither the biggest nor the most distinctive American rail passenger terminal, but its present-day appearance and the combination of uses to which it has been put are truly representative. The big, barrel-vaulted main concourse is no longer the passenger waiting area; this function is now served by a much smaller room, appropriately low ceilinged and vinyl cushioned like the times we live in, adjacent to the Amtrak ticket windows. The concourse itself is jammed with shops.

One of the best ways to begin to get to know Chicago is to put your bags in a station locker and head for the Sears Tower. To reach the Tower from Union Station, turn left on S. Canal Street and walk to W. Adams. Then turn right and cross the bridge over the South Branch of the Chicago River; the Tower is directly ahead at the corner of W. Adams and S. Wacker Drive (total distance from station 2½ blocks).

Since the mid-1970s, the 1,454-foot Sears Tower has stood as the world's tallest building. At the 103rd story is the Skydeck, open 9 A.M.–midnight daily. The Skydeck is completely glassed in and offers a 360-degree view of Chicago. When visibility is perfect, locations as distant as Kenosha, Wisconsin, and the Indiana Dunes can be discerned. But the best thing about the view from this aerie is the opportunity it affords the new visitor to discover the layout and proportions of Chicago.

To the east, of course, is Lake Michigan, and the broad swath of greenery that parallels its shore is Grant Park. In the immediate foreground, between the Sears Tower and the park, is the Loop—Chicago's central downtown business and shopping district. It receives its name from the "loop" of elevated railway tracks that surrounds it. Northeast of the Loop the Chicago River marks the beginning of the city's "Gold Coast," an area of fine shops, hotels, and luxury apartments centered about Michigan Avenue and Lake Shore Drive. Chicago streets, incidentally, carry east, west, north, and south designations. The dividing line for east and west is State Street; for north and south, Madison Street.

Chicago Architecture

Having begun a stay in Chicago with a visit to the summit of the tallest and most exciting of its modern buildings, you might wish to learn a bit more about the city's architecture, one of its major contributions to modern American life, by visiting some of the landmark structures that stand in or near the Loop. A good place to begin is at Archi Center, 310 South Michigan Avenue, second floor (312-782-1776). The center houses an exhibit of well-captioned drawings and photographs documenting the development of Chicago architectural styles and the engineering accomplishments which accompanied it.

The Auditorium Building. 430 S. Michigan. Now the home of Roosevelt University, the Auditorium was built over a period of four years in the late 1880s and represents the first attempt to house a theater, offices, and hotel rooms under one roof. It is the crowning work of the partnership of Dankmar Adler and Louis Sullivan (note Sullivan's decorative efforts inside and out) and was the heaviest building in the world at the time of its completion. As with other landmark Chicago structures, engineering breakthroughs achieved in the Auditorium became standard practices in the twentieth-century builder's trade.

The Rookery. 209 S. LaSalle. The great firm of Burnham and Root built the Rookery in 1886. It is constructed around a soaring inner courtyard, the remodeling of which, early in this century, was the work of Frank Lloyd Wright. Be sure to take note of John W. Root's lacy ironwork detailing in the building's entrance hall.

The Monadnock Building. 53 W. Jackson. When Burnham and Root's Monadnock Building was completed in 1893, it was the world's tallest office structure. At 16 stories, it remains the world's highest building with masonry load-bearing exterior walls. The Monadnock's clean lines retain their austere gracefulness even today, when simplicity of form and absence of ornament are taken for granted in office buildings.

Carson Pirie Scott Building. One State Street. Built in 1899 and enlarged in 1903-4, this recently restored Louis Sullivan masterpiece remains a testament to both the respect for functional, uncluttered lines and talent for rich, organically inspired ornament which fused with such uncanny ease in this great architect's work.

Frank Lloyd Wright District. Oak Park. A visit to this western suburb will take a good half day or more, but is well worth it. Here is where Wright worked for nearly 20 years early in his career, designing homes for his neighbors along the streets that surrounded his own residence and studio. That structure, at Forest and Chicago avenues, Oak Park, is open for guided tours; other Wright buildings in the neighborhood are privately owned and must be viewed from the street. Here also, at the corner of Lake and Kenilworth avenues, is Wright's famous Unity Temple. To get to the Oak Park Visitors' Center, where maps, books, and film presentations on the architect's work are available, take the Lake-Dan Ryan rapid transit line to the Harlem stop in Oak Park (last stop on the line). Follow Harlem Avenue to Lake Avenue (pedestrian shopping mall); turn right and then left on N. Forest Avenue. The Center is at 158 N. Forest, and is open from April through October. Phone 312-848-1978.

Points of Interest

Art Institute of Chicago. Michigan Avenue at Adams Street. 312-443-3600. One of the world's great art museums. Renowned for its French Impressionist collection, American painting and sculpture, European decorative arts, textiles, Orientalia, photography (including the Alfred Stieglitz collection), pre-Columbian and African art, and eighteenth-century French and Italian drawings. Also houses the Thorne rooms, a collection of miniature European and American rooms which illustrate eight centuries of interior design; Trading Room of the old Chicago Stock Exchange, a masterpiece in the turn-of-the-century "Arts and Crafts" idiom. Open Monday, Wednesday, and Friday, 10:30 A.M.–4:30 P.M.; Thursday, 10:30 A.M.–8 P.M.; Saturday, 10 A.M.–5 P.M.; and Sunday, noon–5 P.M.

Museum of Science and Industry. Lake Shore Drive at Fifty-seventh Street (South Side; take rapid-transit Jackson Park line south from Loop). 312-684-1414. Largest museum in the world devoted to the practical applications of science and technology. A pioneer in the "hands on" approach to museum exhibits. The museum and its grounds, which cover fourteen acres, are perhaps best known for two attractions: the U-505, a captured World War II German submarine; and a working coal mine, into which visitors descend by elevator for a train ride and a thorough explanation of mining technology. Open daily, 9:30 A.M.–5:30 P.M., from May through Labor Day. Rest of the year, hours are 9:30 A.M.–4 P.M. Monday through Friday; 9:30 A.M.–5:30 P.M. Saturday, Sunday, and holidays.

Field Museum of Natural History. Lake Shore Drive at Roosevelt Road (southern end of Grant Park). 312-922-9410. One of the nation's great repositories of artifacts and interpretive exhibits chronicling man's physical surroundings and his evolution within them. Extensive dioramas and life-size displays cover anthropology, zoology, botany, and geology (gem collections are particularly interesting—you may never see so much jade under one roof). Open daily, 9 A.M.–5 P.M.; closed only on Christmas, New Year's Day, and Thanksgiving.

John G. Shedd Aquarium. 1200 S. Lake Shore Drive (on Lake Michigan, southern end of Grant Park). 312-939-2438. Indoor aquarium houses over 5,000 individual living specimens representing over 500 species. Ninety-thousand-gallon coral reef exhibit, an accurate simulation of a Caribbean marine ecosystem. Visitors can watch divers feeding fish along the reef each day. Open daily, 9 A.M.–5 P.M. May through August; 10 A.M.–5 P.M. during September, October, March, and April; 10 A.M.–4 P.M. from November through February.

Adler Planetarium. 1300 S. Lake Shore Drive (on Lake Michigan, just east of the Shedd Aquarium). One-hour sky shows (call 322-0300 for schedules); sun telescope; exhibits detailing man's exploration of space. Collection of antique navigation and sky-charting instruments. On clear evenings, visitors can tour **Doane Observatory**, on the lakefront adjacent to the planetarium. Open daily, mid-June through August, 9:30 A.M.–9 P.M. Rest of the year, 9 A.M.–4 P.M. daily; Friday until 9 P.M.

Lincoln Park Zoo. Lincoln Park, 2200 N. Cannon Drive (north from Loop on rapid-transit Howard Line). 312-294-4660. Thirty-five acres; over 2,800 animals, reptiles, and birds. Don't miss the new ape house, American farm, and the only pair of Indian lions in the United States. Open daily, 9 A.M.–5 P.M.

Chicago Public Library and Cultural Center. 78 E. Washington Street. 312-269-2837. Designed by the famous Boston firm of Shepley, Rutan, and Coolidge and built in 1896, the magnificently restored main Chicago library is now a city cultural center as well. The mosaics in the interior are superb. Programs and exhibits change with the seasons and include art and historical exhibits as well as dance, theater, and music. Open 9 A.M.–7 P.M. Monday through Thursday; until 6 P.M. Friday; 9 A.M.–5 P.M. Saturday. Open Sunday for special programs only.

Grant Park and Buckingham Fountain. Between Michigan Avenue and

Lake Shore Drive; fountain is at the foot of Congress Parkway. Scene of the fateful confrontation between Chicago police and antiwar demonstrators during the 1968 Democratic convention, Grant Park is a tranquil place today, with broad lawns and floral plantings in spring and summer. The park's crowning glory is the immense Buckingham Fountain, which is set in operation at intervals throughout each day from late spring through September. Between 9 and 10 P.M. on summer evenings, and on concert nights in the park, colored lights play upon the columns of water.

Around Chicago

For shoppers, the two most important areas are the State Street Mall, in the heart of the Loop, and Michigan Avenue, north of the Chicago River. State Street is the home of the big department stores, Marshall Field and Carson Pirie Scott; upper Michigan Avenue—also known as the "Boul Mich" and "Magnificent Mile"—is known for its chic couturiers and specialty shops, for the John Hancock Center and the sparkling new multileveled Water Tower Place. Whether you are shopping or not, a walk up Michigan Avenue from, say, Congress Parkway to the Water Tower will provide a fine visual sampling of downtown Chicago. At about midpoint, you'll cross the Chicago River; this is as good a place as any to take a long look in every direction. To the west, on the river's north shore is the vast Merchandise Mart; closer by are the twin cylindrical towers of Marine City and the glazed, wedding-cake heights of the Wrigley Building, one of the few structures anywhere that is regularly washed as well as brilliantly illuminated by night. Across Michigan Avenue is the Tribune Tower, which won a famous architectural competition in the 1920s. Just below, along the Chicago River embankment, is the point of departure for Mercury Boat Rides, which offers river and harbor tours of varying durations. The Water Tower, which dominates Michigan Avenue some nine blocks beyond the river, is the only building in this area to have survived the calamitous fire of 1871. Today, it houses a visitor information center.

Wandering back into the Loop, you may wish to look at two striking, and whimsical, pieces of modern civic sculpture, the Alexander Calder Stegosaurus (S. Dearborn Street, between Jackson and Adams) and the "Chicago Picasso," a bizarre avian contrivance that stands before the Richard J. Daley Center on Dearborn between Washington and Randolph.

The South Side is by far the biggest neighborhood in Chicago, yet it is the one least known to outsiders except by hearsay and stereotype. One thing you may have heard is true: the South Side is the home of the Chicago Blues, which evolved here from its original mournful, acoustic Mississippi Delta forms into a driving, amplified style now heard around the world in the work of original bluesmen and rock and roll imitators alike. Buddy Guy owns the Checker Board Lounge, 423 East Forty-third Street, which is as good a place as any to hear this local specialty. Call 312-373-5948 to find out who's playing. This is not the safest neighborhood in Chicago, but then again all bad urban reputations are exaggerated. Use your own judgment and don't be obtrusive.

Public Transportation

Chicago is served by an extensive municipal system of elevated trains, subways, and buses, as well as by commuter rail lines to the outlying suburbs. If you are heading north, west, or south via one of the elevated or subway lines, it's important to make sure that the train you're boarding is destined for the specific stop you have in mind; the lines do branch out beyond the immediate downtown area. All inbound trains, of course, return to the Loop. For route and schedule information, call the Chicago Transit Authority at 312-664-7200.

Lodging

Chicago hotels are not inexpensive, unless you are used only to New York City standards. A tariff that would buy you a spacious, comfortable room in a smaller city further west will purchase only modest, perhaps borderline shabby, quarters here. Acceptable doubles in or within reasonable walking distance of the Loop begin at about $40 per night; at the upper end of the scale, you will have no trouble spending $125 or more.

Harrison Hotel. 65 E. Harrison. 312-427-8000. 12 blocks from station. Located just south of the Loop; convenient to Grant Park and Field Museum. Two restaurants; air conditioning; free in-room movies. No frills but low prices.

Midland Hotel. 172 W. Adams. 312-332-1200. 5 blocks from station. Convenient to Sears Tower, State Street shops. Renovated 1978. One of the better midtown values; location makes it popular with rail travelers. 100 of the 300 guest rooms have personal computers.

Conrad Hilton Hotel. 720 S. Michigan. 312-922-4400. 17 blocks from station. Twenty-three floors, 2,800 rooms—one of the world's largest hotels. Can seem like a small city when a convention is in town. Fine location opposite Grant Park; attractive rooms with spacious tiled baths. If you're traveling alone and don't need much room, ask for a "mini-single," a good value.

Sheraton-Plaza Hotel. 160 E. Huron. 312-787-2900/800-325-3535. 25 blocks from station. Good northside location, near Water Tower Place, Michigan Avenue shops, and Northwestern's Chicago campus. Hotel begins at fourteenth floor of 40-story building. Rooftop pool, health club, sauna, tennis.

Palmer House. 17 E. Monroe. 312-726-7500. 10 blocks from station. Old-fashioned elegance, though recently renovated. Famous Empire Room restaurant. Glass-domed swimming pool. Top two floors contain deluxe Tower suites.

Ritz-Carlton. 160 E. Pearson Street. 312-266-1000. 28 blocks from station. A Four Seasons hotel licensed to carry the famous Ritz name; occupies floors 12 through 31 of new 74-story Water Tower Place. Features such amenities as floor waiters for room service, double basins in bathrooms. Indoor pool and health club. Fine dining, lake views. Concierge service.

Restaurants

Although not noted for any one particular dish or cuisine (though some people make a case for a thick, crusty version of pizza as being a Chicago specialty), Chicago, like other large and ethnically varied cities, offers just about every type of food, in every price range. Proximity to midwestern cattle markets makes beef a good choice; yet, as if to prove that "the grass is always greener," Chicagoans regularly patronize seafood houses, many of which are overpriced. Chicago has a large Central European population, which means that locals and visitors are never at a loss for the type of food associated with cold winter nights. Neither are they at a loss for cold winter nights.

Heartland Cafe. 7000 N. Glenwood Avenue. 312-465-8005. Natural foods. Fish, chicken, and vegetable specialties every day. Good coffee, herb teas, and desserts. Entertainment. Near elevated-train stop.

The Berghoff. 17 W. Adams. 312-427-3170. Perhaps the best Chicago restaurant of the inexpensive-to-moderate category, particularly if you like German food (although the menu has plenty of variety). The atmosphere is strictly *Mitteleuropean* Chicago, with dark paneling and stained glass—perfect for the enjoyment of pickled herring, pork shanks, and mugs of the house beer.

Wrigley Building Restaurant. Wrigley Building, 410 N. Michigan. 312-944-7600. Pleasant and reasonably priced; particularly recommended for lunch, although dinner is also served. Unpretentious American menu runs to items such as oyster stew, broiled whitefish, and pork tenderloin.

The Bakery. 2218 N. Lincoln. 312-472-6942. For a fixed price, owner-chef Louis Szathinary serves a wonderful five-course dinner in the simple and intimate surroundings of an old bakery. Of the eight or so entree offerings, the roast goose and duck are standards—and standouts. The wine list is short but comprehensive; there are Hungarian Tokays available. For dessert, try the Linzer torte.

La Cheminee. 1161 N. Dearborn. 312-642-6654. Elegant and expensive, featuring well-executed dishes from the classic and provincial French repertoire. Stuffed squab and veal florentine are among the offerings. Entertainment.

The *Broadway Limited*

The *Broadway Limited*, another full-service, "Heritage Fleet" train, follows a more southerly route between New York and Chicago. It leaves New York's Pennsylvania Station in mid-afternoon every day, following the main line route of the Northeast Corridor south to Philadelphia, where there is a 20-minute layover before the train heads west into Pennsylvania. (For information on the Northeast Corridor and Philadelphia, see the following chapter. Another train, the *Pennsylvanian*, leaves New York each morning and follows the same route as the *Broadway* as far as Pittsburgh, where it arrives in late afternoon.)

The *Broadway*, incidentally, was named not for the famed New York street but for the six-track main line, nicknamed the "Broadway," which the Pennsylvania Railroad maintained between New York and Philadelphia. The Pennsy began deluxe service to Chicago along this route and the westbound track beyond as early as 1887, although the name *Broadway Limited* wasn't used until 1912. Thereafter, a mighty rivalry with the Central's *Twentieth Century* ensued, a rivalry symbolized by the two trains' racing each other out of Chicago's Englewood Station. The real winners, of course, were luxury-loving New Yorkers and Chicagoans.

The *Broadway* had an entirely different sort of topography to deal with than did the *Century*, and that led to the development of an engine called the Pacific. While the Central's Hudsons were adept at pulling the *Century* along its water-level route, the Pennsy's Pacifics were designed to negotiate the steep grades of the Allegheny Mountains. No one is sure, though, why they were called "Pacifics."

The *Broadway* leaves Philadelphia late in the afternoon, heading westward into Pennsylvania Dutch country. Lancaster, the second stop after Philadelphia, is the chief city of this region and the best layover point for passengers wishing to explore it. There is a railroad museum in nearby Strasburg.

The next stop is at Harrisburg, the capital of Pennsylvania. Near here you can see from the train window the giant cooling towers of the infamous Three Mile Island nuclear power plant. West of Harrisburg, during the longer days of the year, *Broadway* passengers can enjoy a lovely stretch of scenery—the sharp, parallel undulations of Blue Mountain, Mahanoy Ridge, and the Tuscaroras. The precipitousness of this terrain necessitated one of the great wonders of railroad building, the Horseshoe Curve, just west of Altoona. The curve was constructed in 1852 and has not been resurveyed since. Its central angle is 220 degrees, its total length is 2,375 feet, and it is graded at a steep 91 feet to the mile. Unfortunately, westbound passengers must content themselves with seeing only the front and rear lights of the *Broadway* as it rounds the curve. Heading east, in the light of morning, the whole arcing train is visible.

The next stop after Altoona is Johnstown, where in 1889 the rupture of the South Fork Dam caused the great Johnstown Flood, in which twenty-two hundred people lost their lives. West of Johnstown, the valleys and ridges continue their close alternation. At midnight, the *Broadway* reaches the point where the Allegheny and the Monongahela rivers flow together into the Ohio, and where the coal and iron of Pennsylvania and the whole Midwest flow together to create a river of steel.

Pittsburgh

Well into the middle of the twentieth century, Pittsburgh was a living symbol of the Industrial Revolution's dark bargain. "From the manufacturing establishments," said the Federal Writers' Program's 1940 Pennsylvania Guide, "come clouds of devastating smoke that unite with the river fog to form Pittsburgh's traditional nuisance, 'smog'." Poised between a depression and a world war, the writers of that day could surely go no further than to call smog a "nuisance," although they must have known that it was much more than that.

Pictures made as recently as the 1950s show a Pittsburgh in which high noon looked like evening and street lamps burned throughout the day. All through those years, grimmer evidence was accumulating in the lungs of Pittsburghers, until finally the pact with prosperity had to be reexamined.

Immediately after World War II, municipal and business interests began the job of bringing daylight back to Pittsburgh. Their chief weapon was the smokestack scrubber, a device installed atop the chimneys of factories and power plants to trap the soot and other particulate matter. The results have been remarkable; today, Pittsburgh is no longer derided as the "smoky city." Perhaps the best before-and-after evidence can be seen in the facades of old buildings that have been partly cleaned—their stones often show color that is completely indistinguishable in places not yet stripped of decades of soot.

The recovery isn't complete; on occasional days the outline of the hills still loses its sharpness. Also, the increased use of coal brings the less visible danger of sulfur pollution, often carried far downwind in the form of "acid rain." But Pittsburgh's cleaner air has given the city impetus to revitalize the city's downtown "Golden Triangle," so called because its shape is defined by the confluence of the Allegheny and Monongahela. Here there are not only new buildings but a fine state park and magnificent fountain at the very tip of the triangle. It would be wonderful if the spirit of renewal were to spread to the near-derelict Penn Central railroad station at Liberty and Grant streets—Amtrak passengers are now served by a prefab structure set up behind the old depot.

The steel, glass, and canned-goods empires that chose to make Pittsburgh the nation's second city measured in invested capital are not the only reason that the town is on the map. Pittsburgh's three rivers flow between steep ridges; together, the navigable waters and commanding heights made this a prized location for forts during the days when England and France struggled for dominance of the Ohio Valley. Later the rivers invited trade, and as the city grew, the hills, regardless of their pitch, were surveyed for homesites. The problem of near-vertical commuting was solved in 1870 by the introduction of "inclines," best described as a cross between a cable car and an elevator. Two inclines, the Duquesne and the Monongahela, still make the steep climb up Mount Washington. From the upper terminus of either incline, you can see all three rivers, the Golden Triangle, and the hills beyond the city's North Side on a clear day. And, fortunately, clear days in Pittsburgh aren't that hard to come by anymore.

Points of Interest

Fort Pitt Museum. Point State Park. 412-281-9284. On the site of French Fort Duquesne and later British Fort Pitt, the museum does a very thorough job of explaining the strategic history of the Ohio Forks area. Reconstruction of trader's cabin; dioramas; old weapons. Original blockhouse nearby. Open Wednesday through Saturday from 9 A.M.–5 P.M.; Sunday noon–5 P.M. Closed Monday and Tuesday.

University of Pittsburgh Cathedral of Learning—Nationality Classrooms. Bigelow Boulevard near Fifth Avenue. 412-624-6000. On the first floor of this striking neo-Gothic skyscraper are 19 classrooms constructed and designed according to the traditions of different nationalities. The authenticity and craftsmanship are impressive. Open every day; classes sometimes in session.

Conservatory—Aviary. Allegheny Commons, near Ridge and Arch Streets (North Side). 412-322-7855. Many exotic birds in natural tropical settings. Some extremely rare species, such as the African Starling. The mynahs say "hello."

Old Post Office Museum. 1 Landmark Square (North Side). 412-322-1204. The history of Allegheny County and its people, told in photos, documents, and a wealth of artifacts. Open weekdays from 10 A.M.–4:30 P.M.; weekends from 1–4:30 P.M. Closed Monday.

Frick Art Museum. 7227 Reynolds Street. 412-371-7766. European paintings—Italian, French, Flemish—from early Renaissance through eighteenth century. Open Wednesday through Saturday from 10 A.M.–5:30 P.M.; Sunday from noon to 6 P.M. Closed Monday and Tuesday.

The Pittsburgh Visitor Information Center is located in Gateway Center, near the Gateway Towers. Call 412-281-9222 for information.

Public Transportation

Pittsburgh has both trolleys and buses. They're run by Port Authority Transit (PAT); for information call 412-231-5707.

Lodging

Pittsburgh now has more downtown hotel rooms than it did just a few years back, although the budget-minded may find it necessary to locate themselves a little less centrally and use the transit system. The YMCA, at 304 Wood Street, offers basic accommodations. Rates at the four big Golden Triangle hotels run between $65 and $110.

William Penn. Mellon Square. 412-553-5100/800-245-4728. 4 blocks from the station. Pittsburgh's "old guard" hotel, now handsomely refurbished. In the heart of the Triangle. Special "Crown Service" available on two floors; includes continental breakfast, wine, cheese. Restaurants, lounges, entertainment.

Pittsburgh Hilton. Gateway Center. 412-391-4600. 10 blocks from the station. Modern hotel overlooking the Allegheny River, Point State Park, and Pittsburgh's North Side. Spacious rooms; several restaurants and lounges.

Hyatt Pittsburgh. Chatham Center. 412-471-1234/800-228-9000. 6 blocks from station. Comfortable chain hotel, somewhat to the east of downtown and near Civic Arena. Indoor pool, health club. Restaurants, lounges, entertainment.

Sheraton Station Square. 412-261-2000. Pittsburgh's newest hotel is part of the Station Square complex, close to downtown via the Smithfield Street Bridge. Indoor pool, restaurants, lounges, entertainment.

Restaurants

Pittsburgh has made progress on upgrading its culinary image as well as its air quality—but don't overlook small places in ethnic neighborhoods like the North Side. There are also a number of inexpensive eateries in the Station Square restoration, just over the Smithfield Bridge from downtown.

Allegheny Tavern. 537 Suisman Street, North Side. 412-231-1899. Only four owners since 1899, and all have kept it the picture of the German neighborhood tavern. Sausage plates, "Einlauf" dumpling soup, lunchtime buffet. Beer served in mason jars, and a player piano.

Klein's. 330 Fourth Avenue. 412-566-8615. Specializing in seafood—Maine lobsters; soft-shell crabs in season. Also basic steak-house fare. Since 1900.

Grand Concourse. One Station Square, near Smithfield Street Bridge. 412-261-1717. Occupies the entire lower floor of the old Pittsburgh and Lake Erie Railroad station—very plush, with river and city views from a glassed-in terrace. Escargots; paella; fish chowder; steak and shellfish for two. Saloon and oyster bar adjacent.

Pittsburgh to Chicago

The craggy profile of Pennsylvania gives way, after Pittsburgh, to the rolling hills and level farmland of central Ohio, which the *Broadway* traverses in the night. An early morning stop is Fort Wayne, Indiana, named for General "Mad Anthony" Wayne, who was instrumental in wresting the surrounding territory from the British and Indians in the 1790s. Earlier, this was the site of the French fur-trading post of Fort Miamis, so called because of the Miami Indians. Near Warsaw (not a station stop), the *Broadway* crosses the Tippecanoe River, another part of Indiana geography familiar to American history buffs. The battlefield where General William Henry Harrison defeated the Indians is, however, some distance to the southwest, near Lafayette.

The final Indiana stops are Valparaiso and Gary; then, like the *Lake Shore*, the *Broadway* enters the industrial satellites of Chicago, arriving at Union Station at the beginning of the business day.

Hoosier State, Cardinal, and *Capitol Limited*

Service between Chicago and points east is not limited to the *Lake Shore* and the *Broadway.* The *Hoosier State* links Chicago with Indianapolis each day; however, eastbound connections out of the Indiana capital to Cincinnati and other points must be made by bus. The *Cardinal* provides thrice-weekly service between New York and Chicago by way of Washington, D.C., and Cincinnati, taking a southerly route through northern Virginia and central West Virginia. (The route is fairly direct from Washington, although you wouldn't want to take it all the way from New York to Chicago unless time is not a factor. It is, however, the best New York-Cincinnati connection.) The *Capitol Limited* runs daily between Washington and Chicago via Pittsburgh; from Pittsburgh to Chicago, its route is the same as that of the *Broadway.*

Cincinnati

If the railroad had never supplanted the riverboat as the nation's favored means of moving goods from one place to another, Cincinnati might have grown bigger than Chicago. The metropolis of southern Ohio, and the state's second largest city, stands at an ideal location for pursuing Ohio River shipping—on the river, obviously, but also midway between the northern and southern states.

Early in its history, around the turn of the nineteenth century, Cincinnati prospered as a way station for settlers heading westward down the river; later, it succeeded in cornering trade with the southern states. The South was especially eager to obtain meat and produce from the farms of Ohio, since it preferred to plant little else but cotton on its own lands. The Civil War disrupted this arrangement only temporarily. Far more serious was the railroads' usurping of Cincinnati's routes and markets. It took both factory development and the building of a municipally owned railroad to restore the city's economic base. Cincinnati flourished to become what Winston Churchill called America's most beautiful city.

Both Cincinnati's location and its mercantile past make it partly a Northern and partly a Southern city, but what may first strike the visitor attuned to nuances of architecture and style is that it seems partly to be a German city, in much the same way that Milwaukee is. Germans began to turn up in Cincinnati in the 1830s. They congregated in a neighborhood called "Over the Rhine," but soon spread throughout the city to influence its cultural and economic life. Even today, it is not unusual to find German inscriptions on older Cincinnati buildings. On Fountain Square, there is a Munich-built statue called the "Genius of Water." It is a 43-foot structure surmounted by a bronze maiden from whose fingers spray jets of water.

A much larger and even more impressive example of Cincinnati public works will please both preservationists and railroad buffs, but not without touching a sense of irony in the latter. This is Union Terminal, a hemispheric art deco building that cost $43 million in 1943. It stands at the head of Ezzard Charles Drive. Cincinnati realized that it was too good to tear down, but it is a rail depot no longer—instead, it houses restaurants and shops. Amtrak trains arrive and depart from a small new station out on River Road, some distance from downtown.

Points of Interest

Cincinnati Art Museum. Art Museum Drive, Eden Park. 513-721-5204. 118 galleries, housing classical sculpture; Doane collection of musical instruments; period rooms. Also local art, including ceramics from Cincinnati's famous Rookwood Potteries. Open Tuesday through Saturday, 10 A.M.–5 P.M.; Sunday, 1–5 P.M. Closed Monday.

Other Eden Park cultural institutions include:

—**Cincinnati Historical Society.** 513-241-4622. Open Tuesday through Friday, 9 A.M.–4:30 P.M.; Saturday, 9 A.M.–4 P.M. Closed Sunday and Monday.

—**Cincinnati Museum of Natural History.** 513-621-3889. Planetarium. Open Tuesday through Saturday, 9 A.M.–4:30 P.M.; Sunday, 12:30–5 P.M. Closed Monday.

—**Krohn Conservatory.** 513-352-4086. Floral displays. Open every day, 10 A.M.–5 P.M.

Taft Museum. Pike and Fourth streets. 513-241-0343. Fine collection of European Masters; also Chinese porcelain—but the Federal-styled building and lovely gardens are an attraction in themselves. Open Monday through Saturday, 10 A.M.–5 P.M.; opens at 2 P.M. Sunday and holidays except Thanksgiving and Christmas.

Cincinnati Zoo. 3400 Vine Street. 513-281-4700. A splendid zoo harboring many endangered species. Outdoor lowland gorilla exhibit; white Bengal tigers; butterfly aviary. Children's zoo. Open every day, 9 A.M.–5 P.M.

The Greater Cincinnati Chamber of Commerce has offices at 120 West Fifth Street. For information, call 513-579-3100.

Public Transportation

Queen City Metro operates the buses in Cincinnati. For schedules and fares, call 513-621-9450.

Lodging

Cincinnati has only a handful of quality downtown hotels, but they are not expensive by the standards of many cities. Main Street has a few old, low-priced hotels; they are not for the fussy. Otherwise, expect to pay from $45 to $90, except, of course, at the hostels listed immediately below. All are too far from the station to measure in blocks.

Youth Hostels. Two hostels are available here: the **University of Cincinnati**, Sander Hall, U.C. Campus (800 capacity June-September; 513-475-6461/475-6580); and the **Home Hostel** (513-541-1972).

Netherland Plaza. 35 W. Fifth Street. 513-421-9100. A big, nicely kept downtown hotel with spacious lobby and rooms. Convenient to Skywalk shops. Restaurants, lounges.

Holiday Inn—Downtown. Eighth and Linn streets. 513-241-8660. What you'd expect from the popular chain. Pool. Restaurant, disco bar, entertainment except Sunday.

Clarion Hotel Cincinnati. 141 W. Sixth Street. 513-352-2110. Large, modern hotel connected with the downtown Skywalk. Heated pool, saunas, health club. Three restaurants, lounges, entertainment.

Restaurants

Cincinnati is big on chili; you'll find Skyline and other chili parlors throughout town. It comes with or without beans, and various embellishments can be added. At the other end of the spectrum, there are a number of restaurants given five stars by the Mobil Guide.

Lenhardt's. 151 W. McMillan Street. 513-281-3600. German and Hungarian cooking in the old Cincinnati tradition. Eleven kinds of schnitzel. Good desserts.

Pigall's. 127 W. Fourth Street. 513-721-1345. Considered to be among Cincinnati's best; the recipient of many awards. Classic French cuisine; exquisite souffles and pastries. Extensive wine list. Reservations recommended.

A consist of four Amfleet cars, pulled by one of Amtrak's latest AEM-7 electric locomotives, stops at the newly-opened Baltimore Washington International (BWI) Airport station. Connecting buses take passengers directly from the station to BWI's main terminal building.   (Amtrak Photo)

2. The Northeast Corridor

Amtrak's most heavily patronized trains are those which run north and south along the Northeast Corridor, between Washington and Boston. Not all Corridor trains travel the full 456 miles of the route; some go no farther north than New Haven, and others have their southern terminuses in New York and Philadelphia. The premium-service Metroliners (see Introduction) run between New York and Washington (with one trip daily extended to New Haven), although eventual electrification of the entire Corridor could make their use and that of other electric equipment feasible as far north as Boston.

With the exception of the Boston-Washington *Night Owl*, which carries sleeping cars, non-Metroliner Corridor trains mostly use Amfleet equipment, Amcafe and Amclub cars.

The Northeast Corridor is unusual among Amtrak routes in that most of its right-of-way is the property of the National Railroad Passenger Corporation and not that of a contracting private road. Therein lies a story—a story of a great railroad disaster that was not a matter of ruptured boilers and derailed cars but of great plans gone awry, bankruptcy, and reorganization. It is the story of the Penn Central Railroad, a marriage of two giant roads that was clearly not made in heaven.

Merger talks between the New York Central and Pennsylvania railroads began in the late-1950s. Since railroad operation was becoming more difficult, and profit margins smaller—especially in the Northeast—the directors of the two roads believed that money could be saved and efficiency improved if the area's two biggest competitors united. Early in 1968, the Penn Central became a reality; the two carriers combined with the insolvent New York, New Haven and Hartford Railroad to form what was then the world's largest transportation system.

Within two and one-half years, though, the Penn Central was bankrupt, the victim not only of the usual ills of modern-day railroading but of a draining of its capital into subsidiaries that had little to do with transportation. The better part of the 1970s was spent sifting through the corporate rubble. The establishment of Conrail, the quasi-public freight and commuter service, was one outcome of the salvage operations; another was the placing of Penn Central's Washington-Boston corridor in Amtrak's hands.

The northernmost terminal for southbound Corridor trains is Boston's South Station. Trains do serve points north of Boston, but these are operated not by Amtrak but by a local transportation authority and leave from the city's North Station (for Boston information, see trip 1).

Boston to New York

The Corridor right-of-way passes through Boston, skirting (left) the headquarters of the Gillette Company and other South Boston industries before heading through the "triple-decker" neighborhoods, so called because of the dominant style of residential architecture. The first stop, and the last stop in Massachusetts, is at Route 128, the peripheral highway that is home to Greater Boston's booming electronics industry. Soon after leaving Route 128, the train enters Rhode Island and stops in downtown Providence, the state's capital. The Capitol dome is visible nearby. Providence has a large number of restored eighteenth-century homes, and can easily be toured on foot. As of this writing, there are plans to replace the existing Providence station with a handsome new structure—but other plans call for moving the station farther from downtown, which would certainly be a mistake.

After stops in several other Rhode Island towns, the train reaches Mystic, Connecticut, an old whaling center and site of the restored Mystic Seaport. Here the old New Haven tracks meet Long Island Sound, which they follow closely through much of Connecticut. Sit on the left side of the train (on the right northbound) for views of the sailboat-dotted sound and the birds that frequent its tidal marshes.

New Haven, seat of Yale University, is the next major stop; from here, trains run north to Hartford and, around midnight, to Montreal. During the brief pause here, a crew connects the electric engine that will pull the train for the rest of its trip through the Corridor. After passing through the industrial city of Bridgeport and bedroom community of Stamford, the train swings down into New York's Westchester County, runs through the Bronx and across the East River into Queens, and finally reaches Pennsylvania Station, Manhattan, via a tunnel beneath the East River and the city (for New York information, see trip 1).

New York to Philadelphia

Southbound Amtrak trains emerge from the Hudson River tunnels into one of the most maligned stretches of territory in the world—industrial New Jersey. Just before reaching Newark, though, the tracks skirt the Jersey Meadows, portions of which are being saved from development because of their value as wetlands. Newark itself is New Jersey's largest city; it stands at the northern extreme of a smoky corridor of factories and petrochemical plants. The tracks turn southwest after Newark, bisecting the narrowest part of New Jersey and avoiding much of the heavier industry. The last New Jersey stops are at Princeton Junction (Princeton University) and Trenton, the state capital. A bridge carries the train across the Delaware at a place not far from the site of Washington's famous Christmas crossing. The suburbs of Philadelphia grow denser now, and soon the old Pennsylvania Railroad's Thirtieth Street Station is reached.

Philadelphia

It isn't every city that has a patron saint. Not a founder—in Philadelphia, that honor belongs to the distant William Penn—but a guiding spirit, an example of and to the city, a name and face that come to mind almost as quickly as the place is mentioned. Philadelphia's patron is Benjamin Franklin.

Nearly every useful civic institution in Philadelphia was founded by Franklin. Born in Boston, he offered his genius to the service of the city which had taken him in and in which he had made his fortune, as though this offering were a natural part of some social contract. Franklin and Philadelphia are inseparable.

Similarly, the spirit of one era, one series of events, presides over Philadelphia. This, of course, is the time of the signing of the Declaration of Independence, with its attendant deliberations, and the Constitutional Convention, which led, during the uncertain decade following the Revolution, to the creation of a federal authority that briefly sat here.

Americans are inclined to think of their nation as having been born in an atmosphere of reason and Augustan calm, an atmosphere which partook of

The interior of Philadelphia's 30th Street Station features a huge concourse-waiting room, a ticket office and a series of shops and eating establishments.

the rationality and cool brilliance of the Enlightenment. A visit to Philadelphia and a walk amidst the surviving architectural relics of 1776 and 1789 can only confirm this inclination: the symmetry and grace of Independence Hall and the buildings that surround it are like Jefferson's prose translated into brick, and the reasonableness of these rooms mirrors the dispassioned balance of the Constitution.

After imbibing the spirit of Independence Hall, anyone interested in a further lesson in how architecture can reflect social history ought to walk up Chestnut Street to City Hall, an unmistakably Victorian pile hulking beneath a 500-foot tower surmounted by a statue of William Penn. (City Hall, with its carved stone animals lurking in every available crevice, is the largest stone building without steel support in the world. No building in downtown Philadelphia is allowed to be taller.) Had Jefferson and Franklin come back to life for the nation's centennial in 1876 and seen this mansard-roofed extravaganza, they would surely have wondered what imperial pretensions had gripped their little agrarian republic. But they were educated men; having studied the history of Rome, they would have known only too well what was going on.

This is not to say that Philadelphia sprang to the status of a metropolis only in the nineteenth century. The settlement founded by William Penn in 1682 had grown to become the second largest city in the British Empire by the time of the Revolution. Benjamin Franklin was not an anomaly in a wilderness town but an intellect who functioned within a liberal and sophisticated urban environment. To be sure, Franklin helped create this environment, but its beginnings lay in the tolerance and diversity encouraged by Penn. Yet in the nineteenth century Boston, not Philadelphia, became known as the "Athens of America." Philadelphia began instead to rely upon its natural endowments, including a magnificent harbor, to make itself an industrial and mercantile powerhouse and the third largest (later fourth, after Los Angeles) city in America. Rail enthusiasts might be interested to know that Philadelphia was a great builder of steam locomotives. The Baldwin works here turned out many of the largest and most technically advanced engines during the great age of American trains.

William Penn's greatest contribution to the physical appearance of Philadelphia was the layout of its streets. The cities of Europe, and such early American settlements as Boston and New Amsterdam (later New York), grew without any attempts to impose an ordered street design. Penn was an early advocate of the grid system of city planning, and he platted Philadelphia accordingly. The numbered streets run north and south, while Market, Walnut, and Chestnut—the main downtown thoroughfares—run east and west between the Delaware and the Schuylkill, and beyond. He also included in his plan a symmetrical arrangement of open squares. There were five: Franklin, Logan, Rittenhouse, Washington (the names were given later), and Center Square, the city's heart. Don't look for Center Square today—it was chosen as the site for Philadelphia's towering City Hall. The other squares remain. Washington, at Walnut and Seventh streets, was the burial place for more than 2,000 Continental soldiers and British prisoners. An eternal flame burns here in honor of the Unknown Soldier of the Revolution.

Logan Square is now called Logan Circle, for it is the center of a traffic rotary made necessary by the Benjamin Franklin Parkway, a radial artery that is Philadelphia's one major departure from Penn's grid system. The parkway connects the city center with Fairmount Park, and along it are clustered many of Philadelphia's cultural and scientific institutions: the Public Library, the Franklin Institute, the Rodin Museum, the Museum of Art, and the Academy of Natural Sciences.

Philadelphia is a city of parks. Fairmount Park is the largest in the world, and the greenspace along East River Drive is a favorite of hikers, joggers, and picnickers. Here, also, is where you'll find Boat House Row, home of the famous Schuylkill River sculls. Philadelphia parks are graced with an impressive amount of fine statuary, including the world's largest assemblage of work by the French sculptor Jacques Lipshitz.

The shrines of American independence are located along the single-digit streets near the Delaware. This was Philadelphia's original downtown—in fact, when Jefferson rented rooms at the Graff House (Seventh and Market streets) in the summer of 1776, he was fulfilling a desire to live farther out in the country. But the oldest parts of cities often become the most neglected, and by the early years of this century Independence Hall stood amidst severely blighted surroundings. The entire neighborhood has been thoroughly restored, as have the federal row houses of nearby Society Hill, the colonial homes along narrow, ancient Elfreth's Alley, and the old market district— called, ironically, the "Newmarket"—around Head House Square. It is possible now to walk through much of the old city without taking leave of the Age of Reason.

Points of Interest

Independence National Historical Park. Encompassing roughly one square mile of downtown Philadelphia, the park is where most of the city's historic sturctures are located. Those which may be visited by the public are open every day, 9 A.M.–5 P.M., later in the summer. For further information, stop at the Visitor Center at Third and Chestnut streets, or call 215-597-8974.

Major Independence Park attractions include:

—Independence Hall. Chestnut and Fifth streets. Originally the Pennsylvania State House, this Georgian building witnessed the signing of the Declaration of Independence and the Constitutional Convention. The room where the latter took place is arranged as it was for the 13 colonial delegations. A sound-and-light show, "A Nation is Born," is presented outdoors here in summer.

—The Second U.S. Bank. 420 Chestnut Street. An important Greek Revival structure, it now houses galleries of portraits of famous Americans.

—Carpenters Hall. 320 Chestnut Street. The first Continental Congress met here in 1774; it has long been a historical museum. Open 10 A.M.–4 P.M.

—Franklin Court. Market Street, between Third and Fourth. Dr. Franklin's home stood here. It is marked by a steel framework and quotes engraved in slate paving; next door is a museum offering multimedia interpretations of Franklin's life and work. A revolutionary-era printing shop and the **B. Free Franklin Post Office** are nearby.

—Liberty Bell Pavilion. Independence Mall, Chestnut between Fifth and Sixth streets. The famous bell is on display here; during off hours, it is spotlit and may be seen through the pavilion's glass walls.

—Jacob Graff House. 701 Market Street. A replica of the house in which Thomas Jefferson wrote the Declaration of Independence. The upstairs rooms are furnished as Jefferson knew them.

Franklin Institute Science Museum and Planetarium. Twentieth Street and Franklin Parkway. 215-564-3375. Pure and applied sciences; thoroughly explored by means of "please touch" exhibits and frequent demonstrations. There's a Boeing 707 and a Baldwin locomotive; a walk-through heart; nuclear fusion and electro-magnetic displays; also a section devoted to printing. Much more. Open Monday through Saturday, 10 A.M.–5 P.M.; Sunday, noon–5 P.M. Call for planetarium schedules.

Philadelphia Museum of Art. Twenty-sixth Street and Franklin Parkway. 215-763-8100. A world-class art museum. Fine American wing, including many Eakins paintings; Orientalia; a room devoted to Marcel Duchamp; arms and armor collection; period rooms. Open Tuesday through Sunday, 10 A.M.–5 P.M. Closed Monday.

Rodin Museum. Twenty-second Street and Franklin Parkway. 215-763-8100. A small museum housing the largest Rodin collection outside of Paris. The sculptor's *Burghers of Calais* and other important works are here. Open Tuesday through Sunday, 10 A.M.–5 P.M. Closed Monday.

Atwater Kent Museum. 15 S. Seventh Street. 215-922-3031. Located near Independence Park, this museum houses three hundred years of Philadelphiana. Open every day, 9 A.M.–5 P.M.

Christ Church. Second Street above Market. Founded 1695. Many famous Americans worshipped in this beautiful church; Benjamin Franklin is buried in its graveyard at Fifth and Arch streets. Open every day, 9 A.M.–5 P.M.

Philadelphia Maritime Museum. 321 Chestnut Street. 215-925-5439. Everything nautical—models, ship paraphernalia, paintings. Open Monday through Saturday, 10 A.M.–5 P.M.; Sunday, from 1 P.M.

There is a tourist center at John F. Kennedy Boulevard and Sixteenth Street; or call the Philadelphia Convention and Visitors' Bureau at 215-636-3300.

Public Transportation

The Southeastern Pennsylvania Transportation Authority (SEPTA) operates an extensive network of bus, subway, trolley, and commuter rail lines. Subways connect with Amtrak's Thirtieth Street Station. For schedule and fare information, call 215-574-7800.

Lodging

Philadelphia has the downtown hotels you'd expect in a city its size, but most are fairly expensive. Rates vary from $35 to $110 and over, tending toward the higher end of the scale at the half-dozen new hotels that have opened here during the past few years. All of the hotels listed here are across the Schuylkill River from the station; thus distances in blocks are not given.

Apollo. 1918 Arch Street. 215-567-8925. Marginally adequate—small rooms with no private bath. As inexpensive a reputable hotel as downtown Philadelphia offers.

Holiday Inn—Independence Mall. Arch and Fourth streets. 215-923-8660. In the heart of the historic district. Cafe and restaurant, lounge with entertainment. Rooftop pool, poolside service.

Penn Center Inn. Twentieth and Market streets. 215-569-3000. Modern high-rise hotel convenient to cultural attractions, though some distance from Independence Park. Pool, sauna. Restaurant, lounge, entertainment. Shuffleboard. Free coffee in rooms.

Latham. Walnut and Seventeenth streets. 215-563-7474. A small hotel with many amenities—refrigerators, phones in bathrooms, in-room ice dispensers. Cafe and bar. Some studio rooms available.

Warwick. 1701 Locust Street. 215-735-6000. A small, deluxe hotel. Studio rooms availabe; also kitchenette units. Many rooms have refrigerators. Cafe and bar.

Restaurants

Philadelphia is big enough to have everything you might want to eat and well-established enough to prepare and serve it properly. Seafood is big; a few restaurants act as if they'd invented it. Soft pretzels with mustard and cheese steak sandwiches are local fast food favorites. South Philadelphia, an Italian enclave, cooks accordingly. Ninth Street in South Philly is where you'll find the Italian market, one of the largest ethnic food bazaars in the U.S. Ask anyone hereabouts for directions to Pat's, a 24-hour cheese steak haven. Another favorite all-night joint is the Melrose Diner, 1501 Snyder Avenue (215-467-6644).

Saladalley. 1720 Sansom Street (215-564-0767) and 4040 Locust Street (215-349-7644). Very good homemade soups, and a substantial salad bar. Lunch and dinner. You can hardly do better for under $6.

The Saloon. 750 S. 7th Street. 215-627-1811. A favorite among locals for steaks and Italian food, as well as for the decor: antiques, folk art, and a bar moved here from Italy.

Sansom Street Oyster House. 1516 Sansom Street. 215-567-7683. The freshest of fish and shellfish—offerings depend upon the day's catch—at surprisingly low prices. Oysters and clams sold individually; chowders; snapper soup; fried eggplant.

The Commissary. 1710 Sansom Street. 215-569-2240. In the words of one native, a "hip, gourmet cafeteria." Incorporates a piano bar; self-service restaurant featuring pasta, omelettes, soups, salads, and pâtés; and a more formal space offering a variety of ethnic cuisines.

Bookbinder's Old Original. 125 Walnut Street. 215-925-7027. The original location (here since 1865), although the Bookbinder family's restaurant is a separate operation on Fifteenth Street. Here you'll find live lobsters, along with a large variety of fish dishes. The bouillabaisse is thick and hearty, and the strawberry shortcake is superb.

Le Bec Fin. 1312 Spence Street. 215-732-3000. There are many good French restaurants in Philadelphia, but this may be the best. The chef-owner trained at La Pyramide in Vienne, France. Dinners are served prix fixe; two people will spend about $100 without wine. Veal sweetbreads financiere are a standout. Fine pastries.

Philadelphia to Baltimore

The urban landscape is virtually unrelieved from Philadelphia south to the Delaware border. Wilmington has a large Amtrak maintenance yard, where you are likely to see a string of old GG-1 locomotives awaiting their fate. After a quick crossing of the northern portion of the Delmarva Peninsula (so called because it is shared by the states of Delaware, Maryland, and Virginia), Corridor trains pass within sight of the picturesque coves of Chesapeake Bay and near the Army's Aberdeen Proving Grounds and enter the city of Baltimore.

Baltimore

Amtrak trains stop at a small, nicely restored station in Baltimore, a station distinguished by the use of green Rookwood pottery for its interior tile trim. It is no surprise that the station's builders should have turned to Cincinnati's famed Rookwood works for this finishing touch, for Baltimore has long thrived on trade with the Midwest. What is surprising is that the Pennsylvania Railroad decided to get by with such a small depot, one which deceives the arriving passenger into expecting a much smaller city. Baltimore has nearly a million people. But the Pennsy is not solely to blame for this misapprehension—Baltimore's downtown could easily serve as the center for a city half its size.

Baltimore is not a collection of residential satellites clustered around an extensive downtown area. Instead, it is a city of neighborhoods, many of which face their own little squares and seem to exemplify the spirit of insularity and provinciality which has often been identified with Baltimore. Union Square, bounded by Hollins, Lombard, Stricker, and Gilmor streets, is one of these. It was long the home of H. L. Mencken, Baltimore's most famous author and a man who, despite the virulence of his attacks upon American parochialism, has sometimes been taken to task for displaying more than a few of the attitudes associated with lifelong residence on a Baltimore square. Union Square and other squares, incidentally, are focuses for a substantial rehabilitation effort, with different ethnic and income groups appearing to mix with rather than supplant one another.

Baltimore is also a city of markets—not supermarkets or mom-and-pop groceries, but big, city-operated groupings of meat, produce, and seafood stalls that are as popular with natives out to stock their larders as they are with visitors to the city. Two of the largest are the Broadway Market, in the lively, workaday Fells Point district, and the Lexington Market, at Lexington and Eutaw streets. But when Baltimore wanted to develop an attraction on a par with Boston's Quincy Market or San Francisco's Ghirardelli Square, it turned not to the polishing and expansion of one of the old markets—which probably would have been much the worse for a face-lift—but to the building of an entirely new development called Harborplace, on the city's Inner Harbor. Here there are two main pavilions—one divided into shops, and the other given over almost exclusively to food: shellfish, Polish sausages, pastries, and countless other delicacies. One shop sells nothing but horseradish and other fiery condiments.

But before you eat too many soft-shell crabs, take a walk around the tidy harbor that provides the backdrop for these glossy pavilions. Some of the boat cruises from here include a stop at Fort McHenry, the American installation unsuccessfully bombarded by the British during the War of 1812. Francis Scott Key saw the fort's flag still flying after the smoke cleared and wrote "The Star Spangled Banner." If you'd rather stay on land, continue past the marina and head for the park atop Federal Hill, where one of the two best views of the city may be enjoyed. The other vantage point is the Washington Monument, which you can see from Federal Hill. This 178-foot column predates the more famous monument in the nation's capital; it was designed by the same architect. The monument is open Friday to Tuesday. The neighborhood that it dominates is called Mount Vernon, and few places in any American city offer a better sense of good urban design. The combined effect of greenery, statuary, and the facades of public and private buildings is a study in harmony and proportion.

Baltimore has an important place in American railroad history. Here, in 1827, the first major U.S. railroad, the Baltimore and Ohio, was chartered. One of the road's original capitalists was Charles Carroll, the last surviving signer of the Declaration of Independence. Thus the nation's political beginnings were linked with its nineteenth-century commercial growth, and Baltimore was assured a land-based continuation of the old mercantile supremacy it had founded on the high seas.

Points of Interest

Peale Museum. 225 Holliday Street. 301-396-3523. In 1814, the painter Rembrandt Peale built what is now the nation's oldest museum building to house a random collection of curiosities. Today, the Peale Museum exhibits portraits, photographs, prints, and furniture relating to Baltimore's history. Here is where gas was first used for interior lighting in Baltimore, in 1816. Open Tuesday through Saturday, 10 A.M.–5 PM.; Sunday, noon–5 P.M. Closed Monday and holidays.

Carroll Mansion. 800 E. Lombard Street. 301-396-4980. Charles Carroll, last surviving signer of the Declaration of Independence and one of the city's most successful early entrepreneurs, lived out his last days in this, his daughter's home. Exquisite period furnishings; interpretive tapes. Open Tuesday through Sunday from 10 A.M.–4 P.M. Closed Monday.

Walters Art Gallery. Charles and Centre streets. 301-547-9000. An impressively thorough museum that began as a private collection. Every culture and period is represented; classical sculpture, Renaissance and Baroque art, and Oriental porcelains especially stand out. Open Monday from 1–5 P.M.; Tuesday through Saturday from 11 A.M.–5 P.M.; Sunday from 2-5 P.M.

Babe Ruth House. 216 Emory Street. 301-727-1539. The Babe was born here in 1895. Photographs and assorted memorabilia chronicle the career of the immortal Ruth, as well as the Maryland baseball heritage and the Baltimore Orioles in particular. Open October through March, Friday through Monday, 10 A.M.–4 P.M.; rest of year daily, 10 A.M.–6 P.M.

Edgar Allen Poe House. 203 Amity Street. 301-396-7932. The poet lived and wrote here; he's buried not far away, in a corner of the Westminster Churchyard at Fayette and Greene streets. Call for visiting times at the house, which has only recently been reopened.

B&O Railroad Museum. Pratt and Appleton streets. 301-237-2387. A must for rail buffs—includes America's first passenger and freight station, an 1884 roundhouse, steam locomotives, and rolling stock from the passenger train's heyday. Open Wednesday through Sunday, 10 A.M.–4 P.M. Closed Monday and Tuesday.

The Baltimore Office of Promotion and Tourism is at 110 W. Baltimore Street. Call 301-752-8632, or stop at the information booth at Harborplace.

Public Transportation

The Mass Transit Administration of the Maryland Department of Transportation runs Baltimore's buses. Call 301-539-5000 for fare and schedule information. There is a free double-decker "Baltibus" shuttle from downtown points to the Inner Harbor.

Lodging

Downtown Baltimore has a fair number of hotels—small, older establishments as well as members of the chains. Rates vary from $35 to $100.

Abbey. 723 St. Paul Street. 301-332-0405. Eight blocks from the station. Small—it looks like a row house until you see the sign—and convenient to the historic and architecturally interesting Mount Vernon area. The Abbey is quite basic (some rooms lack private bath), but it is reasonably clean and inexpensive and offers free coffee and Danish in the morning.

Holiday Inn Downtown. 301 W. Lombard Street. 301-685-3500. About 1 mile from the station. Suites and studio rooms available. Pool. Restaurants, lounge. Laundromat. Directly opposite the Baltimore Civic Center.

Baltimore Hilton. 101 W. Fayette Street. 301-752-1100. About 1 mile from the station. Suites and studio rooms available. Rooftop pool. Miller Brothers restaurant on premises; also cafe, bars, entertainment. Downtown location.

Restaurants

Oliver Wendell Holmes once suggested that the Washington Monument, on Charles Street in Baltimore, ought to be topped with a canvasback duck. Later, H. L. Mencken remarked that his native city "lay very near the immense protein factory of Chesapeake Bay, and out of the bay it ate divinely." Mencken was referring primarily to the vast store of bivalves and crustaceans which the bay still provides, and which—though themselves invertebrate—form the backbone of Baltimore's menus. Baltimore also has a "Little Italy" neighborhood; Italian restaurants are clustered near Albemarle and Stiles streets.

Phillips Raw and Stew Bar. Harborplace—several locations. Phillips is a good place to try crab cakes, an old Baltimore specialty. Unfortunately, they're served here on soft hamburger buns with a slab of underripe tomato. The cakes at the Broadway Market are more authentically served—with a saltine—but they aren't as good.

Great American Melting Pot. 904 N. Charles Street. 301-837-9797. An intimate spot in the lively Charles Street neighborhood, offering samples of various ethnic cuisines. Open until 3 A.M. on weekends.

Tio Pepe. 10 E. Franklin Street. 301-539-4675. A townhouse restaurant with a Spanish theme and menu. Paella, of course; also pheasant and roast suckling pig. Excellent desserts.

Baltimore to Washington, D.C.

Baltimore and Washington are virtually twin cities: less than 40 miles separate their centers. There are two stops between them for Northeast Corridor trains—the Baltimore-Washington International Airport station, which offers the nation's first and only rail-air passenger connections, and the Capital Beltway station at New Carrollton, Maryland.

The District of Columbia is approached through its northern suburbs. As the train nears Union Station, the landmarks of the capital come into view.

Washington, D.C.

The traveler walks out of Union Station onto Delaware Avenue. Ahead, the brilliantly illuminated Capitol dome floats above the darkness, outlined clearly against a purple sky. With the immense, barrel-vaulted Beaux Arts station behind and the Capitol in the distance, he has a momentary sense of having entered a city that always was, and that will surely always be.

Rome earned the sobriquet "Eternal City" not only by affecting a certain indomitability but by simply predating and outlasting other towns. Capital of the United States since the last decade of the eighteenth century, Washington was deliberately built to look as though it had been there forever. It is no surprise that its builders aped the style and proportions of Athens and Rome. Their achievement is pure theater, but it is nonetheless as impressive as a city can be.

Before Washington, no American city had been created to serve a special purpose. The story of Congress's decision to build a federal city, of the formation of the District of Columbia, and of the hiring of Major Pierre L'Enfant to prepare a master plan is well known. What is not so well known is that the new city did not take shape immediately according to the plan, with broad avenues and white temples of state falling neatly into place. Like most artistic visionaries, L'Enfant was thwarted by people who did not appreciate the breadth of his vision, and by financial constraints. Even after landowners had been compensated and work begun on the Capitol and Executive Mansion, L'Enfant's avenues proceeded slowly through the forest: most were unpaved, muddy tracks even after they were completed. No grand city gates marked the approaches, and no marble facades lined the streets. Landscaping was years away—as late as the Civil War, livestock were penned up on the Mall. The British burnt the city during the War of 1812, and Congress afterward nearly voted to abandon the ruins in favor of New York or Philadelphia.

In the mid-nineteenth century, Charles Dickens called Washington a city of "magnificent intentions." But things began to change during the Gilded Age. Pennsylvania Avenue was finally paved in the 1870s; other modern public works date from the same era. L'Enfant's vision, however, was not really vindicated until the 1920s and 1930s, when many of the neoclassical buildings that give the city its character were completed. Among these are the Supreme Court and the headquarters of the various agencies in the Federal Triangle. Look closely, and you can tell the more crudely monolithic twentieth-century work from the true monuments of the Greek Revival.

The results of this 200-year evolution are arrayed along L'Enfant's radial avenues, which resemble not so much the spokes of a wheel as the spokes of several wheels meshed together, with an overlay of right-angled cross streets. This makes for lovely vistas, but also for a great many diagonal intersections, traffic rotaries, and generally hellish driving conditions. Even if you are on foot, you'll have to pay attention to the compass-direction designations of the city's four quadrants. Relief from the broad, classical boulevards, and from a general sense of bigness, may be found in Georgetown, an old community of merrily painted brick and clapboard row houses lying just beyond the northwestern end of Pennsylvania Avenue. Georgetown is an obviously affluent and self-consciously restored neighborhood, but is has its charm. For one thing, those pastel facades and white-painted cast-iron railings will remind Northerners used to red brick and black enamel that the South begins here—Charleston and New Orleans are, aesthetically, not far away.

Washington is more than a seat of government with Georgetown appended as a luxury bedroom. It is the home of nearly 700,000 persons, most of them black. Only recently granted a modicum of self-rule, the District of Columbia has barely come into its own as a "real" place—something it had been denied even while its physical appearance of solidity and permanence was being cultivated.

Points of Interest

Most people come to Washington to see the federal government buildings, the various monuments and memorials, and the many separate branches of the Smithsonian Institution. The following listings are grouped under four headings: Government, Monuments, Smithsonian, and Other.

Government

United States Capitol. Capitol Hill, between Constitution and Independence avenues. 202-224-3121. Built and rebuilt since 1793, it still serves the House and Senate. Tickets to Visitors' Galleries, from which congressional proceedings may be observed, are available from the offices of your senator or congressman. Tours of the building are given every 15 minutes, every day, 9 A.M.–3:45 P.M.

White House. 1600 Pensylvania Avenue N.W. 202-456-1414. Democracy's answer to palaces is smaller than you might expect, but still impressive. Tours are given Tuesday through Saturday, 10 A.M.–noon; no tours on Sunday and Monday. There's usually a long line.

Supreme Court. Maryland Avenue and First Street N.E. 202-252-3011. The Court sits only between October and June, according to a varying schedule. Buildings open year-round, Monday through Friday, 9 A.M.–4:30 P.M.; lectures when Court not in session.

Library of Congress. 10 First Street S.E. 202-287-5458. Gutenberg Bible; millions of other books. Recordings and public listening rooms. Impressive Great Hall. Tours on weekdays. Open Monday through Friday, 8:30 A.M.–9:30 P.M.; weekends to 6 P.M.

National Archives. Constitution Avenue between Seventh and Ninth streets N.W. 202-523-3000. Declaration of Independence and Constitution—the original copies—plus innumerable other documents. Research rooms open to public. Early March through early October, open Monday through Saturday, 9 A.M.–10P.M.; Sundays, 1 PM. Closes 6 P.M. during winter.

Monuments

Washington Monument. Mall off Fifteenth Street N.W. This 555-foot obelisk was under construction for nearly 40 years. It offers the city's best views. Open every day, 9 A.M.–5 P.M.; 8 A.M.–midnight from late-March to Labor Day.

Lincoln Memorial. Constitution Avenue and Twenty-third Street N.W. Contains engravings of Lincoln's major speeches, flanking the incomparable Daniel Chester French seated statue. Open every day, around the clock.

Jefferson Memorial. North end of E. Potomac Park on Tidal Basin. Graceful classical structure, at the center of which stands an impressive statue of Jefferson surrounded by excerpts from his writings. A tribute to the man, and to the Age of Enlightenment. Open every day, around the clock.

Arlington National Cemetery. In Virginia, across Arlington Memorial Bridge from Lincoln Memorial (Arlington Visitors' Center, 703-521-0772). Graves of John and Robert Kennedy; Tomb of the Unknown Soldier; Robert E. Lee Memorial. Open every day April through September, 8 A.M.–7 P.M.; to 5 P.M. rest of year. Lee House open every day April through September, 9:30 A.M.–6 P.M.; to 4:30 P.M. rest of year.

Smithsonian

All Smithsonian buildings are open every day, 10 A.M.–5:30 P.M.; some later in spring and summer. For information, call 202-381-6264.

National Museum of American History. Constitution Avenue and Fourteenth Street N.W.

Arts and Industries Building. 900 Jefferson Drive S.W.

National Museum of Natural History. Constitution Avenue and Tenth Street N.W.

National Air and Space Museum. Independence Avenue and Seventh Street S.W.

National Portrait Gallery. Eighth and F streets N.W.

Hirshhorn Museum and Sculpture Garden. Independence Avenue at Eighth Street S.W. Mostly nineteenth-century and contemporary art.

Freer Gallery of Art. Jefferson Drive and Twelfth Street S.W. Extensive Whistler collection.

National Museum of American Art. Eighth and G streets N.W. American art. Incorporates Renwick Gallery (decorative arts), 1661 Pennsylvania Avenue N.W.

Other

National Gallery of Art. The Mall, Constitution Avenue between Third and Seventh streets N.W. 202-737-4215. Paintings, graphics, and sculpture of eight centuries; one of the better collections of Impressionists outside France. Houses America's only da Vinci painting. Guided tours available. Open April through Labor Day, Monday through Saturday, 10 A.M.-9 P.M.; closes 5 P.M. fall and winter. Open Sunday all year, noon–9 P.M.

Corcoran Gallery of Art. New York Avenue and Seventeenth Street N.W. 202-638-3211. American and European art of the past three centuries. Open Tuesday through Sunday, 10 A.M.–4:30 P.M. Closed Monday.

Explorers Hall. Seventeenth and M streets N.W. 202-857-7588. The headquarters of the National Geographic Society. A century of NGS explorations chronicled in various exhibits; eleven-foot diameter globe. Open Monday through Friday, 9 A.M.–6 P.M.; Saturday, to 5 P.M.; Sunday, 10 A.M.–5 P.M.

Dumbarton Oaks. 1703 Thirty-second Street N.W. 202-232-3200. Mansion houses Harvard University Byzantine and pre-Columbian art collections; also magnificent gardens. Adjacent to Georgetown section. Open Tuesday through Sunday, 2–5 P.M. Closed Monday. Gardens (entrance at 3101 R Street N.W.) open Monday as well, same hours.

Folger Shakespeare Library. 201 E. Capitol Street S.E. 202-546-4800. America's premier repository of Shakespearean and Elizabethan books and documents. Plays presented October through July. Open April 15 through Labor Day every day, 10 A.M.–4:30 P.M. Closed Sunday fall and winter.

The Washington Convention and Visitors' Association is located at 1575 I Street. Call 202-857-5500 for information. There are also National Park Service Information kiosks throughout the most heavily visited parts of the city.

Public Transportation

Washington has a fine subway system, called the D.C. Metro, serving the city and its suburbs. The Metro also operates the District's buses. For schedule and fare information, call 202-637-2437.

Lodging

If there is one word that characterizes hotels in Washington, it is "expensive." Two people are generally lucky to get by for less than $75 per might, except at the youth hostel listed below and a handful of small, side-street hotels. The upper end of the scale frequently exceeds $175.

Youth Hostel—Washington International Youth Hostel. 1332 I Street N.W. 202-347-3125. 1 mile from the station; 200 beds. Walking distance to all major attractions.

Phoenix Park. 520 N. Capitol Street N.W. 202-628-2300. 1 block from the station. Convenience is the main advantage of this small but elegant hotel; Dubliner pub downstairs, with meals and live Irish music.

Holiday Inn—Connecticut Avenue. 1900 Connecticut Avenue N.W. 202-332-9300. 1 mile from the station. Near Dupont Circle, where major embassies are located. Inexpensive by District standards. Pool. Restaurant, lounge.

Gramercy Inn. 1616 Rhode Island Avenue N.W. 202-347-9550. At Scott Circle, ¾ mile from the station. Wet bar in most rooms; some with refrigerator. Pool. Restaurant, lounge, entertainment.

Guest Quarters. 801 New Hampshire Avenue N.W. (corner of H Street). 202-785-2000. 1 mile from the station. Not cheap, but each unit comes complete with kitchenette. Rooftop pool. Light breakfasts and room service available.

Georgetown Inn. 1310 Wisconsin Avenue N.W. 202-333-8900. 1½ miles from the station. In the heart of Georgetown, this small hotel offers amenities such as bathroom telephones, some refrigerators, and oversize beds. Excellent restaurant, the Four Georges, on premises; bar.

The Madison. 15th and M Streets. 202-785-1000. 1 mile from the station. Exceptionally luxurious, extremely well-appointed: heated towel racks, refrigerators in rooms, massage showerheads; each room is supplied with liquor and soft drinks paid for as consumed. Excellent staff. Very expensive.

Restaurants

Washington's restaurants, like its hotels, come dear. The good news is that the cuisine of a wide variety of nations is available. Georgetown, of all places, is home to some small, reasonably priced bistros. If you wish to eat cheaply at lunchtime, try the cafeterias in large government buildings, and in the Senate wing of the Capitol.

Gepetto. 2917 M Street N.W. 202-333-2602. Homemade pasta. Fettuccini Alfredo; cannelloni. Veal hunter's style. Neapolitan and Sicilian pizzas.

La Chaumiere. 2813M Street N.W. 202-338-1784. French provincial cuisine. Cassoulet; tripe nicoise; fresh seafood casserole; mussels Marseillaise. Excellent wine list.

Gary's. 1800 M Street N.W. 202-463-6470. One of the city's better steak houses, serving excellent cuts and devoting equal attention to side dishes, especially potatoes. The bar gets lively after work.

Jour et Nuit. 3003 M Street N.W. 202-333-1033. French; all a la carte. Veal scallops in cream sauce; tournedos Rossini; trout Wellington for two. Always fresh fish dishes.

Le Montpelier. Madison Hotel, M and Fifteenth streets N.W. 202-862-1600. Classic French menu—Dover sole; rack of lamb. Salads and desserts are excellent. Sunday brunch.

3. The *Montrealer* and the *Adirondack*

Two trains, the *Montrealer* and the *Adirondack,* connect the cities of Amtrak's Northeast Corridor with Montreal. The *Montrealer,* equipped with long- and short-distance Amfleet coaches, lounge, Amdinette, and sleepers, leaves Washington, D.C., early each evening. The *Adirondack,* an Amfleet train offering Amcafe service only, runs daily between New York and Montreal, with morning departures in both directions and same-day arrival. Since the *Montrealer* is an overnight train and the *Adirondack* a day train following a different route, a combination of the two makes for an interesting round trip.

Washington to Montreal: the *Montrealer*

The northbound *Montrealer* follows the same route as Northeast Corridor trains between Washington and New Haven, Connecticut. At New Haven, the train turns off the main Corridor line and heads north toward Hartford, the capital of Connecticut. From Hartford to White River Junction, Vermont, the *Montrealer* follows the Connecticut River Valley. This valley has been a major conduit for commerce and migration since colonial times; in fact, many Vermont towns bear the names of communities left behind by Connecticut settlers who moved north.

The *Montrealer* reaches Springfield, Massachusetts, just after midnight, stopping for a 20-minute layover. Springfield, a small industrial city known for the manufacture of rifles for nearly all this nation's wars (the Springfield Armory is now a museum), is also the northern terminus for several daily trains to New Haven, New York, and Washington. Here the *Montrealer* heads on to Boston and Maine Railroad right-of-way, following the eastern bank of the Connecticut to Holyoke, where it crosses the river and continues north through the Pioneer Valley. Northhampton, the last Massachusetts stop, is within a short distance of four major colleges; Amherst, Smith, Mount Holyoke, and the University of Massachusetts.

It is still dark when the *Montrealer* crosses into Vermont and stops at the small Connecticut Valley cities of Brattleboro, Bellows Falls, and White River Junction. At the Junction, the train rolls onto Central Vermont Railway track and into the lovely foothills of the Green Mountains. Here the Connecticut River is left behind; the mountains rise to the west, on the left side of the train. Much of the terrain through which the *Montrealer* passes here is forested, although a few small dairy farms remain. Dairying has become less profitable in the hillier parts of Vermont, and the industry has gravitated toward the Champlain Valley lowlands on the other side of the mountains.

The *Montrealer* stops at Montpelier Junction, which is adjacent to Montpelier, the capital of Vermont, and then presses on along the Winooski River toward Waterbury. Ask for a wake-up call at Montpelier during those times of year when the sun is coming up between 5 and 6 A.M., so you can see as much as possible of the Green Mountains. Just past Waterbury, to the left of the tracks, stands Camel's Hump, a mountain known to early French explorers as the "Couching Lion." It all depends on the angle from which you view it. To the north (right side of the train), further distant, looms Mount Mansfield, the highest point in Vermont. Mount Mansfield rises above the village of Stowe, Vermont's oldest ski center and still one of its most popular. Amtrak publishes a brochure which describes the best rail/bus/rental car connections for Stowe and other Vermont ski areas; ask for a copy at travel agencies selling Amtrak tickets.

After Essex Junction, the stop nearest Vermont's largest city, Burlington, the *Montrealer* passes through Champlain Valley dairy country as it heads toward St. Albans (home of the annual Maple Festival) and the Canadian border. The uninterrupted flatness of the farmland north of the border comes as a surprise after the hills and mountains of Vermont. The great St. Lawrence River flows through this plain; on an island near its confluence with the Ottawa River stands a French metropolis second only to Paris in influence and size.

Montreal

In all of North America, only three cities stand as reminders of France's vanished New World Empire. One is New Orleans, whose Gallic past is largely contained within its Vieux Carre; another is Quebec, capital of *la belle province*. (see Section III). The third is Montreal, the closest truly "foreign" city to the borders of the United States.

Montreal is very old. Its antecedents date to an October day in 1535 when Jacques Cartier, accompanied by Indian guides, first clambered in his armor to the top of Mount Royal. Over a century later, in 1642, the Sieur de Maisonneuve and a company of 50 settlers came here to found the first permanent French settlement on the Upper St. Lawrence—a little outpost, surrounded by a palisade, that they called Ville Marie. Their ostensible purpose was the conversion of the Indians to Catholicism, but it was not long before an even more ambitious undertaking—a secular one—came to dominate the life of Montreal. The Indians, converted or not, were a great help in this new enterprise, as it involved what was for them a familiar prey—the beaver. As the European demand for the beaver's sleek pelt increased, Montreal became the terminus of a fantastic network of trade, involving the dispatching of brave voyageurs in bark canoes to the furthest reaches of the Canadian forest. There they traded blankets, knives, and sometimes hard liquor for the furs collected by the Indians. As Montreal waxed fat on the trade, it—along with the rest of Canada—passed from French to British hands. The story of the two centuries that followed is largely the story of an attempt to reduce a majority population and culture to the status of a political and economic minority, and of the backlash which that attempt has set off. Today, Montreal, although a branch office of the British Commonwealth, is also a proud French city, and scores of other nationalities have combined to make it one of the most cosmopolitan places on earth.

The Montreal of the old French dominion, of fur traders and evangelizing Jesuits and Sulpicians, has survived in what is called the Old City, a riverside district roughly bounded by Craig, McGill, and Berri streets. Before the early 1960s, the stone buildings of this quarter were threatened with demolition, but municipal and private interests were aroused in time to preserve what was left. They saved enough to create a pleasant neighborhood of residences, small shops, bistros, and outdoor cafes. Although most of the structures that remain were built in the early nineteenth century, the character of these narrow streets was defined much earlier than that, in the days when the settlement had to fit tightly within its now-vanished fortifications. The buildings are stone for an even more fundamental reason: Montreal was so cold in winter that a prodigious amount of wood had to be burned on its hearths, making the danger of disastrous fires an ever-present one.

Hundreds of years later, climate is still dictating the shape of Montreal. Here you will find an extensive complex of underground shops, theaters, and restaurants; the largest component of this "Underground City," Place Bonaventure, is linked not only with a huge above-ground hotel but, via subway, with the rest of the city as well.

There is a good deal more to Montreal that these two extremes of the quaint and the ultramodern. Don't miss a walk along the busy Boulevard Dorchester and St. Catherine, or a tour (with or without cash in hand) of the shops along Crescent Street. And you may compare perspectives with that of Cartier by walking or taking a bus to Mount Royal Park, at the crest of the wooded hill that dominates this island city.

Montreal is a major rail center, with links not only to New York via the *Montrealer* and *Adirondack* but to Halifax, Vancouver, Quebec, and Toronto over the routes of Via Rail Canada, the consolidated successor to the Canadian National and Canadian Pacific passenger services. For information on major Via routes and cities, see Section III.

Points of Interest

Old Montreal. An entire day or more can be spent on a walking tour of Old Montreal. Places to see here include the **Church of Notre Dame; Chateau de Ramezay** (old governor's residence, now a museum); **St. Sulpice Seminary** (built 1685; one of the city's oldest buildings); **City Hall; Old Palace of Justice; Place Royale** (build 1676; Montreal's oldest public square; and the **Youville Stables,** a picturesque courtyard restored and lined with shops. If you wish to take a self-guided tour, pick up the brochure "A Visit to Old Montreal" at the Convention and Visitors' Bureau (address below).

Man and His World. St. Helen's Island. 514-872-6222. The permanent successor to Montreal's Expo '67, Man and His World retains the flavor of a world's fair, with cultural and educational pavilions, exhibits from other nations, lovely botanical gardens, and **La Ronde,** an amusement-theme park with rides, shops, restaurants, and a general carnival atmosphere. Open in summer only; call for exact dates and hours.

Montreal Museum of Fine Arts. 1379 Sherbrooke Street East. 514-285-1600. Special emphasis on Canadian work, but with American and European movements also well represented. Open Tuesday through Sunday, 11 A.M.–5 P.M. Closed Monday.

Botanical Gardens. Maisonneuve Park, 4101 Sherbrooke Street East. 514-872-2681. Acres of plants under glass and, during the growing season, colorful outdoor plantings. Hours vary with season; phone for information.

Olympic Park. Corner of Viau and Pierre de Coubertin, on Metro line. 514-252-4737. The site of Montreal's 1976 Olympics is now open to the sporting public. Visitors can swim and bicycle in the Olympic facilities, and play horseshoes, bocci, croquet, and other games. Spectator sports also. Guided tours available. Open every day. May to October, 9 A.M.–5 P.M.; rest of year to 3:30 P.M.

Old Fort. St. Helen's Island (on Metro line). 514-521-7172. Fortress built in 1820s for defense of Montreal; now houses Military and Maritime Museum. During the summer, full-dress French and British military drills of the eighteenth and early nineteenth centuries are reenacted. Hours vary with season; phone for information.

The Montreal Convention and Visitors' Bureau is located at 155 Notre Dame East. Call 514-872-3561 for information. You may also wish to visit the Quebec Department of Tourism at 2 Place Ville Marie, 514-873-2015.

Public Transportation

Montreal is served by buses and by an extensive new subway system called the "Metro." Metro trains run almost silently on rubber tires; the stations are clean and cheerful. For bus or subway schedule and route information, call 514-288-6287.

Lodging

Accommodations are no problem in Montreal, unless perhaps the Canadiens are playing for the Stanley Cup and you have no room reservations. The buses and Metro make all neighborhoods accessible, so don't worry about sacrificing proximity to downtown for a lower tariff. Among the more centrally located hotels, rates will vary from about $65 to $140 (Canadian dollars). Hostels, of course, are a good deal cheaper.

Youth Hostels. There are many, among them the following:

—**Auberge de Montreal.** 3541 Aylmer Street. 514-843-3317.

—**Auberge Ville-Marie** (summer only). 4211 Esplanade Street. 514-286-9395.

—**YMCA.** 1441 Drummond Street. 514-849-5331.

—**YWCA.** 1355 Dorchester Boulevard West. 514-866-9941.

Chateau Versailles. 1659 Sherbrooke Street W. 514-933-3611. A surprising combination of central location and extremely reasonable rates make this a favorite small hotel. Handy to McGill University, downtown shopping. Lower rates on weekends.

Sheraton Mt. Royal. 1455 Peel Street. 514-842-7777/800-325-3535 (U.S.)/ 800-268-9393 (Eastern Canada)/800-268-9330 (Western Canada). 5 blocks from Windsor Station; 7 blocks from Central Station. A thousand rooms, with a Metro stop just outside. Four restaurants, lounges, entertainment. Family plan.

Ritz-Carlton. 1228 Sherbrooke Street West. 514-842-4212/800-327-0200 (U.S.) 7 blocks from Windsor Station; 9 blocks from Central Station. Montreal's finest traditional hotel. Superb service; excellent dining both indoors and in the outdoor gardens.

Bonaventure. Place Bonaventure. 514-878-2332/800-228-3000. 3 blocks from Windsor Station; 1 block from Central Station. Big, glossy, futuristic hotel, with direct access to the Underground City and Metro. Several restaurants and lounges, entertainment. Fine view from upper floors.

Restaurants

It goes without saying that a French city must be one in which eating and drinking are given due respect, and Montreal is hardly an exception. What sets it apart is that the cuisines of many other nationalities are represented and that in addition to classic French cuisine, you can find the simple, hearty dishes of old Quebec. There are over 5,000 restaurants here, 100 of which are internationally rated. Prices frequently run high, but menus are almost always posted outside. To eat well and still save money, try the prix-fixe lunches at the better restaurants.

Chez Vivienne. 1485 Mansfield Street. 514-845-2894. A tiny, chef-owned establishment—you'll have to look hard to find it—that's hard to beat for sound, French provincial cooking. As unpretentious as they come, but highly recommended.

Les Filles du Roy. 415 Bonsecours. 514-849-3535. It is hard to leave this Old Montreal spot with the faintest sensation of hunger. Authentic French-Canadian dishes, including white-bean soup, cochon de lait (young pig), tourtière (pork pie), baked veal shank.

Le Caveau. 2063 Victoria Street. 514-844-1624. An enormous selection of country French dishes—rabbit, rack of lamb, veal with morels, trout and salmon—served a la carte or in complete dinners for one or two. For dessert, try fresh strawberries with black pepper!

Chez La Mere Michel. 1209 Guy Street. 514-934-0473. Provincial French in ambience and cuisine. Excellent pâtés; coq au vin; sauteed rabbit. Good, home-style desserts.

Cafe de Paris. Ritz Carlton Hotel, 1228 Sherbrooke Street West. 514-842-4212. One of Montreal's leading practitioners of the classic French repertoire. Not only are the more elaborate dishes outstanding, but simpler things—such as Chateaubriand with fresh vegetables—are done well. Outstanding desserts. In the summer, have lunch in the Ritz Garden, the city's most elegant outdoor oasis.

Montreal to New York: the *Adirondack*

If you have taken the *Montrealer* to Montreal and plan to return on the *Adirondack*, it is important to remember that the two trains do *not* use the same station. The *Montrealer*'s terminal is Central Station. The *Adirondack* arrives and departs from Windsor Station. They are only a few blocks apart, but that can be a long way if you are carrying bags and racing the clock.

The *Adirondack* travels south through the same flatlands that the *Montrealer* crosses, but it follows a more westerly route, crossing the St. Lawrence near the Lachine Rapids on one of Canada's longest railroad bridges. To the west (right) at the south end of the bridge is the Indian village of Caughnawaga. After Caughnawaga, the land opens up into farms, distinctive for the pattern of fencing which divides the land into long, narrow fields as opposed to the more square-shaped tracts in the United States. The *Adirondack* crosses the border just to the west of Lake Champlain, stopping next at Rouses Point, New York, named for pioneer farmer Jacques Rouse, who settled here in 1793 and had 26 children. The next stop is Plattsburgh, on Lake Champlain. Plattsburgh is the largest city on the western shore of the lake. It is principally known as the site of a major Air Force base. For 75 miles beginning at Plattsburgh, the *Adirondack* runs south along the rocky banks of Lake Champlain, offering spectacular views of its bays and islands, and of the Green Mountains beyond. Ferry connections for Burlington, Vermont, may be made at Port Kent, except in winter.

In the opposite direction (to the right of the tracks), rise the Adirondack Mountains. The recreational capital of this vast, largely undeveloped area is Lake Placid, located about 25 miles west of the Westport Station.

The *Adirondack* stops at Fort Ticonderoga, held by the British during the Revolution until Ethan Allen demanded its surrender "in the name of the great Jehovah and the Continental Congress," and at Fort Edward, nearest station to Lake George. Perhaps the most famous of all *Adirondack* stops, though, is Saratoga Springs, the nineteenth-century watering spot that is still going strong with its racetrack, performing-arts center, and many mineral springs. The baths at Saratoga are an indulgence not to be missed.

The next stop after Saratoga is Schenectady, after which the route along the east bank of the Hudson is identical to that followed by the New York section of the *Lake Shore Limited*. The *Adirondack*'s New York City terminal is Grand Central Station; keep this in mind if you are making connections for southbound Northeast Corridor trains leaving from Pennsylvania Station.

4. The *Silver Star* and *Silver Meteor* and the *Auto Train*

Amtrak offers travelers a choice of two New York-Florida trains. These are the *Silver Meteor* and the *Silver Star*, both full-service trains with "Heritage Fleet" coaches, diners, lounges, and sleepers. Service from the Northeast to the South is supplemented by the *Palmetto*, an Amfleet train operating between New York and Savannah, Georgia; by two Amfleet trains connecting Boston and New York with Newport News, Virginia—the *Colonial* and the *Tidewater*; and the *Auto Train*, which operates between Lorton, Virginia (in the Washington, D.C. suburbs) and Sanford, Florida. The *Auto Train* is unique among Amtrak trains in that it offers passengers the opportunity to take their automobiles along.

The *Meteor* leaves New York's Pennsylvania Station in late afternoon; the *Star* is scheduled for early morning departure. The *Palmetto* also departs from New York in the morning and follows the same route as the *Meteor*. All of these trains operate daily in both directions.

The southbound route of the *Star*, *Meteor*, and *Palmetto* is identical with that of Northeast Corridor trains as far south as Washington, D.C. From Washington, all three trains head south through Virginia, first stopping at Alexandria, on the tracks of the Richmond, Fredericksburg, and Potomac Railroad. The Fredericksburg stop, halfway between Washington and Richmond, is of particular convenience to Civil War buffs. Near here are the Fredericksburg, Spotsylvania, Chancellorsville, and Wilderness battlefields, as well as the Stonewall Jackson shrine. Richmond, capital of Virginia and of the Confederacy, is noteworthy for its Jefferson-designed Capitol Building; St. John's Church, where Patrick Henry delivered his "Liberty or Death" speech; and Old Stone House (c. 1737), oldest dwelling in Richmond and a memorial to Edgar Allan Poe. Connect at Richmond for buses to Charlottesville (also on the *Crescent* route; see trip 5), home of the Thomas Jefferson-designed University of Virginia and Jefferson's own house, Monticello. We should point out that the train station in Richmond lies at some distance from the city center—a problem common to all major stops along these Atlantic Coast routes south of Washington.

It is at Richmond that the *Colonial* (originating in Boston, Monday through Saturday) and the *Tidewater* (originating in New York, Sunday only) turn east onto Chesapeake and Ohio track toward Williamsburg, site of the restored colonial capital, and Newport News, the great naval port. Bus connections can be made here for Norfolk, Portsmouth, and Virginia Beach.

The parting of the routes of the *Meteor* and the *Star* is at Petersburg, Virginia, where both trains enter the right-of-way of the Seaboard Coast Line. The *Meteor* follows a more easterly course, while the *Star*'s route lies further inland.

Auto Train runs non-stop overnight between Lorton, VA, and Sanford, FL, leaving late afternoon in both directions and arriving the following morning. Service is daily or thrice weekly, depending on the season. Amenities include complimentary continental breakfast and buffet dinner, lounge, and feature movie; sleeping car and coach accommodations are available. The Florida terminus at Sanford is especially convenient, being only 20 miles from Orlando and Disney World.

Petersburg to Charleston: the *Silver Meteor*

It is past midnight when the *Silver Meteor* reaches Rocky Mount, its first North Carolina stop; it continues in darkness through the Tarheel State's tobacco-growing flatlands, entering the South Carolina "Low Country" before dawn. The *Meteor* skirts the borders of the Francis Marion National Forest, named for the "Swamp Fox" of the Revolution, and reaches Charleston around 4 A.M. (On the *Palmetto*, Charleston is an evening stop.)

Charleston

The southbound *Silver Meteor* arrives in Charleston before dawn. So you must hire a taxi; there's no getting around it. The station is 10 miles out of town, and the hour is a bad one for buses. It's a shame that such a lovely city doesn't have a downtown depot.

If you're staying downtown, check into your hotel and head down Meeting Street to the Battery, where you can watch one of America's most beautiful sunrises. Meeting Street and the surrounding neighborhood are rich in stately antebellum architecture. Charleston is one of the few places below the Mason-Dixon Line that lives up to the "Old South" image—only the scene here is one not of vast plantations but of the town-dwelling side of that vanished aristocracy, whose romance and numbers have both been inflated by history. Many wealthy planters of the eighteenth and early nineteenth centuries kept winter homes here; in the summer, they lived on estates such as Middleton Place, Boone Hall, and Magnolia Plantation, all of which are within a short drive of Charleston and are open, along with their fine gardens, to the public. Spring brings the famous Spoleto Festival and the Home and Garden Tour.

Charleston is also where the final act of the Old South's undoing commenced: from the Battery, you can see Fort Sumter, which was fired on by Confederate guns on an April day in 1861. The island fort is accessible now by tour boat (803-722-1691 for information).

Charleston's charm lies in its Georgian elegance and compactness. Here thrived a colonial civilization of Bostonian or Philadelphian sophistication, and one which exceeded both the Puritan and the Quaker capitals in lightheartedness and verve. But it is still a small city. Megalopolis, perhaps, is sobriety's reward.

Points of Interest

Charleston itself is the "point of interest" here; it is one of those places that would be worth visiting even if not one door were opened nor one admission paid. Some of the colonial and early-nineteenth-century interiors, however, are magnificent. Two historic homes are managed by the Historic Charleston Foundation, 51 Meeting Street (803-723-1623). These are the

Nathaniel Russell House (1809), 51 Meeting Street, and the **Edmondston-Alston House** (1828-38), 21 East Battery. Both are open every day, 10 A.M.–5 P.M.; Sunday, 2–4 P.M.

Charleston Museum. 360 Meeting Street. 803-722-2996. Oldest museum in the Western Hemisphere; new building houses local decorative arts, period rooms, natural history exhibits. Open every day, 9 A.M.–5 P.M. The museum also manages the **Heyward-Washington** and **Joseph Manigault** houses; call for details.

Gibbes Art Gallery. 135 Meeting Street. 803-722-2706. Southern artists of the colonial and federal periods; Japanese woodblock prints; miniature portraits of South Carolinians. Open Tuesday through Saturday, 10 A.M.–5 P.M.; Sunday, 2–5 P.M. Closed Monday.

Old Slave Mart Museum. 6 Chalmers Street. 803-722-7313. Photos and artifacts illustrate history of slavery; also native African and slave-made handicrafts. Building was actually a slave market. Open Monday through Saturday, 10 A.M.–4:30 P.M. Closed Sunday.

The Charleston Trident Chamber of Commerce maintains a Visitor Information Center at 85 Calhoun Street, near the Municipal Auditorium. Call 803-722-8338 for information.

Public Transportation

Charleston buses, including a low-fare downtown shuttle, are operated by South Carolina Electric and Gas Company. Call 803-722-2226 for schedule and fare information.

Lodging

Charleston's downtown accommodations are all at least a 10-mile drive from the station; since the *Silver Meteor* gets in so early, it's wise to have advance reservations. (The southbound *Palmetto* arrives in the evening; reservations are likewise recommended.) There are motels and hotels, but the most attractive lodgings can be found in small, antique-filled inns. Expect to pay from $40 to $80 per night.

Golden Eagle Motor Inn. 155 Meeting Street. 803-722-8411. A clean, standard motel, with pool and inexpensive White Horse Inn restaurant adjacent. Near Old Market.

Indigo Inn. 1 Maiden Lane, corner Meeting and Pinckney streets. 803-577-5900. A small and luxurious inn near the old market. Continental breakfast served; bicycles available.

Vendue Inn. 19 Vendue Range. 803-577-7970. Fine old restored building, furnished with antiques. Some rooms with canopied beds. Continental breakfast; wine and cheese served in courtyard.

Battery Carriage House. 20 S. Battery. 803-723-9881. Perhaps Charleston's best location, if your main interest is the architecture and atmosphere of the old city. Inn faces Battery Park and waterfront. Pool. Continental breakfast.

Mills House. Meeting and Queen streets. 803-577-2400. A full-size, first-class hotel, long a Charleston tradition and now part of the Holiday Inn chain, but without resemblance. Meticulously maintained. Elegant courtyard with fountain. Pool. Restaurant.

Restaurants

Charleston is proud of its seafood. Shrimp and fresh fish abound on most restaurant menus, and the one dish found nearly everywhere is she-crab soup, made with not only the meat but also the roe (eggs) of the crab.

White Horse Inn. 155 Meeting Street. 803-723-8639. Downstairs from Golden Eagle Motel. Simple menu, leaning heavily toward steak and southern specialties, but good value. Breakfast (ham biscuits recommended).

East Bay Trading Company. East Bay and Queen streets. 803-577-9060. Restored warehouse with a skylit atrium. Seafood and local specialties; also a few French dishes. Pleasant decor and atmosphere.

Colony House/Wine Cellar. 35 Prioleau Street. 803-723-3424. In restored waterfront warehouse. Colony House serves steaks, local seafoods, shrimp and chicken creoles; Wine Cellar, on same premises, features six-course, prix fixe menu that changes daily and is reputed to be Charleston's best.

Charleston to Savannah

Leaving Charleston, the *Meteor* heads through flat country forested with pine; the ocean is not in sight. There is a stop at Yemassee; near here, along the coast, is the Marine Corps Depot at Parris Island. The Hilton Head Island resorts, although in South Carolina, are best approached from Savannah. Savannah, about an hour's distance from Charleston, is the southern terminus of the *Palmetto*'s run.

Savannah

America has its railroad towns, its market towns, its towns grown large around forts, fur-trading posts, or Spanish missions. It is unusual, though, for an American city to be associated with the colonizing efforts of one individual and to bear that individual's stamp over two hundred years later. Philadelphia, William Penn's city, is the outstanding exception—but Savannah, Georgia, is no less the product of one man's vision.

The founder of Savannah, and of Georgia, was James Oglethorpe, an English aristocrat who launched his colonial experiment as a means of rehabilitating imprisoned debtors. Oglethorpe not only chose Savannah as the new colony's first major settlement but he also—like Penn before him—laid out the plan of his city. This was in 1733, and the precise platting of streets and squares which Oglethorpe conceived is still the hallmark of modern Savannah.

This convenient layout, with its frequent interruptions of exquisite Spanish moss-festooned parks and rows of federal and Italianate brick houses, makes Savannah very much a walker's city. But, like Charleston, Savannah is served by a rail depot located far outside of town, and once again a taxi ride to the city center is unavoidable. Almost as if to tease travelers subjected to this arrangement, the old station stands preserved on downtown's West Broad Street, where it houses the city's visitors' center and a pair of old steam locomotives.

Savannah is proud of its waterfront, which gave it its early prosperity and still figures large in the local economy. Here the first ship to cross the Atlantic under steam got under way, on May 22, 1819. Her name was *Savannah*. Today, the Savannah River harbor is the site of a modest shops-and-restaurants restoration called Factor's Walk and of an impressive building called the Cotton Exchange. In the 1880s, Savannah was the world's second largest cotton-shipping port.

No amount of deliberate "recycling" or renovation, though, can compare with the quiet geometry of Oglethorpe's streets or with open spaces such as

Johnson, Monterrey, and Chippewa squares, the last of which is centered around a Daniel Chester French sculpture of the founder himself. Visually, at least, Savannah is the reasoned and orderly capital envisioned by a reasonable and well-ordered Enlightenment mind.

Points of Interest

Telfair Mansion and Art Museum. 121 Barnard Street. 912-232-1177. A Regency mansion housing both early-nineteenth-century antiques and a comprehensive art collection, including important prints and the drawings of Kahlil Gibran. Open Tuesday through Saturday, 10 A.M.–5 P.M.; Sunday, 2–5 P.M. Closed Monday.

Georgia Historical Society. Whitaker and Gaston streets. 912-944-2128. Oldest Southern historical society; relics and documents relating to the settlement and growth of Georgia. Open Monday through Friday, 10 A.M.–6 P.M.; Saturday, 9:30 A.M.–1 P.M.

Juliette Gordon Low Birthplace. Oglethorpe and Bull streets. 912-233-4501. Not only a finely restored 1820s period home but also the birthplace of the founder of the Girl Scouts; it's stocked with memorabilia of the organization. Open Monday through Saturday, 10 A.M.–4 P.M.; Sunday, 11 A.M.–4:30 P.M. Closed Sunday, December and January.

Ships of the Sea Museum. 503 River Street. 912-232-1511. Ship models, scrimshaw, figureheads, and nautical paraphernalia recalling Savannah's importance as a port. Open daily, 10 A.M.–5 P.M.

The **Savannah Visitors' Center,** 301 West Broad Street (912-233-3067) is a point of interest in itself, especially for railroad buffs. It's in the late 19th century Central of Georgia station, a fine example of the brick depot architecture of the period. Complete literature on Savannah is available at the Center. Open Monday through Friday, 8:30 A.M.–5 P.M.; weekends 9 A.M.–5 P.M. Closed Christmas Day.

Public Transportation

Buses of the Savannah Transit Authority serve the city and its environs. For fare and schedule information, call 912-233-5767.

Lodging

Savannah offers plenty of pleasant bed-and-breakfast accommodations in private historic downtown homes, as well as hotel and motel rooms. Rates will vary from about $30 to $75. All listings are at least 10 miles from the station.

Travelodge. 512 W. Oglethorp Avenue. 912-233-9251. Convenient downtown motel, two blocks from the river. Pool.

Eliza Thompson House. 5 West Jones Street. 912-236-3620. A small and very cozy inn, consisting of a handful of private-entry suites tucked into an 1847 townhouse. All suites have fireplaces and kitchenettes. In-room continental breakfast and sherry provided. Antique furnishings.

DeSoto Hilton. Bull and Liberty streets. 912-232-0171. A big, full-service downtown hotel. Some suites available. Heated outdoor pool. Restaurants, lounge, entertainment.

Liberty Inn. 128 W. Liberty Street. 912-233-1007. Another nicely restored nineteenth-century home. Two- and three-room suites, each with fully equipped kitchens, washer and dryer. Private entrances; close to all downtown points.

Restaurants

Savannah shares with Charleston an affinity for seafood, as well as a tradition of rice cookery. Savannah red rice is a local specialty; it's made with a base of pork scraps and tomatoes and seasoned with onions, garlic, green pepper, and spices.

Morrison's Cafeteria. 15 Bull Street. 912-232-5264. Inexpensive, homemade dishes—soups, salads, main dishes, baked goods—open 11 A.M.–8 P.M. every day of the week.

River House. 125 W. River Street. 912-234-1900. Extensive lunch menu—burgers, omelets, quiche—and a solid dinner menu featuring steak, chicken, seafood. Special seafood casseroles daily.

Garibaldi's Escape. 315 W. Congress Street. 912-232-7118. Something unexpected—a good Italian restaurant. Homemade pasta, mussels, veal dishes. Ask your waiter for the evening's specials, not listed on the menu. You never know what the boats may have brought in.

The *Palmetto*, Amtrak's New York-Savannah train, crosses Bush river near Edgewood, Maryland.

Savannah to Miami

A little after 6 A.M., the *Meteor* leaves Savannah and follows a right-of-way that arches inland into Georgia. There is a stop at Jesup (within easy access to the sea islands), after which the route turns southeastward. The train is now traveling just to the east of the Okefenokee Swamp, a 600-square-mile wilderness that straddles the Georgia-Florida border and is home to rare flowers, alligators, bears, panthers, and deer. The St. Mary's River marks the Florida border, just beyond which lies Jacksonville, the state's third largest city. Bus connections for Tallahassee, Mobile, and New Orleans can be made here. At Jacksonville, the *Silver Meteor* divides into two sections. One heads toward the Gulf Coast cities by way of Orlando, near Walt Disney World. Three buses meet the *Meteor* upon its arrival at Tampa. One goes to St. Petersburg and Treasure Island, one to Clearwater, and one to Bradenton and Sarasota. The other *Meteor* section follows a southerly route out of Jacksonville which takes it along the center of the Florida peninsula, stopping at Ocala, where the famous Silver Springs are located; Winter Haven, home of Cypress Gardens and several baseball spring-training camps; and Sebring, where there is an important auto-racing track. Orange groves are frequently visible at trackside. After Sebring the tracks turn east to meet the Atlantic coast, passing close to the eastern shore of huge Lake Okeechobee. Unfortunately, the lake does not come into view. The run down the coast includes stops at a string of famous resort cities—West Palm Beach, Delray Beach, Deerfield Beach, and Fort Lauderdale. The *Meteor* reaches Miami, its southern terminus, late in the afternoon.

Petersburg to Miami: the *Silver Star*

Having left New York in the morning, the *Silver Star* departs from Petersburg, Virginia, late in the afternoon of the first day of its trip, allowing summer travelers to see rural North Carolina and its tobacco fields before arriving at Raleigh, the state's capital, in early evening. From Raleigh it is a straight, 200-mile run to the South Carolina capital, Columbia. The *Star* reaches Columbia just before 11 P.M. Here visitors can still see damage done to the State House by Sherman's guns during the March to the Sea.

After a final South Carolina stop at Denmark, the *Star* rejoins the route of the *Silver Meteor* at Savannah. The remaining difference between these two trains is in their division into separate sections in Florida. The *Meteor*, as was noted above, divides at Jacksonville. The *Star* remains a single train until Kissimmee, having followed the more easterly of the two north Florida routes, through Palatka, Deland, Sanford and Winter Park to Orlando, the stop for Walt Disney World. Just south of Orlando, at Kissimmee, one *Star* section heads west to Tampa and St. Petersburg (bus connections at Tampa are similar to those available to *Meteor* passengers), while the other continues south, along the route described above, to Miami.

Another Amtrak train, the state-supported *Silver Palm*, makes one daily run in each direction between Tampa and Miami. At Tampa, buses meet the *Palm* and connect with communities along Florida's west coast; near Miami, at Hollywood, there are bus connections to and from Miami Beach and Bal Harbour. At Winter Haven, there are bus connections to and from Cypress Gardens, Circus World, Walt Disney World, and five Orlando stops.

Miami and Miami Beach

Back in the glory years of American railroading, some men were not satisfied simply with building a means of getting somewhere—they had to build somewhere to get to, as well. Such a man was Henry M. Flagler, a one-time partner of John D. Rockefeller whose star rose with that of Standard Oil. Beginning in the 1880s, Flagler assembled a skein of resort hotels linked by rail along Florida's Atlantic coast. Having built extravagantly at St. Augustine and Palm Beach, Flagler was persuaded by the frost-free climate to press south another 90 miles to Miami, a tiny village previously accessible only by water.

Miami's phenomenal growth dates from the arrival of the railroad, in 1896, and from the opening of Flagler's Royal Palm Hotel the following year. Since then, regardless of whatever other pursuits the city may have become involved in, Miami's prosperity has been inextricably bound up with tourism.

Miami shares its prominence as a suntan and night-life capital with Miami Beach, a narrow island community separated from the mainland by Biscayne Bay. The two cities now promote themselves jointly as "Greater Miami and the Beaches," with special emphasis on the recent restoration of a 300-foot-wide swath of ocean beach. The original development of Miami Beach involved a good deal more than restoration—before 1870, neither the hardiest Seminole nor even the most misanthropic recluse called it home. The barrier islands on which Miami Beach later grew were described in those days as a nearly impenetrable mangrove swamp, fronted on the ocean by dunes anchored with glasswort, sea grapes, and pickerelweed. Blizzards of mosquitoes descended upon human invaders of their territory, and crocodiles navigated the island's backwaters. To one with today's more ecologically aware sensibilities, the whole parcel might have presented the same opportunities for preservation as Georgia's Cumberland Island, now a National Seashore. But few people thought that way in those days, and after several thwarted attempts at coconut and avocado farming, the island's owners decided to try subdivision and development. The scheme hinged upon the 1913 completion of the world's longest wooden bridge, which spanned Biscayne Bay between the points now linked by the Venetian Causeway. The avocado farm and bridge were ideas of John S. Collins, for whom Collins Boulevard in Miami Beach is named; the real-estate promotion that followed was the work of Collins's sons and the entrepreneur Carl Fisher.

"The dredge," remarked Will Rogers, "is the national emblem of Florida." In the teens and twenties of this century, dredges were used to transform thousands of acres of Miami Beach swamp and ocean bottom into salable building lots. Meanwhile, the mangroves were uprooted and the dunes were dozed flat. Even though the 1926 hurricane blew down many of Florida's house-of-cards real-estate empires, Miami Beach and its sister resort, Miami, survived and prospered as the developers shaped the terrain to their will.

It is ironic that to reach a city made possible by the railroad, today's Amtrak passenger must get off the train at a station on the outskirts and taxi or bus the rest of the way. One bus leaves right from the Amtrak station for Miami Beach with stops in between. A new rapid transit station is near the Amtrak terminal. Once arrived at the city's center, though, it's generally quite simple to get around. Numbered cross streets intersect with Biscayne Boulevard, along the Bay, and with north-south numbered avenues. Like Washington, Miami is divided into four compass-oriented quadrants.

Miami and Miami Beach have grown in response to the influx of three major groups: tourists, retirees, and Latin American immigrants, particularly Cubans. Miami is, in many ways, the northern-most of the Spanish-speaking metropolises of the Western Hemisphere. Miami Beach appears to be more exclusively a resort community—Collins Avenue, along the Atlantic, is one unbroken row of luxury hotels—but the Beach is a year-round city, many of whose residents have decamped from the snowy Northeast and Midwest. Visitors should see both shores of Biscayne Bay, and the best way to do this is to walk the 2½-mile Venetian Causeway. The causeway is partly a series of bridges and partly a string of tidy, man-made islands landscaped into tame reminders of the riot of subtropical vegetation that once covered the star-crossed barrier beach that lies ahead.

Points of Interest

Little Havana. Centered around Calle Ocho, S.W. Eighth Street, Miami, near the downtown commercial area; crammed with a wide variety of colorful Hispanic stores and restaurants.

Art Deco District. Placed on the National Register of Historic Places in 1979, this square mile of Miami Beach's south shore features restored hotels, shops, restaurants, and theaters that hark back to the heyday of Art Deco.

Vizcaya. 3251 S. Miami Avenue, Miami. 305-579-2708. A well-preserved relic of Miami's days of grand ostentation, this 70-room Renaissance palazzo houses 2,000 years of art treasures. Magnificent ten-acre gardens. Open every day, 10 A.M.–5 P.M.

Historical Museum of Southern Florida. In the new Metro-Dade Cultural Center, 101 West Flagler Street, Miami. 305-372-7747. Traces south Florida history from 10,000 years ago to the present; features Audubon Birds of America collection and traveling exhibits. Open Monday through Saturday, 9 A.M.–5 P.M.; Sunday, 12:30–5 P.M.

Bass Museum of Art. 2100 Collins Avenue, Miami Beach. 305-673-7533. Multimillion dollar Bass collection; traveling exhibits. Open Tuesday through Saturday, 10 A.M.–5 P.M.; Sunday, 1–5 P.M.

Metrozoo. 12400 S.W. 152nd Street, Miami. 305-251-0400. A new, cageless zoo that features 160 acres of natural habitats and free-roaming animals. Open daily, 10 A.M.–5 P.M.

Cloisters of the Monastery of St. Bernard de Clairvaux. 16711 W. Dixie Highway, N. Miami Beach. 305-945-1461. One of William Randolph Hearst's small indulgences—he had this twelfth-century Spanish structure moved, stone by stone, to the United States. Gardens. Open Monday through Saturday, 10 A.M.–5 P.M.; Sunday from noon.

The Metropolitan-Dade County Department of Tourism is at 254 West Flagler Street, Miami; call 305-579-4694 for information. The Miami Beach Visitor and Convention Authority is at 555 Seventeenth Street, Miami Beach; call 305-673-7080.

Public Transportation

Both Miami and Miami Beach are served by the buses of the Metro Transit Agency. Call 305-638-6700 for schedule and fare information.

Lodging—Miami

There are literally hundreds of hotels and motels in the Greater Miami area. Remember that rates are lower in the summer; in winter, you'll pay anywhere from $25 for a small motel room to $150 for a palatial double in Miami Beach.

Everglades. 244 Biscayne Boulevard (near N.E. Second Street). 305-379-5461. Large hotel popular with South American clientele. Views of Biscayne Bay. Rooftop pool. Restaurant, bar, entertainment on weekends. Shuffleboard.

Columbus. 312 N.E. First Street. 305-373-4411. Inexpensive suites and studio rooms available. Restaurants, bar. Sundeck.

Omni International. Biscayne Boulevard at Sixteenth Street. 305-374-0000. Ultramodern hotel is part of indoor shopping, dining, and amusement complex. Some rooms with wet bar and refrigerator. Pool, tennis, health club. Restaurant, bar, entertainment. Round-the-clock room service.

Pavillon. 100 Chopin Plaza. 305-577-1000. Brand-new deluxe hotel in downtown Miami overlooking Biscayne Bay. Restaurants, lounges, sports facilities and Scandinavian health spa.

Lodging—Miami Beach

Art Deco Hotels. 13th Street and Ocean Drive. 305-534-2135. One hundred and forty-six oceanside rooms, done up in their Art Deco best. Good seafood in Carlyle Grill; live jazz and tropical menu in Cafe Cardozo.

Seville. 2901 Collins Avenue. 305-532-2511/800-327-1641. Oceanside hotel; some rooms with balconies. Pool and wading pool. Restaurant, bar, modified American plan available. Some rooms with refrigerators.

Fontainebleu Hilton. 4441 Collins Avenue. 305-538-8811/800-327-8367. An old standby, synonymous with Miami Beach, now newly renovated. Restaurants, lounges, showrooms, pool, and full sports facilities.

Restaurants

There are over 4,000 restaurants in the greater Miami area. Many are all show, with prices to match; others offer serious, fairly priced cuisine. Look for Gulf seafood specialties such as pompano and langoustines.

Wolfie's. Collins Avenue and 21st Street, Miami Beach. 305-538-6626. Miami Beach's favorite deli, with bowls of Kosher dill pickles and pickled green tomatoes at every table. Traditional sandwich offerings; also full menu. Latin dishes, too.

Joe's Stone Crabs. 227 Biscayne Street, Miami Beach. 305-673-0365. A Miami institution, featuring big stone crabs, cottage fries. Non-seafood dishes as well. Open for lunch. No reservations, but worth the wait.

Versailles. 3555 SW Eighth Street (Calle Ocho), Miami. 305-445-7614. Authentic Spanish cuisine in the heart of "Little Havana." Ask to sit in the elaborate "Hall of Mirrors."

5. The *Crescent*

Back in 1891, it was a real treat to be able to walk from one railroad car to another without being pelted by cinders, blackened with soot, and generally disheveled by the breeze. So when the Richmond and Danville Railroad Company that year instituted New York-Atlanta service featuring cars with enclosed vestibules, they capitalized on the innovation by calling their train the *Washington and Southwestern Vestibuled Limited*. The R&D did more than guarantee that you would keep your composure while walking between cars—they even gave you somewhere to walk to, by running the first dining cars between New York and Atlanta.

By 1925, vestibules and diners were commonplace, the R&D had been absorbed by the Southern Railway, and the train—which now ran all the way to New Orleans—was called the *Crescent*, after the nickname of that new terminal city. The *Crescent* was a great train, pulled by huge green-and-gold Ps-4 Pacific steam locomotives, with driving wheels over 6 feet in diameter. For a charge of $5 above the regular fare, *Crescent* passengers could enjoy the services of a valet and ladies' maid and dine splendidly on the best regional cuisine. It is not surprising that such a train should have outlived many of its contemporaries; indeed the Southern's *Crescent* joined the Amtrak system only in 1979, becoming the next to the last privately-run long-distance train to be absorbed into the Amtrak system. (The last was the Denver and Rio Grande Western's *Zephyr*, now a part of the *California Zephyr* route.)

New York to Charlotte

The *Crescent* is a full-service train, with diner, lounge, and sleepers, that leaves New York's Pennsylvania Station early each afternoon. It follows Amtrak's Northeast Corridor right-of-way (see trip 2) as far south as Washington, then heads southwest into Virginia on the tracks of the Southern System by early evening. The first stop on the Southern right-of-way is Alexandria, home of George Washington. His Mount Vernon estate is just downstream on the Potomac, and the George Washington Masonic Temple is visible just west of the station. The stop after Alexandria is Manassas, where a National Park commemorates the bloody battles fought here during the Civil War. The troops brought here by General Thomas "Stonewall" Jackson for the first Battle of Bull Run were the first to be transported by train during the Civil War. Next is Culpeper; about 30 miles to the west, and paralleling the *Crescent's* route, are the beautiful Blue Ridge Mountains and Shenandoah National Park.

Charlottesville, the next stop, is rich in historical associations. Near here are the birthplaces of explorer Meriwether Lewis and revolutionary hero George Rogers Clark, as well as the homes of James Monroe and Thomas Jefferson. The Blue Ridge still rises to the west as the *Crescent* speeds towards Monroe, Lynchburg, and Danville, Virginia, but it rises in darkness now (for northbound passengers, the sun goes down between Lynchburg and Charlottesville), and the North Carolina border slips by just after midnight.

The great spine of the Appalachians takes a southeastward turn as it reaches deeper into the South. The mountains are higher here, but they are farther insland; the *Crescent*'s stops of Greensboro, Highpoint, and Salisbury are located not amidst the foothills of the Smokies but in lower-lying tobacco country. Greensboro is famous as a textile manufacturing center, while High Point is known for its dozens of furniture plants. Salisbury is an old colonial town, rich in eighteenth-century architecture. Charlotte, the next stop, is the trading center of the western Carolinas and the gateway to the highlands along the Tennessee border, 100 miles to the west.

Charlotte

Cities always look larger and more inscrutable when you reach them in the middle of the night. When you add the experience of being woken from a sound sleep by a railroad porter, you have the perfect recipe for disorientation. So it is with Charlotte, otherwise a modest and manageable city, which you first see, bleary-eyed with sleep, from the window of a taxi. It can't be helped: if a train runs from New York to New Orleans, it has to arrive somewhere at three in the morning. It would be nice, though, if the Charlotte station were right downtown.

Charlotte points to its downtown skyline as physical proof of its status as a capital of the "New South." Though its population of 300,000 is small by some standards, it is the largest city in the Carolinas and a regional center of finance. Since the days following Reconstruction, when Southerners decided to put surplus labor to work processing cotton that would otherwise have gone to Northern factories, Charlotte has been a force in the textile industry. Today, over 600 spinning, weaving, and knitting mills are located within 100 miles of the city.

Before textiles the area dealt in gold and pottery. Prior to the California strikes of 1849, the mines around Charlotte provided most of the nation's gold—the federal government operated a mint here until 1916. Red clay was a less valuable but extremely useful local resource, and led to a long tradition of local pottery-making. "Jugtown" ceramics, made not far away, are often represented in museums.

Charlotte may see its new image in the dramatic NCNB Plaza downtown, but you need travel no further than the nearby residential districts to walk beneath the canopies of live oak that are a hallmark of the Old South. As long as that balance can be preserved, Charlotte will still be worth a wake-up call on the *Crescent*.

Points of Interest

Mint Museum of History. 3500 Shamrock Drive, near Alexander Homesite. 704-568-1774. Permanent and changing exhibits concentrating on local and Southern Piedmont history. Open Tuesday through Friday, 10 A.M.–5 P.M.; weekends from 2–5 P.M.

Discovery Place. 301 N. Tryon St. 704-372-6261. At Charlotte's new museum of science and technology you can see marine plants and animals, create electricity and discover more about new methods of energy. Open Monday through Saturday from 9 A.M.–6 P.M.; Sunday from 1–6 P.M. Admission prices are $2.50 for adults, $1.50 for children and senior citizens. Children under 5 can enter free of charge.

Hezekiah Alexander Homesite. 3500 Shamrock Drive. 704-568-1774. Oldest house in Mecklenburg County; built of locally quarried stone in 1774.

Restored and refurnished with period antiques. Open weekends, 2–4 P.M.; group tours by appointment with a charge of $1.00 for adults and 50¢ for children.

The Greater Charlotte Chamber of Commerce is located at 129 West Trade Street. Phone 704-377-6911 for information.

Public Transportation
The buses of the Charlotte Transit System serve the city and its environs. There is a "no fare" zone downtown. For schedule and fare information, call 704-374-3366.

Lodging
You'll have to taxi from the station, but once downtown you'll find an assortment of accommodations, including some inexpensive motels. Since your hour of arrival is so late (or early), reservations are advised. Expect to pay between $20 and $60.

Passport Inn—Downtown. 319 W. Trade Street. 704-376-9841. A large motel, basic yet comfortable, only a couple of blocks from the NCNB Plaza. Restaurant. Pool.

Best Western—Downtown. 900 N. Tryon Street. 704-373-0300. A member of the reliable chain. Convenient downtown location. Pool. Restaurant, lounge.

Radisson Plaza. 2 NCNB Plaza. 704-337-0400. At the heart of everything, this big new hotel offers regular or studio rooms. Lounge with entertainment, Reflections restaurant. Pool. Shopping in adjacent plaza.

Sheraton Center. 555 S. McDowell Street. 704-372-4100. Within walking distanct of downtown. 600 rooms. Two lounges with live entertainment. Marker restaurant. Gift shop. Pool. Fitness trail for jogging.

Restaurants
The old problem: do you want to share Charlotte's enthusiasm for its New South sophistication and eat fancy, or do you want to stick to down-home dishes? If you opt for the latter, there are two local phenomena you should know about: the "fish camp" restaurant, specializing in fried fish, and the preference for pork barbecue rather than beef.

Many of Charlotte's restaurants are located in the city's south end, which is not well served by buses. If you haven't rented a car, ask about transportation when you make your reservations.

The Epicurean. 1324 East Boulevard. 704-377-4529. Long considered one of Charlotte's finest. Continental cuisine at reasonable prices. Complimentary meat and cheese appetizers, open grill charcoaled meats, and homemade hot biscuits.

Open Kitchen. 1318 W. Morehead Street. 704-375-7449. An Italian restaurant serving pizza (try the "Supreme") and lasagna, as well as offbeat dishes such as crabmeat parmigiana.

Great Wall of China. 1600 Montford Drive. 704-525-5803. Offers Cantonese, Mandarin, Szechuan, and Hunan cooking. Reasonable prices; outstanding Oriental fare.

Eli's on East. 311 East Boulevard. 704-375-0756. Small, intimate restaurant located in a restored Victorian home. Menu changes daily; specialties include fresh seafood, veal, beef. Reasonable prices.

Charlotte to Atlanta

Less than an hour out of Charlotte, the *Crescent* stops at Gastonia, North Carolina. In 1929, one of the worst labor struggles in the history of the South took place in Gastonia, as textile workers struck local mills in protest over an exploitative wage structure. By the time the strike was over, a mob had destroyed the workers' headquarters, the city's police chief had been killed, and a woman striker had been shot dead while driving to a meeting. While such strike-related violence has subsided in the past half-century, labor troubles in the South's textile plants continue.

Gastonia stands on the South Carolina border, and for the next two and one-half hours the *Crescent* slices a hundred-mile path across the northwestern tip of South Carolina. The hour is still quite early, and none but the earliest risers are even likely to see South Carolina. But those who awake south of Greenville or across the border around Toccoa or Gainesville, Georgia, will see two unmistakable signs that they are now in the Deep South: red dirt and kudzu. The red dirt is the product of some ancient oxidization of the parent rock of Georgia's clay, but the kudzu is a much more recent and far less benign phenomenon. It is a deep green broad-leafed vine, brought from Japan as a ground cover earlier in this century. It covers the ground, all right—along with anything else it can get a hold of. Kudzu envelops telephone poles, fences, bridge abutments, front porches, and trees both living and dead. You can cut it back, and watch its progress again the next day. People who know the plant must wonder what might happen if the *Crescent* were to stall: could it, too, be smothered in kudzu by morning? No respecter of city limits, kudzu can be seen thriving in the empty lots of the next city on the *Crescent*'s schedule, an old railroad town that is itself no stranger to fast, furious growth: Atlanta.

Atlanta

Whatever Atlanta's other preoccupations may be, two make themselves immediately apparent to the first-time visitor. The first is a penchant for naming things after peach trees, and the second is the idea of becoming a world capital.

Peach trees? Georgia may be known for its peaches, but the trees they grow on do not line the streets of its largest city—not like oranges in Sacramento of maples in Montpelier. Nevertheless, the term "peachtree" holds a peculiar fascination for whoever has been naming things here—the *Crescent* arrives at Peachtree Station (some 3 miles from the heart of town), and two of the city's main drags are called Peachtree Street and West Peachtree Street. Out in the northwest quadrant of town you'll find old Fort Peachtree, and one of the two big downtown shopping-dining-hotel complexes is called Peachtree Center, diagonally across from the Westin Peachtree Plaza, the world's tallest hotel. It's just a few blocks south of West Peachtree Place.

That other preoccupation is a bit more serious. Atlanta is already the capital of Georgia and the unofficial capital of a regional economic entity and state of mind called the New South, but it has its heart set on more. One of the best examples of this ambition is the city's Hartsfield Atlanta International Airport, which bids fair soon to overtake Chicago's O'Hare as the world's busiest air terminal.

Perhaps it is fitting to focus on a transportation facility as a symbol of Atlanta's growth. The city came into being for no other reason than to serve as a railroad terminus, "Terminus" in fact being its original name. But the vigor with which Atlanta has grown is clearly more than a reflection of its desire to ship other people's goods—just a touch of wounded pride and self-vindication may be involved. Atlanta was only in the first promising years of its railroad prosperity when it was burned to the ground by General William Tecumseh Sherman.

Choosing the phoenix as its symbol, Atlanta set about rebuilding. The rebirth of the city dramatized in the last reels of *Gone with the Wind* had its real-life counterpart, and before long the states that had sent Sherman south were losing jobs and markets to the dead Confederacy's live colossus. The railroads returned in force, and soon their cars were freighting a new commodity out of Atlanta: a concoction blended by a local pharmacist and given the catchy name of Coca-Cola. A century later, Coke is still based in Atlanta.

In many ways, downtown Atlanta is the city of the future envisioned by the starry-eyed boosters of 30 years ago. The Peachtree Center is typical of the glass exclamations that have made architect John Portman famous, and the Omni International, with its tiers of shops and hotel rooms, is just as flashy if not as tall. Together, the Omni and Peachtree Center form what some local guidebooks call downtown's two "retail nodes." When a city has abandoned shopping areas in favor of retail nodes, you know it's come up in the world.

Points of Interest

Atlanta Historical Society. 3101 Andrews Drive N.W. 404-261-1837. Three major attractions are situated here, set amidst 22 acres of gardens, woods, and trails. The first is **McElreath Hall**, the society's museum, housing archives, exhibits, and art works. The second is the **Swan House** (404-233-2991), a 1928 Palladian mansion set like a jewel in its gardens. Finally, there is the **Tullie Smith House** (404-262-1067), a modest 1840s Georgia farmhouse that offers a good glimpse at the not-so-glamorous life of a yeoman planter in the Georgia hinterland. Men should wear jackets to dine at the society's restaurant. Open Tuesday through Saturday, 10:30 A.M.–4:30 P.M.; Sunday, 2–4 P.M. Tours throughout the day. Closed Monday.

High Museum of Art. 1280 Peachtree Street N.E. 404-892-3600. Fine and decorative arts of Europe, America, and Africa; especially strong Italian collections. Glass and pottery; silver; colonial Georgia furniture. Open Tuesday through Saturday, 10 A.M.–5 P.M.; Sunday noon–5 P.M. Closed Monday.

Georgia State Capitol. Capitol Hill, Washington Street. 404-656-2844. Houses **Museum of Science and Industry; Hall of Flags; Hall of Fame.** Open Monday through Friday 9 A.M.–5 P.M.; Saturday, 10 A.M.–2 P.M.; Sunday, 1–3 P.M. Tours every hour.

Fernbank Science Center. 156 Heaton Park Drive N.E. 404-378-4311. A planetarium, observatory, botanical conservatory, and exhibit center (the Apollo 6 capsule is here). Forest and walking trails. Open Monday 8:30 A.M.–5 P.M.; Tuesday through Friday, 8:30 A.M.–10 P.M.; Saturday, 10 A.M.–11 P.M.; Sunday, 1–5:30 P.M.

Toy Museum of Atlanta. 2800 Peachtree Road N.E. 404-266-8697. Centuries of playthings from around the world. Open Monday through Saturday, 10 A.M.–5 P.M.; Sunday, 2–5 P.M.

The Atlanta Convention and Visitors' Bureau is located at 233 Peachtree Street N.E., Suite 200, in Peachtree Center. Call 404-521-6633 or 521-6600 for information.

Public Transportation

MARTA is the name of Atlanta's public transit service. It operates both buses and a rail system. Call 404-522-4711 for schedule and fare information.

Lodging

While Atlanta's shiny new downtown hotels command most of the publicity, a good number of less expensive older establishments and motel-type accommodations are available in or near the central city. None of the places listed below are within reasonable walking distance of the station, but then neither is downtown Atlanta. Rates run from around $30 to $100 and up.

Atlantan. 111 Luckie Street N.W. 404-524-7000. Downtown, between Peachtree and Omni. Restaurant, lounge, entertainment. Sauna.

Downtowner—Midtown. 1152 Spring Street N.W. 404-875-3511. Inexpensive motel one block from bus line to downtown. Restaurant, lounge, pool.

Colony Square. Peachtree and Fourteenth streets N.E. 404-892-6000. Part of a big indoor shopping and restaurant complex near Piedmont Park and the Memorial Arts Center and High Museum of Art, but quieter than the downtown developments. Pool, health club, raquetball. Car rental on premises. Restaurants, lounges, entertainment.

Westin Peachtree Plaza. Peachtree Street and International Boulevard. 404-659-1400/800-228-3000. Seventy stories, 1,100 rooms, and a prime downtown location. Pool, health club. Car rental on premises. Several restaurants and lounges, including the revolving rooftop Sun Dial. Weekend discount packages available.

Restaurants

You can get almost anything you want to eat in Atlanta, but a lot of restaurants make a big fuss over their Southern home cooking. So keep this tip in mind: don't pay top dollar for chicken and biscuits that might have been as good or better in a neighborhood cafe.

Trellises. Colony Square Hotel, Peachtree and Fourteenth Street. 404-892-6000. Pleasant, gardenlike surroundings overlooking the Colony lobby. Southern dishes—try the peanut soup. Trellises serves 24 hours a day.

Pleasant Peasant. 555 Peachtree Street N.E. 404-874-3223. A small, airy, plant-bedecked restaurant offering a freely interpreted French provincial menu. Own baking, good service.

The Patio. 3349 Piedmont Road N.E. 404-237-5878. French country cooking. Trout with lemon butter; homemade pâtés; frog legs. Prime steaks are also a specialty.

The Abbey. 163 Ponce de Leon Avenue. 404-876-8532. An old downtown church houses this restaurant, which specializes in classic French cuisine. Roast pheasant Souvarov; Dover sole; filet mignon Aida. Fine wine list.

Atlanta to New Orleans

The diner of the *Crescent,* as it pulls out of Atlanta, is a good place to sit down to a plate of ham, eggs, and grits, while looking out the window and contemplating the terrain. When the train leaves Georgia (Atlanta is the last stop in that state), it also leaves behind the older Southern states, crossing the Appalachian Mountains during the two-hour trip to Anniston, Alabama, and heading into what was wilderness just 40 years before the Civil War. This fact alone should dispel the notion of an Old South dotted with elegant mansions and manicured plantations evidencing generations of husbandry— the fact is that before 1820 most of Alabama looked like the state's Talladega National Forest, through which the *Crescent* passes. Alabama was then a vast woodland and Mississippi a jungle, according to W. J. Cash, whose fine book, *The Mind of the South*, pulls the foundations from under a number of Southern myths. It was the prospect of cheap cotton land that brought settlers from the older, more fertile, and more settled districts along the seaboard, and it was slavery, along with Eli Whitney's cotton gin, that made the clearing and planting of millions of acres between here and the Mississippi profitable. But there was a catch, and the decidedly impoverished appearance of much of the land along the *Crescent*'s route is by no means merely the result of the ravages of the Union army. These old forest lands were nearly destroyed by the very men who planted them to cotton. Cotton exhausts land; the plantation system of agriculture aimed simply at getting the highest yield from the best years of the virgin lands. Modern farming methods were long in taking hold here; even after such practices as crop rotation and "resting" the land gained followers, Southern agriculture had a long wait before it could thrive again. So the region turned to industrialization to help solve its economic problems. The furnaces of Birmingham—like its British namesake, an iron and steel city—were one of the first attempts in this direction.

After Birmingham, the *Crescent* enters the "Heart of Dixie," as Tuscaloosa, Alabama, the Tombigbee River, and Meridian, Mississippi, roll by. Here is the country where the days of summer, in the words of W. J. Cash, are "saturnine and bilious." Past Hattiesburg and the half-million-acre DeSoto National Forest (Hattiesburg is an important lumber center), the landscape grows more and more subtropical, the soil darker, the vegetation more lush. The Gulf of Mexico lies not far south. The border between Mississippi and Louisiana is the Pearl River, a meandering stream that seems to prefigure the Mississippi itself. The Pearl empties into Lake Borgne, which defines New Orlean's eastern border. To the city's north and west, though, lies a larger lake, Pontchartrain. Just after leaving Slidell, its next-to-last stop, the *Crescent* sets out on its crossing of Lake Pontchartrain on a low trestle, or causeway, built in 1886 and still ranked as one of the longest railway bridges in the world: 5.75 miles. This is one of the strangest sections of any roadbed used by Amtrak trains. Bogs and hummocks of marsh grass slowly give way to the open water. Once the *Crescent*'s cars are on the causeway, no land or support at all can be seen on either side. It is like sailing across a lake on a train—or, more exactly, like sailing the ocean, since Pontchartrain spreads so far to the west (right side) that there is no sign of its banks, only an occasional sailboat or oil derrick. The *Crescent* bridges the lake at sunset during early spring and late fall, which adds a suffusion of oranges and pinks to the scene.

The final approach to New Orleans's Union Station (a recently restored intermodel facility, shared with Greyhound buses) is a circuitous one, involving, over the last mile or so, an actual backing of the train into the station. But forward or backward, no matter—the *Crescent* arrives in early evening, when the chefs and musicians of this old city are just warming up.

New Orleans

It is unusual that an American city should be known almost exclusively for its music, for its food, and for a great festival at which the two merge into something ineffably greater. Americans are simply not voluptuaries; they remain suspicious of places obviously dedicated to the pleasing of the senses. Las Vegas is taken seriously only as a resort—and besides, pleasure there is business, not a way of life.

But New Orleans is a city that runs contrary to the mainstream of a culture in which "no-nonsense" is rapidly becoming a favorite descriptive phrase. It shows no shame over its history of pirates and bordellos, and it continues to spew out jazz and crawfish étouffé as if either were as important as aerospace hardware or computer information chips. What sets New Orleans apart?

To begin with, New Orleans is probably the only large American city in which the dour, Calvinist, hardworking cultures of northern Europe and the British Isles never got the upper hand. From the city's founding in 1718 until its assimilation (along with the rest of the vast Louisiana Purchase) into the United States in 1803, the history of New Orleans was a pastiche of French and Spanish influences combined with those of Africa and the Caribbean. As a seaport, New Orleans accumulated its share of colorful and raffish characters, both from upriver and across the ocean.

And then there is the climate. If the South begins somewhere around Baltimore, then the tropics begin in New Orleans. For much of the year, the atmosphere is languid and sultry in the extreme. Vegetation runs out of control, opening cracks even in the roofs of buildings, and tiny, smiling lizards dart along the hedges and iron railings of the Garden District, which begins around the intersection of Jackson and Magazine streets. Behind those hedges and railings are fanciful white houses and lawns that seem made for juleps and discreet assignations.

Since it is too big and too old to ignore, America tolerates New Orleans as though it were some jolly, vaguely disreputable relative, at whose house there is always good food, good music, and a good time—especially during the last two weeks before Lent, when Bourbon Street and environs go completely off their rocker (they are never entirely on it) in the extravaganza known as Mardi Gras. This tolerance is not without its reservations, though. Nearly everyone you meet north of New Orleans will tell you how dangerous it is, especially at night on the side streets of the French Quarter. But the rules here are same as in any big city—that is, don't look or act like an easy mark, and avoid dark alleys. One wonders, though, if the circulation of this "dangerous" reputation isn't some sort of chastisement for all those years of shamelessness and pleasure.

New Orleans is a sprawling city, but its oldest and most interesting sections are easily accessible to the rail traveler. Union Station is on Loyola Avenue, near the Superdome and Civic Center and on the edge of the downtown business district. All of the central city nestles within a huge arc of the Mississippi River; hence the sobriquet "Crescent City"—and the name of the train that got you here.

Once you cross Canal Street south of Rampart, you are in the heart of New Orleans—the Vieux Carré (old square), or French Quarter. While it is true that the French Quarter has been cheapened by bad restaurants, second-rate jazz joints, and stores selling T-shirts that advertise the doltishness of their wearers, it is still the place to go to see the best examples of the city's early architecture. Here you will find the ornate cast-iron railings that have become a local trademark. Jackson Square, with its Cathedral of St. Louis and other historic structures, is a splendid example of dignified, harmonious urban design. Best of all, the French Quarter harbors good restaurants, first-rate jazz spots, and shops selling quality merchandise ranging from homemade pralines to silk lingerie. And with that litany, it seems, we arrive back at the essence and distinction of New Orleans, the American city that enjoys itself.

Points of Interest

The **Louisiana State Museum** incorporates a number of historic buildings and important collections. Each of the places listed below is open Tuesday through Sunday, 9 A.M.–5 P.M.; for information, call 504-568-6968.

—**The Cabildo.** Jackson Square. The "Illustrious Cabildo," the Spanish City Council, met here from 1799 to 1803. The Louisiana transfer was signed here in 1803. Exhibits trace Louisiana history from exploration days to present; also portraits, Napoleon's death mask, and a steamboating collection.

—**The Presbytere.** Jackson Square. Built as a residence for the cathedral's clergy in 1791, the Presbytere houses portraits, crafts, folk and decorative arts, and costumes, with special emphasis on the Mardi Gras. Some of the Presbytere's exhibits will move to the new museum facility in the Old U.S. Mint (see below).

—**The Lower Pontalba.** The 1850 House. Jackson Square. Built by a baroness as New Orleans' first luxury apartment house; now houses decorative arts and domestic furnishings of the pre-Civil War period.

—**Madame John's Legacy.** 632 Dumaine Street. This raised cottage in the French Quarter is one of the oldest buildings in the Mississippi Valley. A fine collection of colonial Louisiana furniture can be seen here.

The Old U.S. Mint. 400 Esplanade Avenue, is now a part of the Louisiana State Museum. It houses Jazz and Mardi Gras museums, the Louisiana Historical Center, and other attractions. For information, call Museum headquarters at 504-568-6968.

Longue Vue Center for Decorative Arts. 7 Bamboo Road. 504-488-5488. Eight acres of gardens and an impeccably furnished mansion, right in the city. Twenty-five fountains. House tour; lower admission fee for gardens only. Open Tuesday through Friday, 10 A.M.–4:30 P.M.; weekends, 1–5 P.M. Closed Monday.

Preservation Hall. 726 St. Peter Street. 504-522-2238 days; 523-8939 nights. The real, unpasteurized New Orleans jazz, played by the city's most venerable musicians. Not a bar, or a lounge, or a "night spot," but a simple, dusty listening room. Records for sale. Performance nightly at 8.

Gallier House. 1118-32 Royal Street. 504-523-6722. James Gallier, a prominent New Orleans architect, built this home for himself in the 1850s. The restoration and tours nicely reveal the flavor of domestic life in the city in those days. Complimentary coffee and pastries on the veranda. Open Monday through Saturday, 10 A.M.–4:30 P.M. (last tour at 3:45). Closed Sunday.

Confederate Museum. 929 Camp Street. 504-523-4522. Civil War memorabilia, both military and civilian; Jefferson Davis collection. Open Monday through Saturday, 10 A.M.–4 P.M. Closed Sunday.

The Greater New Orleans Tourist and Convention Commission is located at 334 Royal Street, in the French Quarter; call 504-566-5011 for information.

From May 12 through Nov. 11, 1984, New Orleans will be host to the **1984 Louisiana World's Fair.** The theme of the Fair, which will be centered on an 80-acre downtown site along the Mississippi, will be "The World of Rivers ... Fresh Water as a Way of Life." Among the special exhibits will be a 19th-century American painting show, "The Waters of America," at the Historic New Orleans Collection, 517/525 Tchoupitoulas Street, and a major display of art and artisanry titled "The Sun King: Louis XIV and the New World," at the Cabildo on Jackson Square (see above). In addition to focusing on the rivers and port of Louisiana and the world, the Fair will feature plenty of local food, music, and folk culture.

Public Transportation

City buses are run by New Orleans Public Service; call 504-486-6338 for information. New Orleans also boasts the country's oldest streetcar line, running along St. Charles Avenue.

Lodging

Downtown New Orleans lodgings include moderate and luxury-priced hotels and motor inns, as well as an assortment of guest houses. Most of the latter are in the French quarter; typically, they are smaller and more homelike in atmosphere than the hotels, and many offer continental breakfast and kitchenette units. Rates at the guest houses vary between $35 and $70. Here is a brief listing:

—**St. Peter.** 1005 St. Peter Street. 504-524-9232/800-535-7815.

—**Ursulines.** 623 Ursulines Street. 504-529-5489.

—**Maison Chartres.** 508 Chartres Street. 504-529-2172.

All of the above are in the French Quarter, between 1 and 2 miles from the station.

Rates in the larger downtown hotels are high; with the exception of the first listing below, most are between $70 and $135 per night. Remember that both hotels and guest houses boost their rates during Mardi Gras.

Rodeway Inn—Downtown. 1725 Tulane Avenue. 504-529-5411. 1 mile from the station. A short walk to Canal Street shopping and the French Quarter. Pool. Room Service. Restaurant, bar, entertainment.

de la Post. 316 Chartres Street. 504-581-1200. A medium sized French Quarter hotel built around an intimate courtyard. Pool. Restaurant, lounge. Transportation to station available.

Bienville House. 320 Decatur Street. 504-529-2345/800-535-7836. A Master Hosts Inn in the French Quarter. Suites available. Pool. Restaurant, lounge, entertainment. Transportation to station available.

Maison Dupuy. 1001 Toulouse Street. 504-586-8000/800-535-9177. In a quiet corner of the French Quarter. Some rooms with balconies. Pool. Le Bon Creole restaurant on premises, lounge, entertainment. Inquire about family rates.

Maison deVille. 727 Toulouse Street. 504-561-5858. A very small, very elegant French Quarter hotel, with a fine restaurant on the premises. Pool. Private patios. Free continental breakfast. One kitchenette unit available.

Restaurants

Gulf seafood and French, Spanish, and Creole culinary traditions have made New Orleans a great dining town. There are more specialties here than there are restaurants in most towns. They include gumbo, jambalaya, crawfish, pralines, and *beignets,* a delicate fried cake eaten with café au lait. No city gives the visitor better reason to avoid the steak-and-beer chains, with their good-time Victorian atmosphere—but somehow these thrive, too. You can get an introduction to New Orleans cooking by having a plate of red beans and rice right at the cafeteria in the Amtrak station.

Buster Holmes. Corner Burgundy Street and Orleans Avenue, French Quarter. 504-561-9375. A favorite of *New Yorker* writer Calvin Trillin. Buster's is a bar, an old lunch joint, serving big platters of rice and beans, sausage, greens, and sometimes duck, rabbit, or turkey wings. You'll pay about $4 or $5, tops.

K-Pauls. 406 Chartres Street. 504-522-3818. Cajun cookery, including the famous "blackened red fish." Try a "Cajun Martini"—the gin is soaked in jalapeno peppers for 24 hours. Dinner only Monday through Friday; no reservations.

Antoine's. 713-717 St. Louis Street. 504-581-4422. Five generations of the same family have made Antoine's a local favorite. Chicken Rochambeau; oysters Rockefeller (they were invented here); pompano en papillotte; also Creole specialties and a fine wine cellar.

Mosca's. Route 90, Waggaman. 504-436-9942. Get a small group together, if you have no car, and share the cost of a cab ride over the Huey Long Bridge to Mosca's. The Italian-Creole cookery served up at this little roadhouse is legendary: baked oysters, spaghetti bordelaise, Italian crab salad. Several days' advance reservation necessary—it's that popular.

6. The *City of New Orleans* and the *Eagle*

Two trains— the *City of New Orleans* and the *Eagle*—run south out of Chicago toward the Gulf Coast. They are both Amfleet trains, equipped with long- and short-distance coaches, sleepers, and Amdinettes. The daily *City* follows a due north-south course, terminating at New Orleans; the *Eagle* heads south through St. Louis, then swings southwest through Arkansas and into Texas where it serves Dallas, Fort Worth, and San Antonio. The *Eagle* runs three days a week. When it reaches San Antonio, two cars—a coach and a sleeper—are uncoupled to await the *Sunset Limited*, to which they are attached for the trip to Los Angeles. Conversely, two cars from the eastbound *Sunset* are detached at San Antonio and joined to the Chicago-bound *Eagle*.

Together, these two trains offer a good way to make a Chicago-Gulf round trip without covering any of the same mileage twice. The connecting link between New Orleans and San Antonio is the *Sunset Limited,* which operates on a thrice-weekly schedule. The trip described here includes a southbound trip on the *City* and a northbound run on the *Eagle*.

Chicago to Memphis: *City of New Orleans*

Early in 1981, Amtrak retired a famous name on its Chicago-New Orleans train, and replaced it with one sure to be recognized by even more travelers. The *Panama Limited* has become the *City of New Orleans*. Back when the Illinois Central Railroad (now the Illinois Central Gulf) ran its own passenger trains along this route, luxury trains traversed this 923-mile stretch under both designations, but it was the *Panama* which survived until the coming of Amtrak. This unlikely name dated back to the patriotic feeling of the early 1900s. When the Panama Canal was completed, the IC could think of no better way to commemorate the event than to rename its showpiece train after the hitherto unknown Central American country. Now, though, the more logical appellation of its sister train has taken its place in the Amtrak timetables, as it has in the imagination of everyone who has heard Arlo Guthrie sing about the *City of New Orleans*.

Each day in early evening, the *City* leaves the South side of Chicago behind as it heads for the Illinois towns of Homewood, Kankakee, and Rantoul, islands in an agricultural sea. The next stop, Champaign-Urbana, is the seat of the University of Illinois. The prairie and the *City* roll south as darkness falls; both pause at Carbondale, where there is a fifteen-minute layover (bus connections for St. Louis may be made here), and where the flatness is relieved by the Shawnee National Forest. The Cherokee Indians passed this way on their "Trail of Tears" after being exiled from their eastern homelands. Cairo, the last Illinois stop, lies at the point where the Ohio River flows into the Mississippi. Near here are burial mounds built by a much earlier Indian civilization.

Sometime around midnight, as the *City* speeds over the ICG track that bisects the western tip of Kentucky, it crosses a boundary that is far less precise than the Ohio River—the boundary between the Midwest and the South. Near Fulton, the only Kentucky stop, is a monument to Casey Jones, who lost his life in the wreck of an IC Chicago-New Orleans train in 1900. We'll pass the spot where the tragedy actually took place farther down the line, just north of Canton, Mississippi. The route followed south from Fulton directly parallels the Mississippi, but it is a lot straighter than the tortuous course taken by Old Man River. This no doubt had a lot to do with the railroad's eclipse of the great paddleboats that once carried nearly all of the passengers and freight between the Midwest and the Gulf. The bed of the Mississippi shifts, but the rails do not, and by three in the morning they take the *City* into Memphis, a cotton-shipping capital of riverboat days that has become an economic power in the New South.

Memphis

Some towns are irrevocably associated with particular commodities. Memphis, for instance, is the world's largest spot-cotton market and a headquarters for the hardwood lumber trade. But neither of these things is likely to come to mind when most people hear the city's name—instead, the mention of Memphis is likely to suggest music.

Memphis is often touted as the birthplace of the blues. But while Beale Street was one of the most musically fertile environments ever to thrive in America, and while W. C. Handy did develop a distinctive, popularly accessible blues style which he carried from Memphis to the world at large, the blues were not "born" here or in any other city. Like any great folk tradition, the blues developed over a long period of time throughout an entire region—in this case, the delta of the Mississippi and the rural South at large. Elements of blues style can even be traced to Africa; during the years of slavery, blacks in America slowly refined this unique idiom, and its bracing, sorrowful strains drifted upriver to Memphis and the world. Handy was a great synthesizer of the blues played and sung up to his time, and his statue—trumpet in hand—fittingly stands in Handy Park facing a revitalized Beale Street. The city celebrated the "reopening" of Beale Street in October of 1983; the street once again features a lively array of restaurants and clubs, along with music—country, jazz, rock, and of course the blues. Lou Rawls has brought the old Daisy Theater back as "Lou's Place;" other spots include the Club Handy and Charlie Rich's country venue, the Silver Fox.

Memphis was destined to incubate a musical phenomenon even more far-reaching than the blues—one which, in fact, owed a great deal to the blues, as it did to the ballad traditions of the southern Appalachians. By the early 1950s, black and white musicians had developed a hybrid style based upon an insistent 4/4 beat. It had barely been christened "rock and roll" when a Memphis truck driver named Elvis Presley recorded his first songs at the Sun Studios here. Elvis continued to make his home in Memphis, and it was here that he died in 1977. He was buried on the grounds of his mansion, Graceland. The Presley grave site has since become one of Memphis's most frequently visited spots. Now, the mansion as well as the grounds are open, and the pilgrimage seems to be without end.

Memphis is a river city, built atop the fourth Chickasaw bluff of the Mississippi. It is no longer entirely concentrated along the waterfront, although the old downtown area (about 1 mile from the Amtrak station at 545

South Main Street) has been kept tidy and functioning with a pedestrian mall, ending at the world's tallest fountain. Just off the waterfront, in the middle of the Mississippi, is Mud Island, attached to downtown by monorail. This new, $63 million dollar cultural, recreational, and educational center includes a River Museum and a 5-block-long scale model of the lower Mississippi. There are also three restaurants serving southern and Creole food, and a 4,500-seat outdoor amphitheater.

Farther from the river are the Victorian Village Historic District, with two carefully restored homes open to the public, and Overton Square, Memphis's chic complex of restaurants and boutiques. Other attractions are scattered through the metropolitan area, making dependence on the bus system a necessity. But don't spend all your time traveling on dry land—the Memphis Queen Line offers narrated tours along the Mississippi in replica stern-wheelers. The best perspective of a city brought into being by a great river can always be had from the river itself.

Points of Interest

Pink Palace Museum. 3050 Central Avenue. 901-454-5600. This was the mansion of Clarence Saunders, founder of the first modern supermarket. Today, it houses a comprehensive collection of exhibits documenting the cultural and natural history of the Mid-South. There's an insect zoo, and the world's largest mechanical miniature circus. Open Tuesday through Thursday, 9 A.M.–5 P.M.; Friday and Saturday, 9 A.M.–10 P.M.; Sunday, 1–6 P.M.

Dixon Gallery and Gardens. 9339 Park Avenue. 901-761-2409. A luxurious former home furnished with fine English antiques. The art collection consists of French and American Impressionists; also eighteenth- and nineteenth-century British art. Lovely gardens; Open Tuesday through Saturday, 11 A.M.–5 P.M.; Sunday, 1–5 P.M.; closed Monday.

Lorraine Motel. The site of Rev. Dr. Martin Luther King's 1968 assassination is at 406 Mulberry Street, in downtown Memphis. There is a memorial to Dr. King on the premises.

Mud Island. Riverside at Adams. See introductory essay, above. Open daily, year round.

Graceland. 3764 Elvis Presley Boulevard. Here in the Meditation Garden alongside his stone mansion, Elvis Presley and his parents are interred. Tour includes main floor and lower level of house, Trophy Room (with Elvis awards, guitars, outfits), and gravesite. Don't miss the multilingual graffiti on the stone wall surrounding the property. Open daily, 9 A.M.–6 P.M. summer; 9 A.M.–5 P.M. winter. Reservations suggested for tours; phone 901-332-3322 in Tennessee; 800-238-2000 elsewhere.

The Memphis Convention and Visitors' Bureau is located at 12 South Main Street. Call 901-526-1919 for information.

Public Transportation

Local bus service is provided by the Memphis Area Transit Authority. For schedule and fare information, call 901-274-6282 or stop at the information kiosk on the Mid-America Mall at Monroe Street.

Lodging

The southbound *City of New Orleans* pulls into Memphis around 4:45 A.M.; going north, it arrives at about 10:45 P.M. This means that advance hotel reservations and a taxi ride are a must, especially since the station is not close to any downtown lodgings. **Holiday Inn** is headquartered in Memphis, and there are ten locations, too many to list here. Double accommodations in Memphis vary from about $22 to $100.

River Rendezvous, P.O. Box 240001, Memphis (901-767-5296) is an organization that arranges comfortable bed and breakfast accommodations in the Memphis area. Rates vary from $25 to $40 for two.

Sheraton Memphis. 300 N. Second Street. 901-525-2511. Large and commercially oriented, but comfortable. Pool. Bar, cafe. Some oversized beds available.

The Peabody. 149 Union Avenue. 901-529-4000. The legendary Peabody reopened in 1982 to much local fanfare. It's a traditional downtown hotel, with all amenities, and a special touch—the "Peabody Ducks," who travel from the rooftop by elevator every morning to take their place in the lobby fountain pool.

Restaurants

Live lobsters travel as well as the best of us, but why not eat them in Maine and stick to catfish in Memphis? Ribs and barbecue are also local specialties, and of course a city approaching three quarters of a million in population has its requisite "continental cuisine" establishments.

Blues Alley. 60 S. Front Street. 901-523-7144. The food is acceptable—try a big basket of shrimp—but the place deserves mention mainly for its music. It's a bastion of Memphis blues.

Captain Bilbo's. 263 Wagner Street, Beale Street Landing. 901-526-1966. Oysters and shrimp in outdoor courtyard; indoor menu features seafood, steaks, catfish. Live music and dancing nightly.

Four Flames. 1085 Poplar Avenue. 901-526-3181. A restored pre-Civil War mansion. It would be another steak-and-seafood house (although a good one) if it weren't for the barbecued oysters and home baking.

Memphis to New Orleans

Leaving Memphis, the *City* crosses into Mississippi, into the rich farm country known as the Delta. This Delta is not to be confused with the one at the mouth of the Mississippi; it comes to an end at Vicksburg, Mississippi, far to the north of New Orleans. The Delta is bounded on the west by the river and on the east by the highlands along which the *City* travels. This roughly lozenge-shaped territory is known for the fertility of its alluvial soil, which is 30 feet deep in some places, but it lives in the American imagination as the source of the blues. Blacks still outnumber whites two to one in the Delta, and the culture of the sharecroppers and small towns that produced the blues has been slow in changing. The Delta is one of the most timeless— and, sadly, one of the poorest—places in America. The soil may be rich, but most of the people are not.

Vaughan, Mississippi, between Durant and Canton, is where Casey Jones met his end on April 30, 1900. Casey was heading south at 70 mph, trying to make up time. Up ahead, a southbound freight lay on a siding—but with four cars extending onto the main line. Casey hit the brakes, and his fireman jumped to safety, but the collision could not be avoided. The engine left the track and turned over, and when they found Casey's body he had one hand on the throttle and the other on the air brake control.

The *City* arrives in Jackson, the capital of Mississippi, just before 9 A.M. From here, the terrain leaves little doubt that you are in the Deep South—not Faulkner's Yoknapatawpha, which is more accurately represented by the hilly uplands in the north of the state, but the Deep South of dark bayous and thick vegetation, alternating with flat, low-lying farms. The land becomes swampier after Hammond, the first Louisiana stop, and in the final miles before New Orleans, as the train passes between Lake Maurepas and the much larger Lake Pontchartrain, water dominates the scenery. A little after noon, the *City of New Orleans* arrives at its namesake, a place whose life and boundaries have been defined by water—by Lake Pontchartrain, the Gulf of Mexico, and the great Mississippi.

San Antonio to Fort Worth-Dallas: the *Eagle*

The *Eagle* replaces Amtrak's *Inter-American*, which ran in two sections originating in Houston and Laredo and joining at Temple, Texas for the trip north to Chicago. The *Eagle*, however, originates as a single train in San Antonio; Houston is served only by the *Sunset Limited* (see trip 10), and Laredo is no longer on the Amtrak system. The *Eagle* leaves San Antonio (for San Antonio information, also see trip 10) thrice weekly just before 9 A.M., heading north through San Marcos for a mid-morning arrival at Austin, the capital of Texas and seat of its university.

Austin stands at the eastern gateway to the Hill Country, a lovely part of Texas with a gentle, rolling appearance completely at odds with many visitors' expectations of flat, arid terrain. Austin, too, is somewhat of a Texas anomaly, for despite the rapidity of its growth in recent years it has managed to avoid the boomtown ambience of Houston and Dallas. Austin owes much of its character to the presence of the University of Texas and also to the vibrant country music scene that has emerged here as a sort of counter-Nashville movement, led by favorite son Willie Nelson.

Things to see in and around Austin include the Lyndon Baines Johnson Library and Museum, the Texas State Capitol Building, 391-acre Zilker Park and the Austin Nature Center, the O. Henry Home and Museum, and the Texas Memorial Museum. The Driskill and the Bradford are the two premier old-style luxury hotels; there are plenty of inexpensive places as well, though many are some distance from the Amtrak station.

The *Eagle* heads north out of Austin on Missouri Pacific track to Taylor, switching there onto the right-of-way of the Missouri-Kansas-Texas or "Katy." Temple, the next stop, is the chief connection point for Waco and Fort Hood. Leaving Temple, the *Eagle* speeds north through fertile grain-farming country, crosses the Bosque River at Meridian (so named because it is near the 98th meridian), and reaches Fort Worth in mid-afternoon.

Fort Worth-Dallas

Fort Worth and Dallas are not really twin cities; they do not even share the same county, and the train ride between them takes over an hour. Nevertheless, they remain linked in the minds of most outsiders, and will no doubt bump squarely into one another if they continue to grow the way they have during the postwar years. They do share a new airport, which, as local boosters will quickly tell you, is larger than Manhattan. People who take comfort in the verification of stereotypes should be pleased to note that, yes, Texans boast about how big things are down here.

Actually, a lot has been said about how different Dallas and Fort Worth are. Dallas, to many easterners the epitome of the damn-it-all, cowboy-Sunbelt style, is perceived locally to be the more Eastern of the twins. Fort Worth, half the size of its neighbor, is a quieter and more casually Western sort of place; businessmen wearing ten-gallon hats are seen more often here than in either Dallas or Houston. (Even here, by the way, that style is the exception rather than the rule.)

Dallas and Fort Worth were founded within eight years of each other in the 1840s. Fort Worth's early history is largely the story of the great Texas cattle drives, while Dallas remained more of a trading center. Not long after Dallas was first settled, it made a fair amount of money selling supplies to forty-niners headed west to join the California gold rush. The arrival of railroads in both cities hastened their growth as manufacturing and distribution centers, but their prosperity and reputation were truly assured when oil was discovered in Texas in the early twentieth century. Fort Worth found its oil to the west, while Dallas's supply came largely from the East Texas fields. Other industries—particularly aviation—continue to thrive, but the world knows these two cities (the "Southwest Metroplex," as they are beginning to call themselves) for their oil. Dallas is, well, Dallas; and most people would suspect that the "Worth" in Fort Worth refers to something other than the general whom the original encampment here was supposed to honor.

Finally, as you roll into either of these cities on the *Eagle*, think about that airport, bigger than Manhattan. You got here without ever seeing it—and you're already right downtown.

Points of Interest—Dallas

Dallas Museum of Fine Arts. Fair Park, Parry and First avenues. 214-421-4187. Art of classical antiquity and pre-Columbian America; also later European and American works. Stillman collection of Congolese sculpture.

Dallas Museum of Natural History. Fair Park, Parry and First avenues. 214-421-2169. One of the best places to learn about Texas wildlife—there is an excellent bird collection, exhibits of local fossils, and 50 dioramas showing the state's animals in their natural habitats. Open Monday through Saturday, 9 A.M.–5 P.M.; Sunday, noon–5 P.M. in winter; noon–6 P.M. rest of year.

Dallas Zoo. Marsalis Park, 612 E. Clarendon Drive. 214-946-5154. Especially strong in primates (a gorilla was born here recently); also indoor rain forest, rare pheasants, hundreds of reptile species, and the world's largest exhibit of flamingos. Open daily, 9 A.M.–5 P.M.

Texas Hall of State. Fair Park, Parry and First avenues. 214-421-5136. Commemorates state's history since independence through exhibits, statuary of founding Texans, and murals. Open Monday through Saturday, 9 A.M.–5 P.M.; Sunday, 1–5 P.M.

The Dallas Convention and Visitors' Bureau is at 1507 Pacific Avenue; call 214-954-1482 for information.

Points of Interest—Fort Worth

Amon Carter Museum of Western Art. 3501 Camp Bowie Boulevard. 817-738-1933. The art of America's pioneer movement and western states, from Frederic Remington and Charles M. Russell to Georgia O'Keeffe. Open Tuesday through Saturday, 10 A.M.–5 P.M.; Sunday, 1–5 P.M. Closed Monday.

Fort Worth Water Gardens. Downtown, adjacent to Convention Center. A refreshing spot on a hot day, just a few blocks west of the train station. Beautiful landscaping, walkways, and three fountain-pools. The fountains are on daily 9 A.M.–11 P.M.

Fort Worth Art Museum. 1309 Montgomery Street, at Will Rogers Memorial Center. 817-738-9215. Twentieth-century painting, sculpture, and graphics. Open Tuesday through Saturday, 10 A.M.–5 P.M.; Sunday, 1–5 P.M.

Fort Worth Zoological Park. 2727 Zoological Park Drive, Forest Park. 817-870-7050. Outstanding exhibits include tropical aviary, primate house, aquarium, and nation's largest herpetarium. Open every day from 9 A.M.; closing hours vary.

The Dallas Convention and Visitors' Bureau's Visitor Information Center is right in Union Station, 400 S. Houston Street. Phone 214-747-2355 for information.

For Fort Worth information, stop at the Fort Worth Convention and Visitors' Bureau at 700 Throckmorton Street, Fort Worth, or call 817-336-8791.

Public Transportation

Dallas buses are run by the Dallas Transit System. Call 214-826-2222 for schedule and fare information. In Fort Worth, bus service is provided by the City Transit Service. City Transit's information number is 817-870-6200.

Lodging—Dallas

Unlike many Sunbelt cities, Dallas and Fort Worth have convenient downtown train stations. The first thing you'll see upon arrival at the Dallas station is the sleek Hyatt Regency, which sets the pricey tone of the area's hostelries. However, many less glamorous but quite reasonable accommodations may be found in Dallas, Fort Worth, and points in between. Rates will vary from $35 to over $100.

Plaza. 1933 Main Street. 214-742-7251. 12 blocks from the station. A nicely restored old-fashioned hotel in the heart of Dallas's business district. Reasonably priced kitchenette units available. Restaurant, lounge.

Holiday Inn—Downtown. 1015 Elm Street. 214-748-9951. 8 blocks from the station. Motel convenience in center of town. Pool. Some units with balconies. Restuarant, lounge, entertainment.

Hyatt Regency. 300 Reunion Boulevard. 214-651-1234. A massing of blue mirror-glass towers—easily the most striking aspect of the Dallas skyline. Pool, tennis, jogging track. Several restaurants and lounges, entertainment.

Adolphus. 1321 Commerce Street. 214-742-8200. The grand hotel of Dallas, recently restored to the tune of $45 million. Built in 1912 by Adolphus Busch, the Budweiser baron, the Adolphus boasts large, luxurious rooms and three restaurants (with as many bars). The French Room is considered by many locals and visitors to be the city's best dining spot.

Lodging—Fort Worth

Rodeway Inn. 1111 W. Lancaster Street. 817-332-1951. 1 mile from the station. Large, seven-story motel near business district. Some inexpensive suites available. Pool. Restaurant, lounge. Laundromat on premises.

Best Western—Park Central Inn. 1011 Throckmorton Street. 817-336-2011. 10 blocks from the station. Reasonably priced rooms and suites. Room service. Restaurant, lounge, entertainment. Some rooms with oversized beds.

Fort Worth Hilton Inn. 1701 Commerce Street. 817-335-7000. 2 blocks from the station. Next to the Convention Center, across from the Water Gardens. Large well-run member of chain. Studios available; also suites. Pool. Restaurant, lounge, entertainment. Some rooms with balconies.

Restaurants—Dallas

A metroplex just wouldn't be a metroplex without a raft of premium "continental" restaurants, and Dallas-Fort Worth has its share. But don't overlook the basics: Tex-Mex, chili, gargantuan sirloins, and a local peculiarity called "chicken-fried steak."

Joe Moseley Barbecue. 1811 Young Street. 214-742-4636. A locally popular downtown barbecue spot. Open for breakfast as well as lunch, it closes mid-afternoon.

Shenanigans. 201 Elm Street (First International Building). 214-651-1212. Carpetbagger steak, usually a hard-to-find item, is on the menu here, as are spareribs and burgers. Closed weekends.

The Pyramid. Fairmont Hotel, Akard and Ross streets. 214-748-7258. A well-deserved reputation for splendid dining. Pheasant Souvarov; filet of sole en croûte; rack of lamb with spring vegetables. Also at the Fairmont is the Brasserie, a twenty-four-hour restaurant.

Restaurants—Fort Worth

The Greenery. Hilton Inn, 1701 Commerce Street. 817-335-7000. A little of everything, all day long. Huevos rancheros; chicken-fried steak; trout; prime rib. Informal.

Joe T. Garcia's. 2201 N. Commerce Street. 817-626-4356. A favorite local Tex-Mex spot, with one item on the menu: a combo platter that sums up the entire Tex-Mex repertory (almost). Good margaritas.

Fort Worth-Dallas to St. Louis

For 150 miles out of Dallas, the Missouri Pacific right-of-way that the *Eagle* travels runs in a straight line, due east. The route is so straight, in fact, that if you look out the rear window of the last car, you can see signal lights recede for a mile or more. This is beautiful country for sunsets, and the *Eagle* happens through at just the right time. To the right of the train, the Sabine River occasionally comes into view. The straightaway through small farms and pine forests runs uninterrupted until Longview, the nearest station to Tyler, Texas, and Marshall, where bus connetions for Shreveport, Louisiana, can be made.

At Marshall, the tracks veer sharply to the north. The *Eagle* reaches Texarkana, Arkansas, around 9 P.M., in time for the nightcap you have been denied until now because of county liquor laws in east Texas. There is a Texarkana, Texas, too, and the Amtrak timetables bear the names of both states at the listing for this stop. So, don't badger the steward until you know you're over the line.

Of the four Arkansas stops that the *Eagle* makes during the night, the most important is Little Rock, the capital, at about 11:40 P.M. Although the stop at Malvern is closer, Little Rock is the best place to get off if you wish to make connections for Hot Springs National Park and the nearby Ouachita National Forest. Between Malvern and Little Rock are many of Arkansas's bauxite mines, which yield the mineral from which aluminum is refined.

The *Eagle* leaves Little Rock after a 15-minute layover just before midnight, but there is little cause for regret in knowing that the remainder of Arkansas is slipping by in darkness. Arkansas is a picturesque state, but most of its more dramatic scenery lies far to the west, on the Ozark Plateau. Southern Missouri is a bit more varied, but current scheduling of the *Eagle* keeps you in the dark along this stretch as well, on both northbound and southbound runs.

As the hills get lower, the train bears east toward the Mississippi, which it follows north to St. Louis. This is a half-hour layover at about breakfasttime, so if this is your stop and you still haven't woken up, you'll have time to do so. If you still don't wake up, blame the porter, or blame the over-enthusiasm in Texarkana that followed the long Texas abstinence.

St. Louis

People in Kansas City—particularly those who hail from Harry Truman's hometown of Independence—often contend that their Missouri River location, and not that of St. Louis, was the one from which most people struck out for the West.

But St. Louis has the Arch. Built in the 1960s, the Gateway Arch commemorates the westward movement in America. And even if Kansas City has a point concerning where most of the pioneers embarked from, no one can disagree that it was in St. Louis that the whole adventure first became politically sanctioned. Here, on March 9, 1804, the United States took official possession of Upper Louisiana (the vast lands drained by the Missouri River, which empties near St. Louis into the Mississippi), according to the terms of the Louisiana Purchase.

St. Louis had been around for 40 years before the transfer took place. Founded by New Orleans merchants as a post for trading with the Indians, the settlement had passed from French to Spanish control and then back to the French again before becoming an American town. It flourished with the boom in river traffic in the 1800s; at mid-century it received a further civic and economic boost with the arrival of thousands of emigré Germans. Along with Milwaukee and Cincinnati, St. Louis was destined to become one of the most German cities in America. A German named Adolphus Busch set up a brewery here; his descendants still make a bit of beer.

By 1904, St. Louis felt prosperous enough to celebrate the centennial of the Louisiana Purchase with a grand exposition—the fair that is mentioned in the song "Meet Me in St. Louis." The exposition was held far to the west of downtown, in Forest Park. Unfortunately, the economic and population trends of the future also led away from downtown, with the result that, by the middle of our own century, St. Louis desperately needed the Arch—not as a memorial but as an anchor—along with a concerted effort at renewing its riverside core. Today, the old business district has come back to life in the shadow of Eero Saarinen's Arch. The Amtrak station is downtown, as are the sports stadium, municipal buildings, hotels and theaters, and a renovated shops-and-dining district called Laclede's Landing. Forest Park, the old exposition site, is also a focus of recreational and cultural activity. But outside these enclaves, St. Louis is making the same brave and sometimes bleak struggle that most old industrial cities are making, trying to assure that there may yet be ages and events worth commemorating.

Points of Interest

Gateway Arch and Museum of Westward Expansion. Jefferson National Expansion Memorial, 11 N. Fourth Street. 314-425-4465. St. Louis's trademark—a graceful, 630-foot arch designed by Eero Saarinen. Trams take visitors to observation deck at the top. Below, there's a museum devoted to the explorers and settlers of the West. Trams run every day between Memorial Day and Labor Day, 8:30 A.M.–9:30 P.M.; 9:30 A.M.–5:30 P.M. rest of year. Museum hours roughly correspond.

Anheuser-Busch Brewery Tour. Broadway at Pestalozzi Street. 314-577-2626. Guided tours of this registered historic landmark, one of the world's largest breweries. You'll get some free beer, and maybe see the Clydesdales. Tours Monday through Friday all year, 9:30 A.M., 3:30 P.M.; Saturday, June through August only.

Eugene Field House and Toy Museum. 634 S. Broadway. 314-421-4689. Federal row house where the children's poet was born. Personal effects and furnishings; also toy and doll collection. Open Tuesday through Saturday, 10 A.M.–4 P.M.; Sunday, noon–5 P.M. Closed Monday.

St. Louis Art Museum. Forest Park. 314-721-0067. American and European art; also other cultures. Sculpture hall. Seventy galleries; fine shop and restaurant on premises. Open Wednesday through Sunday, 10 A.M.–5 P.M.; Tuesday 2:30–9:30 P.M. Closed Monday.

St. Louis Zoological Park. Forest Park. 314-781-0900. Two thousand animals inhabit settings designed to resemble their natural habitats. The big cats alone are worth the admission price. Children's zoo; railroad. Marlin Perkins, of television fame, formerly directed this zoo. Open every day, 9 A.M.–5 P.M.

Missouri Botanical Garden. 2101 Tower Grove Avenue. 314-772-7600. Plants and trees of all climatic regions, growing indoors and out. World's first geodesic greenhouse. Japanese gardens. Buildings include restored **Tower Grove House,** home of Henry Shaw, the garden's founder. Open May to November every day, 9 A.M.–6 P.M.; winter to 5 P.M.

Missouri Historical Society. Jefferson Memorial Building, Lindell Boulevard and DeBaliviere Street, 314-361-1424. Art and artifacts pertaining to the state's past and its contributions to various industries. Particularly interesting is the Charles Lindbergh Gallery. Open Tuesday through Sunday, 9:30 A.M.–4:45 P.M. Guided tours Saturday and Sunday at 1:30 P.M. Closed Monday.

The Convention and Visitors' Bureau is located at 10 South Broadway. Call 314-421-1023 for information; toll-free 1-800-325-7962.

Public Transportation

St. Louis and its suburbs on both sides of the Mississippi are served by the buses of the Bi-State Transit System. For schedule and fare information, call 314-231-2345.

Lodging

As St. Louis grew away from the Mississippi toward Forest Park, it threatened to abandon its old downtown hostelries. However, the core city's revitalization, symbolized by the Gateway Arch, has assured the survival of establishments near the station as well as the building of new places to stay.

Expect to pay between $45 and $85 for a double at the hotels listed below.

Best Western—St. Louisian. 1133 Washington Avenue. 314-421-4727/800-528-1234. 15 blocks from the station. Inexpensive yet convenient to all downtown points. Three suites available. Heated pool. Restaurant, lounge.

Holiday Inn—Downtown. 2211 Market Street. 314-231-3232. 5 blocks from station. Just redecorated. Pool. Restaurant, lounge, entertainment.

Mayfair. 806 St. Charles Street. 314-231-1500/800-325-7100. 18 blocks from station. A traditional hotel in the heart of St. Louis's financial district. Walk to all downtown attractions. Rooftop pool. Restaurant, lounges, live ragtime music.

Bel Air Hilton. 333 Washington Street. 314-621-7900. Luxury hotel near riverfront and Gateway Arch. Indoor pool. Two restaurants, lounge.

Restaurants

St. Louis dining represents the coming together of southern and midwestern traditions, but the French-Continental restaurants common now to all large cities have made their impact as well. In other words, you'll find catfish and hush puppies, sauerbraten and steak, and medallions de veau on St. Louis menus.

Miss Hullings. 1103 Locust Street (314-436-0404). This reliable cafeteria serves breakfast, lunch, and dinner. Homemade desserts.

Dunie's. 1215 Delmar Boulevard. 314-231-8294. A Jewish deli serving breakfast and lunch. The corned-beef sandwich isn't New York, but it's good; also matzohball soup and other homemade dishes.

Catfish and Crystal. 409 N. Eleventh Street, corner of Locust. 314-231-7703. As the name implies. Catfish isn't the only thing on the menu; there are scallops, prime rib, steaks, and an assortment of homemade desserts. Entertainment on weekends.

Froebe's Wine Bar and Restaurant. 75 Maryland Plaza. 314-361-2200. If you've combined a day at Forest Park with a trip to the Maryland Plaza Shopping Center, Froebe's makes a handy lunch or dinner stop. German menu is enhanced by a selection of forty-two wines, thirty of them by the glass.

Tony's. 826 N. Broadway. 314-231-7007. Mobil gives this one five stars. The menu is Italian, with emphasis on fresh seafood and the finest of veal; there are also prime steaks. Get there early and have a drink by the fire.

St. Louis to Chicago

From St. Louis to Chicago, the *Eagle* traverses much the same Illinois countryside as the *City of New Orleans*. The stops are different, though, the principal one being Springfield, the state capital and site of the home and tomb of Abraham Lincoln. Arrival at Chicago's Union Station is in early afternoon.

The *Empire Builder*, Amtrak's Chicago-Seattle train, winds through the mountains of America's west on its 2,281-mile journey to the west coast. The *Empire Builder* was Amtrak's first train to be equipped with the popular bi-level Superliner cars.

7. The *Empire Builder*

The *Empire Builder* travels the northernmost of the routes that connect Chicago with the West Coast (for information on Chicago, see trip 1). It takes its name from the storied limited once run by the Great Northern Railroad; the train, in turn, was named in homage to James J. Hill, the Canadian emigrant to St. Paul who built the Great Northern and the "empire" traversed by its tracks. St. Paul was not connected to Chicago by rail until 1867; by 1893, Hill's enterprise had pushed the road westward to Tacoma, on Puget Sound. Hill, by the way, was also instrumental in putting together the syndicate that built the Canadian Pacific, and hand-picked the great William Cornelius Van Horne to be that road's general manager. Hill pulled out of the CPR, though, when his plans to run the Canadian venture's eastern leg through the United States (to the benefit of his other interests) were rejected by his colleagues on the board and by his protégé Van Horne. For this bit of perceived disloyalty, Hill swore he would get even with Van Horne "if I have to go to hell for it and shovel coal." Such was the world of high-roll railroading in the nineteenth century.

In the days of Jim Hill, several other rail companies operated between Chicago and the Pacific Northwest, most notably the Northern Pacific and the Chicago and Burlington. In 1901, with the help of Edward Harriman and J. P. Morgan, Hill consolidated those roads with the Great Northern. Although that action was soon overturned by the "trust-buster" president, Theodore Roosevelt, the economics of rail service dictated an eventual merger, and today the *Empire Builder* operates between St. Paul and Seattle over the track of the Burlington Northern, successor to the three older firms. Between Chicago and Milwaukee, the *Builder* runs on Milwaukee Road track. Until 1979, Amtrak ran a train called the *North Coast Hiawatha* along a Northern Pacific route parallel to and south of the Burlington Northern. This train, however, succumbed during the system consolidation of that year.

The *Empire Builder* is not the only way to get to Milwaukee and Minneapolis-St. Paul by rail from Chicago. Four other trains, the *Nicollet*, *Radisson*, *Marquette*, and *LaSalle*, all named for early French explorers of the upper Midwest, run between the two Lake Michigan cities. But the *Builder* is the only American train to cross the northern plains beyond Minneapolis, and now it does so daily all year. (Another train, the *North Star*, provides daily connections between Minneapolis and the Great Lakes port of Duluth, 153 miles to the northeast.)

A full-service train, the *Empire Builder* is the first on which Amtrak put its new Superliner equipment into service. The consist includes full coaches, baggage-coach cars, diner, sleeping cars, and lounge.

Chicago to Milwaukee

Leaving Chicago in mid-afternoon, the *Empire Builder* heads north along Lake Michigan, making one Illinois stop, at Glenview, before reaching Milwaukee. (The other Chicago-Milwaukee trains also stop at Sturtevant,

Wisconsin, near Racine). The trip from Chicago to Milwaukee takes about an hour and a half.

Milwaukee

Milwaukee both reinforces and contradicts its reputation. The popular notion has it that Milwaukee is an unsophisticated, blue-collar city and that it is heavily German both in population and character. If you substitute "unpretentious" for "unsophisticated," both impressions are true. A great many heavy industries are concentrated in and around Milwaukee; without exaggeration, it could be called the machine-tool capital of the United States. And yes, this is a German city. Perhaps no other urban area in America ever received such a steady influx of a single nationality.

But no city of three-quarters of a million people can be summed up so simply. In addition to its foundries, Milwaukee has one of the world's great park systems and an important university; along with its tens of thousands of citizens of German descent, it counts representatives of virtually every ethnic group among its population.

Like Chicago, its neighbor 90 miles to the south, Milwaukee got its start as a port on Lake Michigan. In the early 1840s, the only permanent structures near the mouth of the Milwaukee River were the log cabins built by fur trader Solomon Juneau, now regarded as the founder of Milwaukee. With the development of farmland in Wisconsin, Minnesota, and Iowa and the mining of iron ore in the ranges surrounding the upper Great Lakes, shipping became a matter of more than the exchange of furs and blankets with the Indians. Sailing ships and steamers provided the necessary link with the expanding rail terminus of Chicago, but it was not long until Milwaukee had railroads of its own. By 1867, connections with both Chicago and St. Paul had been made. Grain, iron and coal could reach Milwaukee easily. Just as easily, finished products could be shipped out.

Milwaukee's concentration of Germans is the result of a wave of immigration which followed the political tumult of 1848. At that time, large numbers of German liberal sympathizers, along with individuals who were simply disillusioned by the scarcity of land and opportunity in Central Europe, began making their way to the American Midwest. They brought with them a capacity for thoroughness and hard work, particularly as applied to the mechanical arts, and a tradition of civic-mindedness and democratic socialism which inspired conscientious maintenance of public works and institutions. It is generally forgotten that within this century, Milwaukee elected independent socialist mayors for 50 years.

The Germans also brought with them a prodigious thirst. The grain and water for brewing were close at hand, but the beer that Milwaukee made famous was different from what Americans had been drinking before the mid-nineteenth century. It was light, aged, lager beer. A torrent of lager still flows out of Milwaukee, both from the three giants—Pabst, Schlitz, and Miller—and from smaller breweries unheard of outside Wisconsin.

The Amtrak station in Milwaukee is located on St. Paul Street, just a few blocks from Wisconsin Avenue, the main downtown artery. South of the station and the nearby harbor, beyond National Avenue, sprawls Milwaukee's South Side, a neighborhood whose factories, innumerable corner taverns, and rows of neat frame double-deckers and bungalows have given the city its "lunch pail" image. Not far from the station in another direction, however, the city assumes a completely different character. Head up to Wisconsin

Avenue and turn right. Just after you cross the river, look to your left, down Water Street. The *rathaus*-styled building, which could just as easily dominate the skyline of some town along the Rhine, is Milwaukee's City Hall. The streets that crisscross the pocket formed by the river, Wisconsin Avenue, and lakeside Juneau Park make up East Town, an area of small art galleries and specialty shops. From here, head north along Prospect or Farwell avenues into the East Side. The tone of this neighborhood is set by its large student population. The University of Wisconsin–Milwaukee, a large and diverse institution too often eclipsed by its counterpart at Madison, occupies several blocks along the city's border with its northern suburb of Shorewood. The East Side is a virtual college town unto itself, with a large population of artists, craftspeople, young professionals, and aging counter-culturists. To meet at least half of them at once, go into Hooligan's Bar on a Saturday night. It's near the neo-Gothic water tower at the intersection of North and Prospect avenues.

Points of Interest

Milwaukee Art Museum. War Memorial Building, 750 N. Lincoln Memorial Drive (Juneau Park). 414-271-9508. Art from Egyptian to modern American periods. Especially strong in German Expressionism and American Ash-Can School. Open Tuesday, Wednesday, Friday, and Saturday, 10 A.M.–5 P.M.; Thursday, noon–9 P.M.; Sunday, 1 P.M.–6 P.M. Closed Monday.

Charles Allis Art Museum. 1801 N. Prospect Avenue. 414-278-8295. Mansion and collection bequeathed to the city by industrialist Charles Allis. Changing exhibits, including work of local craftspeople. Open Wednesday through Sunday 1–5 P.M.; also Wednesday evening, 7–9 P.M. Closed Monday and Tuesday.

Milwaukee Public Museum. 800 W. Wells Street. 414-278-2700. Exhibits focus on natural and social history of Milwaukee area, also fine arts. A popular attraction is "A Trip through Time," offering a look at old Milwaukee. Also see the European village, African waterhole, Japanese garden, and pre-Columbian tomb. A new wing, "The Third Planet," houses dinosaur dioramas. Open every day, 9 A.M.–5 P.M.

Mitchell Park Horticultural Conservatory. 524 S. Layton Boulevard. 414-278-4383. An outstanding conservatory, housed in three glass domes, each regulated for a different climate. One houses a tropical rain forest; another an arid desert; the third is used for six annual flower shows. Open Tuesday through Sunday, 9 A.M.–9 P.M.; Monday, 9 A.M.–5 PM.

Boerner Botanical Gardens. Whitnall Park, 5879 S. 92nd Street, Hales Corners. 414-425-1131. Beautifully maintained outdoor gardens; something in bloom at virtually every time of the year. Open every day, 8 A.M.–sunset.

Milwaukee County Zoo. 10001 W. Bluemound Road. 414-771-5500/3040. This was one of the first zoos to adopt the idea of allowing animals to roam freely in environments that simulate their native habitats. The gorilla house is a favorite attraction. Open first weekend in May through Labor Day, weekdays, 9 A.M.–5 P.M.; Sundays and holidays, to 6 P.M.; rest of year, 9 A.M.–4:30 P.M. daily. Closed Thanksgiving, Christmas, New Year's Day.

Brewery Tours. Pabst and Miller offer tours of their Milwaukee breweries. Pabst, 901 W. Juneau Avenue, 414-347-7328; Miller, 4251 State Street, 414-931-2153.

The Greater Milwaukee Convention and Visitors' Bureau maintains three Visitors' Information Centers: 756 N. Milwaukee Street, 414-273-7222; General Mitchell Field (Airport), 414-747-4808; and "Discover Milwaukee," at Grand Avenue retail center, 161 W. Wisconsin Avenue, 414-276-8482.

Around Milwaukee

One of the best ways to spend an extra day in Milwaukee is to explore the County Parks, particularly those adjacent to Lake Michigan. It's possible to walk from Juneau Park, downtown, all the way to Lake Park, near the university campus, along this lakeside green belt. On the South Side, Sheridan, Warnimont, and Grant parks extend along the water for over 5 miles. Milwaukee's parks are clean and beautifully landscaped, with lovely views of the lake and the opposite shores of the harbor.

If you are a walker and have an interest in the extravagant domestic architecture of the early years of this century, you might enjoy a trek northward along Lake Drive. Start in the university neighborhood, where the mansions are impressive enough; heading north into Shorewood and Whitefish Bay, you'll pass dozens of shaded, stately homes built by the brewing and industrial magnates of an earlier Milwaukee.

Between July 1 and Labor Day, the Iroquois Boat Line runs harbor cruises lasting one and a half hours. Boats leave from the west bank of the Milwaukee River dock at the Clybourn Street bridge. 414-354-5050.

Public Transportation

Like its parks, Milwaukee's bus system is operated by the county. Routes are extensive, service dependable. The Milwaukee County Transit System information number is 414-344-6711.

Lodging

Although downtown Milwaukee has lost economic ground to the suburbs, there are still good hotels within a short distance of the train station. Acceptable rooms start at about $40; deluxe accommodations at several establishments can reach $90 or more.

Astor Hotel. 924 E. Juneau Avenue. 414-271-4220. 16 blocks from station. A small, comfortable hotel, very reasonably priced and situated near Juneau Park and the lakefront, away from downtown bustle.

Marc Plaza. 509 W. Wisconsin Avenue. 414-271-7250/800-323-7500. 6 blocks from station. A newly renovated Milwaukee landmark. Fine views from upper stories; five-room suites available. Restaurant, two lounges. Year-round pool, and health club.

Pfister Hotel and Tower. 424 E. Wisconsin Avenue. 414-273-8222/800-323-7500. 9 blocks from station. The grande dame of Milwaukee hotels. Main building dates to 1890; it's been restored and joined to a 200-room circular tower with views of Lake Michigan. Rooftop pool, sauna and health club. English Room restaurant, entertainment in the lounge.

Restaurants

The mainstays of this city are schnitzel, beer, dark bread, and the wonderful sausages turned out by local packers. Still, you may arrive during a warm spell or stay for more than a few days, so here is a varied sampling.

Watts Tea Room. 761 N. Jefferson Street. 414-276-6352. An elegant oasis serving lunch and, yes, tea, above the George Watts Company, Milwaukee's finest purveyor of crystal, silver, and fine china. Long popular with lady shoppers, but men can break these barriers now.

Karl Ratzsch's. 320 E. Mason Street, 414-276-2720. Locals and visitors generally agree that Ratzsch's is the best of Milwaukee's German restaurants. Specialties include virtually every variety of schnitzel, sauerbraten, wursts, and roast goose. A truly fine cellar stocking hard-to-find German wines.

Jean-Paul. 811 E. Wisconsin Avenue. 414-271-5400. A serene and uncluttered French establishment offering, but not limited to, the "nouvelle cuisine." Baked salmon mousse, stuffed quail, turbot in hollandaise sauce. Crepes and soufflés. Lunch weekdays only.

Milwaukee is a good place to stock up on nonperishables (see Introduction) if you are packing a transcontinental train lunch. Try the delicatessen on the first floor of Gimbel's department store, downtown on Wisconsin Avenue, or, on the East Side, Beans and Barley, 1901 E. North Avenue.

Milwaukee to St. Paul

During the late afternoon, the *Empire Builder* travels through the farmlands of south central Wisconsin. The stop nearest to the capital and university city of Madison is Columbus; connections may be made by bus. Next is Portage, whose name is a reminder of the days of the fur trade, and then Wisconsin Dells, a town which sprang into existence with the coming of the Chicago, Milwaukee, St. Paul, and Pacific Railroad in the 1850s. Nearby, the Wisconsin River flows through an area of picturesque rock formations. The Winnebago Indians believed that a giant serpent pushing its way southward was responsible for the tortuous course of the river here. Excursion boats ply the river, offering the best views of the Dells.

The last Wisconsin stops are at Tomah and La Crosse. The latter town was named by early traders who observed the Indians playing their variation of the popular French game. At La Crosse, the *Builder* crosses the Mississippi, then runs alongside it at one of its most beautiful sections, stopping at Winona, Minnesota, and arriving at Red Wing around dinner time. Red Wing, with its beautiful river bluffs and remarkably well preserved Victorian architecture, is worth an overnight stop if you have the time. The place to stay is the St. James Hotel.

Leaving Red Wing, the tracks bear west. Late in the evening, the train arrives at St. Paul, with a half-hour stop scheduled.

Minneapolis-St. Paul

The first thing to remember about Minneapolis and St. Paul is that although "Twin Cities" is a convenient name for them, you wouldn't want to walk from one city center to the other—they are about 9 miles apart. Amtrak's aptly named Midway Station, on Transfer Road near University Avenue in St. Paul, is equally distant from both downtowns. Considering the hour at which the *Empire Builder* arrives, your best bet is to take a cab to your destination (and have reservations ahead of time). If you're taking the bus, remember that Minneapolis is to your *right* on University Avenue, and St. Paul is to your *left*.

Minneapolis and St. Paul differ in many ways. Some people even go so far as to suggest that the former is a Western city, while the latter belongs to the East. But one thing that they have in common is the Mississippi River. This is where the navigable portion of the Mississippi begins; from here, it is some fifteen hundred miles downriver to New Orleans. It was the river that first brought French explorers and fur traders to these parts. The Falls of St. Anthony, near which Minneapolis was to grow some two hundred years later, were discovered by Father Louis Hennepin in 1680. This 16-foot cataract was a hindrance to navigation, but eventually proved useful as a source of power when the cities' industrial era began.

Although French domination of the Upper Mississippi lasted until the mid-1700s, the group did little in the way of real settlement. The wealth of New France depended on beaver pelts, and its rulers favored a commerce with the Indians which was unimpeded by the presence of villages and farms. The British next controlled the area, and by 1814 United States dominion was secure. The 1830s saw the growth of two villages, Pig's Eye and St. Anthony, on the opposite shores of the river. Pig's Eye was the nickname of a local whisky trader; the site of his business took on his name. In 1841, a Catholic priest consecrated a chapel to St. Paul in the village, and Minnesota was spared having a capital city named Pig's Eye.

While the eastern twin took a saint's name, its fledgling counterpart followed a more secular course. St. Anthony decided to call itself Minneapolis, a name which joins the Sioux word for water with the Greek word for city.

From the beginning, the two communities set about different pursuits. St. Paul took full advantage of its riverside location and became a trading center. Furs were still the town's chief export. But across the Mississippi, Minneapolis entrepreneurs exploited two resources destined to eclipse the beaver as the source of the region's wealth: timber and wheat. St. Paul stuck to its shipping, and Minneapolis became a city of lumbering and flour milling. This division of labor—accompanied by no small amount of rivalry—continued for many years, and by the time the commercial distinctions began to blur, the political sovereignty of both cities was well established.

Still, the twins could have progressed much further toward becoming a single urban center had not certain topographical features determined a peculiar development of the railroads. Breaks in the bluffs that parallel the Mississippi as far north as St. Paul allowed rail access into that city. Minneapolis, meanwhile, is situated near the most likely spot for trains coming from the north and west to cross the river. Railroad companies needed terminals in both growing cities. Amtrak's modern solution—a station at the halfway point—would not have worked, for before the coming of the automobile, 5 miles was a much greater distance. Today both centers thrive separately, although Minneapolis is larger by far than St. Paul.

The Twin Cities became a conduit not only for the wheat, wood, and iron of the developing frontier but also for the manpower needed to farm, hew, and mine. Great numbers of Scandinavian emigrants began to arrive in Minnesota. To this day, citizens of Swedish, Danish, and Norwegian descent make up a significant part of the upper Midwest's ethnic mix, as anyone who listens to Garrison Keillor's *Prairie Home Companion* radio show is well aware. (If you're going to be in St. Paul on a Saturday night, by all means try to get tickets to the show, which starts at 5 P.M. at the World Theater, Wabasha and Exchange streets, 612-221-1500/623-3444). Interestingly, certain stones found in Minnesota indicate a possible Viking visit to this area—as though the early Norsemen foreshadowed the later influx of their countrymen into the region.

The northern prairie begins at the Twin Cities. If you arrive in Minneapolis on a clear day, go to the Skylook Observation Gallery atop the 775-foot IDS Tower. While the terrain beyond St. Paul, to the east, is more hilly, the western horizon is virtually unbroken. Not until you reach the Rockies, in western Montana, does this landscape change significantly.

The IDS Tower—Minnesota's tallest building—stands at the heart of an indoor mall complex and system of enclosed walkways. Minneapolis is known for its ferocious winters, and these "skyways" provide a practical means for shoppers, office workers, and visitors to avoid the elements.

St. Paul has also built enclosed walkways in its downtown area, although the city does not bristle with the same sort of rakish modern architecture that characterizes Minneapolis. The smaller city, however, excels in the number of fine Victorian homes it has preserved, such as the James J. Hill house, 240 Summit Avenue, and the F. Scott Fitzgerald house, Summit Hill.

Points of Interest—Minneapolis

Butler Square. First Avenue N. between Fifth Street N. and Sixth Street N. An old warehouse, which has been given a quality shops-and-restaurants refurbishment. Most interesting shop is called "Hello Minnesota"; sells everything Minnesotan, from recordings of local humor to long johns.

Minneapolis Institute of Art. Fine Arts Park. 2400 Third Avenue S. 612-870-3046. Extensive collection of oriental art; period rooms. Calder mobile in lobby. Museum open Tuesday through Saturday, 10 A.M.–5 P.M.; Thursday until 9 P.M.; Sunday, noon–5 P.M. Closed Monday. Next door is the museum of the Hennepin County Historical Society, featuring displays of local artifacts.

American Swedish Institute. 2600 Park Avenue. 612-871-4907. A thirty-three-room mansion in the French chateau style, housing exhibits illustrating the Scandinavian experience in Minnesota. Open Tuesday through Saturday, noon–4 P.M.; Sunday, 1–5 P.M. Closed Monday.

Minnehaha Falls and Park. In southern outskirts of Minneapolis, but accessible by bus. This 144-acre park is the site of Minnehaha Falls, made famous by Longfellow in his *Song of Hiawatha*. The 53-foot falls are just above the point where Minnehaha Creek flows into the Mississippi River.

The Minneapolis Convention and Visitor Commission is located at 15 S. Fifth Street. 612-348-4313. There is also an information booth in the Crystal Court, main floor of the IDS Tower.

Points of Interest—St. Paul

Fort Snelling. Highway 5, south of the cities, but accessible by bus. 612-726-9430/726-1171. In the 1820s this was the United States government's main garrison in the upper Midwest—then called the Northwest. The fort is not just a restored building; costumed actors recreate the lives of officers, men, and their families during the garrison's heyday. Open daily, June through Labor Day, 10 A.M.–5 P.M. May, September, and October, 9 A.M.–4:30 P.M. weekdays; 10 A.M.–5 P.M. weekends.

Science Museum of Minnesota. William L. McKnight-3M Omnitheater. 30 E. Tenth Street. 612-221-9488; 612-221-9400 for Omnitheater shows. Museum features anthropological exhibits, natural history, and archaeology of Minnesota. The Omnitheater shows, billed as a "roller coaster ride for the mind," are a changing program of 70-mm film and sound presentations using the world's largest projector and a 7,300-square-foot curving screen. Museum open Tuesday through Saturday, 9:30 A.M.–9 P.M.; Sunday, 11 A.M.–9 P.M. Open Mondays, Memorial Day to Labor Day only. Call for Omnitheater schedules.

Alexander Ramsey House. 265 S. Exchange Street. 612-296-0100. Home of Minnesota's first territorial governor. Built 1872; carefully restored and furnished in high-Victorian style. Open weekdays, 10 A.M.–4 P.M.; weekends, 1–4:30 P.M.

State Capitol. Capitol Complex, just north of downtown. Built in 1905 and inspired by St. Peter's in Rome, the Minnesota Capitol has the world's largest unsupported marble dome. Tours daily.

The St. Paul Convention, Exhibition, and Tourism Commission is located in the Landmark Center, 75 W. Fifth Street, Level B-100; call 612-292-4360. There is also a visitors' information center at the Landmark Center.

Lodging—Minneapolis

There has been a spate of hotel-building in the Minneapolis-St. Paul area, so there are many new hotels to choose from. A double room here will cost from $35 to $100. Because of the location of the station, distances from station to hotels are not noted.

Curtis Hotel and Motor Lodge. 327 Tenth Street S. 612-340-5300. Recently remodeled hotel with adjoining motel. Continental breakfast, lounge. Indoor/outdoor pool, sauna. All rooms with bath.

Regency Plaza Best Western Hotel. 41 Tenth Street N. 612-339-9311/800-528-1234. Indoor pool, sauna. Restaurant and lounge, entertainment. Free shuttle bus to downtown shopping mall.

Sheraton-Ritz. 315 Nicollet Mall. 612-332-4000/800-325-3535. In the heart of downtown; recently remodeled with rooms in contemporary and French Provincial style. Indoor pool, whirlpool, and weight room. Fine restaurant, entertainment.

Lodging—St. Paul

Youth Hostel—Capitol Center YMCA. 475 Cedar Street. 612-222-0771. 20 bunks.

St. Paul Travelodge. 149 E. University Avenue. 612-227-8801/800-255-3050. 3 blocks from state capitol; also convenient bus connections to train station. Some rooms with balcony.

Radisson-St. Paul. 11 E. Kellogg Boulevard. 612-292-1900/800-228-9822. Minnesota is Radisson's headquarters, and this is one of their flagship hotels. Several restaurants, including revolving rooftop. Entertainment. Heated indoor pool. Cabana rooms have direct access to pool.

Restaurants—Minneapolis

D.B. Kaplan's Delicatessen. Butler Square, 100 Sixth Street N. 612-332-0903. Serving all meals; specialties include over 150 varieties of sandwiches. Licensed.

Link Restaurant. 2400 Third Avenue S. 612-870-3180. Tucked between the Minneapolis Institute of Art and the Children's Theater, this quiet, elegant oasis excels when it comes to Sunday brunch—the buffet includes prime ribs and strawberry crepes.

The 510 Haute Cuisine. 510 Groveland Avenue. 612-874-6440. Limited menu, freshest ingredients. Fixed-price dinners include appetizer, soup, and salad; dessert extra. Pheasant véronique, scallops bonne femme, émince of duck. Excellent pastries. Extensive wine list. Lunch served. Reservations recommended for dinner.

Restaurants—St. Paul

MacCafferty's. 788 Grand Avenue. 612-227-7328. An Irish pub, but with food to match the Guinness. Homemade soda bread, scotch eggs, rarebit. Oysters on the half shell. Live music Tuesday through Saturday. Sunday brunch.

Alfredo's. 400 Sibley Street. 612-221-0551. It seems only fitting that fettucini Alfredo is a big item here; so are other pasta specialties, veal, and seafood. Free hors d'oeuvres at happy hour. Live jazz every night.

St. Paul to Seattle

It is late evening on the prairie as the *Empire Builder* pulls out of St. Paul. While you sleep the train heads northwest through fields of wheat and corn (the latter, incidentally, has replaced the former as Minnesota's chief crop), stopping at St. Cloud, Staples, and Detroit Lakes, Minnesota. At Detroit Lakes the Burlington Northern tracks turn due west, taking the *Builder* across the Red River into Fargo, North Dakota, sometime after one in the morning. During the night the train heads north and then west again. Near the scheduled stop of Rugby, North Dakota, it passes the geographical center of North America. At this point, you are less than 50 miles south of the Canadian border.

If you are an early riser, or have left your drapes open, you will probably first see the sun somewhere between Grand Forks and Devil's Lake, perhaps earlier in high summer. It will rise behind you, suffusing the prairie with luminous shades of yellow and pink, colors which dissipate just above the horizon into the lingering deep blue of night. On a clear day, sunrise in North Dakota is one of the most beautiful sights along any American rail route.

Minot, North Dakota, is the state's third largest city and an important distribution center for grain, livestock, and oil. There is a 15-minute layover here. Between Stanley and Williston, the *Empire Builder* passes through the town of Wheelock, which at 2,387 feet is the highest point along the Burlington Northern right-of-way in North Dakota. You'll never notice the elevation—there are no dramatic hills to climb, no switchbacks or horseshoe curves. This is table land, rising imperceptibly in altitude toward the Continental Divide. It is the high prairie. Throughout the remainder of North Dakota and through all but the last third of Montana, the *Empire Builder* is like a ship at sea, pressing westward through a strange and desolate landscape in which farms give way to vast grazing lands where each head of cattle seems master of many acres. Sheep, too, populate the rangelands; they take well to the terrain and climate and since the coming of the railroad in the late 1800s have been a Montana staple. In the terms suggested by Joel Garreau in his 1981 book *The Nine Nations of North America*, you are passing now from the "Breadbasket" into the "Empty Quarter"—the difference being that the latter "nation" receives less than 20 inches of rain per year, and most of the land is owned by the government. But this territory is empty only of people, not resources. The oil and gas reserves in the American West are vast, and pose difficult choices concerning the balance between extraction and preservation of the region's topography and ecology.

This is the country made famous by Charles M. Russell, who was equaled only by Frederic Remington as a painter of the American West. South of the *Empire Builder*'s route, between the Montana towns of Wolf Point and Malta, lies the vast Russell National Wildlife Range. Wild creatures do not respect the borders of such places; from the window of your Superliner coach or sleeper, you may see pronghorn antelope bounding effortlessly across the plain.

Just before Havre, and south of the Burlington Northern route, is the Bear Paws Battleground, where the Nez Percé Indians, led by the brilliant strategist Chief Joseph, made their last stand against the U.S. Army. The Nez Percé were only 40 miles away from sanctuary in Canada, but the tribe's children and old people slowed their retreat.

Havre is a 15-minute stop (Amtrak trains often stop for less than the scheduled time if they are running late) and a good place to stretch your legs. If the prairie is an ocean, places like Havre are its islands. You can well imagine how ranch families might look forward to the occasional visit to Havre—but don't wander too far from the station, or all you will be looking forward to is the next *Empire Builder.*

Havre, Shelby, Cut Bank—the plains roll on through the afternoon. Shelby sits in the heart of Montana's oil fields. Near Cut Bank, to the left (south) the monument to Meriwether Lewis is visible from the train. Lewis, of course, was co-leader of the 1804 Lewis and Clark Expedition, which passed this way in its exploration of the newly-acquired Louisiana Purchase.

At Browning, near the Blackfoot Indian Reservation, the Rocky Mountains finally begin to crumple the horizon; at Glacier Park Station, you are in their midst. Here in East Glacier is the Glacier Park Lodge, a resort hotel built early in this century by the Great Northern Railway. Fishing, riding and backpacking enthusiasts might consider a layover at Glacier if time allows; the stop is made only during the summer months.

Glacier is an early evening stop. As the sky darkens, the *Empire Builder* winds through the mountainous terrain that makes up the rest of Montana. There are few better times or places to have a window seat in an Amtrak diner. By midnight, you will have crossed Idaho's narrow northern panhandle, and a little after 1 A.M. you will be in Spokane. Here there is a half-hour layover, and the *Empire Builder* splits into two trains. One continues west towards Seattle, while the other heads south and west to Portland, Oregon (for Portland information, see trip 12). South of Pasco, Washington, the Portland section follows the Columbia River to its destination, as did Lewis and Clark. The Seattle section crosses the Columbia at Wenatchee, center of apple orchard country, around dawn. Even if you ordinarily do not like to get up at 5, ask for a wake-up call at Wenatchee because for the next couple of hours the *Empire Builder* will wind through the beautiful Cascade Mountains.

Breakfast in the Cascades is as wonderful an experience as dinner in the Rockies. Keep your eyes on the clearings between the forest and the track— more often than not, you will see elk staring passively at the train.

The ride through the Cascades is not a long one. Soon the *Empire Builder* begins its descent through their green, windward foothills and around 8 A.M. reaches Everett, a Puget Sound port and aircraft manufacturing center. From here, the tracks hug Puget Sound on their final southward stretch to Edmonds and Seattle.

Seattle

Seattle is the largest city of the Pacific Northwest, although it has been little more than a hundred years in the making. King Street Station, your destination, is within a few blocks of the area where Seattle's industry and commerce got its start.

The first white settlers of Seattle arrived from Portland, Oregon, in 1851 and built their cabins on a spit of land just south of the city's present location. By early 1852, the permanent site of Seattle had been selected for its superior harbor. Standing as it did between forests full of timber and the shipping lanes of Puget Sound and the Pacific, Seattle's growth was assured. Portlander Henry Yesler set up a sawmill near present-day Pioneer Square, and the long muddy slide down which logs were transported to the mill became known as the Skid Road—a phrase which remained in the language. The original skid road is now Yesler Way, and Pioneer Square, its old waterfront terminus, is no longer the exclusive domain of old loggers and fishermen who are "on the skids." The Square has been nicely restored, although you may still see a few characters waiting for the next gold rush.

It was the great Alaskan gold rush of 1898 that brought Seattle its first real boom. Within seven years of that date, over 90 percent of Alaskan shipping was headquartered here, and nearly everyone who headed north to seek his fortune passed through this harbor. All of the secondary enterprises that accompanied the search for gold flourished in Seattle, creating a greatly expanded industrial and mercantile capacity that remained even after the Alaskan boom died down.

To reach Pioneer Square from the King Street Station, follow Third Avenue S. to either S. Washington Street or Yesler Way and turn left. If you continue through the Square area, you will reach Alaskan Way, which parallels the waterfront. Walk along the harbor to get a sense of Seattle's still-lively maritime life; or head uphill, on James Street or Yesler Way, for a panorama of Elliott Bay, its islands, and the clean, modern city that has spread itself across the surrounding hills.

Like San Francisco, another hilly, oceanside city, Seattle is a city of mists. During the six colder months of the year, this mist often promotes itself into rain, which is why Seattle stores sell T-shirts that say, "Seattle people don't tan, they rust." But many days in summer are vividly clear, and the dampness has a charm—particularly if you choose a drizzly day for a walk along the waterfront or a ferry ride that will end with hot coffee on a quiet island.

Points of Interest

Seattle Space Needle. Off Broad Street near Fifth Avenue N. The Space Needle was the focal point of the 1964 Seattle World's Fair. At 520 feet, it towers above Seattle Center, the park and arts complex that occupies the old fairgrounds. The Space Needle has indoor and outdoor observation decks and, at the 500-foot level, a revolving restaurant serving breakfast (summer only), lunch, dinner, and cocktails. Reservations (206-447-3100) are recommended for dinner. Views of Puget Sound and, in clear weather, Mount Rainier are outstanding. Open every day.

Seattle Art Museum. Volunteer Park, 14th Street East and Prospect Street. 206-447-4710. Widely known for its Oriental art holdings, the museum features an extensive collection of Chinese jade. Examples of Greek, Roman, and medieval art are also displayed. Modern collections are housed in the museum's *Modern Art Pavilion,* located near the Space Needle in Seattle Center. The Seattle Art Museum is open Tuesday through Saturday, 10 A.M.–5 P.M.; Sunday, noon–5 P.M., and on Thursday evenings, 7–10 P.M. Closed Monday. The Modern Art Pavilion is open Tuesday through Sunday, 11 A.M.–6 P.M. (8 P.M. on Thursday). Closed Monday.

Woodland Park Zoo. 5500 Phinney Avenue N. 206-789-7919. The major feature of this zoo is the world's largest exhibit of gorillas in an outdoor setting designed to resemble the natural habitat of the great primates. The zoo is open every day, 8:30 A.M.–dusk.

Burke Memorial Museum, University of Washington. 206-543-5590. The entrance to the campus is at Seventeenth Avenue N.E. and N.E. Forty-fifth Street; the museum is on the right just beyond the entrance. The Burke Museum houses an extensive collection of artifacts from the Indian cultures of the Pacific Northwest, as well as paleontology exhibits. On the museum's lower floor is an indoor-outdoor cafe serving excellent home-made baked goods. The Burke Museum is open weekdays except Monday, 10 A.M.–4:30 P.M.

Underground Seattle. After Seattle's disastrous 1889 fire, the streets were regraded, but the storefronts remained at their original levels. Around the turn of the century, street-level sidewalks were built, and the old ground floors became bricked-over catacombs. One-and-a-half-hour tours take you below the Pioneer Square area. Reservations (206-682-4646) are a must; tours meet at 610 First Avenue. Several tours are scheduled every day.

Seattle Aquarium. Pier 59, Waterfront Park. 206-625-4357. The focus of this aquarium is the marine life of the northwest coast, particularly that which thrives in tidal areas. Visitors walk into a transparent dome that is completely surrounded by water teeming with fish. The aquarium is open every day from 9 A.M.–7 P.M., Memorial Day–Labor Day; 10 A.M.–5 P.M. rest of year; Fridays to 7.

Tillicum Village. Blake Island Marine State Park, Puget Sound. This center for the preservation of northcoast Indian culture is accessible throughout the year by boat from Seattle. Highlights of a visit to Tillicum include traditional interpretive dances; native craft displays, with items available for purchase; and a buffet-style dinner, with salmon baked before open fires. Tours leave Pier 56 at the foot of Seneca Street. Reservations may be obtained from Tillicum Tours Service, 2366 Eastlake Avenue E., Seattle 98102, (206-329-5700). The same company offers sightseeing tours of Elliott Bay and Seattle harbor.

Pacific Science Center. 200 Second Avenue N. 206-625-9333. Over 120 "hands-on" science exhibits; Laserium sound and light shows; 3½-story screen for IMAX films. Also planetarium, Northwest native American exhibits, computers and seismography. Open daily, 10 A.M.–5 P.M.; till 6 P.M. on weekends.

The Seattle-King County Convention and Visitors' Bureau's tourist information center is located at 1815 Seventh Avenue (206-447-7273).

Around Seattle

Like most peninsular cities, Seattle is compact and can easily be toured on foot—provided you aren't averse to climbing hills. The Oriental district, with its numerous Chinese and Japanese restaurants, is just uphill from King Street Station; between there and Seattle Center, site of the Space Needle, Opera, and Repertory Theater, lies the entire downtown and waterfront area.

It is hard to spend much time in Seattle, however, without wanting to get out onto the islands of Elliott Bay and Puget Sound. Fortunately, a fleet of modern, state-run ferries makes this easy. Downtown Seattle's Pier 52 is the point of departure for Bainbridge Island and for Bremerton (home of the Battleship Missouri), on the Kitsap Peninsula. Vashon Island is reached by ferry from Fauntleroy, which lies several miles to the south of the city.

A visit to Bainbridge Island and its principal community of Winslow is an especially pleasant way to pass a morning or afternoon. Ferries ply the half-hour route throughout the day, and reduced, round-trip rates are available.

Public Transportation

The Seattle Metro Transit System maintains frequent bus service throughout the metropolitan area, and has designated a "Magic Carpet" zone bounded by Battery Street, Jackson Street, Sixth Avenue, and the waterfront. But when people think of public transportation in Seattle, they think of the monorail. This elevated train, with rubber wheels that roll against a single concrete track, is cheap, quiet, and fun to ride, and it will get you from downtown to the Space Needle—with no stops in between—in a hurry.

For public transportation information in Seattle, call the Metro transit System, 206-447-4800.

Lodging

Quality Seattle accommodations for two start at just above $35, and range to about $100.

Vance Motor Hotel. Seventh and Stewart. 206-623-2700/800-426-0670 (800-552-7122 if calling from within Washington state). 15 blocks from station. The Vance is a comfortable, medium-sized, modestly priced hotel. Some single rooms available without bath. Restaurant.

Mayflower Park Hotel. 405 Olive Way (corner of Fourth Avenue). 206-623-8700. 14 blocks from station. Recently renovated downtown hotel, 1 block from monorail terminal. Coffee shop, cocktail lounge.

Roosevelt Hotel. Seventh and Pine. 206-624-1400. 15 blocks from station. Another recently renovated, modestly priced hotel, with many rooms facing Puget Sound. Restaurant, lounge, entertainment.

Camlin Hotel. 1619 Ninth Avenue (corner of Pine Street). 206-682-0100. 18 blocks from station. The Camlin is a small, elegant hotel which prides itself in its service and appointments. Rooms in main building or cabanas. Garden terrace and heated pool. Rooftop restaurant and lounge.

Restaurants

The main culinary attraction in Seattle is seafood—fresh Pacific salmon, oysters, Dungeness crab, and (particularly in Oriental restaurants) abalone. The city is large and cosmopolitan enough, however, to support restaurants featuring a variety of cuisines.

Ivar's Acres of Clams. On the waterfront, just north of Washington State Ferry docks. The basics—fresh, served at at sidewalk counter, and eaten at outdoor tables overlooking the harbor. Fried fish, clams, oysters, available in regular or large portions. The perfect place if you've worked up an appetite on the ferry.

Emmett Watson's Oyster Bar. 1916 Pike Place. 206-622-7721. A tiny eatery in the historic Pike Place Market. Several varieties of shucked-to-order oysters, depending on what's in season; steamers, chowder, and codfish seviche; 50 brands of beer available.

Jake O'Shaughnessey's. 100 Mercer Street. 206-285-1897. Smoked filet of salmon; beef roasted in a salt-paste encasement; excellent desserts, all in an old-time saloon setting in the old Hansen Baking Company building.

Amtrak's *Empire Builder* stands in King Street Station, Seattle.

8. The *California Zephyr*

The *California Zephyr* follows Amtrak's longest route—2,427 miles from Chicago to Oakland, California. It is not mere distance, though, that gives the *Zephyr* its unique place among American trains. It owes its distinction instead to the country it traverses and the roadbed on which it rides. It is, from Omaha to Denver and from Salt Lake City to Sacramento, the route of the first transcontinental railway laid by the Union Pacific and the Central Pacific (later incorporated into the Southern Pacific).

Commercial enterprises and feats of construction do not frequently become the stuff of legend, but the spanning of the American continent with steel rails has earned its place in our folklore beside Paul Revere's ride and the siege of the Alamo. It is easy to understand why: the Union Pacific, working from Omaha, and the Central Pacific, working from Sacramento, commenced their tracklaying efforts before the lands they were to cross had even been properly explored and charted, let alone settled. Much of the terrain they had to contend with was among the most hostile on earth—and they not only had to cross it but leave a permanent roadbed, way stations, and telegraph connections. That it was accomplished at all is remarkable; that it took only six years, in the 1860s, nearly defies belief. But there it stands, and you can ride it today—on vastly improved rails and ties—for the price of a ticket on the *California Zephyr*.

The *California Zephyr* is the successor to Amtrak's old *San Francisco Zephyr*. The name was changed in 1983 to reflect a significant change in the route, one which much more closely follows the path of the original *California Zephyr*. That train was a cooperative venture of the Burlington, Denver and Rio Grande Western, and Western Pacific, and ran from the late 1940s to the late 1960s. The three roads shared ownership of the rolling stock used on the *Zephyr*. From Chicago to Denver, the train ran on Burlington track. From Denver to Salt Lake City, it followed the picturesque mountain right-of-way of the D&RGW. From Salt Lake City to the coast, the Zephyr took the Western Pacific road, finishing the trip with a run through California's 118-mile Feather River Canyon that still stands out in the memories of passengers who made the trip twenty or thirty years ago.

The original *California Zephyr* was discontinued when the Burlington and Western Pacific chose to end their participation in the venture, but the middle portion of the run—between Denver and Salt Lake City—survived as the *Rio Grande Zephyr*, operated by the D&RGW using part of the 1949 *California Zephyr* train set. In 1983, the *Rio Grande Zephyr* was finally incorporated into the Amtrak system. The old *San Francisco Zephyr* route between Denver and Ogden, Utah via Cheyenne, Wyoming was abandoned (much to the displeasure of Wyoming residents), and Amtrak trains began taking the more scenic Denver-Grand Junction-Salt Lake City route formerly used by the D&RGW's *Zephyr*. Thus the revival of the old name. The old train set, though, has been retired, as it would not have been compatible with the Superliners used by Amtrak between Chicago and the west coast.

We should note one other difference between the old and new *California Zephyrs*: west of Winnemuca, Nevada, the Amtrak train uses the Southern

Pacific right-of-way, rather than that of the Western Pacific (now part of the Union Pacific system). This makes little difference east of Reno, but it does eliminate the Feather River route and the scenery that goes along with it. Instead, the new *California Zephyr* follows a less spectacular but still quite scenic course through the Donner Pass to Sacramento.

The *Zephyr* leaves Chicago (for information on Chicago, see trip 1) each day in mid afternoon. It is an all-Superliner train, consisting of both long- and short-distance coaches, sleepers, full-service diner, and lounge. Departing Union Station on the tracks of the Burlington Northern, it crosses northern Illinois and what has been said to be the richest, most valuable cropland on earth. Afternoon stops include Aurora, Illinois, once an important stagecoach transfer point, and Galesburg, site of the famous Lincoln-Douglas debate of 1858. About 26 miles west of Monmouth, Illinois, the *Zephyr* crosses the Mississippi River, and reaches Burlington, Iowa, at about 5:30 P.M. It was on a grade along this same right-of-way near Burlington that George Westinghouse perfected the air brake in 1887.

The *Zephyr* crosses another great river, the Des Moines, at Ottumwa, and traverses the broad grain fields of southern Iowa during the evening hours. At about 10 P.M. the *Zephyr* reaches what was, before 1865, the western extremity of American rails. The broad Missouri River is bridged at Council Bluffs, Iowa, and the train enters Omaha, Nebraska, arriving about 10:30 P.M. This is where the great adventure of building the transcontinental railroad began.

Omaha

Omaha is a good example of what we might call urban crawl—the slow, steady creeping of a city away from the place where it began toward expansive new neighborhoods that lie beyond its old periphery. This movement was everywhere related to the ascendancy of the automobile, and nowhere was it more easily accomplished than on the open prairie.

Omaha started life on the banks of the Missouri River. Lewis and Clark explored the area as they made their way west toward Oregon. Near here they held a conference with the Indians and named the site of that meeting Council Bluffs. There was a trading post on the western bank in the late 1820s, but for years afterward Nebraska remained Indian territory, off limits to settlers until the Kansas-Nebraska Act of 1854.

One group of westward-bound emigrants, the Mormons, was given permission to camp on the Indian lands west of the Missouri before territorial status had been granted. A location just to the north of what was to be Omaha became the principal staging ground for their drive toward Utah. Many of them died here during the winter of 1846-47; a commemorative monument, sculptor Avard Fairbank's *Winter Quarters*, at Thirty-sixth and State streets, marks their graves.

Omaha was laid out as soon as the area officially became a territory (actually a few months before). The new town grew rapidly and soon became a center for trade among the settlers pouring in to take advantage of the new Homestead Act, which made 160 acres of farmland available to anyone willing to cultivate it.

All of this was just a prelude to the decision that really ensured Omaha's future as a prairie metropolis. In 1862, Congress chartered the transcontinental railroad, and at the conclusion of the Civil War, the Union Pacific began its work of laying track across the plains. Workers and supplies flooded Omaha during the years that it took to complete the project. In 1871, the rail link to the Pacific, coupled with the new bridge across the Missouri to Council Bluffs, made Omaha an ideal place to do business. Stockmen followed farmers, and in 1884 the Union Stockyards were built. Today, Omaha remains the nation's third largest livestock market and meat processing center. It is also an exchange point for the tremendous harvests of the Corn Belt.

Two huge terminals—the Burlington and the Union Pacific—now stand in disuse in the old riverside neighborhood where Omaha began. Amtrak conducts its passenger operations in a small prefabricated building behind the Burlington station on S. Ninth Street. The station is nearly a mile from downtown. As the *Zephyr* arrives fairly late in the evening, it's a good idea to have hotel reservations in advance, and to take a taxi into the central business district or wherever else your lodgings may be located.

Omaha has moved away from, but has not forgotten, its old downtown. Between the business district and the station, you'll find the Old Market, a restored warehouse neighborhood that makes a good spot for coffee or a drink if you are waiting for a westbound departure on the *Zephyr*. Omahans are moving back into this district, too. Another aspect of recent downtown revitalization is the new Central Park Mall, 2 blocks from the Old Market. The Mall includes a 4-square-block lake with fish and ducks, bridges, and pleasant, well-lit walkways. A number of new restaurants, boutiques, and art galleries have gravitated to the Mall area. Perhaps as dependence on the automobile diminishes, this spread-out city will contract, and the lights may even burn in one of those grand old stations.

Points of Interest

Union Pacific Museum. 1416 Dodge Street. 402-271-3530. The UP's attic, adjacent to corporate headquarters. Exhibits tell the story of the building of the transcontinental railroad, and also reveal the extent to which the UP was the law of the land in parts of the Old West. Lincoln memorabilia; passenger-train nostalgia; lots of photos. Open Monday through Friday, 9 A.M.–5 P.M.; Saturday, 9 A.M.–1 P.M. Closed Sunday.

Joslyn Art Museum. 2200 Dodge Street. 402-342-3300. An art deco pink-marble building housing a collection that is broad, rather than deep in one area. Japanese woodcuts; American furniture; European masters. Open Tuesday through Saturday, 10 A.M.–5 P.M.; Sunday, 1–5 P.M. Closed Monday.

Strategic Air Command Museum. 2510 Clay Street. Bellevue. 402-292-2001. Omaha is SAC headquarters, and this 42-acre indoor-and-outdoor museum contains missiles, planes, and smaller defense-related exhibits, as well as a film theater. Open every day, 8 A.M.–5 P.M.

Omaha Livestock Exchange. Thirty-third and L streets. Overhead walkways enable visitors to view the hundred-acre stockyard operation. Call 402-731-4980 for hours.

Western Heritage Museum. Old Union Station, 810 S. Tenth Street. 402-444-5071. Photos and exhibits chronicle Nebraska history. Profits go to restoration of station. Open Tuesday through Friday, 10 A.M.–5 P.M.; Saturday and Sunday, 1–5 P.M.

Boys' Town. 132nd Street and West Dodge Road. 402-498-1111. Father Flanagan's famous refuge for homeless and underprivileged boys. An entire village, occupying 1400 acres. Self-guided tours year round; guided tours available hourly June through August. Open to visitors Monday through Saturday, 8 A.M.–4:30 P.M.; Sunday 9 A.M.–4:30 P.M.

Fontenelle Forest. 1111 Bellevue Road, Bellevue. 402-731-3140. A perfect country respite for the city-bound rail traveler. Seventeen miles of hiking trails through wooded hills along the Missouri. Open year round, daily, 8 A.M.–6 P.M.

The Greater Omaha Convention and Visitors' Bureau is located at 1819 Farnam, Suite 1200. Call 402-444-4660 for information.

Public Transportation

Metro Area Transit runs buses throughout Omaha and its suburbs. Call 402-341-0800 for information.

Lodging

Since Amtrak's Omaha station is some distance from the city center, distances in blocks are not given here. All hotels listed are in or near downtown. Rates begin around $30, and few double rooms cost more than $80.

Thrifty Scot. 7101 Grover Street. 402-391-5757. Simple but sufficient, and one of Omaha's better bargains, with doubles starting in the mid-$30 range.

Granada Royale Hometel. 7270 Cedar Street. 402-397-5141. All accommodations are two-room suites with kitchen. Indoor pool, health club. Free cocktail hour daily.

Red Lion Inn. 1616 Dodge Street. 402-346-7600. Downtown luxury. 19-story, 400+ room hotel with indoor pool and sauna.

Restaurants

Omaha is "Steak City," and nowhere are the prices for good beef so reasonable. In addition to the steak houses, try Butsy LeDoux (1014 Howard St.) for Cajun/Creole food; and Trini's (1020 Howard) for Mexican dining in the Old Market.

Cascio's. 1622 S. Tenth Street. 402-345-8313. Like several other Omaha steakeries, this one shows Italian influence—you get spaghetti with your beef. Choose from the menu or go back to the kitchen and have your steak custom-carved.

Johnny's Cafe. 4702 S. Twenty-seventh Street. 402-731-4774. Next door to the stockyard, this is a popular spot with the cattle trade. Excellent steaks.

V. Mertz. 1022 Howard Street, in Old Market Arcade. 402-345-8980. A nonsteak alternative. Smoked eel; bundesflesch plate; boned breast of chicken; homemade soups. Good light lunches. Menu always changes. Cappuccino.

Omaha to Denver

Although Omaha was the point at which the Union Pacific began laying track and continues to be its eastern terminus, today's *California Zephyr* follows the more southerly Burlington Northern roadbed west out of Omaha. The UP stays to the valley of the Platte River; the Burlington cuts instead across southern Nebraska, crossing the Platte about halfway between Omaha and Lincoln, Nebraska's capital. There is 15-minute *Zephyr* layover at Lincoln at about midnight. Among Lincoln's more interesting sights, if you plan to get off here, is the Thirties-Moderne State Capitol building, an unusual skyscraper approach to a function usually served by low, domed structures. Middle-of-the-night Nebraska stops include Hastings, Holdrege, and McCook. By the time you reach McCook, you will not only have traveled nearly 300 miles since leaving Omaha but will have gained 1,400 feet in elevation as well.

In its more southerly modern-day route, the *Zephyr* diverges from the way taken by its famous predecessor, the *Overland Limited*. From the 1880s to the 1960s, this luxurious train hustled between Chicago to Oakland as a cooperative venture of the Union Pacific, Southern Pacific, and Chicago and North Western railroads. The *Overland* was really the first of the long-distance luxury limiteds. The proprietors outdid themselves in pursuit of illustrious passengers and prestige for their roads and set a standard for later "name" trains. Its legend is recounted by Lucius Beebe in his book *The Overland Limited* (see reading list at end of this book). Although the *Overland* bypassed Denver, the city gave its name to two other famous limiteds—the UP's *City of Denver*, which set the speed record for a 1,000-mile run (Denver to Chicago, 1,048 miles, at an *average* of 67 miles per hour), and the Burlington's *Denver Zephyr*, one of the first true streamliners.

Many Easterners think of Nebraska as a plains state and Colorado as part of the West. As the border between the two states approaches, they expect to see the prairie erupt in snow-capped peaks. (Actually, it is still dark when you cross the border, and you wouldn't see it if it did.) But the same vast flatness continues as the *California Zephyr* rolls ahead of the rising sun through Akron and Fort Morgan, Colorado. Only at Denver, nearly halfway across the state, does the end of the plains come in sight.

Denver

Denver is a boom town, born again. This time it isn't gold or silver, although precious metals are still mined in the West, but energy—oil, coal, gas. The drive to develop domestic energy resources has centered on the high plains, making Denver into a Houston north. Today, the sheer, high towers of the oil companies and their attendant financial institutions dominate the Denver skyline, adding height to a city that already stands exactly a mile above sea level. But Denver's growth has come so quickly that plenty of downtown anomalies exist; the steel and glass titans often crowd against smaller, aging buildings that belong to an earlier day.

Denver was built at the point where the slow, imperceptible ascent of the Great Plains finally gives way to the abrupt skyward leap of the Rockies. The city is not in the mountains, as many Easterners believe, but rather on a high apron of level land drained by the South Platte River. As in Omaha, the original settlement—what is today the oldest part of town—nestled against the river, and it is there that the railroad depot is located. Amtrak passengers alight at Union Station, Seventeenth and Wynkoop streets, and although they can clearly see the downtown skyscrapers ahead of them (Denver inched its way east, not west), their first reaction is likely to be, *"This* is Denver?"

Well, it is. It is old Denver, the Denver that Sal Paradise and Dean Moriarty haunted in Jack Kerouac's *On the Road*. But already there are signs that new Denver is reaching back to reclaim these tired streets. Within a block of the station, erstwhile fleabags have been turned back into respectable hotels, and not far away you will come upon the extensive Larimer Square restoration and the ambitious overhauling of the old Tivolli Brewery into an entertainment center complete with restaurants, bars, shops, twelve cinemas, and a dinner theater. Around Larimer Square, stained glass, exposed bricks, hanging plants, and expensive Bloody Marys are now common features of what Kerouac remembered as nickel beaneries; you will have to decide for yourself whether to rejoice in this reclamation or, like Kerouac in *Lonesome Traveler*, to lament the passing of nickel-beanery America.

Denver's history is as varied as its present-day appearance. Like so many western cities, it came alive when gold was discovered. The year was 1858, and the place was just a few blocks from Larimer Square, at the confluence of the South Platte River and Cherry Creek. The settlement was originally called Auraria. The town's founders, however, were soon muscled out of their holdings by William Larimer, for whom the modern square is named. The mushrooming villages on both banks of Cherry Creek were later consolidated as Denver City. The name was that of the governor of Kansas Territory. (According to local tradition, the citizens of Auraria dropped their claims to their town and agreed to consolidate with Denver in return for a barrel of whiskey.)

Before 1859, Denver's residents spent more time speculating in land than finding gold, but a strike that year on Clear Creek launched a boom that eventually pumped $85 million into the town and started a cycle of depletion and new discovery in both gold and silver. Denver's fortunes rose and fell throughout the late nineteenth century. In its high times it earned a reputation for ostentation, as personified by men like Henry C. Brown, who spent over a million and a half dollars building the Brown Palace Hotel.

Unlike Nevada's Virginia City, which withered and blew away when the mines gave out, Denver managed to establish itself early as a distribution center and terminus for the great cattle drives. None of this would have been possible without the railroad. In its dash across the plains, the Union Pacific bypassed Denver in favor of a more northerly route; however, the young city's leaders saw that a spur was built to Cheyenne, and of course today the Burlington's line runs directly into the Colorado metropolis.

Points of Interest

United States Mint. W. Colfax Avenue and Cherokee Street. 303-837-3582. See coins stamped from blanks, sorted and bagged. Money-related historical artifacts; gold bullion on display. Tours weekdays, 8 A.M.–3 P.M. in summer; 8:30 A.M.–3 P.M. in winter. Closed holidays.

Denver Art Museum. 100 W. Fourteenth Parkway. 303-575-2755. Striking architecture, and a vertical arrangement of galleries. Highlights are the excellent collection of Orientalia, including early Chinese furniture; the colonial Russell House rooms; the Charles Russell and Frederic Remington western paintings; and a collection of American Indian art works regarded as one of the world's best. Open Monday through Saturday, 9 A.M.–5 P.M. (till 9 P.M. on Wednesday), and Sunday, 1–5 P.M.

Colorado Heritage Center. 1300 Broadway. A trove of artifacts relating to the settlement of the West. Mixed-media exhibits recreate lives of pioneers. Open weekdays, 9 A.M.–5 P.M.; weekends and holidays, 10 A.M.–5 P.M.

Colorado State Capitol. Colfax Avenue and Lincoln Street. 303-839-2604 for tour information. Particularly notable for the murals surrounding the first-floor rotunda, which stress the importance of water on the prairie. A verse accompanies each mural.

Denver Botanic Gardens. 1005 York Street. 303-575-2547. Herb and Japanese gardens; native Rocky Mountain plants; conservatory with tropical plantings. Open every day, 9 A.M.–4:45 P.M.

Denver Museum of Natural History. City Park, Montview and Colorado boulevards. 303-575-3872. Ecology exhibits; Indian artifacts; fine mineral and fossil collections. **Gates Planetarium.** Open Monday through Saturday, 9 A.M.–4:30 P.M.; Sunday and holidays, noon–4:30 P.M.

Forney Transportation Museum. 1416 Platte Street. 303-433-3643. A must for rail buffs. Three hundred steam engines, plus old coaches. Also cars, carriages, cycles, sleighs. Open Monday through Saturday, 9 A.M.–5 P.M.; Sunday, 11 A.M.–5:30 P.M. Also of interest to transportation—and especially rail-buffs—is the **Colorado Railroad Museum,** at 17155 West 44th Avenue between Denver and Golden. You'll need a car to get there; it's open daily, 9 A.M.–5 P.M.

In downtown Denver, be sure to see the new **16th Street Mall.** It starts 3 blocks from Union Station and runs to the Civic Center. This focal point for retail and dining establishments is lined with 200 red oak trees and is dotted with fountains and flowers. Shuttle buses run along the 1-mile length of the Mall.

The Denver and Colorado Convention and Visitors' Bureau is at 225 W. Colfax Avenue (near the U.S. Mint). Call 303-892-1112 for information.

Public Transportation

Denver's buses are run by the Regional Transportation District. Call 303-778-6000 for schedules and fare information. Fares are reduced on weekends and in midday.

Lodging

Denver has grown so fast and frantically that most of its quality hotels are modern. In the middle of it all, though, stands the luxurious Brown Palace, a throwback to the Gilded Age. Double rooms in Denver start around $40; at the Oxford and the Brown, rates can reach $100.

Colburn. 980 Grant Street. 303-837-1261. 20 blocks from station. A modest, recently renovated hotel on Capitol Hill. Short walk to downtown. All outside rooms, some with kitchenette. Lounge, solarium, restaurant.

Hampshire House. 1000 Grant Street. 303-837-1200. 20 blocks from station. A fine new hotel just outside the downtown area. All suites—private balcony, kitchenette, and dining alcove included. Restaurant, lounge, entertainment. Pool.

Denver Hilton. 1550 Court Place. 303-893-3333. 15 blocks from station. In the heart of the city, with mountain views from upper-story rooms. In-room movies. Several restaurants, including Trader Vic's. Pool and terrace deck.

Oxford. 1600 17th Street. 303-628-5400. Denver's oldest hotel (1891), now completely restored. Each of the 82 rooms is decorated with antiques. Two restaurants; art deco bar listed on National Register of Historic Places.

Brown Palace. 321 Seventeenth Street. 303-825-3111. 12 blocks from station. Denver's prestige hotel, built in 1892 and connected to a 22-story modern wing. The central lobby in the old building rises past ornate cast iron balconies to a stained-glass ceiling; the rooms are equally impressive. Fine dining, cocktails.

Restaurants

An old cow town, Denver has always listed steak on its menus, and Mexican dishes are also traditional here. But growth has brought more sophistication to Denver palates. Larimer Square is particularly eclectic.

Buckhorn Exchange. 1000 Osage Street. 303-534-9505. Colorado's oldest restaurant. Old West atmosphere, gun collection, and a menu that runs to buffalo, quail, trout, and a 24-ounce T-bone steak. The bean soup is famous.

Kyoto. 1905 Lawrence Street, Sakura Square. 303-572-3441. In the heart of Denver's Japanese district, Kyoto serves the teriyaki, sukiyaki, and tempura dishes that represent Japanese cuisine to Americans.

Tante Louise. 4900 E. Colfax Avenue. 303-355-4488. French provincial cooking in a country house atmosphere. Menu might include bouillabaisse, trout amandine, or sweetbreads in a vol-au-vent shell. Attentive service. A nice spot for lunch.

Normandy. E. Colfax Avenue at Madison Street. 303-321-3311. Sophisticated French dining, near beautiful City Park. Try the veal scallops Marie Antoinette, sole meunière, or chicken in beaujolais.

Denver to Salt Lake City and Reno

Denver is the point at which the *California Zephyr* diverges from the old route of its Amtrak predecessor and takes to the rails of the Denver and Rio Grande Western. The *Zephyr* heads west out of Denver early each morning, after a half-hour layover, and soon passes through aptly-named Plainview, from which you can look eastward, through the wraparound windows of a Superliner lounge, over one-fourth of the entire land area of Colorado. Near Plainview is the first in a series of 28 tunnels, culminating in the long Moffat Tunnel between East Portal and Winter Park. Crescent (not a scheduled stop) marks the entry to the Roosevelt National Forest; at this point, you can begin to enjoy your first expansive views of the Rockies.

On the Canadian Pacific route through western Alberta, trains cross the Continental Divide at an altitude of only a mile. Here on the D&RGW, though, the divide stands 9,239 feet above sea level. Instead of climbing and looping up to this height, the tracks burrow 4,000 feet beneath the summit of James Peak via the 6.2-mile Moffat Tunnel. Emerging from the western end of the tunnel, the *Zephyr* continues along the canyons of the Arapahoe National Forest, traveling almost due north to meet the Colorado River at Granby, the first scheduled stop after Denver. Granby is the point of entrance to Rocky Mountain National Park, the crown of which is 14,256-foot Longs Peak which rises to the northeast on the right side of the train.

The *Zephyr* follows the Colorado River for 238 miles after leaving Granby. Just past Hot Sulphur Springs, 11 miles west of Granby, the twisting, colorful Byers Canyon offers a preview of the even more vividly hued and precipitous Gore Canyon, west of Kremmling. The Colorado flows through Gore Canyon at the foot of jagged, beetling 1,500-foot cliffs, along which the *Zephyr* makes its way in a sure vindication of Amtrak's decision to adopt the D&RGW route.

Canyon follows canyon as the Colorado gains force. Beyond Gore Canyon is the Red Canyon, with its variegated "pagoda" formations carved by wind and water. Past the confluence of the Eagle and Colorado rivers, the train rolls through the 18-mile Glenwood Canyon with its contrast of verdant coniferous forest and stark, rolling cliffs. Glenwood Springs, the next *Zephyr* stop, is renowned for its hot mineral springs, which feed the world's largest open air, warm water pool, and its "vapor caves," another geothermal phenomenon. The Roaring Fork Rodeo is held here each June. An hour's travel from Glenwood Springs brings the train through the town of Rifle and the De Becque Canyon into the center of Colorado's fruit-orchard region and the city of Grand Junction. Grand Junction is the point of departure for Grand Mesa National Forest and the Colorado National Monument, the rugged cliffs of which are visible to the south. Just ahead, in Ruby Canyon, the *Zephyr* passes the Colorado-Utah border.

The D&RGW right-of-way and the Colorado River finally part company at the Utah line, with the river heading southwest towards Glen Canyon (now inundated by Lake Powell) and the tracks bearing due west towards Green River. South of Thompson, roughly halfway between Thompson and Green River, the erosion-carved spires and arches of Arches National Park rise above the broken table land.

Green River is, at 4,075 feet, the *lowest* point along the Denver–Salt Lake City route. Here the *Zephyr* crosses the Green River and bears north past ancient lava fields to Helper, Utah, so named because it is the point at which "helper" locomotives are added to westbound freights to aid in the ascent of the Price River Canyon. The canyon leads to Soldier summit, the 7,440-foot pinnacle of the Wasatch range, after which the D&RGW road drops through the Spanish Fork Canyon (it's dinnertime now, and the views of the canyon from the upper level of a Superliner diner are superb) towards Provo and the valley of the Great Salt Lake. The lake which appears to the left of the train after you leave Provo is not the Great Salt but freshwater Utah Lake, from which the Jordan River flows north into the larger, brackish body of water.

Past Provo on the right is the Uinta National Forest and 11,750-foot Mt. Timpanagos, which means "sleeping princess" in the local native American tongue. Within an hour after passing Timpanagos, the *Zephyr* makes its late evening arrival at the capital of Utah and of the Mormons, Salt Lake City (for Salt Lake City information, see trip 11).

The *Zephyr* leaves Salt Lake City after a half-hour layover and bears west through the night across the great Basin, the ancient bed of Lake Bonneville. Here young, rugged mountain ridges alternate with alkaline lowlands in a seemingly endless undulation known to geologists as the Basin and Range (*Basin and Range* is the title of a fine book by John McPhee on the geological structure of this area). In the vicinity of Elko, Nevada, the route of the *Zephyr* parallels another topographical curiosity, the Humboldt River, which rises in the hills north of Elko and disappears in the desert to the south, flowing for 1,000 miles within Nevada without a truly discernible beginning or end. The train stops at Elko and again at the mining town of Winnemucca, between the Santa Rosa and Humboldt ranges. The first daylight stop is at Sparks, in the foothills of the Sierras; after a 20-minute layover here and 15 more minutes of travel, the *Zephyr* arrives at Reno.

Reno

Like other Nevada cities, Reno is a twice-born town—it flourished during the silver mining boom of the late 1800s and rose again when legalized gambling arrived to rescue the state's faltering economy.

Silver was discovered in this part of Nevada in 1859. Before that time, the only permanent settlers were Mormons who had set out from Salt Lake City to farm the arable valleys on the east slopes of the Sierras and trade with settlers heading for California. Most of them returned to Utah in 1857 to defend their capital against federal troops in what turned out to be a bloodless confrontation. In their absence, silver fever struck, and the character of the place changed abruptly.

Reno was not the capital of the silver boom; that honor went to Virginia City, 23 miles to the southeast. Sitting astride the Comstock Lode, Virginia City presided over the accumulation and lavish disbursement of $300 million in revenues derived from the precious ore. At its peak, the city was home to more than thirty thousand souls bound together by little more than sheer avarice. It was connected to Reno, a lesser silver town, by the Virginia and Truckee Railroad. But the larger settlement was the less fortunate of the two when the veins gave out. Today, Virginia City is a tourist attraction with a population of about 500, while Reno, situated along the first transcontinental rail route at the point where it begins to climb into the Sierras, survived to become Nevada's second city.

But location alone did not save Reno. Its second era of prosperity began in 1897 with the legalization of prizefighting in Nevada (Reno was the site of the 1910 battle between Jim Jeffries and Jack Johnson). In 1931 the state legislature gave its sanction to casino gambling, and Reno's future was assured.

Harolds Club, the town's first really successful legal casino, opened in 1936. The proprietors, Harold and Raymond Smith, hit on the idea of advertising, which was something new in gambling circles, and their success led to the burgeoning of the casino business in Reno. Today, the passenger arriving at the Amtrak station on Commercial Row beholds a garishly dazzling concentration of gaming palaces.

There is no simple distinction between these places and buildings designed for other purposes, however. In Reno, as in Las Vegas, every hotel lobby has its slot machines, every casino its restaurant and its glittery squad of cocktail waitresses. Stay at a craps table or roulette wheel long enough, and the drinks will start coming for free. The largest casinos, of course, are Vegas-style hotel complexes with big-name entertainment throughout the year. Reno knows no season, just as it can't tell the difference between day and night.

All this on a subalpine meadow set against the Sierra Nevada, along the banks of a swift and lovely little river called the Truckee. If, after a couple of days in Reno, you have forgotten such things as natural light, water, and grass, walk down Arlington Street to Wingfield Park, located on an island in the river. And if you look around and see a few long faces, just be thankful that you still have a couple of rolls of nickels left.

Points of Interest

It almost seems ridiculous to suggest that visitors would come to Reno to do anything other than gamble or get married (there are ten marriages here to every divorce, because of the State of Nevada's "no waiting period" law), but nevertheless the town has a number of attractions that do not involve the shedding of a bankroll or the acquisition of a spouse.

Harrah's Automobile Collection. Off Glendale Road in nearby Sparks. Free shuttle bus (a vintage double-decker) leaves Harrah's Hotel and Casino, downtown Reno, hourly. 702-786-3232. This is the largest collection of rare automobiles in America, with over 1,000 vehicles on display. It is encyclopedic—you may find your first car. Allow three hours or more. Open every day, 9 A.M.–6 P.M.

Sierra Nevada Museum of Art. 549 Court Street. 702-329-3333. Local and regional work; major traveling shows. Open Tuesday through Saturday, 10 A.M.–4 P.M.; Sunday, noon–4 P.M. Closed Monday.

Nevada State Historical Society. 1650 N. Virginia Street. 702-784-6397. Artifacts relating to Nevada history before and after settlement—Indian crafts, mineral displays, costumes. Open every day, 9 A.M.–5 P.M.

Slot Machine Collection. Liberty Belle Restaurant, 4250 S. Virginia Street. 702-825-1776. The name says it all. The building is owned by the descendants of the machine's inventor, Charles Fey.

The Visitors' Information Center is at the Reno Chamber of Commerce, 133 N. Sierra Street. 702-786-3030.

Around Reno

The best way to spend a day outside of Reno is to visit Lake Tahoe, 30 miles to the southwest. At 6,228 feet, it qualifies as an alpine lake and is the world's largest. Bus service available; inquire at Reno Chamber of Commerce (see above).

Public Transportation

Downtown Reno buses are operated by Citifare. Call 702-826-3273 for information.

Lodging

Visitors can stay at the big hotel casinos or at smaller hotels and motels with only a few slot machines. Rates are low, even in the big palaces, and all sorts of bonuses are offered. The reason? You'll have more money to spend at the tables and machines. A double can be as low as $25, as high as $75. Prices are usually lower in winter.

Peppermill Inn and Casino. 2707 S. Virginia Street. 702-826-2121. Nicely appointed rooms at reasonable rates; copious lunch and dinner buffet.

Shamrock Inn. 505 N. Center Street. 702-332-0405. A downtown motel, economical and clean. Free coffee and donuts in the morning (or the end of the night, whichever you happen to call it).

Harrah's. Center and Second streets. 702-786-3232. 2 blocks from station. The quintessential Reno hotel-casino. 325 deluxe rooms. All-night gambling. Restaurants. Splashy production numbers in the showroom. Even a children's recreation center and a kennel.

Restaurants

Reno is big on steak, and there are a number of ample buffets. Again, the tab is kept low so you feel flush.

Circus Buffet. Circus Circus Casino, 500 N. Sierra Street. 702-329-0711. All you can eat, all day, every day. Outlandishly low prices.

Harolds Club—Presidential Car. Harolds Club, seventh floor, Virginia at E. Commercial Row. 702-329-0881. Prime rib, steak, and sole served in an atmosphere best described as early robber baron. Moderately priced.

Reno to Sacramento

Leaving Reno, the *Zephyr* heads through Verdi, Nevada, across the state line into California, and up the Truckee River Canyon to the 7,013-foot summit of the route through the Sierras. Just before the crest lies Truckee, a popular winter sports center. The negotiation of this route through the Sierra Nevada was the most difficult part of the entire U.S. transcontinental railroad project, and the Chinese laborers who blasted and hewed their way eastward suffered as much as or perhaps more than their plains-and-desert-crossing counterparts on the Union Pacific crews. But this pass lives in American legend not because of the railroad but through the tragic tale of the Donner party, for which Donner Lake (8 miles past Truckee, visible on the right), and the Donner Pass were named.

On October 31, 1846, this group of 89 emigrants approached the pass. Heavy snowfalls forced them into encampment. Six weeks later, 15 members of the party set out on snowshoes, stumbling for a month toward the Sacramento Valley. Eight died, and the survivors resorted to cannibalism. Those left back in the camp responded similarly to the deaths of their comrades and the urgency of their hunger. Rescuers from Sacramento finally arrived—but, in all, 42 of the settlers died. It was the most disastrous episode of the California migration.

It is ironic that such a gruesome story should be associated with this, one of the prettiest landscapes along any Amtrak route. The *Zephyr* rides through the pass surrounded by Ponderosa pines and soaring mountains clad through much of the year in snow. How different from the scenery of the day before—here is climatology vividly illustrated, in these hills made verdant by Pacific-born moisture trapped in the Sierras and denied to the deserts of Nevada and Utah. The picture flashes off and on, interrupted by the darkness of wooden snow sheds that overhang the track. After stops along the Old West main street of Colfax, California, the train makes its final descent along the American River into the Sacramento Valley.

Sacramento

The sight of palm trees and the scent of jasmine let you know that you are in California. With the crossing of the Sierras, climate and terrain change more quickly and completely than at any point along the *Zephyr*'s route.

Something else has changed as well. Up until now, you have been traveling the path of westward expansion, visiting places settled by overland migrants from the East and made accessible and prosperous by the coming of the railroad. In California, though, this sequence is broken. Here are valleys that were cultivated and streets that echoed with churchbells when much of the prairie and Great Basin was uncharted wilderness.

The reason, of course, is that California was settled from the south, by the Spanish masters of Mexico, and from the west, by seagoing adventurers and seekers of land. One such individual was Captain John Sutter, a Swiss immigrant who in 1839 received a Mexican grant for 44,000 acres near the point where the Sacramento and American rivers meet. Sutter's dream of a Swiss colony with a diversified economic base evaporated when, in 1848, gold was discovered near the lumber mill that he had built.

The promise of gold made Californians out of thousands of discontented Easterners, and it made a small metropolis—if a somewhat noisy and unkempt one—out of Sacramento. Among the motley assortment of settlers were Mark Twain and Bret Harte, who wrote for the Sacramento *Union*, and a number of visionaries who felt that riverboats were impractical as a means of transportation in the booming valley. Accordingly, they founded the Sacramento Valley Railroad in 1856. Seven years later, at the corner of Front and K streets, the first ties were laid for a much bigger venture: the ascent of the Sierras and the meeting with the Union Pacific.

Sacramento was the western terminus of a much shorter-lived but nevertheless legendary enterprise, the Pony Express. The first eastbound rider left the B. F. Hastings Building, which still stands at Second and J streets, on April 4, 1860.

With its designation as California state capital and the subsiding of the madness over gold, Sacramento settled into a more stable existence and grew to become a lovely city whose streets are lined with palms and orange trees and whose buildings—civic, commercial, and residential—are beautifully maintained.

Rail travelers arrive in Sacramento at the Southern Pacific station on I Street, two blocks from the modern K Street Mall, which forms the city's main shopping district and connects "Old Sacramento," the restored original settlement, with the Capitol district. The mall is an attractive pedestrian thoroughfare highlighted by abstract concrete sculptures and a swift, splashing waterway. At K and Eleventh streets stands the white, Spanish-styled Cathedral of the Blessed Sacrament. Turn right anywhere along here and head up to L Street, which borders the magnificent grounds of the State Capitol. The classical, domed building is surrounded by forty acres of trees, shrubs, gardens, fountains, and quiet walkways. Visitors from the East will be amazed at how tall their familiar species grow here—that is, if they can take their attention away from the lordly palms and the magical aroma of jasmine.

Beyond the Capitol, to the east, are neighborhoods of restored Victorian homes, among them the Leland Stanford house at 800 N Street (not open) and the old California governor's mansion (see Points of Interest).

Old Sacramento, which lies to the west just beyond the Interstate 5 overpass, is 28 acres of gold-rush nostalgia, shops, and restaurants. It is the largest such historic preservation project in the West, and is nearly complete.

Points of Interest

Sutter's Fort. 2701 L Street. 916-445-4209. Fort buildings reconstructed on original site. Exhibits show life of the 1840s. Open daily, 10 A.M.–5 P.M. Adjacent is the State Indian Museum, an interpretive center for native American life of the past and present. Open same hours as fort.

Governor's Mansion. Sixteenth and H streets. 916-445-4209. Built in 1877, this high Victorian structure housed California's governors for 64 years until Ronald Reagan moved out in 1967. Guided tours. Open daily (except Thanksgiving, Christmas, and New Year's), 10 A.M.–5 P.M. (last tour at 4:30).

California State Railroad Museum. Second and I streets. 916-445-7373. This is the premier attraction of its kind in the United States, and no rail enthusiast should miss it. Twenty-one restored locomotives and cars, including plush private cars, the 1862 "Governor Stanford" steam locomotive, E and F-type diesels in their original livery, and the only cab-forward SP steam engine anywhere. Also exhibit galleries, freight cars and track work equipment, and the restored Central Pacific Passenger Station. Open daily, 10 A.M.–5 P.M. except State holidays; later in summer.

California Almond Growers Factory. Eighteenth and C streets. 916-442-0771. Tours of the world's largest almond processing plant. Movies. Tours at 10 A.M., 1 and 2 P.M., Monday through Friday.

The Sacramento Convention and Visitors' Bureau is located at 1311 I Street. Call 916-442-5542 for information.

Public Transportation

Virtually all of Sacramento is accessible to the walker; however, good bus service is provided by the Sacramento Regional Transit District. Call 916-444-BUSS for information.

Lodging

Caravan Lodge. 1212 Sixteenth Street. 916-440-8600. 12 blocks from station. Pleasant, inexpensive rooms in a quiet part of town. Each unit has own refrigerator.

Mansion Inn. Sixteenth and H streets. 816-444-8000/800-952-5604 (California)/800-824-5815 (other states). 11 blocks from station. A modern luxury inn across the street from the old governor's mansion. Restaurant, lounges. Pool. Beautifully landscaped courtyards.

Capitol Plaza Holiday Inn. 300 J Street. 916-446-0100. A new, deluxe addition to the chain located in old Sacramento. Restaurant, pool, easy access to all downtown attractions.

Restaurants

Los Padres. 106 J Street, Old Sacramento. 916-443-6376. Mexican. Also special steak dishes. Watch tortillas being made. Entertainment.

Americo's. 2000 Capitol Avenue. 916-442-8119. Homemade pasta, ravioli, assorted sauces. Also veal, chicken, and calamari. Nice atmosphere.

Sacramento to San Francisco

The final miles of the *Zephyr*'s run take you through the university town of Davis and the rich farmlands that lie between the Sierras and the Coast Range. To the south lies the San Joaquin Valley; to the north, the wine country of the Napa, accessible by rented car to passengers getting off the train at the Suisun-Fairfield stop. The next stop, just beyond the bridge over Carquinez Strait, is the Contra Costa County seat of Martinez, an oil shipping port. Beyond Martinez, the *Zephyr* follows the shores of San Pablo and then San Francisco Bay on its way to Richmond, where there are connections with San Francisco and other Bay Area points via BART, the Bay Area Rapid Transit (see San Francisco transportation, below). Between Martinez and Richmond, you should be able to look across the Bay to the Marin Hills and Mt. Tamalpais. Five miles past Richmond the *Zephyr* reaches Berkeley (not a scheduled stop), home of the main campus of the University of California, and within minutes makes its mid-afternoon arrival at Oakland.

San Francisco

A peculiar thing about the *San Francisco Zephyr* is that it does not go to San Francisco. Its terminus, instead, is at Oakland—to be exact, at the Southern Pacific station on the corner of Sixteenth and Wood streets. A bus meets through passengers here and shuttles them across the Oakland Bay Bridge to the Transbay Terminal, just 2 blocks from Market Street in downtown San Francisco.

Rather than simply be perplexed or feel inconvenienced by this last-minute break in what otherwise has been an uninterrupted railroad passage across the continent, the Amtrak traveler might take note of the way in which it reflects the special status of San Francisco among American cities. For much of its history, San Francisco faced west. Its commerce revolved around its wharves, and its harbor welcomed ships that had made the perilous journey around Cape Horn or across the Pacific. Even its discovery and settlement was the accomplishment not of eastern Americans migrating to the west but of Spanish colonials, who traveled from Baja (lower) into Alta (upper)

California to found, on the peninsula by the bay, the last and northernmost link in Junipero Serra's chain of missions: that of San Francisco de Asis, (Saint Francis of Assisi), in 1776.

Even at the time of Mexico's ceding of California to the United States in 1848, San Francisco—despite the presence of many Yankee settlers in the Bay Area—continued to live its life apart from the tide of westward expansion. Even in its tent-and-cabin days, it was already a world city. The geographical determinant of this isolation was not, of course, the bay; it was the lofty Sierra and the desert beyond.

The gold rush (see preceding section on Sacramento) followed hard upon the raising of the United States flag over California, and it caused a population and commercial boom in San Francisco. Suddenly, swarms of Easterners converged upon the city, but many of them came by water, and that was how goods moved in and out as well. It must have been hard to think of San Francisco as a point at the end of a continental journey—instead, it must have seemed like a place apart, a beginning rather than a destination. Never a pioneer way station but a metropolis almost from the start, San Francisco still faced west.

The completion of the cross-country railroad (an event which, incidentally, took place after the gold years had ended and a more diversified economy had begun) did not immediately make possible direct travel from the Golden Gate to the East. It remained for men like Mark Hopkins and Leland Stanford to put together over the following ten years the rail network that, by way of San Jose, linked San Francisco with Sacramento. The preferred route for transcontinental trains, however, has long been via the more direct connection with Oakland. From there, the bay could be crossed by ferry or later by bridge. The "apartness" of San Francisco remains for arriving train passengers.

What to say about San Francisco? It is tempting to construct social parallels to the city's historical and geographical separateness and point to its long tradition of independence and innovation in the arts. San Francisco is virtually synonymous with the Beat Generation, and Lawrence Ferlinghetti's City Lights Bookstore and publishing company is still one of its great cultural enterprises. The Bay Area's tradition of literary idiosyncrasy goes back much further than that, to the days of Jack London, Bret Harte, and Ambrose Bierce. A more recent cultural notoriety has less to do with literature than with the bittersweet chaos of hippiedom that rose out of Haight-Ashbury in the mid-1960s. Finally, there is San Francisco the gay city, the virtual capital of homosexual America. This substantial minority asserts its presence not so much in the *outré* aspects of its behavior as in its stable and sustained involvement in the economic life of the city.

Yes, the parallels could be neatly drawn. But perhaps it is better simply to say that San Francisco is thoroughly unlike any American city; that its shaggy-bearded, nonconformist image is everywhere countered by urbanity, polish, and elan; that although it stands at the extremity of the West, its manners are curiously Eastern, though without the flint and caustic of New York; that—perhaps most important of all—it is an almost impossibly beautiful city, poised upon hills and surrounded by water, subtle in its fogs yet blissfully frank on days when the view is clear toward Tamalpais and Marin across the Golden Gate.

Amtrak's *California Zephyr* provides one of the nation's most scenic runs.
This Superliner-equipped train travels daily between Chicago and Oakland/
San Francisco.   (Amtrak Photo)

Points of Interest

Golden Gate Park. Just over 1,000 acres, this is the world's largest man-made park. In addition to its natural splendor (there are actually fields where buffalo roam), the park is the home of:

—**Asian Art Museum (Avery Brundage Collection).** 415-558-2993. Jades, porcelains; also arts of India and the Middle East. Open daily, 10 A.M.–5 P.M.

—**M. H. de Young Memorial Museum.** 415-558-2887. An extremely comprehensive art museum, with collections ranging from classical sculpture to contemporary photography. Open Wednesday through Sunday, 10 A.M.–5 P.M. Closed Monday and Tuesday.

—**California Academy of Sciences.** 415-221-4214. Aquarium, planetarium, and hall of anthropology, all under one roof. Open daily, 10 A.M.–5 P.M.

Golden Gate Park also contains the **Conservatory of Flowers, Japanese Tea Garden,** and **Strybing Arboretum.**

California Palace of the Legion of Honor. Lincoln Park. 415-558-2881. A museum devoted to French art—paintings, sculpture, graphics, and furniture. Excellent Rodin collection. Open Wednesday through Sunday, 10 A.M.–5 P.M. Closed Monday and Tuesday.

Palace of Fine Arts. Marina Boulevard and Baker Street. This huge and improbable piece of baroque stage-setting was built for the Panama-Pacific Exposition of 1915 and was too endearing to tear down. It consists of an elaborate rotunda rising from a lagoon. An adjacent building houses the **Exploratorium** (415-563-7337), a series of exhibits designed to refine awareness of various perceptions. Exploratorium open Wednesday through Friday, 1–5 P.M. (Wednesday evening, 7–9 P.M.); weekends, 11 A.M.–5 P.M.

Coit Tower. Top of Telegraph Hill Boulevard. A 210-foot tower in art deco style. Take elevator to top for fine views of city, mountains, and bay. Open daily, 10 A.M.–4:30 P.M.

San Francisco Zoo. Zoo Road and Skyline Boulevard. 415-661-4844. One of America's best zoos: snow leopards, white rhinos, excellent aviary, Monkey Island. Children's zoo features tortoise rides. Open daily 10 A.M.–5 P.M.

California Historical Society. 2090 Jackson Street. 415-567-1848. Housed in an ornate mansion that predates the 1906 earthquake and fire, this collection concentrates on fine arts, furniture, and historic artifacts and graphics. Open Wednesday, noon–4 P.M., and Sunday, 11 A.M.–4:30 P.M.

National Maritime Museum. Aquatic Park, foot of Polk Street. 415-556-8177. Exhibits and rare photos chronicle the history of San Francisco as a port, as well as the ships and men that have served her. Beautiful model collection. Open every day from 10 A.M.–5 P.M.

The San Francisco Visitors' Information Center is in Hallidie Plaza, at Powell and Market streets. Call 415-974-6900 or dial 415-391-2000 for a recording of the day's events.

Around San Francisco

Although a number of specific attractions have been listed above, the city itself is what people come to see. San Francisco is a collection of hills, a collection of neighborhoods. Russian Hill has lovely homes and the beflowered hairpin turns of Lombard Street. Telegraph Hill, nearer the bay, is also a fine residential district. Chinatown, the largest Chinese district in North America, centers around Grant Avenue roughly between Pacific Avenue and California Street. Fisherman's Wharf, although commercialized, still bristles with the masts of small craft; here you can buy fresh seafood boiled in street-side caldrons. Adjacent is Pier 39, a renovated waterfront complex of shops and restaurants. Ghirardelli Square and the Cannery, both near Fisherman's Wharf, were models for the nationwide trend of "recycling" sound old industrial structures to make shopping and dining centers.

Farther west on the peninsula stands the Presidio of San Francisco, descendant of the 1776 Spanish military post and still headquarters for the U.S. Sixth Army. The beautiful grounds are open to visitors, and the army conducts tours. Not far from the Presidio stand the gingerbread Victorian houses of Pacific Heights and the Western Addition. (The latter is not a particularly safe area, especially at night.) At the edge of the Pacific, between Lincoln and Golden Gate parks, you'll find Seal Rocks—exactly what their name implies. The barking of these hundreds of sea mammals can be heard from the rugged shoreline, where the historic Cliff House stands.

Back downtown, compare the modern, all-business design of Embarcadero Center with the fabled sleaziness of North Beach—the latter, please, by day. Every bit of it is San Francisco, and awfully hard to tire of.

Across the bay to the east lie Oakland (visit Jack London Square, a restored old-time neighborhood) and Berkeley, best known for its University of California campus. To the north—and accessible by either bus or ferry—is Sausalito, a pretty little town where you can feel the "laid back" ethos of Marin County begin to take hold. If you are going to rent a car anywhere on your trip, do it in San Francisco and take a drive out of Sausalito and on to Stinson Beach, along a road that winds through green hills and hugs the Pacific atop high cliffs. Sunset is the best time; you'll never forget it.

Public Transportation

Public transportation in San Francisco is an interesting combination of old and new elements; however, as of this writing and for at least a year to come (into 1985) the oldest components of the system—the beloved cable cars—will be out of commission as they and their underground cable network undergo major renovation. Take consolation in the fact that the work being done will assure the jaunty little vehicles a secure future along their Powell and Mason, Powell and Hyde, and California Street routes.

BART—Bay Area Rapid Transit—is the newest part of San Francisco's transportation system. Sleek, automated BART trains run far beyond the city limits in three directions. You can even take BART to Richmond Station, north of Berkeley, and connect with the *Zephyr* (check schedules first). BART runs as far south as Fremont, as far east as Concord. Excursion tickets are available. For information, call 788-BART from San Francisco, or 465-BART from Oakland/Berkeley.

Neither old nor new but certainly convenient, the buses, subways, and streetcars of the San Francisco MUNI (Municipal Railway) serve all parts of the city and its suburbs. For information call 673-MUNI.

The Southern Pacific Railway (415-981-4700) runs trains south to Palo Alto and San Jose. Golden Gate Transit buses (415-332-6600) serve the Marin County towns of Sausalito, Mill Valley and San Rafael.

Lodging

Nothing is very far from anything else in San Francisco; hotels in every price bracket are found within a short distance of the main downtown attractions. (The Amtrak station is in Oakland, so distances in blocks are not given.) The city's luxury hostelries are clustered in two major areas, Nob

Hill and Union Square, and a good cross section may be found on Lombard and Van Ness streets.

Comfortable rooms start at around $45 to $50 in San Francisco. Luxury accommodations do not come cheaply here; it's easy to spend $140 or $150 per night on a Nob Hill room with a view. Budget-minded travelers, though, can take advantage of bed-and-breakfast arrangements through the agencies listed below.

Youth Hostels. San Francisco International Hostel. Building 240, Fort Mason. 415-771-7277. Also operates other hostels in the Bay Area.

Bed and Breakfast. For comfortable lodging in private homes, call or write Bed and Breakfast International, 151 Ardmore Road, Kensington, Calfornia 94707 (415-525-4569) or American Family Inn/Bed & Breakfast San Francisco, 2185-A Union Street, San Francisco 94123 (415-931-3083).

El Cortez. 550 Geary Street. 415-775-5000/800-223-5695. Remarkable value for a downtown hotel. Near Union Square; just 6 blocks from Nob Hill. Most rooms have kitchenettes. Corner suites available. Lounge, good restaurant.

Oxford. Mason and Market streets. 415-775-4600/800-221-6509. 1 block from Hallidie Plaza, near Union Square. Powell Street BART and cable-car stops nearby. Not a new hotel, but renovated and clean. Restaurant, lounge.

Kyoto Inn—Best Western. 1800 Sutter Street. 415-921-4000/800-528-1234. Near new Japan Center, in the heart of San Francisco's Japantown. All rooms have two double beds; some with steam baths. Northern Chinese restaurant on premises; many Japanese restaurants nearby.

Quality Inn—San Francisco. 2775 Van Ness Avenue. 415-928-5000/800-228-5151. A short walk from the fascinating Ghirardelli Square shopping and dining complex and from Fisherman's Wharf. Restaurant, lounge. Free van service to downtown mornings and evenings

Westin St. Francis. Union Square. 415-397-7000/800-228-3000. An impressive, elegant hotel—1,200 rooms and a full complement of services. Central to everything. Victor's Restaurant on 32nd floor; also others. Entertainment in The Penthouse. Visit the Lobby Court even if you don't stay there.

Mark Hopkins. 1 Nob Hill, 415-392-3434/800-327-0200. To many, this is San Francisco's best address, and it certainly has some of the city's finest views. Some suites with glassed-in terraces. Fine dining in Nob Hill Restaurant and Top of the Mark. Entertainment and dancing.

Stanford Court. 905 California Street. 415-989-3500/800-227-4736. Another Nob Hill tradition, right on the cablecar line. Lovely courtyard lobby with fountain. Rooms with authentic early 1900s decor, marble-walled bathrooms (with phones). Dining places include Fournou's Ovens (see Restaurants).

Restaurants

San Francisco has an international reputation as a restaurant town. It would be foolhardy even to attempt to offer a systematic sampling from among the city's more than 2,000 eateries. Here, instead, is a small and completely random list. Keep in mind the local specialties—sourdough bread, cioppino (sort of an Italian bouillabaisse), Oriental foods of all descriptions, abalone, and Dungeness crabs. And don't forget—the Napa and Sonoma valleys, America's Bordeaux, are right nearby.

Tung Fong. 808 Pacific Street (Chinatown). 415-362-7115. One of San Francisco's favorite spots for *dim sum*, those endlessly varied Chinese snacks, steamed in dough, of which a whole meal can be built. The waiter will keep track of your tab by counting empty plates.

Tadich Grill. 240 California Street. 415-391-2373. One of San Francisco's oldest restaurants. Extensive menu of American favorites—steak, chops, pot roast, fried oysters. Wood-paneled private alcoves flank old-fashioned bar.

Osteria Romana. 2183 Greenwich Street. 415-346-6737. On most nights, there are nearly 20 different pasta preparations to choose from; also fine fresh seafood. Piano bar. Reservations a must.

Ronayne's. 1799 Lombard Street. 415-922-5060. Essentially a seafood house; notable for serving Hangtown Fry, an oyster omelet with a long San Francisco history.

Top of the Mark. Mark Hopkins Hotel, 1 Nob Hill. 415-392-3434. There are other restaurants in this hotel, but go to the Top for a superlative luncheon buffet. Cocktails only in evening. Wonderful views.

Fournou's Ovens. Stanford Court Hotel, 905 California Street. 415-989-1910. French provincial, specializing in meats roasted in the huge brick ovens on view in the central room. Rack of lamb especially recommended. Salmon in season.

Visitors interested in moderately priced international cuisines should head for Clement Avenue, in San Francisco's Richmond neighborhood. A few names: **Alejandro's, The Courtyard, El Mansour Moroccan Restaurant.**

9. The *Southwest Limited*

The western terminus of the *Southwest Limited* is the beautiful Spanish-styled Union Depot in Los Angeles, which was built in 1939 as a cooperative venture of the Union Pacific, Southern Pacific, and Santa Fe railroads. Sixty years before, these same roads—particularly the SP and the Santa Fe—had been the force behind a much vaster yet largely unheralded venture, that of luring emigrants to a little cow town in this southwestern corner of their empires. In the years between 1880 and 1890, the population of Los Angeles increased tenfold, from just over 10,000 to more than 100,000.

Los Angeles

"El Pueblo Nuestra Señora La Reina de Los Angeles" is the original, grandiloquent Spanish name for the city that New Yorkers love to hate. It means "the village of Our Lady Queen of the Angels," but in deference to brevity and church-state separation it has long since become known as Los Angeles, or simply L.A.

The site of the Spanish settlement of 1781—the "pueblo" of Los Angeles—was long ago swallowed up by the modern city, which in turn has been encircled by a complex of suburbs so vast that it is futile to attempt the fine distinctions between what lies within its boundaries and what lies without. Los Angeles, Hollywood, Beverly Hills, Santa Monica—it's all L.A., and it occupies over five hundred square miles of a coastal plain that stretches between the San Gabriel Mountains and the sea. That ancient Spanish nucleus, however, can serve as a convenient point of reference for the train traveler, thanks to the location of Union Depot directly across from the Pueblo de Los Angeles State Historic Park and its main thoroughfare, Olvera Street.

If you have just come into Los Angeles on the *Coast Starlight*, or have made the trip from the East on the *Southwest Limited*, visit Olvera Street for an inexpensive Mexican meal and a reminder that great enterprises can have the most inauspicious of beginnings. The original pueblo was settled by only 11 families, numbering 44 people in all; for many years after their arrival, it could easily have been suspected that time and prosperity would forget this place.

Even this "unwalkable" city yields some of its more interesting neighborhoods to the rail passenger who hasn't yet rented a car or begun coping with the bus system (see Public Transportation). Among these are Chinatown, just a few blocks west of Olvera Street, and Little Tokyo, directly south of Union Depot. Both of these neighborhoods have expanded significantly during the early 1980s; in Little Tokyo, there is now a beautiful new Japanese theater where kabuki and Noh plays are performed. Another major cultural institution within a short walk of Union Station is the Music Center, where the Joffrey Ballet now has permanent residence. Downtown Los Angeles, long believed to have been forgotten in the race to colonize the city's outlying valleys, has become the focus of intensive development—from the ambitious Bunker Hill condo-theater-art museum-hotel complex to the high-rise headquarters of major corporations formerly given to making such architectural statements only in Manhattan and Chicago. Los Angeles, far from being a city without a center, is backtracking in its evolution and is finally hard at work building a central core for itself.

Eventually, though, you must come to terms with the whole enormous, amorphous city beyond downtown. If you have chosen accommodations located at some distance from the city's center, the moment of truth will come sooner; so much, perhaps, for the better.

The first thing to do is to get a map. In no other American city is it as possible to get so completely disoriented, to lose, almost immediately, the remotest sense of where you are. It doesn't matter whether you are in a car or on a bus. The freeways will be the medium of your confusion if you're driving; if you're taking the bus, your downfall will be the bus route chart, which resembles a detailed diagram of the circulatory system.

All of this is not to suggest that there is no overall scheme of things or that it cannot be mastered. Think in terms of north-south and east-west axes, with downtown Los Angeles roughly at the center. Most of what visitors wish to see lies west and northwest of downtown. The main arteries in these directions are the Hollywood and Santa Monica freeways; in between them run Hollywood, Sunset, Santa Monica, and (farther south) Wilshire boulevards.

If you take Sunset Boulevard or the Hollywood Freeway northwest from downtown, you'll get to Hollywood. Here is where, in the second decade of this century, filmmakers sought refuge from the capricious weather of the East Coast and where, today, you can visit Mann's Chinese Theater, with the stars' footprints preserved in cement; a number of TV, recording, and movie studios; and the considerable and often rugged expanse of Griffith Park.

Santa Monica and Wilshire boulevards lead west into Beverly Hills. The whole of this separate municipality was once a Mexican land-grant ranch. Now it is quite likely the most manicured town on earth—a place where stars' mansions dot the foothills of the Santa Monica Mountains and where the rich can have their Bentleys valet-parked while they shop for diamonds or socks on Rodeo Drive.

Beyond Beverly Hills lies Century City, home of a huge futuristic shopping complex; Westwood, dominated by the lovely UCLA campus; and finally Santa Monica, which faces the open Pacific some 15 miles from downtown L.A. A walk here along Palisades Park, toward Malibu, is always pleasant, and at sunset it is unforgettable.

Los Angeles itself is unforgettable, whether you love it or despise it, whether you have arrived at Union Depot weighted down with preconceptions or not. In the end, what is likely to win your affection is not Beverly Hills or Universal City or the Tar Pits or Gable's footprints at the Chinese Theater but the purple light of evening above a still, palm-lined street in a quiet neighborhood, with the dark mountains rising to the north and east. That, of course, is a sight that the *pobladores* of old Olvera Street might also have enjoyed.

Points of Interest

Avila Adobe. Olvera Street, Pueblo de Los Angeles State Historic Park. 213-628-1274. This is the oldest (1818) house in Los Angeles; it was once owned by the family of the city's founder. Tour reveals much about Spanish colonial life and culture. Open daily, 10 A.M.–5 P.M.

George C. Page Museum and Rancho La Brea Tar Pits. 5801 Wilshire Boulevard. 213-936-2230. The Page Museum is the repository for the wealth of plant and animal fossils retrieved from the adjacent La Brea Tar Pits since their discovery in 1769. Skeletons; murals; films. Museum open Tuesday through Sunday, 10 A.M.–5 P.M.; closed Monday. Observation pit open Tuesday through Friday, 1–5 P.M.; Saturday and Sunday, 10 A.M.–5 P.M.

Los Angeles County Museum of Art. 5905 Wilshire Boulevard. 213-937-2590. Very comprehensive museum, including costumes and textiles along with major visual arts. Contemporary galleries. Sculpture Garden; also one of the largest U.S. collections of Tibetan, Nepalese, and Indian art. Completion of the Atlantic Richfield Gallery of Modern Art is expected during 1984. Open Tuesday through Friday, 10 A.M.–5 P.M.; Saturday and Sunday, 10 A.M.–6 P.M. Closed Monday.

J. Paul Getty Museum. 17985 Pacific Coast Highway, Malibu. 213-454-6541. A hilltop recreation of a Roman villa, housing the personal collection of the late billionaire, the Getty is the most lavishly endowed art museum in the world. Three main areas: Greek and Roman; Baroque and Renaissance painting; French decorative arts. The building itself is exquisite; so are the grounds. Get pass from driver if you take the bus. Open Tuesday through Saturday, 10 A.M.–5 P.M. in winter; Monday through Friday, 10 A.M.–5 P.M. in summer; closed Sunday all year.

Griffith Park. Los Feliz Boulevard at Riverside Drive. Los Angeles's largest park has miles of trails, picnic areas, outdoor theater. Main attraction is **Griffith Observatory** (213-644-1191), with its twin Zeiss refracting telescopes through which visitors can peer; also fine planetarium shows, Foucault pendulum, and Hall of Science. Open every day in summer; closed Monday in winter. Call for times and planetarium schedule.

Universal City Studio Tour. 3900 Lankershim Boulevard, Universal City. 213-877-1131. A tram ride through the Universal back lot, revealing sets used in famous movies and TV shows; also demonstrations of special effects and some surprises. Children love it. Also restaurants, shops, entertainment, film museum—see Shirley Temple's teddy bear. Open every day; tours begin at 10 A.M. fall, winter, spring (last tour 3:30 P.M.); at 8 A.M. in summer (last tour 6 P.M.).

University of California at Los Angeles (UCLA). 405 Hilgard. Visitor center at Room 1215, Murphy Hall. 213-825-4338. Many things to see here, including the **Franklin D. Murphy Sculpture Garden**, a 62-piece outdoor museum featuring works by Moore, Calder, and others; the **Wight Art Gallery** with both permanent and changing exhibits; and the **Botanical Gardens**, an 8-acre preserve that teems with local and exotic plants. Follow quiet walkways through laurel and jasmine, past fine palm and fern specimens. UCLA tours are given by appointment; or stop at the information office (see above) for self-guided tour brochures.

Watts Towers. 1765 E. 107th Street (Watts). These 100-foot-high towers took Simon Rodia 33 years to build. They are built of concrete, steel, and "found" materials such as shells and broken crockery. Fountains adjacent; also art center. Open daily 10 A.M.–dusk.

Queen Mary. Pier J, Long Beach. 213-435-4747. A three-hour tour takes visitors through the great liner. There's a museum, but the upper decks are kept as they were. Entertainment every day. Open Monday through Friday, 10 A.M.–4 P.M.; 10 A.M.–5 P.M. weekends and holidays and during the summer.

The Greater Los Angeles Convention and Visitors' Bureau is located in the ARCO Plaza, 505 S. Flower Street, downtown. Call 213-488-9100 for information. Other area visitors' centers include: Hollywood, 6801 Hollywood Boulevard, 213-466-1389; Beverly Hills, 239 South Beverly Drive, 213-271-

8126; and Santa Monica, Santa Monica Boulevard at Ocean Avenue, 213-393-7593.

Public Transportation

The history and present state of public transportation in Los Angeles deserves more than passing mention and a phone number. The city that is often reviled for having made little or no concession to the needs of people for mass transit once could boast an excellent light-rail system, over which the "big red cars" of the Pacific Electric Company moved tourist and commuter alike. The evolution of Los Angeles County into a galaxy of settlements with no true center is often attributed to the automobile and the freeway, but in fact it was the electric interurban that made this style of development not only possible but attractive.

The heyday of Pacific Electric and its red cars was the first quarter of the twentieth century. After that, buses began to replace the streetcars, and the tracks were ripped up—at the instigation, some say, of those corporate powers tht had the most to gain from the ascendancy of the buses and of private automobiles. Today, the interurban rail system is a memory, and public transportation in the Los Angeles area is the province of the Southern California Rapid Transit District or RTD. RTD depends exclusively on buses to move its patrons around.

According to a widely held belief, public transit is virtually nonexistent in greater Los Angeles. This is obviously not true, but it isn't hard to see how disillusionment and cynicism can begin to dominate a discussion of the subject. It isn't bad equipment or poor scheduling that gives L.A.'s bus system a bad name; it's the sheer size of the city and its environs. If you are in Hollywood, say, and want to see the Queen Mary at its berth in Long Beach or the J. Paul Getty Museum in Malibu, your bus time is likely to exceed the time that you spend at your destination. Clearly, there is a need for a rapid (read "rail") transit revival in Los Angeles, and one is on its way: the 14-mile Wilshire Boulevard subway is scheduled to be completed in the late 1980s. For many mass-transit advocates, however, this isn't nearly enough. They'd like to see a full-scale return to above-ground, light-rail vehicles, possibly operating along the municipally owned rights-of-way that already exist alongside flood-control channels and on the median strips of freeways.

For the time being, though, the buses are all you've got. The number to call for schedule, fare, and route information is 213-626-4455; or, visit the RTD Customer Service Center at the ARCO Plaza, Sixth and Flower streets, downtown. Economical tourist passes and brochures describing self-guided bus tours are available there and at the Amtrak ticket counter at Union Station, as well as at a number of other downtown locations.

Lodging

As developers' attention increasingly focuses on downtown Los Angeles, the number of hotel rooms there—mostly in the upper price bracket—rises accordingly. Other parts of the vast metropolitan area, of course, have their own accommodations. It's best to decide where most of the things you want to see are and to stay near there, despite distances from the station. Prices can range from $30 to infinity.

American Youth Hostel for Los Angeles. 1502 Palos Verdes Drive North, Harbor City. 213-831-8109. Overlooking Long Beach Harbor; not close to downtown but on bus line. There's also a hostel at the Hollywood YMCA, 1553 North Hudson Avenue (213-467-4161).

Stillwell Hotel. 838 South Grand Avenue. 213-627-1151. An old hotel that wears its years well; very inexpensive but convenient to most downtown locations if not to Union Station (about 1 mile away). Indian restaurant on premises.

Mayflower. 535 S. Grand Avenue. 213-624-1331/800-421-8851. One of downtown's older hotels, fully renovated and very much in fashion. Restaurant, 24-hour coffee shop.

Hollywood Roosevelt. 7000 Hollywood Boulevard. 213-469-2442. In the middle of Hollywood (7 miles from station) opposite Chinese Theater. Remodeled rooms, suites, and pool-side villas. Restaurant. A local institution.

New Otani Hotel and Garden. 120 S. Los Angeles Street. 213-629-1200/800-421-8795. 8 blocks from station. A modern luxury hotel in the heart of downtown L.A.'s Little Tokyo section. Restaurant.

Alexandria. 501 S. Spring Street. 213-626-7484/800-421-8815. 8 blocks from station. Once a favorite of silent-film stars, this elegant old hotel has been completely restored. Convenient to all downtown points. Restaurant.

Biltmore. 515 S. Olive Street, facing Pershing Square. 213-624-1011/800-421-0156/800-252-0175 (California). 14 blocks from station. One thousand rooms, and a lobby you should go see even if you aren't staying there. Some kitchenette units available. Restaurants, bar (the latter stately, impressive, and quite expensive). Downtown's traditional luxury hotel.

Westin Bonaventure. Fifth and Figueroa streets. 213-624-1000/800-228-3000. 16 blocks from station. Downtown luxury in a different vein, housed in cylindrical towers of glass. Pool, tennis. Nine restaurants and an enclosed shopping gallery.

Restaurants

Los Angeles cannot point to a particular dish or style of eating and call it its own; the city's culinary tastes are as varied as its largely emigrant population. You can expect good, inexpensive Mexican food (try the burritos at Yuca's, on Hillhurst Avenue near Ambrose in the Los Feliz neighborhood), and some of the restaurants in Chinatown vie with those of San Francisco. Lately, also, the city has seen a trend toward chef-owned "in" spots where gifted imaginations run riot with super-fresh local ingredients in the idiom recently dubbed "the New American Cuisine"—an amalgam of French nouvelle, Oriental, northern Italian, and a rash of other influences. You'll also find sushi bars all over town. Watch out for places whose chief specialty is an astronomical bill: this town is full of them.

Phillippe's. 1001 N. Alameda Street, just a few blocks from the train station. 213-628-3781. Phillippe's claim to fame is the invention of the French-dip roast beef sandwich. Try this or one of the other simple, inexpensive cafeteria-style selections.

Mon Kee. 679½ N. Spring Street. 213-628-6717. This Chinatown establishment serves wonderful seafood dishes. Try crab with garlic sauce, squid with ginger and scallions, or a whole poached sea bass. Chinese beer available.

Spago. 8795 Sunset Boulevard, West Hollywood. 213-652-4025. Wolfgang Puck, formerly of Ma Maison, is the owner-chef; he comes up with things like lobster-filled ravioli, tuna steaks broiled over mesquite, black pasta with grilled salmon trout and arugula, and duck sausage. Terrific pastry. Breezy, new wave decor. Reserve for dinner well in advance.

Il Rex Ristorante. 617 South Olive Street. 213-627-2300. Named for the famous gambling ship that moored off L.A. in the thirties, Il Rex is a temple of art deco style as well as of the Italian version of "new cuisine." All pasta is homemade; the wine list is exhaustive. The exquisite period bar, in the words of our L.A. correspondent, "makes Scott Fitzgerald look like Charlie Weaver."

The Tower. 1150 S. Olive Street. 213-746-1554. One of downtown's finest restaurants. Among the house specialties are smoked trout, noisettes of lamb in a tarragon-laced sauce, and the hard-to-find turbot. The 32nd-floor view is spectacular.

Los Angeles to Albuquerque

The ghosts of two great trains ride out of Union Station with the *Southwest Limited*. One is the Santa Fe's *Super Chief*; the other, the Union Pacific's *City of Los Angeles*. These limiteds shared, in the words of Lucius Beebe, "probably the handsomest train compartments in the world." Back in the 1930s and 1940s, these were the trains of choice for eastbound film stars. Gary Cooper or Rita Hayworth could hop the *Chief* or the *City* and be in Chicago in less than forty hours; from there they could connect with the *Twentieth Century Limited* for New York. The total time from coast to coast (not counting the Chicago layover) would be a scant 56 hours. Along the western part of the trip—if the choice was the *Super Chief*—both the famous and the merely comfortable could enjoy such appurtenances as an observation lounge decorated in Navajo motifs and a beautiful rolling dining room called the Turquoise Room.

The *City* and the *Chief* parted ways at Barstow, California, and this is where today's *Southwest Limited* turns due east, along Santa Fe track that leads through the Mojave Desert toward the Arizona border at Needles. This division of the Santa Fe—from Barstow to Winslow, Arizona—has always been a tough and demanding one. There are numerous grades as steep as 1.8 percent, and the land is so dry that, during the days of steam, it was sometimes necessary to transport 3 million gallons of water *per day* to one point along the line. These conditions led the Santa Fe to pioneer in the use of diesel locomotives for freight service, beginning in 1941.

Needles, California, is a small oasis on the Colorado River and the point at which Atchison, Topeka, and Santa Fe rails first reached California soil, in 1883. They managed to press on further, toward Los Angeles, after a series of confrontations and an eventual compromise with the older and more powerful Southern Pacific. The spirit of cooperation which led to the joint construction of Union Depot was hardly in evidence in those days.

The *Southwest* heads into Arizona along the route later followed by US 66 and by the migrants immortalized in John Steinbeck's *Grapes of Wrath*. The train crosses this desert terrain, stopping at Kingman and Seligman, Arizona, just before dawn. Kingman is the seat of Mohave County, which has the richest diversified mineral deposits of any county in the Southwest. Also near here are the Mohave Museum of History and Art and Hualapai Mountain Park. Between Kingman and Seligman the train passes through the southern corner of the Hualapai Indian Reservation. By 7:30 A.M. you are in Flagstaff, which is the winter-sports capital of Arizona and the point at which passengers can disembark for bus connections to the Grand Canyon. Other day trips out of Flagstaff (this is as good a place as any to get off the train and rent a car for a few days) include the pueblo ruins in Wupatki National Monument, the Painted Desert, Monument Valley, and Oak Creek Canyon. Humphreys Peak, about 15 miles north of the city (view from left side of train heading east) is at 12,670 feet the highest point in Arizona. To the right, just after leaving Flagstaff, you can see the Lowell Observatory.

The next stop is Winslow, also a good "base camp" for explorations of the Painted Desert and Petrified Forest. It's a good deal closer to these natural phenomena than Flagstaff, although not as centrally located with regard to other attractions (principally, the Grand Canyon), and not as extensively equipped with visitor services.

By mid-morning the *Southwest* has crossed the border into New Mexico, arriving at Gallup, where there is a Museum of Indian Arts and Crafts and, each August, inter-tribal Indian ceremonies. The scenery in this part of New Mexico, as the tracks cross the Continental Divide in a region of 8,000-foot peaks, is spectacular. Just to the south lies the Cibola National Forest; Spanish conquistatores roamed the Southwest for many years in search of the fabled "Seven Cities of Cibola." These cities, of course, never existed, but the remains of the pueblo villages that inspired the legend still dot the desert landscape north of Albuquerque.

Albuquerque

One of the first things you notice about Albuquerque is the light. It is the piercingly clear light of one of Georgia O'Keeffe's desert paintings, and it does immense justice to the things on which it falls—the ruddy faces of the Sandia Mountains, the smooth, pleasing neo-pueblo architecture of the University of New Mexico, and of course the city itself.

The second thing you are likely to notice, even if your stay in Albuquerque is only limited to the 20-minute layover during which crews wash the desert dust from the *Southwest Limited*, is that Albuquerque is the turquoise-and-silver jewelry capital of the world. Each day, before the *Southwest Limited* arrives from either direction, Indian women set up tables at the station and bedeck them with silver, set with fragments of the desert sky. The vendors here are only harbingers of what awaits in the city's Old Town section, however; shop after shop, plus tables and blankets crowding the sidewalks, all heavily laden with turquoise and silver. Squash-blossom pendants, elaborate belt buckles, rings and earrings and bracelets and money clips. Turquoise and silver, acres of it.

Old Town, as the name tells you, is the original part of Albuquerque; its San Felipe Church dates from 1706. (Nearby Santa Fe is even older—the Palace of the Governors there was built in 1610 and is the oldest capitol building in the United States.) Much of Old Town has been restored to suggest the flavor of the Spanish territorial period. A visit to this historic section, as well as a tour of the university's cultural attractions and beautiful campus, can easily be accomplished during a day's *Southwest Limited* layover. But the clear, dry weather, along with that incredible light, might persuade you to stay longer—particularly if you can get out to the Sandia Mountains, where an aerial tramway ascends to the 10,400-foot level. From there, you can look down on a city which is itself over a mile above sea level.

Points of Interest

Indian Pueblo Cultural Center. 2401 Twelfth Street N.W. 505-843-7270. A multifaceted center devoted to the preservation and interpretation of Southwest native culture. Museum exhibits show pueblo life; arts program sponsors crafts, dances, and Indian-produced drama and films. Also arts and crafts market. Restaurants. Indian-owned. Open every day, 9 A.M.–5 P.M. Closed weekends, September through April.

Maxwell Museum of Anthropology. University of New Mexico campus, between Central and Grand streets. 505-277-4404. UNM excels in the field of anthropology, and the Maxwell is a very comprehensive museum dedicated to man's history and, in particular, the indigenous peoples of the Southwest. Open Monday through Friday, 9 A.M.–4 P.M.; Saturday, 10 A.M.–4 P.M.; Sunday, 1:30–5 P.M. Closed holidays.

Rio Grande Zoo. 903 Tenth Street S.W. 505-766-7822. Excellent reptile collection; tropical rain forest; herd of Greater Kudu. In-town location. Open every day except Christmas and New Year's. Memorial Day to Labor Day, 10 A.M.–7 P.M.; rest of year, 10 A.M.–5 P.M.

University of New Mexico Fine Arts Museum. University campus, off Central Avenue. 505-277-2111. Specializing in photography and graphics, particularly work of local artists. Open Tuesday through Friday, 10 A.M.–5 P.M.; Sunday, 1–5 P.M. Closed Saturday and Monday.

The Albuquerque Convention and Visitors' Bureau is located at the Convention Center, 401 Second Street N.W. Call 505-842-0220 for information.

Public Transportation

Albuquerque and environs are served by the buses of Sun Tran. Call 505-766-7830 for schedule and fare information.

Lodging

A double motel room in Albuquerque can be had for under $30; luxury hotel accommodations are unlikely to exceed $80.

Town House Motor Hotel. 400 Central Avenue N.E. 505-255-0057. 5 blocks from station. Nothing fancy—but clean, cheap, and centrally located between downtown and the university.

Regent of Albuquerque. Second and Marquette streets N.W. 505-247-3344. 6 blocks from station. A modern, 15-story hotel in the heart of downtown. Pool. The rates go up with the elevator; if you choose an upper floor, ask for view of Sandia Mountains.

Sheraton Old Town Inn. 800 Rio Grande Boulevard. 505-843-6300. 1 mile from station. A modern hotel, despite its name. Convenient to Old Town attractions, though not as close to downtown as above listings. Pool.

Restaurants

Albuquerque's specialty is Mexican cuisine, headquarters for which is Old Town. The steak houses and continental restaurants have gravitated toward the northwestern and northeastern outskirts.

Drell's Barbeque. 311 Central Avenue N.W. 505-243-9595. Western-style barbecue, slow-cooked over hickory fires. A 40-year Albuquerque tradition.

La Hacienda. Old Town Plaza N.W. 505-242-4866. All the Mexican standbys—enchiladas, tamales, refried beans—in a Spanish colonial atmosphere. Strolling musicians, also classical and flamenco guitar.

Albuquerque to Kansas City

Travelers on the *Southwest Limited* are likely to look at their timetables, notice that the train is running on Santa Fe track, and wonder why it doesn't stop at Santa Fe, the old Spanish colonial town that is the capital of New Mexico. The answer is that it never did—the road's builders found the terrain that lay between the main line and Sante Fe too difficult to deal with, and the city had to raise the money to build a connecting spur. Amtrak does not use this spur; the nearest stop to Santa Fe is at Lamy, 18 miles distant. Bus connections are better from Albuquerque, however. Inquire in that city at the Transportation Center, 300 Second Street S.W.

After Lamy the *Southwest* skirts the southern foothills of the Sangre de Cristo Mountains, and stops at Las Vegas, New Mexico, before heading nearly due north toward Colorado. Las Vegas is where General Stephen Kearney took possession of New Mexico for the United States in 1846. The route beyond Las Vegas features an exciting series of switchbacks and also a good deal of hard climbing, with four diesel units at the head end of the train.

This is the way of the old Santa Fe Trail, one of those legendary routes that conjure up images of a brief but colorful era in the pre-railroad West. Adventurers began making their way along the trail to seek trade with the Spanish (later Mexicans) at Santa Fe as early as 1812; they defied harsh weather and Indian attacks along the 850-mile, 12-week trip, which ended with a tidy profit and a month's stay in the old capital. By 1846, when New Mexico was annexed by the United States, one of these caravans might haul more than $1.5 million in goods. The eastern terminus of this enterprise was Independence, Missouri, and it was from there that stagecoach service to Santa Fe originated, starting in 1849. The rail link was not completed until 1880.

At the Colorado-New Mexico border the *Southwest* crosses Raton Pass, which was the prize in a race between the Santa Fe and Denver and Rio Grande Western railroads, both of which were itching to build south in 1878. The D&RGW grading crew pressed ahead all through one night to stake its claim, only to find a Santa Fe work gang, recruited from local saloons only hours before, picking and shoveling at the pass.

By early evening the *Southwest* is in Trinidad, Colorado, in the shadow of the 13,000-foot Spanish Peaks, which may be seen to the left in the foreground of the Sangre de Cristo (Blood of Christ) Range. But as the sun sets behind you along the way to La Junta and Lamar, you become aware that this part of Colorado offers one of those topographical turnabouts that are so clearly revealed to the train traveler: the desert and mountains are past, and the high plains lie ahead. From La Junta, the Santa Fe tracks follow the valley of the Arkansas River into Kansas; somewhat after midnight, they lead the *Southwest* into one of the most famous cow towns a railroad ever spawned—Dodge City.

Many Western legends are more embroidery than fact, and movies and television have blurred the reality of those times. But there really was a Front Street and a Long Branch Saloon, and gunslingers who were too slow on the draw really were buried on Boot Hill. Wyatt Earp did patrol Dodge with a Colt on his hip, and Bat Masterson helped him tame the Texas cowboys who came into town to raise hell. What we tend to forget, though, is that it was all over so soon. By 1880, a schoolhouse stood on Boot Hill, and Wyatt Earp had left for Tombstone, Arizona. The great cattle drives ended not long afterward. Civilization—dull, predictable, and safe—arrived, and Dodge City became just another stop on the Santa Fe.

The *Southwest* speeds eastward in darkness through fields of Kansas wheat, stopping at Newton, Emporia, and Topeka, the capital. From there it follows the Kansas River to the Missouri, crosses that broad, brown stream, and enters Kansas City, Missouri, by 7 A.M.

Kansas City

Union Station, in Kansas City, is one of the most impressive of the old-time, grand-scale train depots. Not the architecture of the place but rather its sheer size commands the attention of arriving passengers: this is the third largest station in the country. It was built in 1911–14 to handle a volume of over 300 trains per day, at a cost, including trackage and viaducts, of $50 million. Today, six Amtrak trains—the eastbound and westbound sections of the *Southwest Limited*, the Chicago-St. Louis-Kansas City *Ann Rutledge* and the Kansas City-St. Louis *Mule*—stop here. What more can be said about changing American transportation habits? The numbers, though, will no doubt increase, even if they never approach the 1914 figure. Meanwhile, Amtrak now operates its ticketing and waiting room services in an air-supported structure within Union Station while it undergoes renovation.

Before you leave Union Station, take a look at the marble foundation stone that supports the first column to the left of the east entrance. The chip in the stone about seven feet off the ground is a bullet hole made during the Union Station massacre of 1933. Waiting mobsters gunned down police officers in order to free a prisoner being transported to a local penitentiary.

Events like the Union Station massacre, along with a corrupt political machine and a cow-town and jazz-joint image, gave Kansas City a dubious reputation in the early part of this century. Today, however, Kansas City's morals seem to be in no more a state of dishabille than those of any other town its size; for a while, in fact, its chief public relations problem had to do with a popular perception of Kansas City as *too* Middle American a place. Today the pendulum seems to have stopped in the middle, with Kansas City acquiring a reputation for general civic attractiveness that has made it one of the ten most popular convention cities in the United States. That fact alone, of course, does little to advertise a city's virtues to the casual traveler. But Kansas City is worth a stop. It's a case study in the benefits of freedom from both the boom-bust cycles of the energy capitals and the advancing dereliction of certain Northern cities whose time has come and gone—a circumstance peculiar to Midwestern cities whose economy is based on our continued attachment to staple foods.

When you arrive in Kansas City, the first thing you'll see on the other side of Pershing Road from Union Station is the glossy, extravagant Crown Center, a climate-controlled enclave of shops, restaurants and two luxury hotels. But right alongside Crown Center sprawls evidence of Kansas City's subtler and more endearing side—Penn Valley Park, its heights surmounted by the Liberty Monument. This is a city of parks, and surprisingly, of more fountains than any other metropolis save Rome. It also harbors some interesting conceptions in city planning. The most notable among these is the Country Club Plaza, billed in local promotional literature as the nation's first suburban shopping center but actually a far cry from today's versions, with their acres of asphalt and shoebox architecture. The Country Club Plaza is, instead, a unified neighborhood of shops, stitched securely into the cityscape that surrounds it. Its design is characterized not by sterility but by the richness and whimsy of its tile-roofed Spanish Colonial buildings and by its generous complement of sculptures and fountains.

The Country Club Plaza lies to the south of downtown. In the opposite direction, north of and closer to Union Station, stands the city's old downtown, built on hills against a curve of the Missouri River. Here, in September of 1806, Lewis and Clark stopped on their return trip from the West (a plaque marks the spot, near Eighth and Jefferson streets). Here, also, as the nineteenth century progressed, there arose a staging area for the westward migrations and a great distribution center, founded on rail and river transport, for the cattle and grain industries. Perhaps more than anything else, modern Kansas City remains an agribusiness capital.

Downtown is not Kansas City's most exciting district (the Westport area, just north of the Country Club Plaza, is a good deal livelier and more interesting), although you may enjoy a ride to the 30th floor observation deck atop City Hall or a browse through City Market, a quarter of meat and vegetable stalls near where Main Street meets the river. Curiously enough, Kansas City failed to make a go of its River Quay restoration in this part of town, even while cities across America were cashing in by exposing old warehouse beams and selling gourmet cookware in one-time machine shops. It's just as well—America has enough of these sanitized districts. The admirable thing about Kansas City is that it just keeps working, cooking barbecue, and playing jazz, and has not found it necessary to put any part of itself under glass.

Points of Interest

Harry S. Truman Library and Museum. US 24 and N. Delaware Street, Independence. 816-833-1400. Mementos of the 23rd president's administration recreate that time in America's history. A huge Thomas Hart Benton mural makes the trip worthwhile even for those who aren't Truman buffs. Truman home nearby. Museum open every day except Thanksgiving, Christmas, and New Year's, 9 A.M.–5 P.M.

Nelson Gallery of Art. 4525 Oak Street. 816-561-4000. Eclectic, but with particular concentration on American and Oriental art. Colonial period rooms; recreation of room from home of donor, William Rockhill Nelson. Open Tuesday through Saturday, 10 A.M.–5 P.M.; Sunday, 2–6 P.M. Closed Monday.

Kansas City Museum of History and Science. 3218 Gladstone Boulevard. 816-241-3660. Strong emphasis on regional history, both natural and social. Indian artifacts and costume displays. Planetarium shows on weekends. Call for museum hours and planetarium show times.

Kansas City Board of Trade. 4800 Main Street. 816-753-7802. What you will see here is as fascinating as it is incomprehensible. Speculators shout bids for grain futures while standing in the "pit" below the visitors' gallery. Boards show prices in other two markets at Minneapolis and Chicago. Trading takes place Monday through Friday, 9:30 A.M.–1:15 P.M.

Kansas City Livestock Exchange. 1600 Genessee Street. 816-842-6800. One of the country's major cattle markets. Here you can see livestock auctioned on the hoof. Auctions take place Tuesday and Wednesday at 9 A.M.; Thursday at 10 A.M. Thursday auction is largest, but Tuesday is "Fat Cattle" day.

Kansas City Zoo. Swope Park. 816-333-7406. Located in the second largest municipal park in the United States, this zoo features an excellent tropical habitat exhibit, as well as a "Cat Walk" which weaves through the feline cages. Excursion railway. Open every day, 9 A.M.–5 P.M.

Excursion Boats. The Kansas City Excursion Boat Company (pier at 1 Grand Avenue, 816-842-0027) runs narrated Missouri River cruises Wednesday, Friday, Saturday, and Sunday at 2 P.M., May through October.

The Convention and Visitors' Bureau of Greater Kansas City operates an information booth at City Center Square, 1100 Main Street. Call 816-221-5242, or 816-474-9600 for a recorded list of events.

Public Transportation

Kansas City Area Transportation Authority (Metro, for short) operates buses in the city and suburbs. Call 816-221-0660 for schedule and fare information.

Lodging

Kansas City is not one of those towns with a large number of downtown hotels in all price ranges; nevertheless, there is a sufficient assortment, as well as luxury accommodations at Crown Center and Country Club Plaza. Expect to pay from $35 for a modest double room to $100 or more in the best places.

Howard Johnson's Central. 610 Washington Street. 816-421-1800. 20 blocks from station. One of several HoJos in the area, but the most centrally located. Overlooks Missouri River. Some rooms with balconies. Heated pool. Restaurants, lounges, entertainment.

Radisson Muehlebach. Baltimore at Twelfth streets. 816-471-1400/800-228-9822. 13 blocks from station. Long considered Kansas City's premier hotel; recently purchased and restored by national chain. No chrome and glass here; it's a stately old place. Rooftop pool. Several restaurants and lounges (see Kansas City restaurant listings).

Alameda Plaza. Wornall Road at Ward Parkway. 816-756-1500/800-323-7500. 4 miles from station. Modern luxury hotel some distance from downtown, but right next to Country Club Plaza. Also convenient to Nelson Gallery and Board of Trade. Restaurants, lounge, entertainment. Two pools (one for children).

Westin Crown Center. One Pershing Road, Crown Center complex. 816-474-4400/800-228-3000. Directly opposite station. This ultramodern hotel is an experience in itself—expensive, but an experience—with its five-story landscaped indoor waterfall, balconied rooms, year-round pool, tennis courts, and selection of restaurants and lounges. It's all connected to the Crown Center indoor shopping and dining complex.

Restaurants

Like Omaha, Kansas City, with its history as a railhead for the cattle trade, has a reputation for good steaks. The reputation stands, but of course there's more—including a wonderful barbecue establishment. And on Sunday morning, go to the Radisson Muehlebach for a sumptuous brunch buffet, a fixed-price feast that will keep you going till dinner or beyond.

Arthur Bryant's Barbecue. 1727 Brooklyn Street. 816-231-1123. Beef, ham, mutton, and ribs barbecued on the premises and served with the secret Bryant sauce. You can order a sandwich, or you can order by the pound. French fries, pickles, and pitchers of beer. The portions are enormous. Dinner-hour lines can get long—service is cafeteria style. A must in Kansas City.

Annie's Santa Fe. 100 Ward Parkway, Country Club Plaza. 816-753-1621. Mexican in atmosphere and cuisine; a few variations on the standard tacos and tostadas, notably crabmeat served with tomatoes, avocado, olives, and sour cream (all on a tortilla) and a steak and enchilada combo.

Golden Ox. 1600 Genessee Street. 816-842-2866. A steak house next to the stockyards, and a good one. All cuts; the strip steak is especially fine. At lunch, they serve a small steak nearly as high as it is wide, and also feature something called "steak soup."

La Bonne Auberge. 8th and Main streets. 816-474-7025. A chef-owned French restaurant offering dishes such as crispy duck in apricot, almond, and brandy sauce. Veal and trout are also specialties.

Kansas City to Chicago

The eastbound traveler has an option here; he or she can stay on the *Southwest* bound for Chicago or change for the *Ann Rutledge* or *Mule* to St. Louis, where connections can be made with the *Eagle* for Chicago or Texas points. The Santa Fe tracks that the *Southwest* follows slant northeastward in a near beeline across Missouri, which is here mostly agricultural flatlands and low, rolling hills. The route also nips off a small southeastern corner of Iowa. Fort Madison is the only Iowa stop. Here the Santa Fe tracks cross the Mississippi River on an eight-span, 3,300-foot steel bridge, at the head of what is virtually a 40-mile-long lake created out of this section of the great river by a dam at Keokuk, south of here at the Iowa–Illinois–Missouri border. Now begins the final midday run through the farmland of Illinois. After Galesburg the route of the *Southwest* is virtually identical with that of the *California Zephyr*, although we are now on Santa Fe track rather than the *Zephyr*'s Burlington Northern, and the *Southwest* uses the North Broad Street station in Galesburg, not the one on South Seminary Street.

The small towns begin to wear a decidedly Midwestern aspect now, and the prairie is heavy with grain. But less than five hours after the Mississippi is crossed, both prairie and town give way to freight yards and factories at the grey back door of Chicago (for Chicago information, see trip 2).

Amtrak's Sunset Limited cruises through the desert of New Mexico enroute from Los Angeles to New Orleans.

10. The *Sunset Limited*

Few American railroad men were more voracious in their appetite for trackage and power than the Southern Pacific's Big Four—Leland Stanford, Charles Crocker, Mark Hopkins, and Collis P. Huntington. Having started the Central Pacific on a shoestring, they successfully met the challenge of joining with the Union Pacific to provide the first transcontinental service. Not long afterward, they purchased the small Southern Pacific road; it outgrew their original venture and went on to become the rail colossus of California. But California was not the limit for the Big Four—the SP's track stretched north into the Pacific Northwest and east into Arizona, New Mexico, and Texas as well. It was along this latter route, in 1894, that the SP introduced its *Sunset Limited*, a San Francisco-New Orleans train designed to compete with the more northerly, Rocky Mountain routes. So vast were the SP's holdings that the owners were actually able to combine this rail service with cruises on their own passenger steamers from New Orleans to New York—an early, lavish example of "intermodal" transportation.

The steamers are gone, but the *Sunset* has survived to become one of those Amtrak trains that kept the name it made famous. Today's *Sunset* links New Orleans with Los Angeles, not San Francisco (connections between the two California cities are made easily enough), and operates in both directions on a thrice-weekly basis. As of this writing, New Orleans departures are scheduled for Monday, Wednesday, and Saturday; the train leaves Los Angeles on Sunday, Wednesday, and Friday. When planning a layover at any *Sunset* stop, keep in mind that you will not be able to catch the train on the next day.

Los Angeles to Phoenix

The *Sunset* departs Los Angeles's Union Station late in the evening (for Los Angeles information, see trip 9). Because of the hour, dinner is not served on departure, although the lounge is open. There are stops at Pomona and Indio, California (connections here for Palm Springs, although not at this time of night), after which the *Sunset* heads into the Colorado Desert, at California's extreme southeastern point. Along the way, it passes the Salton Sea, a saline lake which lies 235 feet below sea level.

A bridge across the Colorado River leads the *Sunset* into Yuma, Arizona. Damming of the river near this point makes possible the irrigation and cultivation of California's Imperial and Coachella valleys. The Colorado, of course, is also the source of much of Los Angeles's water.

Sunrise on the *Sunset* comes between Yuma and Phoenix, as the train follows the course of the Gila River in a near-straight line across the Sonoran Desert. The surrounding territory is not entirely arid, though—the Wellton-Mohawk Canal brings irrigation water that makes possible the growing of crops such as lettuce and melons. Just before passing through the small town of Buckeye, the tracks bridge the Hassayampa River. An old legend had it that anyone who drank from the Hassayampa would never tell the truth again.

By 8 A.M., the *Sunset* has left Buckeye and its irrigated fields of cotton and grain behind, and has entered the rapidly expanding suburbs of Phoenix, the capital of Arizona.

Phoenix

The cities of the American Southwest are the gift of irrigation. That there could have been any permanent settlements of any sort here before Europeans arrived with their technology seems impossible to many people, but in fact, an Indian culture called the Hohokam thrived on the site of modern Phoenix for many hundreds of years, finally withering just before the beginning of the Spanish era.

The secret of the Hohokam people's mastery of this fiercely inhospitable desert environment was, of course, also irrigation. The first white settlers uncovered the ruined canals of the Hohokam and actually rebuilt them for use in the 1860s. One of the settlers who knew mythology predicted that a city would arise, like the legendary phoenix, above the ancient and abandoned haunts of the Hohokam. The railroad was one vehicle for the fulfillment of his prophecy, but not until 1911, when Roosevelt Dam was completed 75 miles north of the city, did the bird truly soar clear of its ashes. To describe Phoenix's growth since then, one would have to invent a new myth. Its population of 11,000 in 1910 increased tenfold by 1950, to 107,000, then mushroomed again to 600,000 in the early seventies. Today, the population of the Greater Phoenix area is closer to one million.

Phoenix got so big so fast not only by hoarding water but also by capitalizing on the very sunshine that made it such an arid place to begin with. People flock to Phoenix both as winter vacationers, and as wide-eyed emigrants, for whom the city represents perpetual freedom from moisture—moisture being something that is always more welcome captured behind a dam than it is in its airborne state.

Although some may miss the presence of anything manmade that is truly old (one exception: the ruins at the Pueblo Grande Museum), most visitors will find Phoenix a pleasant, attractive city. The same may be said for neighboring Scottsdale. Beyond Scottsdale, however, one encounters what is truly engaging about the Phoenix area and all of Arizona—the unearthly, dessicated beauty of its mountains. If it is at all possible, take one of the tours into the Superstition Mountains. The scenery is entrancing, and the story of the Lost Dutchman Mine comes along with it.

Points of Interest

Heard Museum. 22 E. Monte Vista Road. 602-252-8848. The anthropological history of the Southwest; emphasis upon Indian cultures. Contemporary arts and crafts are exhibited. Open Monday through Saturday, 10 A.M.–5 P.M.; Sunday, 1–5 P.M.

Heritage Square. Sixth and Monroe streets. 602-262-5071. A corner of old Phoenix. Victorian architecture; shops; restaurants. Also an open-air "lathe house."

Pueblo Grande Museum. 4619 E. Washington Street. 602-275-3452. Ruins left behind by the ancient Hohokam culture; archaeologists believe these early Arizonans occupied this site before the time of Christ and abandoned it some 500 years ago. Open Monday through Friday, 9 A.M.–4:45 P.M.; Sunday, 1–4 P.M. Closed Saturday.

Phoenix Art Museum. 1625 N. Central Avenue. 602-257-1222. Fine arts from the Renaissance through the modern period. Special emphasis on eighteenth-century French painting, Oriental art, and the art of the West and Southwest. Open Tuesday through Saturday, 10 A.M.–5 P.M.; Sunday, 1–5 PM. Closed Monday.

Arizona Historical Society. 1242 N. Central Avenue. 602-255-4479. The history of Phoenix and surrounding territory, told through exhibits that include a costume gallery and turn-of-the-century pharmacy. Children are encouraged to touch certain exhibits. Open Tuesday through Saturday, 10 A.M.–4 P.M.; closed Sunday and Monday.

The Phoenix and Valley of the Sun Convention and Visitors' Bureau is located at 2701 E. Camelback Road, Suite 200 H. Call 602-957-0070 for information.

Public Transportation

Bus service in Phoenix and environs is provided by Phoenix Transit. Call 602-257-8426 for schedules and fares.

Lodging

Phoenix, Scottsdale, and the surrounding communities have no shortage of accommodations; many hotels are actually full-service resorts offering a broad range of activities. Because of the agreeable climate, rates are often higher in winter. Expect to pay from $35 to $90, although a tab of $100 per night or more is not unusual at the best resorts. The Phoenix and Valley of the Sun Convention and Visitors' Bureau can arrange hotel and resort reservations; call toll free 800-528-6149.

Sandman. 2120 W. Van Buren Street. 602-258-8357. A small motel; most units are kitchenettes. Pool. Not right downtown, but with transportation to the train station.

Downtown Travelodge. 402 W. Van Buren Street. 602-254-7247. Near Park Central Mall; close to downtown attractions. Pool.

Hotel San Carlos. 202 N. Central Street. 602-253-4121. Downtown, 2 blocks from Civic Plaza. Free continental breakfast and wine. Pool. Restaurants nearby.

Phoenix Hilton. Central and Adams streets. 602-257-1525. Handsome, convenient, and well-run. Pool, sauna, health club. Jogging track. Restaurant, lounge, entertainment. Many other services.

Restaurants

Phoenix has plenty of the steaks and Mexican food you'd expect in the Southwest, along with a surprising number of good Italian restaurants. Keep in mind that nearby Scottsdale boasts many of the Phoenix area's better dining spots.

Marie Collender's. 3434 E. Thomas Road. 602-956-7060. Specializing in homemade noodle dishes—fettuccini Alfredo, steak and shrimp linguine; also steamed fresh vegetable platter and famous pies.

John Domonick. 4622 N. Seventh Avenue. 602-266-9594. Mostly northern Italian—saltimbocca; cannelloni Alfredo; chicken Agnesi; abalone; sand dabs.

Golden Eagle. Valley Bank Center, 201 North Central Street. 602-257-7700. On the 37th floor, with fine city views. Rack of lamb; Dover sole; steak Diane. Lounge with live music.

Phoenix to San Antonio

Leaving Phoenix, the *Sunset* heads south again, at the beginning of a long day of desert travel. The SP tracks cross the Gila and continue on toward the Picacho Peak Saguaro Forest, which is visible on the right (south) side of the train. This is the perfect time of day to see these stately cacti, as they stand silhouetted against the brightening desert sky. Picacho Peak itself is also impressive, not so much for its height as for the abruptness with which it rises.

Tucson, the next stop, has sprung no less abruptly out of the desert. Although nearly three hundred years old, its boom years date only to the 1880 arrival of the railroad, and to the beginning of Americans' infatuation with year-round sunny weather. Today, over a third of a million people live here.

The last Arizona stop is at Benson. The nearby Dragoon Mountains were the stronghold of Cochise, the guerrilla-style Apache leader. Marble is mined in the mountains now. Just south of Benson is Tombstone, once a notorious mining town. Its newspaper was called the *Tombstone Epitaph*.

The *Sunset* crosses into New Mexico a little after noon, by way of a pass through the Peloncillo Mountains. The fierce beauty of the southern New Mexico landscape conceals the area's economic importance: considerable amounts of gold, copper, and silver have been found here. Roughly halfway between the mining and ranching towns of Lordsburg and Deming (both scheduled stops), the SP tracks cross the Continental Divide. This is the lowest elevation—4,587 feet—at which any railroad crosses the divide in the United States.

Deming, New Mexico, and El Paso, Texas, are separated by one of the blankest spots on the Amtrak map. To the south (right) rise the lonely Florida Mountains, crested by 7,400-foot Florida Peak. This barren country was visited in 1916 by Pancho Villa and his band, who attacked the border town of Columbus. This was one of the occurrences that provoked President Wilson to send an expeditionary force under General John J. Pershing into Mexico to hunt down Villa.

The *Sunset* makes a wide, looping approach to El Paso, which lies along the north bank of the Rio Grande. Depending on the season, this river can be a torrent or a trickle. The city that you see on the opposite bank is Ciudad Juarez, in Mexico's Chihuahua province. Ciudad Juarez is a terminal town for the Mexican National Railways; connections may be made here for Chihuahua and Mexico City. The *Sunset* stops for 20 minutes in El Paso; even if you're not planning a layover here, you still have enough time to get off and inspect the 1904 Baldwin steam locomotive, with Southern Pacific insignia, that graces the station grounds.

The terrain just east of El Paso has a deceptively cultivated look about it, and there are trees. This leads many travelers to suspect that the desert is behind them, but this is hardly the case. The sere peaks and dry, pastel-colored flatlands and foothills soon dominate the landscape again. As evening comes on, the aptness of this train's name becomes evident. If one were to give only a half-dozen reasons for riding about the country on trains, one of them would have to be sunset in the desert.

As dusk gathers, the *Sunset* turns away from the Rio Grande Valley. In summer you may be able to see the McDonald Observatory, the country's second largest, to the left (north) of the tracks about a half hour before the train arrives in Alpine. The highest point along the *Sunset*'s route—5,074 feet at Paisano Pass—is also in this vicinity.

The *Sunset* stops for 20 minutes before midnight at Sanderson, Texas, and soon crosses the Pecos River just east of the town of Langtry, where Judge Roy Bean once dispensed a species of justice—when he wasn't selling whiskey.

It was near Langtry that the last spike was driven on the Southern Pacific's Sunset route on Jan. 12, 1883, making this the second transcontinental line to be completed. The *Sunset* reaches its southernmost point just beyond the border town of Del Rio, then curves eastward for a crack-of-dawn rendezvous with San Antonio. (Here, a sleeper and a coach are disengaged from the *Sunset* consist and connected with the *Eagle* for the trip to Chicago.)

San Antonio

The combination of over 250 years of history, a legendary struggle against a colonial oppressor, and the influx of dozens of nationalities over the past century suggests a Northeastern city—Philadelphia, perhaps, or Boston. But all of these attributes apply to San Antonio, a Texas city of remarkable charm which has become America's tenth largest metropolis.

As they were in much of the Southwest, Franciscan missionaries were the earliest European pioneers in this area. They built their first mission here in 1718, thus anchoring a settlement that was to grow in importance under Spanish colonial and, later, Mexican rule.

Eventually, the followers of Saint Francis built four other missions in San Antonio—but one was destined for a special sort of fame. By the 1830s, American settlers in Texas were chafing under Mexican rule. War broke out in 1835; in late February of the following year, a company of 187 men assembled under colonels William Travis and James Bowie within the walls of the abandoned mission of San Antonio de Valero, otherwise known as the Alamo. For nearly two weeks, this garrison held off General Santa Anna and five thousand troops. Finally, though, the Mexicans triumphed, leaving all of the Texas defenders dead. Their struggle may have been, as one historian put it, "a compound of courage and stupidity," but it gave Texans heart, Texas a myth, and San Antonio a sacred shrine.

If the siege of the Alamo contributed to the image of Texans as fierce and independent, San Antonio's later incarnation as a hell-for-leather cow town helped create the popular notion that the state's residents spent their time fighting, drinking, and embroidering on their own reputations. Fortunately for Texas, modern San Antonio has been able to present a third impression— one of sophistication, diversity, and physical attractiveness.

The city's assimilation of immigrants representing 26 different ethnic groups has helped; Mexican- and German-Americans constitute significant minorities. But San Antonio has also carefully cultivated its appearance. The focus downtown is the Paseo del Rio, or River Walk. This is a winding arcade of shops and restaurants which lines the banks of the San Antonio River—two arcades, actually, connected by lovely stone bridges. The effect is part Venice, part American Southwest. The whole Paseo is especially beautiful at Christmastime, when thousands of candles flicker in the windows of the restored buildings along the river.

San Antonio has done a good job of historic neighborhood preservation. The two outstanding examples are La Villita, the oldest, most thoroughly Spanish part of town, and the King William district, where nineteenth-century German burghers put up fanciful Victorian homes. Not only the old has been preserved: the grounds and buildings of San Antonio's 1968 HemisFair still attract visitors. Dominating the HemisFair site is the 750-foot Tower of the Americas, from which the city can be surveyed. And somewhere, down amongst those bright lights, the old Alamo still stands.

Points of Interest

The Alamo. Alamo Plaza. 512-222-1693. The building all Texans remember was the chapel of the Mission San Antonio de Valero, once part of a much larger complex of structures. The Alamo today contains a museum and a multimedia recreation of the battle. Open Monday through Saturday, 9 A.M.–5:30 P.M.; Sunday, 10 A.M.

Institute of Texas Cultures. HemisFair Plaza, S. Alamo Street. 512-226-7651. Texas, and particularly San Antonio, has benefited from the contributions of a wide range of ethnic groups. Their stories are told here, on film and in various exhibits. Open Tuesday through Sunday, 9 A.M.–5 P.M. Closed Monday.

Hertzberg Circus Collection. Library Annex, 210 W. Market Street. 512-299-7810. The circus is permanently in town at this museum, which contains thousands of items related to the Big Top and its outstanding stars. Open Monday through Saturday, 9 A.M.–5:30 P.M.; Sunday and holidays, 1–5 P.M. Closed Sunday in winter.

Witte Memorial Museum. 3801 Broadway (at Tuleta Street), Brackenridge Park. 512-266-5544. A combination art, science, and history museum, with emphasis on Texas. Colonial Texan buildings on premises. Open Tuesday through Friday, 10 A.M.–5 P.M. Closed Saturday, Sunday, Monday.

Spanish Governor's Palace. 105 Military Plaza. 512-224-0601. Over two centuries ago, Spain administered the vast territory of Texas from this building. Refurbished now in Spanish colonial style. Open Monday through Saturday, 9 A.M.–5 P.M.; Sunday, 10 A.M.

The San Antonio Convention and Visitors' Bureau maintains an information center opposite the Alamo, at 321 Alamo Plaza. Phone 512-299-8155 for information (out of state 800-531-7500; Texas 800-292-1010).

Public Transportation

VIA Metropolitan Transit serves San Antonio and environs with an extensive system of bus routes. Call 512-227-2020 for information on fares and schedules.

Lodging

As the San Antonio area has grown, its lodging industry has gravitated toward the city's periphery. But more than most boom cities, San Antonio has retained a variety of comfortable downtown accommodations, both modern and traditional. Rates vary from about $35 to $100.

La Quinta Motor Inn—Downtown. 1001 E. Commerce Street. 512-222-9181/800-292-5200. Spanish Colonial-styled motor hotel close to River Walk. Some suites available. Room service. Restaurant, lounge. Car rental on premises.

Menger Hotel and Motor Inn. 204 Alamo Plaza. 512-223-4361/800-323-1776. On the Alamo battle site, across from the historic structure. Established 1859. Free in-room movies. Heated outdoor pool. Restaurant, bar. Beautifully landscaped courtyard.

St. Anthony. 300 E. Travis Street. 512-227-4392/800-531-5766. San Antonio's grandest old hotel, with a huge fireplace in its lobby and spacious, elegant rooms. This was the first centrally air-conditioned hotel in the world. Two restaurants, lounge.

Restaurants

As outsiders might expect, San Antonio serves a lot of Mexican food, but the city's size and sophistication assure more than the usual taco-enchilada selection. For instance, goat (*cabrito*) is a local specialty. Germans have also made their culinary mark, and there are always Texas-sized steaks.

Mi Tierra Cafe and Bakery. 218 Produce Row. 512-225-1262. A 24-hour restaurant and bar that serves baked cabrito as well as pan dulce, a light, sweet Mexican roll. Other homemade pastries are also excellent. Mariachi bands provide entertainment.

Kangaroo Court. 512 River Walk. 512-224-6821. A perfect location along San Antonio's Paseo del Rio. Several Gulf shrimp preparations grace the menu. Good desserts. Indoor or terrace dining.

Fig Tree. 515 Villita Street. 512-224-1976. A converted home in the historic La Villita neighborhood, right on the River Walk. Expensive, but one of San Antonio's best. Rack of lamb; beef Wellington; fresh trout and other seafood. Dine indoors or overlooking river.

San Antonio to Houston

Along certain stretches of some of Amtrak's longer routes not only the scenery but the climate seems to change overnight, and this is one of them. You will notice—particularly if you have slept through San Antonio—that the terrain through which the *Sunset* travels along the last miles before Houston is vastly different from the desert of the night before. The Gulf of Mexico dictates the climate here; it is humid, and the landscape is infinitely greener. River flows are more constant, year round, and agriculture seems far less marginal.

There are no scheduled stops between San Antonio and Houston. The *Sunset* passes through the oil-producing territory around Luling, and crosses the Colorado River (Texas's Colorado, not the one that flows through the Grand Canyon in Arizona) at Columbus. Beason's Ford, nearby, was where the Texan forces under General Sam Houston camped prior to their victory over the Mexicans at San Jacinto. Beyond Rosenberg there are more oil wells, and, at Sugarland, a huge sugar refining plant is visible from the train. Arrival in Houston is at mid-morning.

Houston

It is hard to get a handle on Houston. Its image looms even larger than the place itself. Amtrak trains arrive at a small, modern station on Washington Street, near Buffalo Bayou, and the first thing the traveler notices are the glassy monoliths of Houston in the 1980s. Impressive—but this hardly seems the downtown of a city that boasts a population of a million and a half. Houston has grown in true Sunbelt fashion: rather than grow up, it has grown out. These downtown skyscrapers, obligatory for the banks and corporations that matter, are the exception to the way Houston has developed. It's easy to tell how recent a phenomenon they are just by walking the streets around them. Within a few blocks of the shiniest towers are old commercial neighborhoods for which "urban renewal" is a concept as foreign as the nationalization of oil.

The oil-company logos that stand out from Houston's big new buildings tell you what built this new Houston. Not that Houston was a sleepy village before the energy boom—in fact, its East Texas location had long made it a capital of the cotton trade—but the discovery and exploitation of huge deposits of petroleum beneath the Gulf of Mexico and its environs ended the exclusive reign of cotton and made Houston a world metropolis and the largest city in the South. (As of this writing, there is a lull in the Houston boom, caused by more plentiful world supplies of oil.) What nature did not provide, the people built. Houston's greatest man-made asset is its 50-mile Ship Channel, which connects the city with its Gulf port of Galveston and assures easy market access for the hundreds of petrochemical and other industries that have grown up in the area. For visitors, tour boats ply the channel along with the tankers and freighters.

Houston's size and prosperity can be easily explained; the fact that it is there at all presents more of a mystery. Southerners pushing west for more cotton lands founded the city in 1836, the year in which the Republic of Texas was proclaimed. The site was a boggy lowland crisscrossed by bayous, and the mosquitos—along with the heat and humidity—must have been nearly unbearable. The insects are somewhat under control these days, but the heat and humidity have never abated. Houston is made habitable in summer only by artifical refrigeration; it is probably the most air-conditioned city in America, if not the world. A Northerner might shake his head over the consumption of all that electricity. But he'd better be quiet, because chances are he needs oil to survive his winters.

Points of Interest

Sam Houston Park. Bagby Street, between Dallas and McKinney streets. 713-223-8367. A collection of restored and reconstructed nineteenth-century buildings, including **The Long Row** (Houston's first business block); **Pillot House** (built in 1868, it had Houston's first indoor kitchen); **Nichols-Rice-Cherry House** (fine Greek Revival style); **Old Place** (oldest structure in Harris County); **St. John Church**; and more. Tours of park and buildings on the hour. Tuesday through Friday, 10 A.M.–4 P.M.; Saturday, 11 A.M.–3 P.M.; Sunday, 2-5 P.M. Last tour begins one hour before closing. Closed Monday.

Lyndon B. Johnson Space Center. NASA Road 1, off I-75 between Houston and Galveston. 713-483-4321. Huge complex includes **Mission Control Center** for moon flights; training facility; exhibits pertaining to past, present, and future space missions. Self-guided tour; also guided tours (call for reservations) through areas off-limits to unguided visitors. Open every day, 9 A.M.–4 P.M.

Houston Museum of Natural Science and Burke Baker Planetarium. 1 Hermann Circle Drive, Hermann Park. 713-526-4273. Anthropological and natural history displays including 65-foot dinosaur skeleton; petroleum technology and Texas coastal habitat exhibits; space science planetarium shows average ten times weekly. Open Tuesday through Saturday, 9 A.M.–5 P.M.; Sunday and Monday, noon–5 P.M.; Friday and Saturday evenings, 7:30–9 P.M.

Museum of Fine Arts. 1001 Bissonnet. 713-526-1361. A Mies Van der Rohe-designed building housing 5,000 years of art treasures—European, American, African, pre-Columbian. The work of Western artist Frederic Remington is well represented. Open Tuesday through Saturday, 10 A.M.–5 P.M.; Sunday, noon–6 P.M. Closed Monday.

Bayou Bend. 1 Westcott Street. 713-529-8773. The home of Houston philanthropist Ima Hogg houses American decorative arts of three centuries.

Tours given Tuesday through Saturday; reservations necessary. Open house second Sunday each month except March and August.

Houston Arboretum and Botanical Garden. 4501 Woodway. 713-681-8433. 155 acres of local and exotic plantings. Self-guided nature trails. Open November through April every day, 8:30 A.M.–6 P.M.; May through October, 8:30 A.M.–8 P.M.

The Greater Houston Convention and Visitors Council's Information Center is located at 3300 Main Street. Call 713-523-5050 for information.

Public Transportation

The Metropolitan Transit Authority operates Houston's buses. Call 713-635-4000 for schedule and fare information.

Lodging

Houston has grown tremendously during the past 20 years, and the number of rooms available for its visitors has increased as well. Much of Houston's growth, though, has taken place away from the core city, centering instead upon the areas around Rice University, the Space Center, and other outlying districts. The establishments listed below are all downtown.

Hotel rates are higher in Houston than in many other Southern cities, largely because of corporate expense-account travel. Expect to pay at least $40 for a double; the top end should be about $125 but of course can go higher in a town that likes to spend money and expects that you do, too.

Center City Motor Inn. 1015 Texas Avenue. 713-224-4511. 10 blocks from station. Seven-story downtown motor inn. Four suites available. Restaurant, coffee shop. Pool. Renovated in 1979.

Harley. 101 Main Street. 713-225-1781/800-321-2323. 7 blocks from station. Allen's Landing location, near Buffalo Bayou. Some rooms with private balcony. Pool, patio. Coffee shop, restaurant. Car rental on premises. Formerly Ramada Inn—Downtown.

Whitehall. 1700 Smith Street. 713-659-5000. 17 blocks from station. Deluxe, cosmopolitan downtown hotel, near Cullen Center. Pool, 18-hole putting green, shopping arcade. Rib Room restaurant, lounge, entertainment. Fine service.

Restaurants

You can't eat oil (we're not talking olive oil), but you can pump it into the local economy to the advantage of a lot of fancy restaurants. Amidst all of Houston's sophistication and haute cuisine, though, don't forget that you are at the point where South meets Southwest—that means barbecue, chili, Tex-Mex, and Gulf seafood.

Steve's. 600 Jefferson Street. 713-659-8590. The specialty here is Texas beef barbecue (not pork, as in other parts of the South), along with homemade soups and a variety of salads.

Hebert's Ritz. 1214 McGowan Street. 713-659-3459. For over 40 years, a local favorite for aficionados of fresh Gulf seafood and Cajun specialties. Also good steaks.

Kaphan's. 7900 S. Main Street. 713-668-0491. Fine seafood—try the redfish Pontchartrain. Also crab, trout, oysters, escargots. The beef dishes are attended to with equal care.

Houston to New Orleans

Less than 100 miles separate Houston from the Louisiana border. This is a span of no small consequence to the nation's energy industry, though—it was here that oil was first discovered in Texas. The wells are still producing, and Beaumont, the *Sunset*'s last Texas stop, is the center of Gulf Coast refining activity. The Sabine River marks the Texas-Louisiana boundary, but the sight of oil derricks is common on both sides of the border. Lake Charles, the first Louisiana stop, is surrounded by fields that produce a different kind of staple—rice. The elevation of Lake Charles is only 16 feet above sea level; that of Lafayette if 40 feet. The high water table is perfect for rice cultivation. This was doubtless small consolation to the French Acadians, exiled here from their Nova Scotia home by the British in the 1700s. Their descendants, the Cajuns, have learned to live the bayou life, and many of them cling to their traditional culture despite intrusions from the world outside. No trip to Louisiana is complete without hearing some good Cajun music.

New Iberia is a sugar town, but it is famous for a product far more unique—Tabasco Sauce, which is made from locally grown hot peppers marinated in vinegar and salt. The Tabasco Sauce factory is actually just outside New Iberia at a place called Avery Island. This "island" really isn't; it is one of several salt domes which was once surrounded by water but is now connected to the mainland by sedimentary deposits. The founder of the Tabasco business, Edward McIlhenny, also established a bird sanctuary which still thrives just south of New Iberia. Hundreds of American egrets roost here, as do ibises, herons, ducks, and geese. East of New Iberia flows the Bayou Teche, along which Longfellow's Evangeline lived.

The *Sunset* next makes its way along the edges of the Chacahoula Swamp, stopping at the tiny village of Schriever. Beyond here the landscape gets increasingly wet; soon it seems that the ground must surely be about to give up its attempt to stay above water. It never does, of course, and soon you're mounting the levee, crossing the Mississippi, and, before 8 P.M., entering New Orleans. (For New Orleans information, see trip 5.)

11. The *Pioneer* and the *Desert Wind*

Two Amtrak routes— the *Pioneer* and the *Desert Wind*—head northwest to Seattle and southwest to Los Angeles, respectively, out of Salt Lake City. According to Amtrak timetables, the eastern terminus of these trains is Chicago—but if you look closely, you'll see that both the *Pioneer* and *Desert Wind* are incorporated into the *California Zephyr* between Chicago and Salt Lake City. Following a brief layover in the Utah capital, the consist of the *Zephyr* is broken up so that through cars from Chicago continue on their separate ways to Los Angeles, Oakland (San Francisco), and Seattle. Eastbound, the three trains unite at Salt Lake City for the trip to Chicago.

Salt Lake City

"This," said Brigham Young on a July day in 1847, "is the place." Along with a party of several hundred emigrant Mormons, he had arrived at the valley of the Great Salt Lake. The land that he identified as "the place" would have appeared, to most people, to be little more than a desert. But it was the very desolation of the site which appealed to Young and the long-persecuted Mormons, who had been traveling for three months. Fortunately, there was enough fresh water in the springs of the surrounding mountains to make Brigham Young's dream of "making the desert bloom" come true.

For a long time, Salt Lake City—and the territory that surrounded it—was only grudgingly a part of the United States. The Mormons' sureness of the revelations on which their faith was founded, as well as their practice of polygamy, alienated them from the rest of the American nation. In 1849, the Mormon leaders proclaimed the Provisional State of Deseret. Although Utah became a territory of the United States one year later, feelings of intense nationalism continued to pervade the Mormon community, and in 1857 federal troops were sent to force Washington's will upon the Latter-Day Saints. The "Mormon War" was over by the following year, but hostility between Utah and the rest of the United States began to disappear only after the Civil War. The migration of non-Mormons into the territory no doubt contributed to this lessening of tensions, as did the withdrawal of the church's sanction of polygamy—an act which paved the way for statehood in 1896. But perhaps the greatest impetus for the integration of Mormon culture with that of the country at large was the growth of commerce and resource development.

The railroad was crucial both to the opening of the West and to ending Utah's isolation. The Union Pacific trunk line was built to the north of the Great Salt Lake through Ogden, but the 1870 completion of the Utah Central Railroad, which was Mormon backed and built, provided a connection with the capital. Today, the *Desert Wind* and *Pioneer* roll into Salt Lake City on Denver and Rio Grande Western track and leave via the right-of-way of the Union Pacific, and passengers arrive at the old Union Pacific station at the head of South Temple Street.

Few cities reveal themselves to the railroad traveler as plainly and quickly as Salt Lake City. First, murals on opposite walls in the station depict the two most important moments in the city's early history: Brigham Young leading the faithful into the valley and the driving of the Golden Spike. Then, South Temple Street, immediately in front of the station, introduces the traveler to the simplicity of Young's grid street plan, drawn up within weeks of the Mormons' arrival. Directly ahead is Temple Square, the point at which all street numbering begins. Uphill, to the left of the Temple spires, stands the Corinthian-style Utah State Capitol. With these two landmarks as your guide, it is difficult to lose your sense of direction.

It is pleasant to walk uphill on any of the streets near the Capitol until you reach a point where the pavement ends. Here you have a commanding view of the city, the valley, and the Wasatch Mountains to the east. Turn to your right, and you will see the Great Salt Lake itself and the bleached flats that surround it.

Points of Interest

Temple Square. Bordered by Main Street and North, South, and West Temple streets. This is the home of the Church of Jesus Christ of Latter-Day Saints. The principal structures in the Square include the **Temple**, completed in 1893 (open only to church members in good standing); the **Tabernacle**, built in 1867, an acoustically remarkable building which houses one of the world's greatest organs (concerts each day) and is the home of the Mormon Tabernacle Choir; and the two **Visitors' Centers**, which offer multimedia displays explaining the doctrines of the church. Also enclosed within the Square are the **Sea Gull Monument**, which commemorates the 1848 deliverance of the settlers from a plague of crickets by the arrival of vast flocks of gulls; and the century-old **Assembly Hall**, where guest artists perform Friday and Saturday evenings.

Temple Square gates are open from 6 A.M.–11 P.M. in summer; 6 A.M.–10 P.M. in winter. Guided tours are offered throughout the day, all year.

Beehive House. Corner State Street and South Temple Street. This was the home and office of Brigham Young. Rooms have been restored to period style. Beehive House is open daily; guided tours given from 9:30 A.M.–4:30 P.M., Monday through Saturday, and at mid-day on Sunday.

Pioneer Memorial Museum. 300 N. Main Street. 801-533-5759. Extensive displays of pioneer crafts and household artifacts. Many of Brigham Young's personal effects. The museum is open Monday through Saturday, 9 A.M.–5 P.M.; open Sundays, April to October, 1–5 P.M. Closed holidays.

Utah Museum of Fine Arts. Art and Architecture Complex, University of Utah campus. 801-581-7332. Collections include Cypriot antiquities, Navajo weavings, contemporary American prints and ceramics. The museum is open weekdays, 10 A.M.–5 P.M.; weekends, 2–5 P.M.

Utah Museum of Natural History. University of Utah campus. 801-581-6927. Exhibits focus on the remarkable geological and biological past of the state of Utah and include dinosaur bones and tracks, Indian artifacts, mineral collections. Many "please touch" exhibits. Open Monday through Saturday, 9:30 A.M.–5:30 P.M.; Sunday, noon–5 P.M.

Hansen Planetarium. 15 S. State Street. 801-535-7007. Star shows; Foucault pendulum; giant rotating Earth globe. **Space Science Library** open to public. Open every day; star shows presented four times daily Monday through Saturday; twice on Sunday.

The Salt Lake Valley Convention and Visitors' Bureau maintains visitor information centers at 180 South West Temple, and at the west entrance to Trolley Square, 700 East between 500 and 600 South Streets. Call 801-521-2822 for information.

Around Salt Lake City

Trolley Square, on 700 East Street between 500 and 600 South Streets, is Salt Lake's "recycled" restaurant-and-boutique complex; the buildings that it occupies were once street railway barns.

If you have the time and can arrange transportation, a trip to the Great Salt Lake itself should be on your agenda. Unfortunately, no public bus service runs to the lake, which lies 15 miles distant from the city. To get there, it is necessary to rent a car, hire a taxi, or take a Gray Line bus tour. One-quarter of the lake's volume is salt, suspended in a water solution so thick that bathers find it difficult not to bob on the surface like a cork. There are public beaches at South Shore State Park, off I-80. Saltair Beach State Park and Saltair Resort have water amusements, shopping, an arcade, bath house, and entertainment pavilion.

Public Transportation

Bus service is provided throughout Salt Lake City and the valley suburbs by the Utah Transit Authority. For schedule and route information, dial 801-263-3737.

Lodging

Hotels are not expensive in Salt Lake City—not by the standards of the East or the larges cities of the West. A comfortable double room can be had for $40; $60 or more buys considerable luxury.

Howard Johnson's Motor Lodge. 122 W. South Temple Street. 801-521-0130. 3 blocks from station. Convenient to everything in downtown Salt Lake; features some dormitory-style rooms with four beds, as well as wheelchair facilities, cocktail lounge, and heated pool.

Temple Square Hotel. 75 S. West Temple Street. 801-355-2961. 4 blocks from station. An older hotel, recently renovated. Overlooks Temple Square. Restaurant.

Hotel Utah. South Temple and Main street. 801-531-1000. 4 blocks from station. This is the premier hotel of Salt Lake City. Free feature movies in rooms. Several restaurants, including rooftop dining room with fine view of Wasatch Mountains. Pool available nearby. Lower rates for travelers willing to forego a guaranteed advance reservation.

Restaurants

Salt Lake City has the variety of restaurants you would expect in any regional center with a half million population, but its liquor laws are a bit different. Eating places will serve hard liquor only with meals, although those that are not licensed to dispense spirits often permit patrons to bring their own. Bars sell beer only; cocktails without meals are available only at private clubs.

R.J. Wheatfield's. Trolley Square. 801-364-8963. Menu leans toward natural foods; some vegetarian dishes and some with meat. Vegetable curry, beef Stroganoff, sweet-and-sour chicken. Some Mexican specialties. Good desserts. Open for all meals.

Rio Grande Cafe. 270 South Rio Grande. 801-364-3302. A Mexican menu, served in a refurbished train station. Nice atmosphere. Liquor available.

Le Parisien. 417 South 300 E. Streets. 801-364-5223. Italian and French cuisine; dover sole. Wine list; liquors. Continental breakfast. Outdoor seating.

Salt Lake City to Portland and Seattle: *Pioneer*

The *Pioneer* heads north out of Salt Lake City late each evening to join the Union Pacific main line at Ogden. This route takes the *Pioneer* due north along the eastern shores of the Great Salt Lake and into Idaho. Pocatello, second largest city in the state and chief market town for its agricultural region, is reached just after 1:30 A.M. After Pocatello the train crosses the Snake River and heads for Shoshone. Mammoth Cave is near here, as are the Shoshone Ice Caves. There is currently no passenger service on the spur running north from here to Ketchum—an ironic note, since Union Pacific was the developer of the huge Sun Valley Resort near that town. When the Sun Valley Lodge and the surrounding ski area were built in the 1930s, UP public relations men lured several well-known people into summering there. One of them was Ernest Hemingway, who died at his Ketchum home in 1961 and lies buried nearby.

Around daybreak the *Pioneer* reaches Boise, the capital of Idaho. Soon the Snake River is crossed again; at this point, it forms the boundary between Idaho and Oregon. From here the route heads north toward the Columbia through hilly, forested terrain. The UP built this rail line in 1884 to bring the agricultural products of the Oregon river valleys east. It enabled Portland and other Oregon cities to compete more effectively with Seattle and Tacoma, which had their own rail links with the Midwest (trip 7).

North of La Grande is sheep country, as the name of the next stop—Pendleton—implies. Just past here, at Hinkle, the roadbed begins to closely parallel the Columbia River. "Dalles," in the jargon of the French fur traders, referred to a swift dangerous spot where the river flowed over flat rocks. It is the name of the next stop and a reminder that French fur traders were among the first white men in these parts. Past The Dalles, some 20 miles to the south, stands 11,235-foot Mount Hood, highest point in Oregon.

The *Pioneer* reaches Portland in late afternoon. As you arrive, think about the prediction made in 1828 by a New Jersey senator. He stated that Oregon could never be admitted to the Union, because it would take an Oregon congressman 350 days to travel to and from Washington, D.C.!

From Portland, the *Pioneer*'s run to Seattle is identical to that made by the *Coast Starlight*. (For information on that route, and on the cities of Portland and Seattle, see trip 12.)

Ogden to Las Vegas: the *Desert Wind*

The *Desert Wind* is another late-night train, traversing the vastness of west central Utah in darkness. The train leaves Salt Lake City about half past ten, and sets out upon a Union Pacific route to Los Angeles completed in 1905. The tracks lead southwest away from the lake and across the Oquirrh Mountains into the Sevier Desert. Beyond is the Great Pahvant Valley, where irrigation has made agriculture feasible; Delta, the first stop after Salt Lake City, is a center for the production of alfalfa seed. Farther south, and also along the *Pioneer*'s route, the 100-mile-long Escalante Valley yields harvests of potatoes and sugar beets. The last Utah stop is at Milford, in the shadow of Frisco Peak and the Wah Wah Mountains (there are no shadows, though, at 2 A.M.).

Crossing the border into Nevada, the *Desert Wind* stops at Caliente, a mining and ranching town, and heads due south along the Meadow Valley Wash. Just north of Las Vegas, at the right time of year, you will catch a glimpse of the desert sunrise. Look at this vast, empty country in the gathering light of day, and reflect on Gertrude Stein's remark, "In the United States there is more space where nobody is than where anybody is."

This, said Stein, "is what makes America what it is." Yes—but just south of here, on the other side of the Valley of Fire and the Muddy Mountains, lies something else that rounds out that definition.

Las Vegas

Las Vegas got off to more than its share of false starts. If it hadn't been for the railroad, the town would probably never have survived until Nevada legalized gambling. The Mormons gave up a 2-year-old settlement here in 1857; a 37-year ranching enterprise came to an end in 1899. Salvation came in 1905 with the arrival of the Union Pacific, and the town was chartered in 1911. In the 1930s it began legalized gambling on a small scale along with the rest of the state and boomed after World War II when gangsters like Bugsy Siegel started to move in on the casino action. Nevada, however, has long since wrested control of its number-one industry from the mob. Today's resorts are mostly in the hands of big business, and stringent licensing and control laws are in effect.

The most popular casino games are blackjack, in which players try to exceed the dealer's card count without going over 21; keno, which simply involves picking a series of numbers and hoping they come up when numbered balls are drawn; the familiar roulette and craps; bingo; and baccarat, in which the object is to hold a two- or three-card combination totaling 9 or as close to it as possible.

Las Vegas has acquired such a jet-set image that it seems odd to go there by train. Nevertheless, this has become a popular means of getting to the tables for many Los Angelenos. It's also a good way to sense the barrenness that surrounds this improbable city, and the *Desert Wind*'s lounge is a good place to hear stories that start with, "I get here on Friday, right, with four hundred bucks, and . . ."

Points of Interest

Las Vegas's main attractions, obviously, are its casinos and entertainment. But if you are taking some time off from the tables, a visit to the **University of Nevada**, 4505 S. Maryland Parkway (main phone 702-739-3011), is worthwhile. The university's **Museum of Natural History** (702-739-3381) houses Indian and pioneer artifacts; also live reptiles. Open every day, 8 A.M.–5 P.M.; closed Fourth of July and Christmas. Also on campus are an art gallery (702-739-3751), **Desert Research Institute**, and a thousand-specimen mineral collection, all open to the public.

Scenic Airlines runs one-day, round-trip air-and-bus excursions to the **Grand Canyon** from Las Vegas's McCarran Airport. Call 702-739-1900 for schedules and information.

Getting back to gambling, the **Mint Hotel,** 100 E. Fremont Street, offers a "Behind the Scenes" tour showing the casino counting room and one-way mirrors; also demonstrations of how slot machines operate and lessons in basic games. Call 702-385-7440.

The Las Vegas Convention and Visitors' Authority is located in the city's Convention Center, Paradise Road, downtown. Call 702-733-2323.

Public Transportation

Buses are run by the Las Vegas Transit System. Call 702-384-3540 for schedules and information.

Lodging

Las Vegas is as famous for the sumptuousness of its resort hotels as it is for its casinos and name entertainment—in fact, the three are inseparable, since every big hostelry has its own gaming tables and stage shows. The major hotel-casinos on the Strip are about 2 to 3 miles from the station; smaller motels in the downtown district are within walking distance. Look for three-day, two-night package deals, which average from $50 to $90 per person (double occupancy).

Western. 899 E. Fremont Street. 702-384-4620. Small, downtown motel. Twenty-four-hour bar; free breakfast at El Cortez Hotel nearby. Snack bar. Small casino, bingo.

Circus Circus. 2880 Las Vegas Boulevard. 702-734-0410/800-634-3450. On the Strip. Circus acts every day in main arena. Inexpensive packages include buffet luncheon and dinner, two breakfasts, tips.

Union Plaza. 1 Main St. 702-386-2110. This is a large, moderately-priced hotel, complete with casino, dinner theater, and a big plus for the rail traveler—the Amtrak station is under the same roof.

The Sands. 3355 Las Vegas Boulevard S. 702-733-5000. One of the biggest—a Strip landmark. Two pools; tennis; access to Paradise Valley Country Club golf course. Fine restaurants. Always top entertainment.

Riviera. 2901 Las Vegas Boulevard. 702-734-5110/800-634-6855. In style, appointments, and entertainment, the Riviera sums up the Strip. Versailles Theater, four major restaurants. Ten tennis courts, Olympic pool.

Restaurants

The sandwich was invented by a gambling earl who preferred not to leave his games; today's Vegas bettors are fed at dozens of generous buffets whose low prices say something about the local cash flow. Sit-down restaurants include:

Cafe Cortez. El Cortez Hotel, 600 East Fremont Street. 702-385-5200. The place to go for a good steak dinner, without divesting yourself of your own stake.

Cafe Gigi. MGM Grand Hotel, 3645 Las Vegas Boulevard South. 702-739-4111. Believe it or not, this restaurant's decor is actually the set from the film "Marie Antoinette"—another MGM production. Seafood; steak tartare and au poivre; French dishes.

Bacchanal. Caesar's Palace, 3570 Las Vegas Boulevard S. 702-734-7110. Features a fixed-price seven-course dinner with three wine selections. French cuisine; Roman atmosphere. Reservations required. Very expensive.

Las Vegas to Los Angeles

After a 15-minute layover in Las Vegas, the *Desert Wind* continues southward through a ferociously uncompromising landscape, past places with names like the New York Mountains, the Old Dad Mountains, and the Devil's Playground. The peaks in these ranges are in the 4,000- to 6,000-foot range, and they appear as moonlike and forbidding as the country from which they rise. If you look at a map, you'll see that dotted lines border the lakes here, which means that they are dry most of the year. This is the Mojave Desert.

The first California stop is at Barstow, a junction town for the Union Pacific and the Santa Fe. From Barstow, bus connections are available with Bakersfield. Beyond Barstow are the San Gabriel and San Bernardino Mountains, and the Cajon Pass (alt. 3,285 feet) that takes you through them to the next stop at San Bernardino. The trip through the Cajon Pass provides a lesson in the climatological effect of mountains, in the difference between leeward and windward. Once you breach the San Gabriels (the highest peak, on your right [west] is 10,000-foot Mount Baldy), the world becomes green again. From San Bernardino on, toward Pasadena, civilization is there to take advantage of this moisture—although for the metropolis at the end of this route, no amount of water seems enough. Los Angeles slakes its thirst by reaching far beyond the desert you have crossed (for Los Angeles information, see trip 9), all the way to the Colorado River itself.

An Amtrak bi-level superliner car.

12. The *Coast Starlight* and the *San Diegan*

Two trains—the *Coast Starlight* and the *San Diegan*—provide connecting service along the Pacific Coast. The *Coast Starlight* is a full-service, Superliner train. As the *Starlight*'s Seattle to Los Angeles trip takes roughly one and a half days (departure from Seattle is at midday; from Los Angeles in mid-morning), sleeping accommodations are provided. The *San Diegan,* an Amfleet train, plies Amtrak's second-busiest corridor, the 127-mile stretch between Los Angeles and San Diego. Numerous daily trains are scheduled in each direction.

Seattle to Portland

Like the *Empire Builder,* the *Coast Starlight* enters and departs Seattle via the right-of-way of the Burlington Northern. (The BN roundhouse at Interbay, near here, is open to visitors Saturday mornings by reservation.) At Tacoma the *Starlight* reaches the southern tip of Puget Sound, which divides the Washington mainland from the rain-forested Olympic Peninsula, and at East Olympia it begins to follow a due-south course through farm and pasture land that must surely have reminded early Eastern and Midwestern settlers of home. After Kelso-Longview, the train holds to the east bank of the Columbia River, main artery of the old Northwest fur trade, until it reaches Vancouver, Washington. Here stood Fort Vancouver, once a British outpost. Crossing the Columbia, the *Starlight* enters Portland, Oregon.

Portland

The *Coast Starlight*—along with the *Pioneer* and the Portland-Eugene *Willamette Valley*—enters and departs Portland at Union Station, a handsome, tile-roofed Union Pacific depot built against a crook in the Willamette River. The station stands in a neighborhood that has been changing a great deal over the past few years. Not long ago, the old Burnside district that commenced here was the local skid row, but it has receded almost to the point of disappearing as new office construction and the recycling of buildings in Portland's "Old Town" have surged ahead. Within a few years, in the opinion of one local observer, "the Burnside district as we know it today will probably cease to exist."

Portland, which calls itself the "Rose City" because of that flower's profusion here in spring and early summer, can seem a model of civic order to the Easterner used to more tawdry and chaotic surroundings. It shares this aspect with Seattle, its northern neighbor. Portland appears to have gotten off to an orderly start; it was never the hell-raising frontier town of Western legend. The settlers of the Willamette Valley (the Willamette joins the wide Columbia just north of Portland) were mostly sober Midwestern farmers who migrated over the Oregon Trail in the 1840s. Their attitude is suggested by a diary entry of the time: "Friday, October 27—arrived at Oregon City on the Falls of the Willamette. Saturday, October 28—went to work."

The emigrants were attracted by fertile soil, mild temperatures, and ample rainfall. Its early monopoly of road and river traffic with the mining and farming hinterlands gave Portland ascendancy over other western Oregon settlements. Railroads came later; the first line to San Francisco, in fact, was begun only in 1868 and took 20 years to complete. When the rails did come, they changed the local economy from one based on cattle to one whose staples were sheep and wheat.

The natural setting of Portland must also have been an inducement to build a city. The urban center, along the river, is flat, but an encirclement of steep hills made for attractive residential developments and a variety of expansive views—both of the valley and, to the north and west, the mountains. In May 1980, the northerly view was more spectacular than usual: Mount St. Helens, the volcano, is a mere 40 miles away. If you rent a car, you can get out amidst the surrounding scenery in no time at all; but even if you are traveling by bus, it's possible to gain enough altitude to enjoy majestic panoramas. One suggestion is a trip to the Pittock Mansion, listed under Points of Interest. Both the mansion and the Japanese Gardens, on the west side of the city, are accessible not only by city bus but via a Gray Line Tour (503-226-6755).

Portland, the "Rose City," is proud of its roses. The climate favors them; there are rose test gardens at Washington Park, and a Rose Festival is held each June. But even if you arrive when the roses aren't in bloom, you are likely to find Portland an agreeable place. Don't let the Burnside mislead you.

Points of Interest

Western Forestry Center. 4033 Southwest Canyon Road. 503-228-1367. A very informative look at forests and what they mean to the ecology and economy of the Northwest. Learn about logging, fires, wood processing. (Rail buffs take note: there's a 1909 Shay-type locomotive on display.) Open every day, 10 A.M.–5 P.M.

Portland Art Museum. S.W. Jefferson Street at W. Park Avenue. 503-226-2811. One of the two oldest art museums on the West Coast. European art since the Renaissance; nineteenth- and twentieth-century American art; Northwest Indian and pre-Columbian pieces. Open Tuesday through Sunday, noon–5 P.M.; till 10 P.M. Friday. Closed Monday.

Pittock Mansion. 3229 N.W. Pittock Drive. 503-248-4469. Built in 1909-14 by a Portland newspaper publisher, this fine house offers examples not only of vanished craftsmanship but of then-innovative ideas such as indirect lighting and central vacuuming. Exquisitely restored. Good views; nature trails. Open Wednesday through Sunday, 1–5 P.M. Closed Monday and Tuesday.

Oregon Museum of Science and Industry (OMSI). Off US 26, near Western Forestry Center and Washington Park Zoo. 503-222-2828. Everything from aerospace exhibits to a walk-in model of the human heart to a "transparent lady" designed to illustrate anatomy. Planetarium shows. Open every day, 9 A.M.–5 P.M. Call 503-248-5947 for planetarium schedules.

Oregon Historical Society Museum. 1230 S.W. Park Avenue. 503-222-1741. Local history; particular emphasis on exploration and settlement of Oregon Territory in nineteenth century. Open Monday through Saturday, 10 A.M.–4:45 P.M. Closed Sunday.

Oregon Preservation Research Center. 26 N.W. Second Street. 503-243-1923. Portland's architectural heritage and present efforts to preserve and recycle explained through rotating exhibits. Open Tuesday through Friday, 10 A.M.–3 P.M.; weekends, noon–4 P.M. Closed Monday.

The offices of the Greater Portland Convention and Visitors' Association are at 26 S.W. Salmon Street, in the new office complex near the river. Phone 503-222-2223 for information.

Public Transportation

Portland's bus system, operated by Tri-Met, may well be the nation's finest. At its heart is the Portland Mall, a section of downtown closed to auto traffic. Along the streets of the mall are 31 passenger shelters, each equipped with color-coded route maps and closed-circuit television that tells when the next buses are departing. Most of downtown is a fare-free zone. The Tri-Met information number is 503-233-3511.

Lodging

Portland, for some reason, has more cheap downtown hotels than most cities its size. Perhaps this has something to do with the transience of workers in the fishing and logging industries. There are plenty of shopworn but acceptable rooms starting at $20; at the other end of the scale, deluxe doubles can run to $110.

Imperial. 400 S.W. Broadway. 503-228-7221. 13 blocks from station. Older hotel, recently renovated, in downtown location. Restaurant, lounge.

Riverside West Motor Hotel. 50 S.W. Morrison Street. 503-221-0711. 12 blocks from station. Near Willamette River and central to all downtown locations. Restaurant, lounge. In-room movies.

The Westin Benson. 309 S.W. Broadway. 503-228-9611/800-228-3000. 12 blocks from station. A Portland landmark, known for its understated elegance, fine service, and details like electric blankets. Two restaurants, including excellent London Grill; lounges.

Portland Hilton. 921 S.W. Sixth Avenue. 503-226-1611. 20 blocks from station. Modern luxury hotel; convenient downtown location. Heated pool, sundeck, landscaped garden. In-room movies. Restaurants, lounge.

Restaurants

As in Seattle, diners are advised to choose local seafood—especially crab and salmon—over "continental" cuisine.

Henry Thiele's. 2305 W. Burnside Street. 503-223-2060. A visit to Portland isn't complete without one of Henry Thiele's German pancakes. The extensive (and inexpensive) selection of entrees includes sturgeon (when available), Oregon crab cakes, sweetbreads, and chicken with parsley dumplings.

Jake's. 401 S.W. Twelfth Avenue. 503-226-1419. An old-time Portland establishment—they've been serving seafood since 1892. Dungeness crab, Chinook salmon, steamers, and, in season, Jake's specialty—crawfish.

London Grill. Westin Benson Hotel, 309 S.W. Broadway. 503-228-9611. The traditional place in Portland for a big night out. Prime ribs with creamed horseradish; chicken stuffed with crabmeat; gingered rack of lamb. Lobster tank.

Portland to Oakland

The *Coast Starlight* rolls south out of Portland on Southern Pacific roadbed. The route that it follows, as evening approaches, runs the length of the

Willamette Valley. The Willamette is Oregon's Nile; farms may still be found along its banks, and around it is clustered the bulk of the state's population. At the university town of Eugene the river forks southeastward toward its source in the southern Cascades, and the *Starlight* follows it, negotiating a series of mountain passes. Klamath Falls, reached shortly after 10:00 P.M., is the closest stop to Crater Lake National Park.

The train enters California in darkness. Unfortunately, this makes it impossible to see 14,000-foot Mount Shasta, which looms only 10 miles from the track. Mt. Lassen, which before the 1980 eruption of Mt. St. Helens was thought to be the only live volcano in the continental United States (it is currently dormant), is 45 minutes east of the scheduled stop of Redding. At Tehama the SP tracks fork, and, unlike in years past, the *Starlight* now bears onto the more easterly line which leads into Sacramento (for Sacramento information, see trip 8). From Sacramento, the route into Oakland is the same as that followed by the *California Zephyr*. As with the *Zephyr*, Oakland is as close as you can get to San Francisco via Amtrak. Buses across the bay, of course, connect with all trains (for San Francisco information, see trip 8). Oakland is also the terminus for Amtrak's *San Joaquin* trains, which follow the San Joaquin Valley to Bakersfield. Get off at Merced for Yosemite National Park, and at Fresno for Sequoia and Kings Canyon National Parks.

Oakland to Los Angeles

The route south to Los Angeles was that taken by the Southern Pacific's famous *Daylight*—and, indeed, this part of the trip is completed in daylight by both the northbound and southbound *Starlights*. Rail historian Lucius Beebe called the old SP *Daylight* "probably the most spectacular train ever designed." Drawn in its heyday by a streamlined 4-8-4 locomotive, its 12 stainless-steel cars were painted in orange, red, and black lacquers.

The *Coast Starlight* roughly follows El Camino Real, the old Spanish highway that linked colonial California's Franciscan missions. The building of a railroad along this route began in 1857, but it was not until 1901 that through service to Los Angeles was achieved. While traveling on the *Starlight*, you will be able to see the formidable physical obstacles to the road's completion.

The train holds close to the shore of San Francisco Bay as it makes its way toward "Silicon Valley," so called because of the concentration of computer firms here. The first southbound stop is San Jose, site of the mission of San Jose of Guadalupe. The 200-year-old structure was not only a religious but a social and cultural center during Spanish rule. To the east is Mount Hamilton; to the west, the Santa Cruz Mountains. The tracks continue south, paralleling Route 101, into Salinas, the boyhood home of John Steinbeck and capital of the region where many of his novels were set. The California Rodeo is held here each July.

There is currently no scheduled stop at Soledad, but it was here that the rails from San Francisco terminated between 1874 and 1887. Get off at Salinas if you wish to see the Soledad Mission Ruins or visit Pinnacles National Monument, a few miles to the east. The rail route south bisects the fertile Salinas Valley, a livestock center, passes a working oil field just south of San Ardo, and enters the town of San Miguel (not a scheduled stop), where on the left (east) side of the track you can see the Mission of San Miguel Archangel (1797), the only California mission that still stands in its original condition.

Beginning at Santa Margarita, the *Starlight* has to negotiate a spectacular series of switchbacks and tunnels through the Santa Lucia Mountains, emerging finally at another old mission town, San Luis Obispo. Here is where California's ubiquitous red tile was first produced. It is also the point of departure for visitors to the Hearst Castle in San Simeon. Next come the sand dunes of Pismo Beach, winter home of monarch butterflies, and a 113-mile skirting of the Pacific Coast. This oceanside segment of the trip includes a stop at Santa Barbara, where Franciscan friars still operate the local mission and where flowers bloom almost everywhere.

The *Starlight* finally heads inland at Ventura, stops at Oxnard, and enters the Simi Valley by way of the Santa Susana tunnel. Once out of the tunnel, you are in Los Angeles County. The 6,000-foot San Gabriel Mountains rise to the north, and the suburban sprawl of the San Fernando Valley lies ahead. After a stop at Glendale, the *Starlight* reaches its southern terminus at Los Angeles. (For Los Angeles information, see trip 9.)

Los Angeles to San Diego

The *San Diegan* follows the Santa Fe Railroad's old "Surf Line" between southern California's two largest cities. The original, early 1880s route bypassed Los Angeles in favor of San Bernardino, but that mistake was soon rectified. Current plans, being developed by a private concern with assistance from Amtrak, call for implementation of the first U.S. versions of the Japanese "bullet trains" in the Los Angeles–San Diego corridor during the late 1980s or early 1990s. If the scheme is successful, it could spell the beginning of a new era in short to medium distance rail service between major cities: Chicago–Detroit and the Northeast Corridor immediately come to mind.

The first notable sight south of Los Angeles is the Matterhorn, visible on the right (west) side of the train in Anaheim, just past the Fullerton stop. The Matterhorn? Yes—the Disney version. Disneyland's 185 acres lie just across the Santa Ana Freeway. Now you enter into a region whose long-established orange groves (hence the name, Orange County) vie with runaway suburban development. The *San Diegan* stops at Santa Ana, and then at San Juan Capistrano, the mission town to which the swallows return each October 23. Here the Santa Fe tracks meet the sea, pass Dana Point, and head toward the oceanside station at San Clemente, where Richard Nixon once lived. Oceanside and Del Mar are the next stops. After Del Mar, as the train turns inland, look to your right (west) to see the famous Torrey Pines, a gnarled, bonsai-like species indigenous only to this part of California. The route from here through the Soledad Canyon provides fine views. Once the canyon has been passed, the San Diego suburbs are at hand. The train follows the shore of Mission Bay into the city.

San Diego

San Diego is where California began. The Cabrillo Monument, which stands on Point Loma at the southwestern extremity of the United States, commemorates the discovery of the area by Juan Rodriquez Cabrillo on September 28, 1542. The lands north of here became, for the Spanish settlers and administrators, Alta California; Baja California, still Mexican territory, begins just 16 miles to the south.

The settlement of San Diego has existed since 1769 when the first California mission was established by Father Junipero Serra, but the growth

With the Pacific coastline as a backdrop, one of Amtrak's San Diegan trains heads south from Los Angeles in this growing California rail corridor.

Amtrak's San Diego rail passenger station combines the traditional California architecture with the latest in modern rail passenger equipment, Amfleet.

of the city dates to 1885, when the Santa Fe Railroad made it a western terminus. Modern San Diego owes its prosperity chiefly to the aerospace business and to its status as a major naval base. (There's usually at least one ship open to the public at Broadway Pier on weekend afternoons.) Few cities anywhere are favored with as expansive and well protected a harbor. Because of the residential popularity of its seaside district, though, and because its boom years followed the development of freeways, San Diego appears to lack a center. Its downtown looks appropriate for a city of 100,000, perhaps, but not for one of nearly a million. Visitors must be willing to venture a bit further than usual in order to see what the place has to offer. Fortunately, bus service is good, and there is even a new trolley that runs from the train station through downtown and the suburbs all the way to San Ysidro on the Mexican border, making Tijuana even more easily accessible from San Diego than before. American travelers do not need a passport to cross the border (a visa is necessary only for trips that take you more than 75 miles from the border, or for stays of longer than 72 hours) and Mexican shops and restaurants accept U.S. currency. Tijuana's reputation for tawdriness and danger is not entirely fair to this small, workaday city, and its food is often superior to what passes for Mexican fare in the States. You can see the town on a morning or afternoon excursion and return to San Diego for the remainder of the day.

Points of Interest

Sea World. Sea World Drive, Mission Bay. 619-224-3562. World's largest marine life park. Seals, walruses, killer whales, dolphins, sharks, and more. Don't miss the new penguin exhibit. Live shows; opportunities for children to touch some animals. Exotic birds. Open every day, 9 A.M.–5 P.M.; later in summer (ticket office closes 1½ hours before actual closing).

Balboa Park. Northeast of downtown; main access streets are Laurel Street and Park Boulevard. This vast park was developed for the Panama Canal exposition of 1914 and the 1935 California-Pacific International Exposition; today, its buildings house the city's major museums, including:

—**San Diego Museum of Art.** 619-232-7931. Open Tuesday through Sunday, 10 A.M.–5 P.M.

—**Aerospace Museum.** 619-234-8291. Open every day, 10 A.M.–6 P.M.

—**Natural History Museum.** 619-232-3821. Open every day, 10 A.M.–5 P.M.

—**Museum of Man.** 619-239-2001. Open every day, 10 A.M.–4:30 P.M.

Balboa Park's most famous attraction, however, is the **San Diego Zoo**, one of the world's best. Rare creatures are a specialty—Komodo dragons, Australian koalas, and lesser pandas are but a few. Aerial tramway; children's zoo. 619-234-3153. Open daily. Hours vary with season; call for information.

Firehouse Museum. 1572 Columbia Street. 619-232-FIRE. Antique firefighting equipment, displayed in an old fire station. Open weekends only, 10 A.M.–4 P.M.

Scripps Institution of Oceanography. 8602 La Jolla Shores Drive, La Jolla. **Scripps Aquarium-Museum** (619-452-4086) at the institution houses live specimens as well as recreations of undersea scenes. A famous research center. Open every day, 9 A.M.–5 P.M.

The San Diego Convention and Visitors' Bureau is at 1200 Third Avenue; call 619-239-9696 for information.

Public Transportation

San Diego Transit runs the buses here; the fare and schedule information number is 619-239-8161. Mexicoach makes the San Diego-Tijuana circuit several times daily. Call 619-232-5049, or visit the ticket booth at the Amtrak station. For information on trolley service to the border, call 619-233-3004 or 231-1466.

Lodging

As spread out as San Diego is, it still has a cluster of variously priced hotels downtown, near the station; others are more distant, in the "Hotel Circle" complex on Interstate 8, or facing the bays north and south of the city. Prices range from $35 to $100 or over for double occupancy.

Pickwick. 132 West Broadway. 619-234-0141. 5 blocks from station. One of the more convenient of San Diego's lower-priced accommodations, at least as far as the rail traveler is concerned. Older hotel with cheerfully redecorated rooms. Restaurant, lounges.

Best Western Shelter Island Marina Inn. 2051 Shelter Island Drive. 619-222-0561/800-528-1234. 7 miles from station. Right on North San Diego Bay, across from downtown. Marina location ideal for water-sports enthusiasts. Boat rentals; also heated pool. Some kitchen suites available. Restaurant, lounge. Fine views.

Westgate. 1055 Second Avenue. 619-238-1818/800-522-1564 (in California). 7 blocks from station. San Diego's most elegant downtown hotel. No two rooms alike; eighteenth-century period furnishings. Formal and casual restaurants, lounges, entertainment.

Del Coronado. 1500 Orange Avenue, Coronado. 619-435-6611. 5 miles from station. The oldest and most charming of San Diego's resort hotels, on a peninsula in San Diego Bay. 1888 original section and new tower wing. Heated Olympic pool, all water sports, golf. Fine restaurants, lounge, entertainment.

Restaurants

Opt for fresh Pacific seafood whenever available; otherwise, selections run the usual gamut from prime rib to Polynesian.

Anthony's Seafood Mart. 555 Harbor Drive. 619-232-2933. A fish market with a dining room; freshness assured. Reasonably priced.

Ten Downing. 1250 Sixth Avenue. 619-235-6566. Mostly steak and seafood, with a British atmosphere. Late suppers, including quiche, omelets, and an imaginative sandwich featuring prime rib, shrimp, and asparagus.

Cafe Pacifica. 2411 San Diego Avenue. 619-291-6666. Fresh fish gets an honest treatment in this popular Old Town spot. Outdoor seating.

III. Routes and Cities:
Via Rail Canada

Grain elevators are the most prominent and ubiquitous features on the Canadian prairie landscape.

1. Introduction to Via Rail Canada

"Canada," wrote Pierre Berton in his superb account of the building of the Canadian Pacific Railway, *The Last Spike*, "is deceptively vast . . . for practical purposes Canada is almost as slender as Chile." Berton was referring, of course, to the concentration of much of the country's population along a slender corridor of land just to the north of the United States border. This is demographic evidence of one of the salient facts of Canadian history and life: Canada, and particularly its west, is a creature of the railroad.

Just as there was a San Francisco before there was a Denver or an Omaha, there were settlements on British Columbia's Vancouver Island back when the prairies and interior mountains of Canada—the "North West" as they were collectively called—were still the exclusive preserve of nomadic Indian tribes and vast herds of buffalo. When Canada became a nation in 1867, the new confederation consisted only of the eastern provinces; British Columbia remained just that—a British colony. Virtually the entire center of the continent north of the United States line belonged to the Hudson's Bay Company.

In 1870, Canada's first prime minister, John A. Macdonald, got British Columbia to agree to join confederation with full provincial status. In order to do so, he made what a good many of his colleagues in the government considered a very rash promise: a railway connecting the Pacific settlements with the East would be built within ten years. In 1871, Canada got the land to build it across, when the Hudson's Bay Company's North West holdings were formally ceded to the new nation. But the logistics of laying track through the muskeg wilderness north of the Great Lakes, across the prairie, and through passes as yet undiscovered, much less surveyed, staggered the imaginations of even the most sanguine of Canadian expansionists.

And yet 14 years later the Canadian Pacific Railway was complete. The story of how it was built—in stages, first under government contract and, after 1881, under the direction of the private yet federally subsidized CPR syndicate, is best left to Pierre Berton, whose books *The National Dream* and *The Last Spike* cannot be recommended too highly (an edition in which these two works are abridged and published in a single volume is listed in the bibliography). The construction of the CPR was one of the nineteenth century's most impressive engineering achievements, a sublime act of will on the part of everyone involved, from the Irish, Chinese, French Canadian, and other laborers on the track crews to the debt-plagued yet financially nimble entrepreneurs who worried the task through at their desks in Montreal and Winnipeg. At center stage in the CPR drama stood the colossal figure of William Cornelius Van Horne, general manager and later president of the road, who could balance a ledger, drive a locomotive, send and receive telegraphic messages, walk miles through the wilderness on inspection tours, and still find time for painting, art collecting, gardening, and a study of geology so thorough that several fossils bear his Latinized name.

The Canadian Pacific Railway was the dominant force in Canadian western development throughout the remainder of the nineteenth century and well into the twentieth. It led the way in the promotion of tourism by rail as well, building hotels in the major cities along its line and also creating resorts such as Banff Springs and Lake Louise. Long before the Harrimans and their Union Pacific turned their attention to Sun Valley, Idaho, and even before Flagler and the railroads built Miami Beach, the CPR pioneered in the marketing of the scenic places accessible by means of its trains. To this day, tourists flock to the mountain retreats first promoted by William Van Horne, and a good many of them stay in CP-owned hotels when they get there. But they no longer arrive on CP trains.

The other great transcontinental rail enterprise north of the border was the Canadian National Railways. The CN lines were not conceived and built in the same deliberate fashion as the CPR; rather, the company is the product of the amalgamation and eventual nationalization of a number of smaller roads. The coast-to-coast culmination of the Canadian National came in 1913, when the line between Moncton, New Brunswick, and Winnipeg was completed, and 1914, when Winnipeg was linked with Prince Rupert on the northern British Columbia coast. This ambitious program of expansion was begun by the Grand Trunk Railway, an old eastern operation; it proved to be too much for the Grand Trunk to handle, and the government stepped in to pick up the fiscal debris. So the Canadian National was born.

The CN route to the Pacific followed a more northerly path than that of the CPR, linking the northern prairie cities of Saskatoon and Edmonton and crossing the Rockies at Jasper rather than at Banff and Lake Louise. Prior to the early 1980s, transcontinental through trains still traversed this route; now, although all major prairie province and northern B.C. points are still connected by rail, the main link between Montreal and Toronto and the Pacific is the older, southerly CPR course.

As was noted in the general introduction to this book, interest in passenger trains on the part of both the CNR and CPR was dwindling, by the mid 1970s, in inverse proportion to the amount of the losses sustained in passenger operations. (We won't go into the chicken-and-egg conundrum implicit in this equation.) Those losses combined to amount to $260 million in 1976, and everyone knew something had to be done. The simplest thing would have been to stop carrying passengers, but Canada balked at that prospect just as the United States had six years before. In early 1977, Via Rail Canada was created as a subsidiary of Canadian National; a little more than a year later, it assumed separate Crown Corporation status. Roughly equivalent in terms of its quasi-governmental standing to Amtrak in the United States (if the United States had a crown, Amtrak would be a Crown Corporation), Via is charged with the operation of all Canadian long distance and corridor trains. In so doing, it is expected to cut the losses the government must absorb (even in pre-Via days, the Dominion agreed to underwrite 80 percent of the private roads' operating losses) and has been making headway in this direction through the consolidation of duplicate routes and stations and by attracting more travelers to the rails.

Equipment

Like Amtrak, Via inherited its rolling stock from the railroads whose passenger services it took over. Restoration similar to that undertaken by

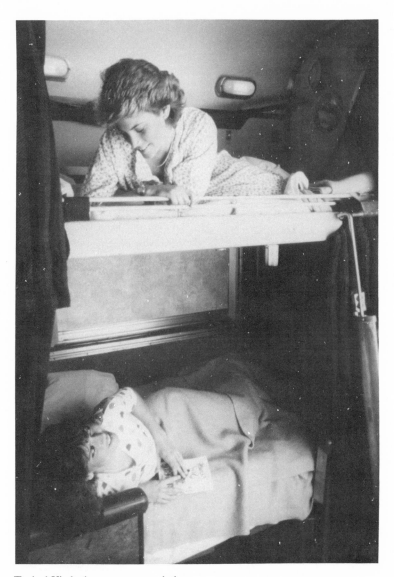

Typical Via bedroom accommodations

Amtrak on its "Heritage Fleet" was begun, and today's Via rolling stock is generally comfortable and reliable even though much of it dates to the mid-1950s. Among the newer equipment in service in Canada is the LRC (light-rapid-comfortable) rolling stock; see below, Quebec-Montreal, for details.

Travelers will find that Canadian and U.S. non-Superliner long-distance rolling stock have more than age and recent rehabilitation in common. The layout of Canadian sleeping cars corresponds to that on Amtrak, with one major difference: in addition to roomette and bedroom accommodations, Canadian sleepers still employ Pullman sections, which are made up as facing bench seats by day and upper and lower curtained berths by night. Also, sleeping cars in the "Chateau" and "Park" series each contain one drawing room, a larger version of the bedroom which sleeps three and by day resembles a private parlor. (Incidentally, if you are traveling coach class on Via, you can usually upgrade your accommodations in mid-trip. Simply ask the conductor what's available; you'll be charged accordingly. If you know you're going to want a sleeper, however, it's best to reserve ahead.)

There's one noteworthy detail of roomette design on Via trains that differs from the U.S. norm. In Amtrak roomettes, all beds fold down from the wall. In Via roomettes on cars built for CN, roomettes with fold-down beds alternate with those in which the bed slides out horizontally from the wall opposite the seat. In these roomettes, it's necessary to store your suitcase either underneath your seat or in with the bed during the day. There is no overhead rack. At night, the suitcase will have to be under the bed, so remember to take out what you'll need before you go to bed. One advantage of this layout is that it's easy to reach behind the flap that conceals the bed for a pillow at afternoon nap time.

Long-distance coaches include both regular seating and, at extra charge, "dayniter" seats, with greater leg and fold-back room, along with leg rests.

Dining cars and lounges on Via are arranged much the same as they are on Amtrak trains using "Heritage Fleet" equipment. On the Canadian, the best lounge seats are in the boat-tailed car at the end of the train. These cars have comfortable armchairs, a small service bar, a writing desk and a supply of magazines, and booth seating in a separate area farther to the front. There are also three bedrooms and a drawing room on the lower level and an observation dome up above. Dome seating is also available elsewhere on the train in Dome cars equipped with a small dinette-lounge.

Via has streamlined its dining services in recent years by limiting selections to two at each meal, with menus changing each day. Prior to lunch and dinner, attendants walk the aisles of coaches, sleepers, and lounges taking reservations for the upcoming meal, even asking for menu preferences and sometimes taking payment in advance. Some people find it irksome to have to decide what they're having for dinner an hour after lunch, but the real cause for regret is that the food isn't as good as it was on the CPR ten years ago. In the 1980s, though, the alternative to lackluster food on trains seems to be no food at all.

Baggage, Stations, and Ticketing

All long-distance Via trains carry baggage cars. Passengers paying full fare are allowed to check up to 150 lbs. of baggage into baggage cars without extra charge, in addition to the hand luggage which is brought into coaches and sleeping compartments. All baggage must be checked at least a half hour before the train is scheduled to depart. Pets are also allowed to travel in baggage cars as checked baggage; it is the responsibility of passengers, however, to feed, water, and walk their animals at layover stops. With the exception of see-eye dogs, no pets may be taken onto the other sections of the train.

One unusual bit of baggage sometimes seen on trains traversing the wilderness is the canoe. For an extra fee, you can bring a canoe on board a Via train (trains with baggage cars only) and have yourself dropped off at any milepost along the route, with arrangements to be picked up later for your return. Before you head for the station with your canoe, though, make sure you have examined the relevant topographical maps of the area you intend to travel through, and that you have sufficient experience—and a guide, if necessary—to make the trip.

Reservations are required for all accommodations on Canadian long-distance trains. The best bet is to see your travel agent well in advance of your planned trip, or to stop in at a Via station equipped with reservation and ticketing facilities, as are all major stations along the routes described in the following pages. Via's new RESERVIA computerized reservation and ticketing system can give instant information on the availability of bookings for all trains, and is integrated with the Air Canada ticketing network. Eventually, Via hopes to expand RESERVIA capacities to include complete intermodal travel planning, along with hotel reservations and car rentals.

For information on Via schedules, services, and the many package tours offered by the Canadian carrier, contact Via Rail Canada, P.O. Box 8116, 1801 McGill College Avenue, Suite 1300, Montreal, PQ H3C, 3N3, 514-286-2311.

Via dining car.

2. The *Ocean*: Halifax to Quebec

Halifax, the capital of Nova Scotia and, unofficially, of the Maritime Provinces, is the terminus for Via's *Ocean*, which departs daily for Moncton, Quebec and Montreal. But Nova Scotia service is not limited to this main-line route. Two other Via trains connect Halifax with the northeastern and southwestern extremes of the province.

The Evangeline Route

The Evangeline Route connects Yarmouth with Halifax. Diesel rail cars, equipped with bar and snack service, operate daily. The eastbound train runs in daylight and offers a better look at the scenery than the evening train westbound out of Halifax. Also, the departure from the Yarmouth terminus affords travelers from the United States the opportunity to begin their Canadian rail trip by taking passage on either the Blue Nose ferry (operated by Canadian National Marine) out of Bar Harbor, Maine, or the Scotia Prince (Prince of Fundy Cruises) out of Portland, Maine.

Yarmouth is a pleasant little city with ample overnight accommodations, restaurants, and the interesting Firefighters' Museum of Nova Scotia and Yarmouth County Historical Museum. The Via Station is on Water Street less than a mile from the ferry terminals downtown. Board here for the five-hour trip to Halifax along the northern Bay of Fundy coast of Nova Scotia. This is the route of the Dominion Atlantic Railway, now a part of the Canadian Pacific system. Some segments date back to the 1850s, and the entire Halifax-Yarmouth route was complete by 1891.

Highlights along the 200-mile route include Digby, home of the famous Digby scallops dragged by local vessels from the floor of the Bay of Fundy; the 1,600-foot Bear River Bridge, a little over 6 miles past Digby; Cornwallis, one of the largest naval training centers in the British Commonwealth; and Annapolis Royal, a picturesque country town located near the site where, for several years following its discovery in 1604, Samuel de Champlain and a party of settlers maintained the first French outpost in Canada. There are several comfortable inns here, as well as galleries specializing in regional arts and crafts.

The Annapolis Valley, which extends east from here to the vicinity of Kentville, is famous for its apple orchards and miles of gently rolling, pastoral scenery. It is also known as the country of Evangeline, Longfellow's heroine, and the French Acadian settlers who were dispersed from Nova Scotia by the British explulsion edict of 1755. The site of Evangeline's village is on the grounds of Grand Pré National Historic Park. The park is just to the north of the rail route, about 10 miles past Kentville. The nearest stop is Wolfville.

The Dominion Atlantic route bears to the south after Wolfville and Grand Pré, crossing the Avon River on a 3,000-foot causeway and passing through a region of lakes and hills on the way to Windsor Junction and Canadian National tracks at Windsor Junction. From here, only 16 miles remain before the train reaches Halifax.

The Cabot Route

The other Nova Scotia route supplementing mainline service on the *Ocean* extends from Truro (64 miles north of Halifax via three trains per day, including the *Ocean*) to Sydney, near the eastern tip of Cape Breton. The 230-mile Cabot Route is the rail gateway to Newfoundland, via the CN ferries which leave North Sydney for Port-aux-Basques (west coast) and Argentia (east coast, nearer to St. John's). Once on Newfoundland, the rail enthusiast has the opportunity to ride on some of North America's last mixed freight-and-passenger trains. There are three: Corner Brook to Bishop's Falls, Clarenville to Bonavista, and Argentia to St. John's. All are ably described in Bill Coo's *Scenic Rail Guide to Central and Atlantic Canada*, which is recommended reading for anyone traveling by rail through this region.

Rail diesel cars leave Truro daily for Sydney. The route begins by traversing a region east of Truro which is today primarily agricultural, but which not long ago was famed for its coal output: a seam near Stellarton was once the world's thickest, at nearly 50 feet. The coal deposits gave rise to industry, as the town name New Glasgow might suggest. Near South River, the waters of St. George's Bay come into view on the left. The tracks roughly follow the bay as far as Havre Boucher. Then, having reached the Canso Strait, they head out across the 4,500-foot man-made Canso Causeway, a 30-year-old link which makes Cape Breton Island technically more cape than island.

Beyond the causeway lies the land which truly earns Nova Scotia—"New Scotland" in Latin—its name. The jewel of Cape Breton is Bras d'Or Lake, a huge saltwater inlet almost entirely surrounded by land. Past Orangedale, the lake is occasionally visible to the south (right); at Grand Narrows, the Barra Strait is crossed and "Little" Bras d'Or, the northern branch of the lake, appears along the north (left). The train soon approaches Sydney Mines, still producing coal after more than 200 years. Get off at North Sydney if you are ferrying on to Newfoundland; otherwise, the trip terminates in another 15 miles at the small industrial city of Sydney, which despite its modest size contains the largest self-contained steel plant in North America. Sydney is the point of departure, by rental car or bus tour, for the vast, restored French town and fortress of Louisbourg, which fell to British colonial forces in 1745. This is the largest historical reconstruction project in Canada, and is well worth the visit.

Halifax

Halifax is a peninsular city, enjoying one of the most beautiful and useful harbors in the world. In terms of size, it is exceeded only by that of Sydney, Australia, and as for shipping volume, it is third on the east coast of North America, and second to no Canadian port in the amount of container traffic it handles. But where other great maritime centers might have yielded entirely to utilitarian considerations—one could imagine the whole of this peninsula from Bedford Basin to the Northwest Arm cluttered with manufacturing and commerce—Halifax has kept to a modest urban scale. Its downtown is compact and tidy; its harbor accessible. Virtually the whole of the long Northwest Arm is the preserve of weekend sailors. (Haligonians, as they are called, sail with a passion and talk about it in bars the way people in other cities chew over baseball and politics.)

Halifax is the oldest British city in Canada. It was founded in 1749 as a coastal bulwark against the soon to be eclipsed French presence in Quebec and what remained of old Acadia. It gained in importance when Great Britain lost her American ports in the Revolution. Halifax received many of the loyalists who left the American colonies with the triumph of rebel forces. In view of its position as the last North American coastal bastion in the British Empire, its military defenses were substantially upgraded. Evidence of this strategic importance looms over the entire city in the form of the Halifax Citadel. Now a national historic park, the Citadel was built between 1828 and 1856 on the site of earlier fortifications. The fact that its guns were never fired in anger may have a good deal to do with the fact that for its time, the Citadel was virtually impregnable, impossible to besiege with any tactic short of wholesale suicide. Visit the Citadel (see "Points of Interest") not only for a superb education in local history—military and otherwise—but simply for the views of the city this commanding height affords.

Via trains arrive at Windsor Station, a CN facility located conveniently at downtown Halifax's front door. Barrington, Hollis, or Lower Water streets— all of which begin to the right of the station entrance—will take you downtown in a matter of a few blocks.

All of central Halifax can easily be explored on foot, although the buses are there when you need them. Start with "Grand Parade," the small park bound by Barrington, Prince, Argyle, and Duke streets. The two buildings which face each other across the Grand Parade are the 1890 City Hall and the Episcopal Church of St. Paul's, built in 1749, the oldest Protestant church in Canada. If you walk into the vestibule of St. Paul's and look just above the inside doors to the left, you will see a scrap of iron protruding from the plaster wall. This is a reminder of the greatest disaster ever to strike Halifax, and perhaps the worst sudden calamity ever to befall a city on this continent.

It happened on Dec. 6, 1917. Halifax Harbor was busy with shipping related to the war in Europe. A Norwegian ship, the *Imo*, collided with the French vessel *Mont Blanc*, which was carrying 5,000 tons of explosives, along with hundreds of barrels of benzine. The benzine caught fire; the crews panicked and headed for shore in lifeboats. The *Mont Blanc*, now a burning derelict, drifted towards the docks near the present site of the A. Murray Mackay Bridge. As Halifax firemen rushed to extinguish the blaze, the flames reached the deadly cargo below decks. The result was the largest man-made explosion prior to Hiroshima. It levelled 1 square mile of downtown Halifax and killed 1,600 people instantly; hundreds more died later of their injuries. The force of the blast cracked the floor of the harbor. Ships were thrown across the channel to Dartmouth, and railroad freight cars landed 2 miles from their yards.

That evening, Halifax was hit by a blizzard.

Walk from the Grand Parade up to the Citadel, past the 1803 Old Town Clock designed by the Duke of Kent, father of Queen Victoria, while he was commander of the British garrison here. The harbor immediately below not only shows no sign of the devastation of 1917, but evidences little of the grit and bustle now centered largely amidst the working docks and container facilities located farther east towards Bedford Basin. Instead, the waterfront of downtown Halifax has been largely refurbished and given over to shops, restaurants, and public promenades, much in the style of similar districts throughout North America. The centerpiece is the Historic Properties, a complex of old warehouses, chandleries, sail lofts and wharves built between 1800 and 1905. There is a visitors' information center here, and nearby are two of Halifax Harbor's best attractions—the Maritime Museum of the Atlantic and the magnificent schooner, *Bluenose II* (see "Points of Interest"). The *Bluenose* takes passengers on three harbor cruises a day in July and August; but even if you don't get a chance to sail with her, you can enjoy a splendid perspective of Halifax by taking the Dartmouth ferry—oldest operating salt water ferry service in North America—from its dock at the foot of George Street. After 5 P.M., the blocks in and around Historic Properties grow livelier as bistros fill with tourists and downtown office workers alike. Rum and waterfronts go hand in hand—even in the once staunchly Calvinist Maritimes—except on Sunday night.

Sunday or any day is fine for a stroll through the most charming holdover from Victorian and Edwardian Halifax—the Public Gardens, which can be entered at the corner of Spring Garden Road and South Park Street. The gardens, begun in 1867, comprise 18 acres of beautiful and profuse formal plantings. There are walkways and benches, a lagoon with ducks and swans, and summer evening concerts in a picturebook bandstand. Point Pleasant Park, roughly 1 mile west of the Gardens via South Park Street and Young Avenue, is another matter altogether: 186 acres of virtual wilderness, on the promontory that was once crucial to Halifax's defenses. Several old forts and a squat, brooding Martello Tower punctuate the coast and forests as reminders of those days. The park is closed to cars and is Halifax's favorite jogging spot; there is a map posted at the Tower Road entrance. Enjoy it, thanks to a 999-year lease from Queen Victoria on which Haligonians pay a shilling a year in rent.

Points of Interest

Halifax Citadel National Historic Park. Entrance at Brunswick and George Streets. 902-422-5979 (Army Museum). The state of the art of fortifications, roughly 150 years ago, now largely renovated. British troops were garrisoned here until 1906, but the massive ironstone walls were never tested by enemy assault. At the Citadel, an excellent multiprojector show relates the history of Halifax. There is also an Army Museum in which uniforms, armaments, medals, and displays tell of Canada's military accomplishments over two centuries. Try to visit at sunset, when pipers play as the Union Jack is lowered. Open June 15 through Labor Day, 9 A.M.–8 P.M.; 9 A.M.–5 P.M. the rest of the year. Phone ahead for museum hours.

Maritime Museum of the Atlantic. 1675 Lower Water Street. 902-429-8210. A spacious new museum filled with detailed ship models, full-scale examples of smaller craft, and nautical artifacts ranging from a *Titanic* deck chair to debris from the Halifax explosion. An interesting annex is the old Robertson Building, equipped as it was when it was a working ship chandlery earlier in this century. Also visit the 1913 steamer *Arcadia*, moored behind the museum. Open June 15 through Labor Day 9 A.M.–9 P.M., Monday through Friday; weekends, 9 A.M.–5 P.M. Closed evenings remainder of year.

Nova Scotia Museum. 1747 Summer Street. 902-429-4610. Specializing in geology, Nova Scotia history, and marine and terrestrial natural history exhibits. The animal specimens are particularly well mounted and displayed, and include the coelacanth, a prehistoric fish which survives to this day, and a whale skeleton. Open Tuesday through Saturday, 9 A.M.–5 P.M.; Sunday, noon–5 P.M. Closed Monday.

Halifax Water Tours. Privateers Wharf, Historic Properties. 902-423-7783. A narrated tour on the *Haligonian III* takes you completely around the peninsula on which Halifax is situated, from Bedford Basin to the head of Northwest Arm. It's a great way to orient yourself to the city or to conclude a visit. Two sailings daily spring and fall; four in summer. Call for schedules.

The Halifax Visitors and Convention Bureau operates a Tourist Information Center at Historic Properties; call 902-426-8736 or write the bureau at P.O. Box 1749, Halifax.

Public Transportation

City buses are run by Halifax Transit. Call 902-421-6600 for information. The ferry to Dartmouth leaves from the foot of George Street, and operates on a frequent schedule June through September.

Lodgings

Accommodations in central Halifax are plentiful and start right at the train station. The roster of area hotels ranges from traditional properties like the Lord Nelson, which overlooks the Public Gardens, to a new Sheraton scheduled to open on the waterfront in 1985. Rates for doubles vary from about $50 to $100.

Nova Scotian. 1181 Hollis Street. 902-423-7231. The Nova Scotian directly adjoins Windsor Station and is only a short walk from downtown. It is nicely appointed and quite reasonable; about half the rooms are air-conditioned and many have fine harbor views. Lounges, two restaurants.

Chateau Halifax. Scotia Square. 902-425-6700 or 800-268-9411. A downtown hotel, part of the nationwide CP chain. Indoor shopping complex adjacent; dining and lounges; heated indoor-outdoor pool and sauna.

Citadel Inn. 1960 Brunswick Street. 902-422-1391 or 800-565-7162 in Canada. Along with the Citadel itself, the upper floors of its namesake inn offer some of the nicest views of Halifax. All rooms have refrigerators. There is a heated pool and solarium as well as a dining room and lounge with entertainment.

Restaurants

Halifax is a seafood town, and the bounty here includes not only lobster and the dozens of saltwater fish species common to North Atlantic ports but also Digby scallops from the Bay of Fundy and the incomparable Nova Scotia salmon. Many restaurants feature "Solomon Gundy," which is pickled herring in sour cream; and the tasty combination of shredded salt cod, salt pork, and onions.

In addition to the places listed below, try *Clipper Cay* and the *Privateer's Warehouse*, both at the waterfront's Historic Properties; The *Guru* on Argyle Street for East Indian food; and *Gabriel's* at Barrington and Morris Streets for traditional Acadian dishes. Halifax also has what one native calls "lots of greasy spoons that aren't."

A note on Nova Scotia drinking laws: you can't have any alcohol on Sundays, except with meals.

Five Fishermen. 1740-44 Argyle Street. 902-422-4421. This popular downtown spot supplies its tables from its own fishing boat. The menu features smoked, poached, and pan-fried Nova Scotia salmon, baked or fresh Bras d'Or oysters, Digby scallops, lobster and sometimes shark and Arctic char. Dinner includes not only a salad bar but also complimentary steamed mussels or clams. A good value.

The Henry House. 1222 Barrington Street. 902-423-1309. This registered historic landmark houses two restaurants. Upstairs, the Henry House offers a solid beef and seafood menu ranging from bouillabaisse for two to Chateaubriand and carpetbag steak (stuffed with oysters). Downstairs at the Little Stone Jug, join in "Champlain's Feast" Tuesday through Sunday. This is an audience-participation reenactment of the communal meals the explorer organized to while away winter evenings at France's 1607 Nova Scotia outpost.

Fat Frank's. 5411 Spring Garden Road. 902-423-6618. Probably the most novel and ambitious menu in Halifax. The offerings change, but recent items on the fixed price menu include coquille of scallops and pears with leeks and Pernod, and veal kidneys with chanterelles. The desserts are equally interesting.

Halifax to Moncton

The *Ocean* leaves Windsor Station, Halifax, daily in the early afternoon. This is the beginning of a convenient schedule for those wishing to arrive in Moncton at dinnertime or in Montreal at the beginning of the next business day, but it means that you will be having your croissants in Quebec, should you detrain there, at a very early hour. No matter. For now, let's consider the first leg of the trip, from Halifax to Moncton, by way of Truro and the arm of land at the head of the Bay of Fundy which separates Nova Scotia from New Brunswick.

As you leave Halifax and the vast yards of the Canadian National, look on your right for the Mackay Bridge and the great container shipping docks which contribute so much to the local economy. Past the container port, the waters of the Narrows open up into the Bedford Basin, one of the largest protected harbors in the world. The CN tracks hug the Basin for several miles before entering into a region of lakes and coniferous forests which serves Haligonians as an inland summer resort area. To the east is the Waverley Game Sanctuary, spreading out beyond the town of Waverley where an 1861 gold rush increased the local population by twentyfold. Grand Lake, Shubenacadie Lake, and farther east, the Stewiacke River, all within a few miles of the route, are popular salmon fishing spots. Just beyond Elmsdale, the *Ocean* passes over the first iron railroad bridge in North America (1877). About an hour and a half after leaving Halifax, the *Ocean* arrives at Truro, a city of 13,000 people, nestled in a tamed, rolling countryside. Truro was an important Acadian settlement prior to the expulsion of that group in 1755 and was later resettled by Northern Irishmen and American loyalists. It is a railway hub and agricultural market town today.

The *Ocean* heads east and due north out of Truro through Debert, where there is a waterfowl sanctuary frequented by Canada geese migrating along the Atlantic flyway, and past Folly Lake, visible to the east (right) about 23 miles past Truro. The "Folly" was an early settler's attempt to farm an unproductive tract nearby. Looking to the other side of the train about 10 miles past Folly Lake, you will see Sugarloaf Mountain—not exactly a towering peak at 929 feet, but a good deal higher than the surrounding territory and a contributor to the gently handsome scenery of the Wentworth Valley region. Oxford Junction, up ahead near the 415-foot bridge over the River Philip, is a forest industry center.

The stop at Springhill Junction gives little indication of the proximity of the town of Springhill and its one-time importance as a coal-mining capital. Some Springhill residents might well wish to forget that era, punctuated by mine disasters that claimed hundreds of lives. The mines were closed after a 1958 calamity that took 76 lives. A Miners' Museum at Springhill, staffed by veterans of the coal pits, tells the story of 140 years of coal mining in the area.

The station at Amherst, the next *Ocean* stop, is a solid and attractive brownstone structure. Amherst, which before 1759 was an Acadian settlement, stands above the fecund Tantramar Marshes, another haven for wildfowl. You are now at the geographical center of the Maritime Provinces. Beyond Amherst, the tracks hug the outline of the Cumberland Basin, an arm of the Bay of Fundy, and enter into New Brunswick just before the town of Sackville. Beyond the border, but before Sackville, is the French Fort Beauséjour (right, on a rise of land), taken by the British in 1755. You can see the gun emplacements from the train.

Sackville stands on land reclaimed by the Acadians through a system of dikes. In fact, it was once called Tantramar, after the marshes. This name is a corruption of the French "tintamarre" for "thundering noise"—the sound that hundreds of geese make on takeoff. Sackville was a seaport until a 1920 landslide changed the course of the Tantramar River.

From Sackville, the *Ocean* makes a straight run through the lengthening afternoon shadows to Moncton. You'll see sheep farms interspersed with the dense pine forests that characterize so much of this province. To the left lie the flats surrounding the muddy, tidal Memramcook River, crossed just beyond the town of Calhoun. In another 10 miles the *Ocean* reaches the outskirts of Moncton, passing the campus of the University of Moncton (right). The station is part of a vast CN complex which lies along the Petitcodiac River. Change here (after an overnight stop) if you are heading on to the western New Brunswick cities of Saint John and Fredericton, reached via the picturesque, 153-mile Gull Route. (Trains leave Moncton daily in early afternoon).

Moncton

Moncton was first settled by Americans and named after a British colonel who defeated the French at nearby Fort Beauséjour. (His name was actually Monckton, but accurate spelling was a sometime thing in the eighteenth century, and the simplified version stuck.) Today, it is the most bilingual of all major population centers in the Maritimes—about 40 percent of all Moncton residents are Francophones. Evidence of the French presence is particularly strong at the University of Moncton, founded during the Acadian revival of the late 1800s as the College of St. Joseph. Classes are taught here in French, and there is an excellent museum spotlighting Acadian culture.

And Moncton is a railroad town. Canadian National is the largest single employer here. Many of the CN workers maintain diesel electric locomotives and other equipment at the company's Atlantic Region repair shops. The first railroad presence here was that of the 107-mile European and North

American Railway. This was absorbed into the Intercolonial Railway, built between Halifax and Quebec city between the 1850s and 1870s. Moncton was well-situated to serve as a major division point on this road, which later became part of CN's main east-west line. (The chief engineer for the building of the Intercolonial, by the way, was Sandford Fleming, who later made the preliminary surveys for what became the Canadian Pacific route across Canada.)

The Via station is a short distance from Main Street, the principal thoroughfare of downtown Moncton, but one whose commercial vigor has largely been sapped by shopping malls outside of town. But Moncton is small enough for the job of downtown revitalization to be manageable. During the next few years—the economy permitting—Main Street is due to be put back into shape. City Hall and the shopping complex anchored by the Hotel Beauséjour are early steps in the right direction.

Moncton is the site of an unusual natural phenomenon that occurs twice each day—the famed Tidal Bore of the Petitcodiac River. This may sound like a double-entendre, but this bore is really quite fascinating. The Petitcodiac is an arm of the Bay of Fundy, known for having the highest tides in the world. At low tide, the river is hardly more than a trickle through mud flats. But with the force of the powerful Fundy tides behind it, the resurgent flood of the Petitcodiac arrives as a virtual wall of water—a tidal bore. It can be a few inches high or as much as several feet if the moon is right (tides are usually more dramatic in spring and fall). The river will rise 25 feet in barely an hour, filling the mud flats. Watch the whole thing at Bore Park (see "Points of Interest") where you will be joined not only by fellow visitors but by natives who apparently never tire of the spectacle.

There are two general directions in which you should head to complete a tour of Moncton. One is towards the university by way of the Moncton Museum. Walk up Steadman Street from Main, and stop at the corner of Mountain road to visit not only the museum but the 1821 Free Meeting House, next to which are buried the original settlers of Moncton—Jacob Trites and a group of Pennsylvanians who arrived in 1766 and received a land grant from the British crown in 1778. The university is at the end of Archibald Street, which runs north off Mountain Road half a mile to the west. The Acadian Museum and art gallery are located here.

About a mile and a half west of the downtown center, off St. George Boulevard, is Centennial Park. This is a spacious retreat, an ideal place to stretch your legs after a train ride. But you'll be reminded of the railroad as you enter the park. Here is a Pacific Class steam locomotive, formerly in the service of Canadian National. Nearby, stuffed and mounted like the old locomotive, is a CF-100 jet fighter, linked to Moncton's prominence as a Canadian Forces base.

Moncton is your point of departure by bus or rental car for the Cape Tormentine ferry to Prince Edward Island. There are no longer any passenger trains on Prince Edward Island, but the beautiful island province deserves to be forgiven this failing. Contact Via for information on ferry-bus tours.

Points of Interest

Acadian Museum. Clement Cormier Building, University of Moncton. Tells the story of the French Acadian presence in the Maritimes since 1604 through art, photography, and artifacts such as clothing, tools, and farm implements. The gallery hosts changing exhibits by local artists. Open June,

July, August, Tuesday through Friday, 10 A.M.–8 P.M.; weekends, 1–5 P.M. September to May, Tuesday through Friday, 12:30–4:30 P.M., weekends, 2–4 P.M.; Wednesday evening until 9. Closed Monday.

Moncton Museum. 20 Mountain Road. 506-854-1001. The museum does a good job of supplementing its regular local history collections with special exhibits focusing on aspects of Moncton's past such as railroads, shipping, and the press. There is also a lecture and film program. Open daily in summer, 10 A.M.–5 P.M.; winter, 1–5 P.M. Tuesday through Friday, 10 A.M.–5 P.M. Saturday and 1–5 P.M. Sunday. Closed Monday in winter.

Bore View Park. Pleasant Street, off Main Street, at the Petitcodiac River. This is the best spot to observe the famous tidal bore. The times are posted daily, and it's a good idea to get there a few minutes in advance. In the summer, a piper in full Highland regalia heralds the bore's arrival, as do the seagulls which precede the rippling vanguard of Fundy water—over 28 million gallons in one hour—that fills the Petitcodiac flats.

The Moncton Central Business Development Corporation maintains a visitors' information center in an old CN caboose at the foot of Pleasant Street near Bore View Park.

Public Transportation

Moncton buses are operated by the Codiac Transit Commission. Call 506-855-2008 for information during business hours.

Lodging

Moncton has several hotels within a half mile or so of the train station. They vary in size and sophistication from the Beauséjour down to some that have been converted from houses. Nearly all are good values by any North American standard—from about $30 to $80 for a double.

Hotel Canadiana. 46 Archibald Street. 506-382-1054. A small hotel in a big white house—only 20 units, and a coffee shop on the premises, but very inexpensive and centrally located.

Midtown Motel. 61 Weldon Street. 506-388-5000. Near the station, with 14 rooms, 5 housekeeping units, and 2 one-bedroom suites. Fully equipped; individual heat and air-conditioning controls.

Hotel Beauséjour. 750 Main Street, P.O. Box 906. 506-854-4344. Moncton's best, at a reasonable price. Cheerful furnishings and nice touches like radio speakers in bathrooms. Very good service (including room service). Outdoor pool; 2 restaurants; lounge. A CN Hotel.

Restaurants

Moncton is a convention and trade show capital. Consequently much of the restaurant activity is centered around the hotels—in particular, the Beauséjour. Chez Jean-Pierre is the upscale French spot. It's on Toombs Street some distance from downtown.

Cy's Seafood. East Main Street just past the Tidal Bore Park (506-382-0032). A cheerful, busy restaurant specializing in fried or broiled plates of good fresh seafood. The fisherman's platter includes salmon, haddock, scallops, and shrimp. Excellent rolls and homemade pies. If you get a window table and are there at the right time, you can watch the bore come in.

The Windjammer. Hotel Beauséjour, 750 Main Street (506-854-4344). The flagship restaurant of Moncton's plushest hotel. Rack of lamb, steaks, lobster, coquille St. Jacques. *L'Auberge* is the Beauséjour's less ambitious dining room.

Moncton to Quebec

The *Ocean* lays over for about a half hour in Moncton before beginning the overnight run to Quebec. Its route, which roughly follows that of New Brunswick Route 126, leads away from the more thickly settled coastal area of the province into the evergreen forest which is more truly representative of the local topography. Like Maine, most of New Brunswick is a vast sea of conifers, partly through natural design and partly because of the silvicultural preferences of paper companies. One of nature's responses to forest monoculture is the proliferation of a creature called the spruce budworm, which has visited cyclical depradation on the timber industry on both sides of the border.

And the *Ocean* crosses rivers: the Cocagne, the Richibucto, the Kouchibouguacis, and the Kouchibouguac. Some 30 miles past Rogersville (the Brussels sprout capital of Canada), the CN tracks bridge New Brunswick's most famous river, the Miramichi, just east of the point where its two main branches converge. The Miramichi is home to a major population of Atlantic salmon and is the setting for the exploits of anglers such as baseball great Ted Williams, one of the few people ever to have taken over 1,000 of these elusive fish on the dry fly. Williams has released the vast majority of his catch, setting an example for everyone who pursues this beautiful and increasingly threatened fish.

The bridge over the Miramichi is more than 1,200 feet long. On the other side is Newcastle, where the famous press magnate Lord Beaverbrook grew up and is buried (his ashes are in a monument in the town square). It seems fitting that a newspaper baron should come from a province whose major industry is pulpwood. Leaving Newcastle, the *Ocean* takes an hour to cross the peninsular forestland which lies between Miramichi Bay and the city of Bathurst on Nepisiguit Bay—itself an arm of the Bay des Chaleurs. The Bay des Chaleurs, widening from the mouth of the Restigouche River to meet the Gulf of St. Lawrence, separates New Brunswick from Quebec's Gaspé Peninsula. It was first explored by Jacques Cartier, who gave it its name after a cold Atlantic passage. *Chaleur* means "warmth" in French.

During the summer, daylight lingers long enough for *Ocean* passengers to enjoy the views along the bay between Bathurst and Charlo. It is after 10 P.M. when the train reaches Campbellton, a port city of 10,000 people. The last battle of the Seven Years' War between England and France, a 1760 naval engagement called the Battle of the Restigouche, was fought here. (Americans are more familiar with this conflict as the French and Indian War, in which Britain gained control of French Canada.) There is a 20-minute layover at Campbellton. In another 10 miles the Restigouche is crossed, and the train reaches Matapedia, Quebec (no stop).

Although no connection is possible in Matapedia, and transfers at other Quebec points would involve inconvenient wee-hours layovers, we should point out that the *Ocean* has now reached track which also serves Via's daily *Chaleur* trains, which run from Montreal by way of Riviere du Loup and Matapedia to the coastal towns of the Gaspé Peninsula. This is a wonderfully picturesque route, following the outline of the Bay des Chaleurs; it is best taken directly from Montreal or Quebec.

The *Ocean* follows the Matapedia River across the Gaspé, reaching the St. Lawrence at Mont-Joli. The time is about midnight, so there is no view of the 40-mile-wide river. Now the tracks turn sharply to the southwest, following the river shore through Rimouski, Trois-Pistoles, and Riviere-du-Loup. This was the road of the French North American empire from the time of Cartier's first voyage, in 1534, until the British took all on the Plains of Abraham. The last word on the Great St. Lawrence or the shades of its explorers and fur-traders has belonged for the past hundred years to the American historian Francis Parkman. He writes here of the vision of Samuel de Champlain:

"On (the St. Lawrence's) banks, as he thought, was the true site for a settlement—a fortified post, whence, as from a secure basis, the waters of the vast interior might be traced back towards their sources, and a western route discovered to China and Japan. For the fur-trade, too, the innumerable streams that descended to the great river might all be closed against foreign intrusion by a single fort at some commanding point, and made tributary to a rich and permanent commerce. . . ."

Just before 5 in the morning, the *Ocean* reaches Levis on the river shore opposite that commanding point at which Champlain set up his "fortified post" in the year 1608. Here, magnificent upon its rock, stands the walled city of Quebec.

Quebec

The *Ocean* uses the Levis station on the south short of the St. Lawrence. This means that the final leg of your rail journey to Quebec will be made by ferry. (We'll take a closer look at current Via station arrangements and future plans in the following section as we move on to Montreal.) The ferry ride takes about 15 minutes and at sunrise offers a spectacular view of the old city—the same view that has fascinated voyagers arriving by the river route for 450 years.

The same view, but with quite a few different features. The skyline of modern Quebec is dominated by a structure which could easily pass for one of the mightiest chateaux on the Loire, but which has stood in its present form only since the 1920s. It is the Chateau Frontenac, a Canadian Pacific hotel begun in 1892 as part of the railroad's campaign to encourage transcontinental and even transglobal travelers to pause and enjoy the charms of Quebec. Built on the site of the official residence of the old French governors and named after the greatest of them all—Louis de Baude, Comte de Frontenac—the CP's chateau was built in a style which, though far more characteristic of late medieval France than her New World colony, has nonetheless managed to establish this great pile as the symbol of Quebec. This is perhaps the only city in the world whose visual trademark is not a government building, ancient ruin, or cathedral, but a hotel. But one look, and there can be no quarrel.

The history of Quebec itself begins at the foot of the promontory on which the Chateau Frontenac stands. Jacques Cartier arrived here in 1534 to find an Indian village called Stadaconna. By the time of Champlain's voyages in the early 1600s, all traces of this settlement had vanished, probably because of migration and tribal warfare. In 1608, Champlain founded Quebec as the headquarters of the French colonial enterprise in Canada. Those were the days when the St. Lawrence was thought of as a direct highway to China, a notion Champlain himself must have begun to suspect when he later tasted fresh water in Lake Huron. But the great river was the path to riches in the fur trade and to Indian nations starved, so the Jesuits and Recollets felt, for the gospel.

Thus Quebec became both staging area and bastion as Champlain's village grew, under the protection of a clifftop fortress of his design, to the status of capital of New France. As an outpost which literally commanded access to the rich Canadian interior, Quebec became the chief object of British military attention throughout repeated attempts to pry from the French their fur trade hegemony and northern flanking of New England. Success finally came in 1759 at the Battle of the Plains of Abraham, the rolling high ground which spreads northward from the heights of Quebec. New France became part of British North America, and Quebec was to be challenged militarily only once more—when American colonial forces unsuccessfully attempted to "liberate" the city in 1775. Since then it has waxed as an English and again as a French city (40 percent Anglophone in 1860, 4 percent today), and while it long ago lost economic ascendancy to Montreal, Quebec thrives as the seat of provincial government and center of an enormously successful tourist industry.

The ferry from Levis takes you close to the heart of the "Lower Town," as the part of the city below the cliffs of Cape Diamond is called. Here are buildings which date to the late seventeenth century, and which—particularly in the area around Place Royale—have recently been restored to present an excellent picture of what Quebec was like in the days of Frontenac and Bishop Laval. At the head of Place Royale stands the church of Notre Dame des Victoires (Our Lady of Victories), built in 1688. It is the oldest surviving church in North America. Champlain's second Quebec house stood on the site of the church.

Just a block from Place Royale is Rue Petit-Champlain, the oldest street in North America. Among its stone houses—now all restored, and mostly harboring shops, restaurants, and cafes—is the home built in 1684 for Louis Jolliet, explorer of the Mississippi River. The interior of the Jolliet House was not treated to the same degree of restorative accuracy as were many of the Lower Town structures, as it serves as the terminus for the funicular car which makes a quick, scenic ascent to the Dufferin Terrace at the summit of the cliff. Access to the upper city is also afforded by the perhaps too dramatically named "breakneck stairs" at the head of rue Petit Champlain. From here, head up Côte de la Montagne to the vicinity of the post office (statue of Laval in front) and Montmorency Park. In the park there is a monument to Louis Hebert, one of Champlain's original colonists who in 1618 was the first Canadian to harvest a crop of wheat. Think of Hebert as you ride through Alberta and pass trains made up of hundreds of grain cars bound for the port of Vancouver.

The buildings which stand opposite rue Port Dauphin, just to the north of Montmorency Park, constitute the Quebec Seminary and until the 1950s also housed the University of Laval. (At Laval's present campus, in the Pavillon Casault, are housed Quebec's National Archives, open to the public. The university is located in suburban St. Foy.) The warren of narrow old streets which stretches along the old ramparts between the Seminary and the Hotel Dieu (hospital) makes for one of the best, and least outwardly tourist-oriented, walker's neighborhoods in all of Quebec. This is a residential district, ancient and quiet; a visit in the early morning hours is especially pleasant. For detailed descriptions of its historic associations and a suggested pedestrian route, pick up a copy of the excellent *The Four Seasons in Quebec City,* available at most hotels, bookstores, and gift shops.

If you choose instead to leave the Lower Town by the funicular route, you will find yourself whisked up 180 vertical feet and deposited on the wooden planks of the Dufferin Terrace in the very shadow of the Chateau Frontenac. The terrace, which is only slightly older than the Chateau, was lengthened and widened to its present appearance in 1878 by the Canadian Governor General Lord Dufferin. It extends for 1,400 feet along the clifftop and connects with the Promenade des Gouverneurs, which leads past the brooding walls of the Citadel (see "Points of Interest") to the Plains of Abraham.

The beginning of the Dufferin Terrace, with the adjacent park of the Place d'Armes, makes an ideal point from which to strike out on explorations of the city within the walls (this is the only walled city north of Mexico) and, via Rue St. Louis through the main gates onto Grande-Allée, to the more modern and spacious quarters which lie beyond. On a warm summer night, though, the terrace is a destination in itself. If there is a good accordionist playing at the foot of the statue of Champlain, this is one of the most impossibly romantic spots on the continent.

To reach the Plains of Abraham, take either the Promenade des Gouverneurs, as mentioned above, or the Grand-Allée to any of the major streets which lead off to the left (right, if you are coming into town) in the vicinity of the Legislative Assembly buildings. The Plains, now a vast, 235-acre park, were the site of the fateful confrontation between invading Americans under British General Wolfe and the French defenders under their commander, Montcalm. Montcalm met the invaders in the open field with a numerically inferior force; the battle was over in 15 minutes, and Quebec was France's no longer. Both Wolfe and Montcalm were killed as they led their troops that day.

When visiting the Plains of Abraham, make sure you inspect one of the Martello Towers, built by the British in the early 1800s as part of the outlying Citadel defenses. Similar to the one in Halifax and others elsewhere in Canada, these pepperbox structures were designed to be virtually impenetrable to attackers but easily breached by cannonfire from behind if they ever were captured. The secret was the varying thickness of the walls.

Visitors to Quebec in 1984 will be able to enjoy the special celebrations being planned to commemorate the 450th anniversary of the arrival here of Jacques Cartier. In the summer, tall ships from all over the world will sail up the St. Lawrence in honor of the event. There is also an annual celebration in Quebec that is not associated with the commemoration of any event other than the triumph of the Canadian winter. This is the Carnival, a February unravelling of inhibitions that rivals New Orleans' Mardi Gras, including tobogganing, snow and ice sculpture, canoe races across the half-frozen St. Lawrence, torchlight skiing, and a citywide disposition towards eating and drinking and having a good time.

Points of Interest

The Citadel. Côte de la Citadelle. 418-694-3563 (Military Museum). The Citadel of Quebec, built in the 1820s, is a massive star-shaped fortress commanding the heights above the Plains of Abraham. It was used by the British as part of Canada's defenses until 1871, and still serves as headquarters for an active Canadian Forces regiment, the Royal 22nd. The principal attractions for visitors are the military museum (open only to participants in tours) and the Changing of the Guard, an intricate and impressive ceremony held daily at 10 A.M. from mid-June until the first Sunday in September. Times for visiting the museum and other buildings vary considerably throughout the year; call for information.

Ursulines' Museum. Donnacona. 418-694-0694. The Ursuline nuns arrived in Quebec early in the colony's history. At the convent's museum are kept a good collection of 17th-century furniture and household artifacts and a stunning exhibit of hand-embroidered church vestments, some nearly 300 years old. Also on display is the skull of General Montcalm. Tuesday through Saturday, 9:30 A.M.–noon, and 1:30–5 P.M.; Sunday, 12:30–5:30 P.M. Closed Monday.

Quebec Museum. Parc des Champs de Bataille (Battlefield Park). 418-643-2150. The permanent collection includes both traditional and modern work by Quebec artists; the country paintings are especially charming. Also ecclesiastical silver. Open daily, 9 A.M.–5 P.M.; Wednesday until 11 P.M.; Sunday, 10 A.M.–5 P.M.

Musee du Fort. 10 rue Ste. Anne, Place d'Armes. 418-692-2175. A very well-done sound and light diorama, giving a thorough history of the six sieges of Quebec. This is an excellent background for visits to the sites discussed. Narrations given alternately in English and French. Call for schedules.

In the Lower Town, there are informative exhibits at the Fornel House, 25 rue St.-Pierre, and the Musee de la Habitation, just off Place Royale. The 1724 Fornel House is also the district's interpretation center.

For information on Quebec attractions, contact the Tourism and Convention Bureau of the Communauté Urbain de Quebec, 60 rue d'Auteuil, 418-692-2471.

Public Transportation

Quebec's bus system is operated by the Transportation Commission of the Communauté Urbain de Quebec, 418-627-2351. The Commission is also the local franchisee for Gray Line Tours.

Lodging

In addition to the CP's landmark Frontenac and an assortment of luxury chain hotels such as the revolving-rooftop Loew's Concorde (those in the latter group are outside the old city walls), Quebec offers a good selection of small tourist homes, all government-inspected and varying in accommodations from simple to luxurious. Some have kitchenettes. The cost for a double will range from $25 at a modest tourist home to over $125 at a fine hotel. Among the several youth hostels is the **Auberge de Jeunesse de la Paix**, 31 rue Couillard, 418-694-0735, located in the quiet Seminary-Hotel Dieu neighborhood mentioned above.

Maison Marie Rollet. 81 rue Ste. Anne. 418-694-9271. The Marie Rollet could pass for either a small hotel or an imposing tourist home. It is well run, nicely furnished, and all rooms have private baths. Central location within city walls.

Chateau Frontenac. 1 rue des Carrieres. 418-692-3861. The great, oak-panelled Frontenac is nearing the end of its first century with reputation and facilities intact, thanks to recent renovations. If you are going to stay here, spend a bit more and reserve on one of the upper floors with a view. Restaurants; lounges, including Bar St. Laurent, commanding a fine prospect of the river. Tours of the hotel are given daily; call for schedules.

Restaurants

The French have little tolerance for bad food. This is as true in the New World as it is in the old, and the result is that there are a great many good places to eat in Quebec. This is especially true in the lower to middle price ranges, where tedium or worse is the hallmark of menus in other parts of North America.

There is classical French cuisine here, of course. But you will also find an abundance of French-Canadian dishes, born not only of local ingredients but of the need to stay warm, full, and ready to work hard in a cold climate. Pea soup, pork pie (*tourtière*), pork and beans, wild game preparations, and sugar pie—made with maple or cane—are a few of the standards of Quebec's hearty *cuisine bourgeois*. Apple tart (*tarte aux pommes*) is also a dessert mainstay.

The restaurants in the Old City are nearly innumerable; some, catering mostly to tourists, are a bit overpriced. Among the nicer spots are **Le Bilboquet** on Cote de Palais, a pleasant little night club where you can order French and Italian specialties as well as a good *entrecote* (steak) and fried potatoes; **Biarritz** on Rue Ste. Anne, excellent for an inexpensive lunch, and **Cafe Bonaparte** on Grande Allée, with moderately priced lunches outdoors and higher priced dinners inside. Grande Allée is the street to head for if you like sidewalk cafes.

Menus in smaller Quebec restaurants are not always bilingual, so try to familiarize yourself with some of the French names for popular dishes.

Aux Anciens Canadiens. 34 rue St. Louis. 418-692-1627. A bastion of French-Canadian cookery in a seventeenth-century house within the Old City walls. Pork and beans, ragout of pig's knuckles and meat balls, partridge, duck, salmon in puff pastry, *tourtière*. Lunch, which is considerably less expensive than dinner, may well last you all day.

Chez Rabelais. 2 rue Petit Champlain, Lower Town. 418-692-1503. Located at the head of the "breakneck stairs," this is one of the Lower Town's more ambitious restaurants. The bar is small, lively, and often noisy; try to reserve ahead and get a table in the main dining room. Veal scallop with apples and calvados; duck breast au poivre; fish pâté with watercress sauce. The steak tartare, prepared to order, is excellent.

Le Champlain. Chateau Frontenac. 418-692-3861. The main dining room of the Frontenac is a grand, formal space overlooking the Dufferin Terrace. The presentations are elaborate, and VSOP cognac is used for tableside flambés. Selections include a boneless quail stuffed with goose liver, sauteed with cream and Calvados; sweetbreads with chanterelles; Dover sole with filberts; and a generous appetizer portion of smoked Nova Scotia salmon that is among North America's best.

Quebec to Montreal

At this point in the westward trip along the St. Lawrence Valley, several new options open up. The traveler heading from Quebec to Montreal has three rail alternatives.

The first is to continue west on the *Ocean*. This entails a ferry trip across the river to the station at Levis where the *Ocean* departs for Montreal once each day, shortly after its early morning (about 5 A.M., as of this writing) arrival. The trip to Central Station, Montreal, takes just under four hours, and the south shore route is followed. The second option is to take one of

Via's "Rapido" trains, which employ the new LRC (Light, Rapid, Comfortable) equipment, paring the time on the south shore route down to two and a half hours. These trains also have reserved club car service with complimentary meal service and even a free newspaper as you check in for boarding. They leave from Via's station in suburban Ste.-Foy (north shore, west of Quebec), which is connected to the central city by a half-hour shuttle bus ride. Rapido trains cross the St. Lawrence shortly after leaving Ste.-Foy and follow the route of the *Ocean*. There are three trains on weekdays—early morning, early afternoon, and early evening. On Saturday, only the early morning train runs westbound, and on Sunday there is service only in the evening. The Montreal terminal is Central Station.

The third possibility is the most leisurely and, in the opinion of many, the most picturesque. This is the so-called "Frontenac Route" (not to be confused with the Frontenac Rapido), taken by rail diesel cars from Ste.-Foy to Windsor Station, Montreal. These are, at present writing, the only trains to follow the north shore route between the two cities. There are three each day Monday through Saturday in the early morning, mid-morning, and late afternoon; on Sunday, only the latter two trains operate. The trip takes approximately three and a half hours.

There are some changes coming: the big old station on St. Paul Street in downtown Quebec, closed back in the days of coal smoke pollution and now the center of a farmer's market, is scheduled to be reopened by Via within the next three to five years. When this happens, *Rapido* trains will come right into town rather than terminate and originate at Ste.-Foy, and they will follow the more direct north shore route once the track has been upgraded for high-speed LRC travel.

The south shore route currently used by the *Ocean* and *Rapido* trains takes you through flat terrain. Not long after leaving Levis the tracks enter pine woods that soon break up to reveal the characteristic farms, farmhouses, and church steeples of the St. Lawrence valley. The red tin roofs on the older farmhouses are a traditional Québécois touch, and you will often see them repeated on brand-new suburban homes. Not for nothing is the Quebec motto "Je me souviens"—I remember. The sole major city along the route is Drummondville, an industrial center and gateway to Estrie, or the Eastern Townships, quiet farming communities that spread to the south between here and the U.S. border. At Drummondville is Le Village Québécois d'Anton, a re-creation (complete with costumed townspeople) of a typical Quebec village of the nineteenth century.

About 15 miles outside of Montreal near the Beloiel Station (no stop), the train crosses the Richelieu River, called the "River of Death" by early French settlers because it so often bore the canoes of the murderous Iroquois. Just before the river on your left stands Mt. St. Hilaire, one of the eight Monteregian Hills that rise in the outskirts of Montreal. These are exposed volcanic intrusions, hundreds of millions of years old, uncovered by the erosion of sedimentary layers. There is a fine nature center at Mt. St. Hilaire that is well worth a day trip from Montreal.

The *Ocean* and *Rapido* enter Montreal via the turn-of-the-century Victoria Bridge, terminating at Central Station, adjacent to Place Bonaventure. (For Montreal information, see trip 3.)

The route along the north shore of the St. Lawrence followed by the diesel rail car *Frontenac* trains winds out of Ste.-Foy on Canadian Pacific track. As with the south shore route, the terrain is essentially flat, although there are hills in view to the north (right side of train) throughout much of the trip, pretty towns and villages, and several dramatic bridgings of streams feeding into the St. Lawrence. Batiscan, some 60 miles out of Ste.-Foy, is a small village grown up near the site where, in 1609, Samuel de Champlain and a party of Hurons agreed on a loose "alliance"—in effect, the securing of the Hurons' friendship by French promises to help them against their foes, the Iroquois. The unfortunate legacy of this policy for New France was the securing of a merciless and implacable enemy.

At a point roughly halfway between Quebec and Montreal, the *Frontenac* reaches Cap-de-la-Madeleine, where to the south can be seen glimpses of one of Quebec's premier religious shrines—the circular basilica of Notre-Dame-du-Cap (Our Lady of the Cape). This is the gateway to Trois-Rivières, reached after crossing the broad St. Maurice River. Now a busy pulp mill city of 100,000 people, Trois-Rivières was the site of the earliest Quebec ironworks. Just past the city, the St. Lawrence widens. This portion of the river is known as Lake St. Pierre. It is fed by numerous fast streams that gather force in the snows of the Laurentians, nearly 100 miles to the north. The *Frontenac* takes a wide swing around the north shore of Lake St. Pierre, through farmland and pine forest which both once comprised the old seigniories of New France. These were quasi-feudal domains granted by the crown to entrepreneurs who would promise to sublet them to farmers (the "habitants" of Quebec lore) and assist in their development. At Terrebonne, about 10 miles outside of Montreal on the Rivière des Mille-Iles, the mills, storehouses, and other stone buildings of one of these seigniories have been extensively restored. After Terrebonne, the *Frontenac* crosses Ile Jesus and Rivière des Prairies and enters Montreal by way of its northern and western suburbs. The terminus, as we noted before, is Windsor Station, a handsome Romanesque structure on Peel Street just 3 blocks west of Central Station. (For Montreal information, see trip 3.)

The *Canadian* (lounge-observation car at the rear) negotiating a mountain pass near the British Columbia-Alberta border in winter.

3. The *Canadian*: Montreal to Vancouver

Montreal to Toronto

The *Canadian* is one of the half-dozen most famous trains in the world. By virtue of the magnificent scenery along its route and the great distance which it covers, it ranks with the *Trans-Siberian* and the *Empire Builder*, with South Africa's *Blue Train* and the Australian *Indian Pacific*. As a monument to the sheer force of will, the legend of the route's construction—of the building of the Canadian Pacific Railway—will probably never be equalled, no matter how far into space we travel.

The *Canadian* leaves Montreal late each afternoon. Watch out for confusion over nomenclature; the Montreal-Toronto leg of the journey is listed in some timetables (notably, *The Official Railway Guide*) as the *Bonaventure*. The train is the same, though, and you will board at the signboard marked *Canadian* in Montreal's Central Station. If you have reserved sleeping accommodations, you will be given a daynighter seat between Montreal and Toronto and may occupy your bedroom or roomette after the Toronto layover.

There are actually three types of service between Montreal and Toronto, all of which follow the same route along the St. Lawrence River and Lake Ontario. The first, of course, is the daily *Canadian*. There are also several other trains of conventional consist (including an overnight run, the *Cavalier*) and five LRC *Rapido* trains daily. The *Rapidos* make the trip in about four and a half to five hours; the others take between five and a half and seven hours.

Back before the days of Via, the main line route followed by the *Canadian* headed nearly due west through Ottawa, the Canadian capital, and along the Ottawa River valley towards Sudbury. Ottawa is no longer on the main line, although it is connected with Montreal by six trains daily, including three *Rapidos*. There is also no rail diesel car service between Ottawa and Sudbury, at which point connections can be made with the westbound *Canadian*.

The route of the *Canadian* and her sister trains follows Canadian National right-of-way out of Central Station, along a route pioneered by the Grand Trunk Railway as one of Canada's first in 1856. The narrow waterway which the train crosses shortly after leaving the station is the Lachine Canal, completed in 1848. Although no longer used, the canal was the St. Lawrence Seaway of its day, extending river navigation by circumventing the dangerous Lachine Rapids. The tracks loop through the industrial neighborhoods to the south of Montreal, with Mount Royal visible to the right, before crossing the canal once again and heading west towards the confluence of the Ottawa and St. Lawrence.

The first stop is Dorval, an "intermodal" station of sorts given the proximity of Dorval Airport. Just past Dorval a brief view of the St. Lawrence opens up on the left; then, the *Canadian* passes through Ste. Anne de Bellevue, home of Macdonald College and its famous Morgan Arboretum, and crosses the Ottawa River just south of the point where it widens at the lovely Lake of Two Mountains. Coteau is the last stop in the province of Quebec; soon after—barely 45 miles from Montreal—the *Canadian* enters Ontario, which it will not leave for a day and a half. Surprising as it may seem, nearly half of the *Canadian*'s entire route—over 1,400 miles—lies within this vast province.

The first Ontario stop is at Cornwall. About a half hour out of Cornwall, looking to the left, you will catch your first glimpse of the St. Lawrence Seaway, completed in the late 1950s as a joint United States–Canadian effort to extend the head of navigation for huge seagoing tankers and freighters to the ports of the Great Lakes. The Seaway does not stay in view for long, although the river can be seen in the middle distance at various points between here and Kingston. Most of the view along this stretch is of rolling farmland and apple orchards, their tailored, well-cultivated appearance reminding us that this is one of the longest-settled parts of Canada and—along with the settlements of Quebec and the Maritimes—*was* Canada before the railroad broke through to the prairies and beyond. Take notice also of the tidy limestone stations at several of the stops along the way. They are among Canada's oldest.

Brockville calls itself the "City of the 1,000 Islands." The Thousand Islands begin to dot the St. Lawrence to the south and west of here; they are accessible by the Via-CN cruise boat *Gananoque*.

The largest city along the route between Montreal and Toronto is Kingston (population 60,000), a one-time shipbuilding center that now serves as an important stop along the St. Lawrence Seaway. It is at Kingston where, amidst the tangle of the westernmost of the Thousand Islands, the St. Lawrence could be said to have its source at the northeastern tip of Lake Ontario. A good view of the lake cannot be had until the train reaches the vicinity of Cobourg, some 90 miles farther along the route. What you see of the lake—and there are frequent vistas to your left after Cobourg—will depend on what train you are on and the time of year. The *Canadian* reaches this point only after 9 P.M., but the lake is beautiful in the light of the long Ontario summer evenings. As that light dwindles, you will see the lakeside farmland beyond Cobourg give way past Oshawa to the sprawling suburbs of Toronto. Don't be too quick to leave your seat, even after the Guildwood stop—the sprawl goes on and on, until at last taller buildings appear (here, the scene is more spectacular at night). The *Canadian* does not reach Union Station until after 10 P.M. (For arrival time of other Montreal-Toronto trains, consult schedules.)

Toronto

Toronto is the largest city in Canada, and now the preeminent city in the nation's commercial life. While Montreal grew into middle age on its banking and shipping laurels and Vancouver and Calgary grew sassy as primary-industries boom-towns, Toronto just sat on its lakeside and grew, enjoying not only its advantages as a port but also the favors of everyone in Canada—and not a few people and businesses from throughout the world—who felt, for whatever reason, that it was time to move to a new location. Toronto was so many people's new location that it *became* a new location, transcended its old image as "Toronto the Good" (without becoming noticeably bad), and shucked the role of beef-and-turnips foil to Montreal's veal with morels. It grew not only in size but in sophistication to the point that "cosmopolitan" is the hands-down winner for most hackneyed local term. All of this has happened in a scant 20 years.

First impressions may be deceiving, at least for the railroad passenger. Toronto's Union Station is a somber, pillared exercise in sun-never-sets-on-the-British-Empire architecture, and though busy, it appears a little gray and worn at the heels. But if you walk out onto Front Street, or head down into the corridors which lead past the Royal York Hotel into a vast underground shopping mall, the new Toronto readily shows its face. The skyscrapers commence almost directly across from the station, and the most striking of the lot looks gold not because of any mirror tricks but because it *is* gold: there are 2,500 ounces of the stuff dusted into the glass.

Underground Toronto spreads beneath a complex of bank towers in an area roughly bounded by Front, Bay, York, and Adelaide Streets, but even beyond Adelaide, there is a tunnel leading to City Hall. Thus it is possible to walk nearly halfway across downtown (the subway trains, of course, take you much farther) without having to emerge into the outer atmosphere. The perceived advantages of this setup depend on the weather, which can be pleasant as often as not. You may just want to take to the streets.

Yonge Street (pronounced "Young") is the main downtown thoroughfare, forming the dividing line between the "east" and "west" designations prefixed to the names of crosstown streets. It begins just a block east of Union Station near the O'Keefe Center (performing arts) and extends through mid- and uptown Toronto to become—if we count its continuation as Highway 11—the longest street in the world. Like many older downtown streets, Yonge shows a bit of wear and has attracted its share of video arcades and cut-rate stereo shops, although anyone holding Yonge up to U.S. standards of downtown deterioration will be pleasantly surprised. But what really sets Yonge Street apart is the fact that it provides two blocks of frontage for Eaton Centre, probably the bravest challenge to the suburbanization of shopping ever mounted anywhere. Eaton Centre (the anchor is a five-story flagship of Eaton's, the big Canadian department store chain) was loosely modeled after the vast Galleria in Milan, as is most strikingly apparent in its enclosure beneath a barrel-vaulted glass roof. Beneath that roof are more than 300 shops on three levels, as well as restaurants, an 18-theater "Cine Plex", and even 60 sculpted Canada Geese suspended in mock flight above the main plaza. At certain points in the Centre, it is possible to get a view of all three levels at once, with glass elevators soaring up and down among them. This is mercantile grand opera, likely to overawe even the most strident critics of shopping malls.

The other most talked about building (buildings, actually) in downtown Toronto is the new City Hall, located in Nathan Phillips Square at Queen Street W. and Bay Street. It is one of those landmark '60s structures, like the Sydney Opera House or Eero Saarinen's TWA terminal in New York, in which an attempt was made at bringing a touch of lilt and lyricism to the International Style. Viljo Revell, its Finnish architect, saw Toronto City Hall as the "Eye of Government"; more prosaically, the twin-curved towers and ellipsoid Council Chamber call to mind two hands cupped around a clamshell. The complex is interesting, though, for the way in which its aspects constantly change in accordance with the onlooker's point of visual reference. Free tours of City Hall are conducted daily; call 947-7341 for information.

For all that has been said and written about the new City Hall, you may well find the old one more interesting. It stands on Queen Street, between Bay and James, just a block from its austere and aloof replacement. Designed by Edward J. Lennox in a fine interpretation of the Richardson Romanesque style and built between 1891 and 1899, the old City Hall features rich polychromatic stonework, a bold clock tower, and wonderfully intricate detailing—especially in the medieval monsters that surmount the main portals, and the assortment of grotesque yet whimsical faces that leer out at passersby from the capitals of the front columns. The story has it that these are the caricatures of public officials who refused to grant the architect additional funds for completion of the building. This is an appealing tale, but it presents three problems: first, the building was finished; second, the faces don't look much like real people; and third, why would there be funds available for such fanciful ornamentation if project costs had already been overrun? In any event, we are fortunate that this quirky old pile survives as a courthouse, and was not razed when the new City Hall was built.

Another treat for fans of the Romanesque Revival is the main building of the Ontario government complex in Queen's Park at the head of University Avenue. Designed by Richard Waite and completed in 1892, this is a massive, cathedral-like structure. In front of it stands a statue of John A. Macdonald, founding father of confederation, first prime minister of Canada, and—remember this as you head west on the *Canadian*—chief political visionary of the transcontinental railway.

Toronto, though, is less a city of buildings than a city of neighborhoods. Even in commercial districts, a residential character is preserved and night-time desolation avoided by zoning regulations that provide for apartment space to be included in new business towers. But it is the survival of older, low-rise neighborhoods as viable residential quarters within a few blocks of the busiest downtown streets that really sets Toronto apart from so many large cities. The distinctive architecture of these neighborhoods is often the gothic brick cottage, separate, attached in pairs, or in rows—a British transplant that took hold even in a nation awash in lumber.

Toronto has for years been a magnet for immigrants and many of its neighborhoods are ethnic. The Chinese, West Indians, and some Portuguese have settled in the blocks around Dundas Street west of Spadina Avenue. East of downtown, many East Indians make their homes around Gerard and Coxwell streets. Around Dufferin and St. Clair streets is an Italian neighborhood, and the street signs along Danforth Street east of Yonge are printed in Greek as well as English. There has also been a strong recent influx of Southeast Asians, most of whom live on the east side of the city.

One neighborhood with a reputation extending well beyond Toronto is Yorkville, centered around Bloor Street W. and Bay Street. In the late 1960s, the warren of little alleys and sidestreets behind Bloor was counterculture territory, its coffeehouses the haunts of American expatriates and young Canadians who had migrated to Toronto to see what was happening. A lot has happened since; the area has grown with the income and tastes of the postwar generation. Yorkville is now a district of upscale bars and boutiques, cheerful and expensive, and you won't recognize it if you last passed through in '67. (For a taste of the old days, stop in at the Cafe La Gaffe, on Kensington Avenue just off St. Andrew Street in the lively Kensington Market district.)

Toronto is the second largest theater capital in North America, and third largest in the world behind London and New York. There are no fewer than 40 troupes headquartered here, and Toronto is on the itinerary of dozens and dozens of road shows. The Toronto Symphony (Roy Thomson Hall; all seats within 120 feet of the stage) and the National Ballet of Canada (O'Keefe

Center) also contribute mightily toward making this city the cultural capital of Canada.

This is a lakeside city, but one that had grown so large that it was in danger of losing touch with its waterfront. This tendency has been reversed by two developments, Harbourfront and Ontario Place, which make good use of their Lake Ontario shore locations and of an assortment of pre-existing structures. Harbourfront, a 92-acre site on Queens Quay W. almost directly south of Union Station, comprises artisans' workshops and stalls, art galleries, a theater, restaurants, and a yacht basin, as well as a huge antiques market. Ontario Place is farther west along the harbor, out past Exhibition Stadium and the grounds of the Canadian National Exhibition—the oldest annual event of its kind in the world, held each year from mid-August to Labor Day. Ontario Place (open from mid-May through Labor Day) is a playground for children and adults, featuring the world's longest water slide, free concerts in an open air amphitheater, an "Adventure Playground" where kids can put their imaginations to work on castoff items, and a cinema (in the building that looks like a big golf ball) with a six-story screen for showing lifelike IMAX films.

Predating these manmade attractions are the Toronto Islands, lying just offshore near Harbourplace. Ferries leaving from the foot of Bay Street (367-8193) take visitors out to the formal gardens, quiet parks, tennis, cycling, and canoeing facilities, and beaches that make the islands a favorite Toronto retreat.

Toronto will be 150 years old in 1984, a milestone which will be celebrated by the summertime arrival of tall ships from throughout the world and dozens of other special events. For much of that century and a half, Toronto was an important town in Ontario, or at best a big city in Canada. It's safe to say, though, that by now it has taken its place among the great cities of the world without having lost its accessibility or its unpretentious charm. Toronto knows when to be showy and when to be staid.

Points of Interest

CN Tower. 301 Front Street W. 416-360-8500. Toronto's preeminent landmark is, at 1,815 feet, the tallest freestanding structure (no guy wires) in the world. It was built for Canadian National Railways radio communications. Glass elevators take you to the 1,465-foot level, where a little hand-held audio device describes the sights. On a clear day, you can see the mist rising from Niagara Falls. Open daily, 10 A.M.–10 P.M.

Royal Ontario Museum. 100 Queen's Park Crescent. 416-978-3692. The recently expanded ROM is particularly strong in two areas: its "Gallery of Evolution," explaining—with mounted specimens—the logic behind life's diversity; and its thorough sequence of exhibits illustrating the development of civilization in the Near East, Egypt, and the Mediterranean Basin. There are also special shows of high quality. Open Monday through Saturday, 10 A.M.–8 P.M.; Sunday, 10 A.M.–6 P.M.

Art Gallery of Ontario. 317 Dundas Street W. 416-977-0414. While art of all schools and periods is represented here to some degree, the two standout collections are of Canadian art in a separate wing; and of the sculptures of Henry Moore—the world's largest assemblage of Moore's work, given by the sculptor to the museum. Open Tuesday through Sunday, 11 A.M.–5:30 P.M.; Wednesday and Thursday, until 9. Closed Monday. Behind the Gallery in a small park stands the Grange, built in 1817 and the oldest brick house in Toronto. The elegant Georgian residence is open Tuesday through Sunday, noon–4 P.M.; Thursday and Friday, 6–9 P.M. Closed Monday.

Ontario Science Center. 770 Don Mills Road. 416-429-4100. Most of the 800 exhibits at the OSC were designed with the Museum's motto "Please Touch" in mind, so that the result is a lively combination of education and fun. The Exploring Space Hall with its astronomy exhibits is fascinating. Open daily, 10 A.M.–6 P.M.

Casa Loma. 1 Austin Terrace. 416-923-1171. Between 1911 and 1914, Sir Henry Pelliatt poured $3 million into this 98-room castle, a place so extravagant he was forced to sell it *before* the Depression. One of the better North American manifestations of the perennial castle fantasy. Open daily 10 A.M.–4 P.M.

Metro Toronto Zoo. Highway 401 at Meadowvale Road. 416-284-8181. Within little more than a decade, this 700-acre zoo (3,500 animals) has become one of the world's best. The reason is that each creature is allowed maximum freedom in as natural an environment as possible; there are six separate areas set up to represent the world's great climatic zones. Don't miss the train ride. Open daily, 9:30 A.M.–4:30 P.M.; last admissions at 3:30 P.M.

The Metropolitan Toronto Convention and Visitors Association is at the Eaton Centre, 220 Yonge Street, Suite 110, Box 510, Toronto M5B 241. Call 416-979-3143 for information, or check any of the video-display "Tele Guide" terminals around town.

Public Transportation

Toronto's system of buses, trolleys, subways, and commuter trains is among the best in North America. The Toronto Transit Commission (484-4544, daily, 7 A.M.–11:30 P.M.) runs the subways, buses, and trolleys; the clean, rapid subways are especially recommended. Union Station is one of the main stops—look for the red and yellow "TTC" logo. Be careful with the tokens; they look like dimes. GO trains connect Toronto with suburban points; in fact, they run as far as Hamilton. Call 630-3933 for information between 7 A.M. and 11 P.M. daily, and 8 A.M. to 11 A.M. Sunday.

Lodging

There are dozens of Toronto hotels within either a short walk or subway ride from Union Station. Most of the chains—Hilton, Westin, Ramada, Sheraton—are represented, along with independent establishments. One of the more interesting hotels in the expensive price range is the small, European-style Windsor Arms on St. Thomas Street near Yorkville (416-979-2341). At the opposite end of the price scale, there is the Toronto International Hostel at 223 Church Street (416-368-0207). Comfortable housekeeping suites are available for weekly rates at the Inn Toronto Apartments, 95 Pembroke Street (416-862-1064). For information and reservations at any Toronto hotel, call Accommodation Toronto at 416-596-7117.

Rates for double accommodation in Toronto hotels range roughly from $45 to $150.

Royal York. 100 Front Street W. 416-368-2511. Few North American hotels are more convenient to a major train station. The CP-owned Royal York, at 1,600 rooms still the largest hotel in the British Commonwealth, is connected by walkways beneath Front Street with Union Station. Unlike many older downtown hotels, the Royal York is a first-class, well-maintained, full-service establishment. Five restaurants, a half dozen bars, night clubs. The Royal York is a comfortable and convenient alternative to slicker modern hotels; for the train traveler, the location can't be beat.

Chelsea Inn. 33 Gerrard Street W. 416-595-1975. Part of the Delta chain, the 10-year-old Chelsea is centrally located 2 blocks north of the Eaton Centre. It is popular with tour groups. Pool and saunas; several restaurants. Jazz on weekend afternoons. No smoking floors are an interesting Chelsea innovation.

Neill-Wycik College-Hotel. 96 Gerrard Street E. 416-977-2320. If you're staying in Toronto in the summer, this is one of the better bargains. From the end of May to about September 1, this college dormitory turns into a comfortable midtown hotel. A cafe and restaurant on premises serve all meals, or choose a room with communal kitchen and bath or a housekeeping suite. Weekly rates available. Sauna, weight room. Call well in advance to reserve.

Restaurants

There is one restaurant for every 725 residents of metropolitan Toronto. This is a phenomenon which came about quite as rapidly as the transformation of the city from a staid, closed-on-weekends provincial capital to the lively and diverse metropolis it is today. These two developments are closely linked, for in fact it is the popularization of the ethnic cuisines brought by the new immigrants which has added so much to the number and variety of Toronto restaurants.

A note on locations: there is no single "restaurant district" in Toronto, downtown or otherwise. Instead there is a liberal scattering of 4,000 institutions throughout the metropolitan area. All the major concentrations are accessible by public transportation. You'll find the chic bistros of Yorkville near the intersection of Queen's Park Avenue and Bloor Street W.; Chinatown along Dundas Street west of Beverley Street; Greek places in the East End along Danforth Street; East Indian spots around Gerard and Coxwell Streets; and Italian restaurants around Dufferin and St. Clair Streets. The Chinese-Jewish establishment of **Ginsberg and Wong** is on McCaul Street, around the corner from the Art Gallery.

In Toronto of all places, the idea of limiting restaurant recommendations to a mere handful seems sheer folly. Think of the spots listed here as a representative introduction, rather than a culling of the best.

Sam Woo BBQ. 476 Dundas Street W. 416-591-9312. A cheerful and very inexpensive little spot one flight down from Chinatown's busy main street. In addition to tasty barbecued pork and duck, Sam Woo offers an extensive assortment of noodle dishes and at least a half-dozen preparations of *congee*, a rice gruel which can be flavored with meat or fish. No liquor, but plenty of complimentary tea.

Bangkok Gardens. 18 Elm Street, in the Elmwood Building. 416-977-6748. Thailand offers one of the world's subtler and more complex cuisines, and this restaurant does it justice with ingredients flown in from Bangkok and dishes like coconut chicken soup, oyster beef noodles, and curries flavored with lime leaves, basil, and the ginger-like kha root. The menu employs little pepper pod symbols to indicate chili content—order an extra beer for each pepper. Special banquet menus for two or more; after-theater supper. Try the mango ice for dessert.

Le Provençal. 23 St. Andrew's opposite Windsor Arms Hotel. 416-924-3721. A cozy French restaurant popular with Toronto residents for 25 years. Lobster bisque with Armagnac, quail pâté, whole salmon baked with fennel, rack of lamb dijonnaise, Grand Marnier soufflé. A four-course table d'hôte menu is offered, with choice of two entrees; otherwise all selections are a la carte. The wine list is adequate if a little expensive. Attentive service. If you reserve in advance ask for a table in the room with the fireplace.

Toronto to Winnipeg

North and west of Toronto, the *Canadian* travels through some of the most remote—and, to the builders of the railway, the most forbidding—territory in any of the sub-arctic or sub-alpine regions of North America. It comes upon the traveler quite suddenly, because the northern suburbs of Toronto and the rolling resort country of the Muskoka Lakes, pass by in darkness, with dawn breaking over the barren outskirts of the nickel-smelting city of Sudbury and nothing beyond but forests and lakes.

But before following the *Canadian* west, we should return briefly to Toronto for a look at several of the other rail routes which terminate in Canada's largest city. In addition to the lines running north and east to Ottawa and Montreal, Toronto is also served by the *Maple Leaf*, which departs three times each day for Niagara Falls and Amtrak connections for New York, and by several trains each day—some of them in the LRC *Rapido* class—to London, Windsor, and Sarnia, Ontario. At Windsor there are connections to Detroit and at Sarnia to Port Huron, Michigan, with Amtrak service to Chicago from these points.

Toronto is also the southern terminus of a non-Via line, the Ontario Northland, which runs due north to Timmins, Cochrane, Kapuskasing, and Moosonee, the last stop a James Bay seaport. The ON trains are considered by Canadian rail guide author Bill Coo to be Canada's "most luxurious," and in fact one hears no end of praise for the Northland's meals and accommodations. As for scenery, it is if anything a distillation of all the lonely boreal splendor encountered to the west along the route of the *Canadian*.

The *Canadian* itself leaves Toronto each day about midnight, and before daybreak traverses the Georgian Bay territory explored by Champlain and Brule in 1615. North of Parry Sound—the very earliest point at which you will see daylight even in summer—are the first glimpses of Georgian Bay, a vast appendage of Lake Huron. Also near Parry Sound is the point at which the *Canadian* enters the right-of-way of the Canadian Pacific Railway, on which it remains for the rest of its transcontinental journey. Between here and Sudbury the tracks cross at least half a dozen rivers; the French River connects Lake Nipissing (to the east) with Lake Huron and, thus, formed an important part of the old fur trade routes.

The *Canadian* reaches Sudbury about 7:30 A.M. and lays over for a half-hour. Sudbury, founded in 1883 after railway links made vast local ore discoveries profitable, remains a center of the nickel industry as well as the center—thanks to mining, slag dumping, and acidic smoke—of some of the least appealing terrain on the continent. Nearly everyone who looks upon the outskirts of Sudbury is reminded of the moon. The people who live here may well feel the same way, but they find it preferable to unemployment. It is one of those sad tradeoffs of industrial development, which reforestation and acid rain awareness are just beginning to redress.

West of Sudbury, the great expanse of the Canadian Shield arches across the northern shores of Lake Superior towards the prairies. The Shield is the armor plate of northern Ontario, Quebec, and much of the Northwest Territories; it is bedrock, at or near the surface, formed during the Precambrian era more than 600 million years ago and remaining relatively geologically stable ever since. Outcroppings of the Shield are everywhere along the *Canadian*'s route, as is its surface legacy of muskeg swamps and running or standing water. You are likely never to see so much water, so many named and nameless ponds and lakes, as in northern Ontario. One-quarter of the world's fresh water is said to be in this province. This expanse of rock and water and birch forest seemed such an insurmountable challenge to the builders of the Canadian Pacific that a number of the road's early promoters favored the adoption of an American route south of the Great Lakes over the idea of slogging through muskeg and blasting through rock to build the Ontario section.

But slog and blast they did, all through the early 1880s. Muskegs swallowed whole locomotives; men were blown to bits while backpacking nitroglycerine (dynamite was invented in Europe while the road was under construction) to the bastions of intransigent rock. At one point, a mile of track was laid at the cost of $700,000. Three dynamite factories set up north of Lake Superior turned out a ton of explosives a day; eventually $7.5 million in nitroglycerine and dynamite were consumed. In the telling of the tale of the CPR most of the glamor usually accrues to the Rocky Mountain episodes—but the laying of the line across the shield took just as much sweat and courage, and it would not have been surprising had the last spike been driven in Ontario instead of at Craigellachie.

The 8 A.M. departure from Sudbury marks the beginning of the first full day of travel on the *Canadian*, a long day spent in a wilderness of lakes and birches broken only by small settlements such as Roberts (note the pretty little wooden church); Sultan and Kormak with their pulp mills; and Nemegos with its single house and wooden-bench train station (the station doesn't *have* a bench; it *is* the bench). There is a brief layover at Chapleau, the first sizeable town west of Sudbury; here you may visit a small museum and an old steam locomotive in Centennial Park.

About 10 miles past Chapleau is the divide between the Hudson's Bay and Lake Superior watersheds. As you travel along this section, watch for beaver lodges, loons, and an occasional browsing moose. All three of these quintessentially Canadian creatures are common in these forests and lakes. The town of Franz, reached in mid-afternoon, is the junction point with the Algoma Central Railway, whose "Black Bear" passenger train runs through here on its way from Sault Ste. Marie to Hearst, 100 miles to the north.

The next layover—a scant 10 minutes—is at White River, a pulpwood center whose sleepy appearance belies the fact that thousands of gold-mining claims have recently been staked here. The lowest temperature ever recorded in Canada did not occur in the Yukon or on Baffin Island, but at the weather reporting station in White River: 72 degrees below zero, Fahrenheit, not counting wind chill.

From White River the *Canadian* strikes west for Lake Superior. The vast inland sea comes into view around 6:30 P.M. between Heron Bay and Marathon. From here, through Terrace Bay and Schreiber, then to Nipigon and south to Thunder Bay, the tracks hug the shore. Building this section was one of the most challenging feats of engineering and labor for the CPR.

While it was under construction, lake steamers linked eastern Great Lakes ports with the railhead at Thunder Bay. During ferocious Lake Superior storms, the waters of Gitchee-Gumee have made a similarly nautical experience out of the shoreline rail run, with waves cresting over tracks and train. (Don't worry; this is a mercifully rare occurrence.)

Thunder Bay, the northern terminus of shipping on the Great Lakes (there is storage capacity here at the "Lakehead" for 100 million bushels of grain), is reached (westbound) at about half past 12 in the morning. There is a 35-minute layover, which you may as well sleep through. If you wake up at around 7, the *Canadian* should be just coming into Kenora, Ontario, on the northern shores of the Lake of the Woods. The views are still of forests and lakes, still characteristically Ontario, but not for long. Less than an hour out of Kenora, the train crosses into Manitoba, and soon the Canadian Shield makes its last breach of the surface. The forests begin to thin out; grassy, open spaces appear. Nothing in word or picture could prepare you for the sheer spaciousness of what lies ahead. Of his first arrival at this point as part of a rail survey crew in 1872, George Monro Grant wrote, "As you cannot know what the ocean is without having seen it, neither in imagination can you picture the prairie."

At speeds of 90 to 100 mph, the *Canadian* closes the distance between daybreak and Winnipeg. The grain elevators clip by. Once across the Red River floodway, you are in the suburbs of Manitoba's capital and the first of the prairie cities built by agriculture and the railroad.

Winnipeg

Winnipeg is one of the most pleasant surprises among North American cities. It is that rare thing—a city neither in the throes of any great boom, nor sliding into economic lassitude; it has no need of any vast publicity apparatus to tell the world that it is "coming back," since it never went anywhere all that bad in the first place. It is prosperous; it is clean; it gives a good account of itself culturally. It is, in short, a place of remarkable equilibrium.

This wasn't always so. For a delirious period in 1881 and 1882, Winnipeg was the focus of an exercise in greed and black comedy called the great Manitoba land boom. As the CPR drove its trunk line and spurs westward, speculators whipped up interest in towns both real and imaginary, said to be slated for rail connections with the east, as well as in lots in Winnipeg itself. The fever caught and values escalated by the day—even at times by the hour. Lots changed hands sight unseen, the prices rising with each transaction. It mattered little that some of the "towns" in question would never see a railroad; everyone had faith in the prairie metropolises that would rise in short order on land that they had been clever enough to buy when it was fallow. Winnipeg, of course, did have a future—but not one that rated downtown frontage at $2,000 a foot in 1882.

The house of cards came down in April of 1882, victim of a devastating flood (many "choice lots" were seen to be potential lake bottoms), new CPR land sale policies favoring actual settlers over speculators, and a belated return of common sense following the failure of an expected Edmonton boom to get off the ground. The legacy of the crash was not only a slew of ruined paper tycoons, but also a soberer city better fit for sound and deliberate growth. Today it has 600,000 citizens—two-thirds the population of Manitoba—and serves as a central exchange point for goods and services between eastern and western Canada. As long as people eat wheat, there need not be another 1882 in this city.

The *Canadian* arrives in Winnipeg in mid-morning and stays for three and a half hours, time enough for a good walk around the central city or a bus tour of the greater metropolitan area. Reservations for Rouge Line double-decker sightseeing buses can even be made on the train before arrival at Winnipeg.

The Winnipeg Via depot is the old Canadian National station on Main Street at the foot of Broadway. The site is near the confluence of the Red and Assiniboine Rivers, where fur traders used to rendezvous long before any permanent settlement was made. Unlike many cities which began life near a riverbank and spread to the horizon, Winnipeg has maintained a vigorous downtown neighborhood near the source of its roots. Consequently, the train station is as well-located as any in Canada—a few blocks in one direction from the main business district and in the other from the impressive provincial legislative building (follow Broadway to Memorial Boulevard).

The real history of settlement in the Red River Valley and the Winnipeg area began with an experiment by Thomas Douglas, the Earl of Selkirk, in bringing colonists to establish farms on lands obtained from the Hudson's Bay Company, of which Selkirk was governor. The emigrants started arriving in 1812. The colony survived early clashes with the Northwest Company, archrival of the Hudson's Bay traders, the most notable of which took place in 1816 near the house called Seven Oaks (see "Points of Interest"). Absorption of the Northwest Company by Hudson's Bay settled this score, but the Selkirk colonists never achieved great numbers. By the mid 1870s, when the first rail link with the United States was begun, Winnipeg was still a fur-trading, river-oriented city of barely 6,000 people.

The other great influence on local settlement patterns was the *Métis*, descendants of French fur traders and Plains Indians who shaped their lives around the semiannual buffalo hunt. Their leader, by the late 1860s, was the firebrand Louis Riel, who spurred the founding of Manitoba in the temporal breach between the Hudson's Bay Company's relinquishing of its land and the new Confederation's assumption of control. But the incorporation of Manitoba into the Dominion of Canada did not go smoothly. Riel was involved in armed conflict with the central government in 1870 and again in the Saskatchewan rebellion of 1885, for the latter of which he was hanged at Regina. He lies buried in the graveyard of St. Boniface Cathedral in the old French neighborhood of the same name which lies across the Provencher Boulevard Bridge more or less directly behind the Via station. Here, also, is the grave of Jean-Baptiste Lagimodière, the first white settler of the Canadian Northwest (the old name for the prairie provinces) to have brought his family along.

The French-speaking Métis and the Scottish Selkirk pioneers were the original European ethnic groups of Winnipeg, but they were followed by many others. With the obvious exception of Toronto, no other Canadian city has grown to be such a mosaic of languages and cultures—a fact which is due, no doubt, to the success of the railroad in attracting immigrants to the prairies and the tendency of some to congregate in the city rather than disperse over the surrounding farmland. There are healthy congregations of Ukranians, Italians, Poles, Scandinavians, and numerous other nationalities here, as is revealed not only by a sampling of Winnipeg restaurants but by a stopover in the city during its biggest annual event: Folklorama, a week-long August festival of ethnic song, dance, food, and crafts which draws half a million visitors to 40 national pavilions spread all over town. Just about the only comparable extravaganza on Winnipeg's social calendar is the Folk Music Festival, held each July in Birds Hill Park.

Winnipeg is a large but walkable city, with a good variety of neighborhoods and attractions accessible by foot or reliable public transportation. One nice touch that helps to put Winnipeg on a human scale is the absence of downtown expressways, which can so often intimidate native and visitor alike and make the core city little more than a backdrop for auto traffic. Heading from the station, an exploration of Winnipeg might well begin with a turn to the right towards Portage Avenue, the main downtown shopping street. You'll have to go underground to cross the intersection of Portage and Main Street; here you'll find the subterranean shopping mall of Winnipeg Square, with connections to office towers and hotels.

On the other side of Portage Avenue, 2 blocks from its intersection with Main Street, is the neighborhood of Albert Street and McDermot Avenue. This is an old warehouse district now beginning to brighten with boutiques and cafes. It culminates in Market Square, where a number of the older commercial buildings have been renovated and where, on weekends in summer, there is an open-air food and crafts market. During July and August, guided tours of Market Square focusing on history and architecture leave from the Museum of Man and Nature. Phone 204-985-5287 for information. Just beyond Market Square, the area between Princess and Main Streets as far as Rupert Avenue comprises Winnipeg's small Chinatown.

If you head up Broadway past the legislative building (especially beautiful at twilight, when the dome is illuminated) and turn left on Osborne Street, you will cross the Assiniboine River into the chic district of shops and restaurants called Osborne Village. The Village extends as far as Stradbrook Avenue; turn right here to reach Wellington Crescent, a handsome residential street that follows a horseshoe bend in the Assiniboine. The tongue of land on the other side of the river is called Armstrong Point. It also contains one of Winnipeg's more comfortable neighborhoods, with elm-shaded streets made for quiet strolling. You may reach it by following Wellington Crescent to the next bridge, crossing the river and turning right onto West Gate. These are the last of the eastern-style upper-middle-class neighborhoods you will see on your trip west; beyond here, residential architecture becomes more distinctly western and contemporary, less historically eclectic.

In a broader sense, the East itself could be said to end at Winnipeg. With the forests of the Shield left behind, the scale of the land itself changes. Past Winnipeg the word "old" strikes a shallow bottom of meaning: in these places, the white man's world really began only a hundred years ago, with the arrival of the Canadian Pacific Railway.

Points of Interest

Museum of Man and Nature. Manitoba Centennial Centre, 190 Rupert Avenue. 204-956-2830. This is one of the best museums of its kind in North America and is easily worth a half-day's visit. Seven galleries containing specimen displays and wonderfully detailed dioramas cover ecological and ethnographic subjects ranging from the life of the Arctic and sub-Arctic to contemporary life in the prairie provinces. Of special interest is the reconstruction of the 17th-century fur-trading ship *Nonsuch* in an authentic harbor setting and the re-creation of a street and shop interiors of turn-of-the-century Winnipeg. Open daily. Hours vary with the seasons. Call ahead for schedules.

Winnipeg Art Gallery. 300 Memorial Boulevard. 204-786-6641. Respectable European and international collections are supplemented by a fine representation of Canadian art (including works of the Group of Seven) and the largest collection of Inuit (Eskimo) art in the world. Restaurant; film and concert series, including "Jazz on the Roof" in summer. Open Tuesday through Saturday, 11 A.M.–5 P.M.; Sunday, noon–5 P.M. Closed Monday.

Lower Fort Garry National Historic Park. Selkirk, Manitoba, 20 miles north of Winnipeg. 204-949-3600. Take a cruise on the M.S. *Lady Winnipeg* up the Red River from the Louise Bridge in downtown Winnipeg to visit Canada's only restored stone fur-trading fort. Lower Fort Garry was built in the 1830s by the Hudson's Bay Company. Today, costumed guides welcome visitors to the "Big House" and many outbuildings, explaining the operation of the fort when it was the center of Manitoba's social and mercantile life. Everything is in perfect period detail right down to the craftspeople working at their trades. Grounds open daylight hours all year; buildings open daily, 9:30 A.M.–6 P.M., mid-May to mid-October. Phone 204-669-2824 for cruise information.

Living Prairie Museum. 2795 Ness Avenue. 204-832-0167. A most unusual urban park, consisting of unplowed, virgin, tall-grass prairie. The 26 acres and 160 species of native plants are a reminder of what the vast Canadian plains were like before the white man arrived. Guided trail walks leave from the interpretive center, open 10 A.M.–6 P.M., July and August. The park and trails are open daily all year.

Assiniboine Park Zoo. Corydon Avenue west of Shaftsbury Boulevard. 204-888-3634. Set in Assiniboine Park, the zoo features over 1,000 animals, including an extensive Canadian collection: bison, wapiti (elk), and other indigenous northwestern creatures. Tropical house with birds, monkeys, reptiles; also children's farm zoo. Open daily, 10 A.M.–sunset. (Children's zoo June through Labor Day only.)

Seven Oaks House. Rupertsland Avenue, east of Main Street. 204-339-7429. The oldest habitable house in the province, Seven Oaks was built in 1851 near the site of the 1816 battle between fur traders and Selkirk colonists. The house is filled with authentic furniture and personal items of a century ago. An interesting point: there are no nails in Seven Oaks. It's held together with wooden pins. Open 10 A.M.–5 P.M. on weekends, mid-May to mid-June; daily (same hours), mid-June to Labor Day.

Prairie Dog Central. St. James CNR Station, 1661 Portage Avenue. 204-284-2690. A 36-mile excursion via an 1882 4-4-0 steam locomotive and turn-of-the-century coaches. A must for rail fans. Departs from St. James station twice each Sunday, June through September.

The Winnipeg Convention and Visitors Bureau is located on the second floor of the Convention Center, 375 York Avenue. Call 204-943-1970 for information (204-944-3777 evenings and weekends).

Public Transportation

Winnipeg Transit runs the local buses, including the free downtown "Dash" service, weekdays, 11 A.M.–3:30 P.M. Bus routes have names, not numbers. For schedule and fare information, call 204-284-7190.

Lodging

Thanks to the central downtown location of the Via station, many good Winnipeg hotels are just a short walk or taxi drive away. The **Knappen House Youth Hostel** is at 210 Maryland Street (204-772-3022); other establishments range in price from $35 to $120 or more for double accommodations.

Charterhouse Hotel. 330 York Avenue. 204-942-0101. A small, centrally located hotel with restaurant, lounge, and outdoor pool. Prices are quite reasonable for a downtown spot but full services are offered, including room service and color cable television.

The Fort Garry. 222 Broadway. 204-942-8251. Winnipeg's chateau-style *grande dame* is less than a five-minute walk from the Via station. An excellent value for a hotel of its caliber, the Fort Garry offers fine dining at the Factor's Table, a cozy lounge, a night club/disco, and a wood-panelled old Canada atmosphere. Spacious suites available at reasonable rates.

Westin. 2 Lombard Place (Winnipeg Square, near Portage and Main). 204-957-1350. The top end of the scale in price and modern style. The Westin is a new, high-rise hotel, very much in keeping with the tone of the chain's other properties. Pool; several restaurants, including one on the roof with a terrific view; dancing. This is the part of Winnipeg least distinguishable from the rest of the late-20th-century world.

Restaurants

You expect ethnic diversity among the restaurants of Toronto, Montreal, and Vancouver, but in Winnipeg it comes as an unexpected bonus. Of 650 eating places in the city, some 130 specialize in ethnic cuisine. You'll find Chinese and Italian spots, of course, but also Ukranian, Czechoslovakian, Greek, East Indian, Hungarian—the list goes on and on. But don't overlook the native specialties, such as Manitoba Goldeye (a local fish, served smoked) and buffalo meat. The latter is nicely prepared as a ragout, served in a puff pastry shell, at the **Factor's Table** in the Fort Garry Hotel.

King's Palace. 260 King Street. 204-943-1077. Perhaps the best Chinese restaurant on the prairies, and unbelievably inexpensive. Boiled whole pickerel with ginger and green onions; fried crab with garlic and black bean sauce; also a superb whole cut-up chicken in ginger-vinegar-soy sauce. How about "miscellaneous ingredient soup?"

Tee Pee. 236 Edmonton Street. 204-942-7491. An American Indian-owned and operated restaurant featuring native Indian cuisine updated and seasoned to modern tastes. Still, the ingredients are authentic components of Plains Indian cooking—pickerel, buffalo (in steaks or stews, or served as the dry, finely-ground pemmican), wild rice (excellent in pilaf or the Tee Pee's unique dessert flan), quail and Arctic char. Entertainment nightly in adjoining cafe; open for lunch and dinner, except dinner only in summer.

Restaurant Dubrovnik. 390 Assiniboine Avenue. 204-944-0594. A Yugoslavian restaurant—but with more conventional continental items as well—located in a comfortable old house on the Assiniboine River a few blocks from downtown. (In fact, you can dock your boat out back.) The menu includes schnitzel, trout and salmon, borscht, pork tenderloin with dates and walnuts; the homemade bread is very good.

Winnipeg to Regina

Before you head straight off across the prairies to Regina, consider your options. Winnipeg is the southern terminus of the *Hudson Bay*, which embarks three days each week upon the 1,055-mile journey to Churchill on the southern shores of Hudson Bay. The trip takes a day and a half and follows a northwesterly route on Canadian National track into Saskatchewan before looping back to The Pas, Manitoba, and bearing northeast into total wilderness. For a good part of the way it is the conventional wilderness of lakes, rivers, and forests, but this eventually gives way to interminable muskegs set in permafrost and finally to the "barren lands" on which nothing grows except scant boreal mosses. Churchill, an old Hudson's Bay Company outpost, is a wheat-shipping port when the ice is out between July and October. In fact, wheat transport was the reason for building the railway, which was completed in 1929. It is perhaps more famous, though, for the visits of polar bears to its outskirts and even its downtown streets during their spring and fall migration seasons.

A trip to Churchill and back will add the better part of a week to a cross-Canada train journey and is recommended if at all feasible. Call Via or inquire at any major station regarding package tours, which are offered each summer.

The *Canadian* leaves Winnipeg for Regina daily in early afternoon. The trip takes you right into a prairie sunset, through the territory across which CPR General Manager William Cornelius Van Horne vowed to lay 500 miles of track during the summer of 1882. To the amazement of everyone concerned, Van Horne and his crews very nearly succeeded. This accomplishment was a tremendous morale-booster, even though the hard parts of the job—laying track through the mountains and the Shield—still loomed ahead. There was, of course, no "easy" part to building the CPR, although tackling this level stretch of prairie may have seemed such by comparison.

In its primeval state (and primeval, here, means only a hundred years ago before the CPR came through), the land now characterized by wheat fields and grain elevators was tall-grass prairie. Just as the first plains farmers had to turn the sod and break the prairie earth, so too did the railway builders have to prepare the ground for laying track. To do this, teams of horses dragged scrapers that cleared vegetation and leveled the roadbed, which had to be built up to a grade of 4 feet above the level of the surrounding terrain and ditched for 20 yards on each side. This was a precaution against snowdrifts. The scraping and grading crews followed the survey engineers and, according to Pierre Berton in *The Last Spike*, sometimes even caught up with them. Still farther behind were the track-laying crews themselves, working with tremendous speed and precision. Serving the whole operation were supply lines, with Winnipeg as their main base depot, which rivalled in volume and efficiency those of any military campaign ever mounted. Of all the statistics Berton offers in his book, perhaps the one which tells the most about the magnitude of this enterprise has to do with feed for the CPR's horses. At one point, 4,000 bushels of oats had to be distributed to the draft teams *every day* along a 150-mile section of track construction.

On they bore, and on bears the *Canadian*. Portage la Prairie, 55 miles from Winnipeg, carries in its French name a reminder that this was the staging ground for the early 18th-century explorations of the plains and Rockies made by Pierre La Verendrye and his sons. It was here that the first homestead in western Canada was established in 1872. Also at Portage La Prairie is the Fort la Reine Museum and Pioneer Village, which exhibits reconstructions of early settlers' structures as well as the office car used by Van Horne during that heroic 1882 track-laying season.

Brandon, Manitoba, reached in late afternoon, was a CPR town from the start. It stands where it does because the company built its station where it did, and the reason for the station's location is that the original proposed site, 2 miles to the east, was adjacent to land held by a settler who demanded twice as much money for it as the CPR offered. The company's agent told him to keep his land. He did and watched it wither in value as Brandon blossomed 2 miles away. On a small scale, greed goes unrewarded.

By nightfall, the *Canadian* is in Saskatchewan. Well before Broadview, it has also passed from the First Prairie Plain to the Second, a distinction not readily apparent to the observer in these days of universal prairie cultivation, but one which was defined by the original vegetation of the region. The First Plain is the tall grass prairie. On the Second, the shorter mixed grasses prevailed. Farther west still, in the lee of the Rockies, is the Third Prairie Plain—the short-grass prairie where rain is minimal.

About 10 P.M., the *Canadian* reaches Regina, the small, handsome prairie city chosen in 1882 as the capital of the North West Territories, and which has been the provincial capital since Saskatchewan joined confederation in 1905.

Regina

The first passenger train steamed into Regina on Aug. 23, 1882. Eleven days earlier, the name of the new territorial capital had been chosen by Queen Victoria's daughter, Princess Louise, wife of Canadian Governor General Lord Lorne. In choosing the Latin word for "queen," she was naming the place for her mother, but the choice was not a popular one. Still, no one seemed too interested in continuing to call the capital by its old name, Pile o'Bones. The suggestion for *that* improbable moniker had come not from a princess but from the Indians' old practice of dumping buffalo bones at a certain spot in a local creek.

When that first train pulled into Regina, carrying W. C. Van Horne's private car in which the formal dedication of Regina as territorial capital was made, Easterners on board who had never been out to the end of the track must have been struck by the prairie isolation of the new townsite. (So were a good many Westerners, who had thought the more protected and hospitable slopes of the Qu'Appelle Valley, northeast of Regina, were a better location for the capital. They hadn't taken into account Edgar Dewdney, lieutenant governor of the North West Territories, who was speculating in land at Pile o'Bones.) A hundred years later, Regina seems like a man-made oasis, a contrived but welcome bastion of people and things in the middle of a limitless golden expanse of spring wheat. Part of the illusion is due to the presence of trees. The citizens of Regina have planted hundreds of thousands of trees—more, probably, than there are between here and Winnipeg in one direction and Calgary in the other.

The Via station in Regina is on Saskatchewan Drive, at the foot of Rose Street. This location does not seem so much in the middle of things as is the case in Winnipeg, nor does the station seem as busy. Nevertheless, you are within only a few blocks of the busiest parts of downtown (though it won't look that way at the *Canadian*'s scheduled arrival time) and most of the better hotels. Before you leave the station, take note of the tile inserts depicting buffalo in the wall of the main concourse, and the art deco chandeliers.

The hotels suggested below are all on Victoria Avenue, which puts any of them within easy walking distance of the city's principal attractions. Scarth Street, which crosses Victoria Avenue and runs alongside Victoria Park, has been blocked between 11th and 12th Avenues as a pedestrian mall. There is a farmers' market here on Thursdays and Saturdays in summer. At the head of the mall, on the corner of 11th Avenue, stands the mansard-roofed old City Hall, which now houses the Plains Historical Museum (see "Points of Interest," below) and Globe Theater. Just across 11th Avenue is the entrance to Cornwall Centre, Regina's successful attempt at keeping the retail trade downtown. Cornwall Centre is a 94-shop complex, reminiscent in spirit if not in design of Toronto's Eaton Centre (of course, Eaton's is the anchor store) and quite capable of convincing Easterners that this hub of the prairie provinces is up to far more than dealing in feed grains and farm implements. While you're at the Centre, be sure to take a look at the columned facade of the old Bank of Commerce building, which was imaginatively incorporated into the central enclosed courtyard of the new structure.

Plenty of North American cities have shiny new downtown shopping galleries and pedestrian malls: these things do not by themselves make for stopovers on long train trips. But you will look far and wide for a city anywhere that has anything so vast, ambitious, and defiant of description as Wascana Centre. This is a project which could only have been undertaken in a place blessed with plenty of land and plenty of foresight. Wascana Centre is 2,300 acres of open space in the heart of Regina, surrounding a man-made lake (the result of the dredging and impoundment of none other than Pile o'Bones Creek, "Oscana" in the Cree language) and incorporating the city's premier cultural, political, and educational institutions. The fact that such a diverse collection of civic furniture is not out of place in a park is a tribute to the thoroughness and careful implementation of the Wascana master plan, which has now run approximately one-fifth of its 100-year course.

Set aside the better part of a day—at the very least—for an exploration of Wascana Centre. There are guided tours via double-decker bus in summer (inquire at Wascana Place, the main visitor center on Wascana Drive, 306-522-3661), but the place is made for walking. Wascana Place is a good starting point; nearby is the marina, offering boat rentals in summer, and the inlets and islands of Wascana Waterfowl Park. On the other side of the lake are the Saskatchewan Centre of the Arts, where internationally prominent performers regularly appear; the main campus of the University of Regina; the Diefenbaker Homestead (see "Points of Interest," below); and the imposing buildings of the Saskatchewan legislature. The main legislative building was dedicated in 1912. The principal material used in its construction is Manitoba Tyndal stone, in which tiny prehistoric fossils are often visible. Thirty-four kinds of marble were used in the interior of the building. Inside, visit the Assiniboine Gallery with its portraits of prairie Indian chiefs; on the grounds

The *Canadian* crosses the prairies in springtime.

facing Wascana Lake, don't miss the formal gardens, Trafalgar fountain, and the impressionistic statue of Louis Riel.

As Regina had been chosen as the capital of the North West Territories, it followed that it should also be the headquarters of the quasimilitary force entrusted with the maintenance of law and order throughout that vast expanse. This was the Royal North West Mounted Police, now the Royal Canadian Mounted Police. Regina is still the R.C.M.P's home town, and a visit here ought to include the short bus ride along Dewdney Avenue to the force's training center and museum (see "Points of Interest"). In addition to the reinforcement of some and the dispelling of other myths and romantic notions about the Mounties, a tour of the headquarters is instructive in the patterns of settlement of western Canada. Americans will learn the differences between the ways Canada's frontiers and their own were formed: up here, there was more land and a far smaller number of people to live on it. The very word "frontier," in fact, is not so musty and dated, once you get north of Edmonton and Saskatoon, as it is in Butte or Cheyenne, and the railroad, stretching out from Regina to its meeting with the mountains west of Calgary, is still very much the lifeline it became just a hundred years ago.

Points of Interest

Museum of Natural History. Albert Street and College Avenue. 306-565-2815. A broad array of exhibits, with a strong focus on the ecology of western Canada. Before you go in, note the frieze around the building depicting 300 native animal species. The museum features animal dioramas arranged according to habitat groups. See the largest lake trout ever caught—a Saskatchewan giant that weighed 102 lbs. Open daily, 9 A.M.–9 P.M., May 1 to October 1; rest of year, 9 A.M.–5 P.M. weekdays, 10 A.M.–6 P.M. Saturday, Sunday, and holidays.

Plains Historical Museum. 1801 Scarth Street (old City Hall). 306-352-0844. The location, across the street from Cornwall Centre, makes these reminders of prairie life at the turn of the century all the more poignant. Here are reconstructions of a bachelor's sod house and small town schoolroom; also Indian artifacts, early surveying tools, and the goods that once lined the shelves of Main Street shops. Open Monday through Friday, 11:30 A.M.–5 P.M.; weekends, 1–5 P.M.

Diefenbaker Homestead. Lakeshore Drive, Wascana Centre. (No telephone.) The late John Diefenbaker, prime minister of Canada during the late 1950s and early 1960s, lived in this house in Borden, Saskatchewan, as a boy at the turn of the century. Typical of pioneer homesteads of the period, it was moved to Regina in 1967 and furnished with family possessions. From the looks of the place, one gathers that Mr. Diefenbaker's boyhood was rigorous yet serene. Open summer, 10 A.M.–8 P.M.

Centennial Museum. At R.C.M.P. Depot Division, Dewdney Avenue West. 306-359-5838. The Mounties have been stationed at Regina for just over 100 years, and this extensive collection of R.C.M.P. memorabilia—papers, photographs, firearms, uniforms—tells much of the story of western Canada. Also on the grounds are the 1883 R.C.M.P. Chapel, Regina's oldest building, and training facilities open to tour groups on weekdays. There are dress parades Monday through Friday, outdoors in summer, indoors in winter. Museum open 8 A.M.–8:45 P.M., June 1 through Sept. 15; 8 A.M.–4:45 P.M. rest of year.

The Regina Tourist and Convention Bureau is at 2145 Albert Street; call 306-527-6631 for information.

Public Transportation

The Regina Transit System runs city buses. For routes and schedules, call 306-569-7777.

Lodging

As was noted above, Victoria Avenue is downtown Regina's hotel row. All of the places listed below are within 6 to 10 blocks of the Via station; prices range from $35 to $80 and up for double accommodations.

Plains Motor Hotel. 1965 Albert Street (just off Victoria Avenue). 306-527-8661. Small, inexpensive hotel at the southwestern corner of the city center, just 4 blocks from Wascana Centre. Air conditioned; licensed dining room.

Regina's Westwater Inn. 1717 Victoria Avenue. 306-527-0663; toll-free reservations 800-665-8818 or 800-268-8993 in Canada, 800-528-1234 in United States. Part of the Best Western chain. Special quarters available for non-smokers. Room service, color cable television, restaurant, and lounge.

Hotel Saskatchewan. Victoria Avenue at Scarth Street. 306-522-7691; toll-free reservations 800-667-5828. The lone representative of the traditional hotel style in Regina, the Saskatchewan faces Victoria Park and offers comfortable, recently renovated rooms at reasonable prices. Full services, cozy lounge, good restaurant. A welcome destination after a late-night arrival.

Restaurants

As throughout western Canada, the first suggestion that comes to mind is to concentrate on beef and local freshwater fish, simply prepared. But Regina has grown sufficiently to support several decent "continental" establishments, as well as an ethnic restaurant or two (the Copper Kettle, a steak house at 1953 Scarth Street, has "Greek night" on Saturdays).

Meika's Kitchen. 1810 Smith Street. 306-522-6700. The chef was trained at the Cordon Bleu, and offers a French-accented dinner menu and a good selection of soups, salads, and light entrees at lunch. Reservations suggested for dinner.

Ranch Room. Hotel Saskatchewan, Victoria Avenue at Scarth Street. 306-522-7691. The setting is prairie-baronial, the service formal; this is the spot for a Big Night Out before getting back on the train (watch the clock). The prime rib is good, if not cut quite thick enough, and the wine list perhaps as extensive as any in town.

Regina to Calgary

In addition to daily evening departures of the *Canadian* for Calgary and points west, there is also one train each day operating between Regina and Saskatoon, Saskatchewan. This train, which originates in Winnipeg, leaves Regina in the early evening on its four-hour, 163-mile trip to Saskatoon, at which point (after an overnight layover) the traveler can make daily morning connections for Edmonton, Alberta. Edmonton is the eastern terminus of Via's *Skeena*, which follows a route whose scenic attractions are rivaled only by those along the way of the *Canadian* west of Calgary. The *Skeena* travels nearly a thousand miles to the northern British Columbia port of Prince Rupert. For a fine description of the route, see Bill Coo's *Scenic Rail Guide to Western Canada.*

Because of the way the *Canadian*'s schedule works, you aren't going to see much between Regina and Calgary (the same would be true if you were traveling eastward). Forty miles west of Regina is Moose Jaw, where there is a half-hour scheduled layover. Moose Jaw was once the premier rail center of Saskatchewan, and made a serious bid to become the province's capital when the old territorial status ended in 1905. Today it is the site of one of Saskatchewan's four Western Development Museums, and a market town serving nearby farms and ranches. Swift Current, 110 miles farther across the dark prairie, started life as a tent village from which, in the spring of 1883, CPR track-laying crews began their push to the Rockies. It is still important as a railroad division point and market center for grain and dairy products, and as the site of a major federal agricultural research station.

Beyond Swift Current to the north lie the Great Sand Hills, formed from sedimentary deposits left behind as the glacial lake which once covered this area receded. Some of the dunes here advance up to 10 feet per year; the advancing edges of the largest dunes reach 50 feet in height.

The region south of Maple Creek, the last Saskatchewan stop on the *Canadian* route, was mistakenly named the "Cypress Hills" by early French Canadian fur traders. The dominant vegetation here is lodgepole pine, not cypress or jack pine (*cyprès* in French), but the area is also known for a variety of plants and animals more commonly associated with the higher elevations to the west. The reason they prevail here is that during the last ice age, the height of the plateau which the Cypress Hills occupy was an "island" not covered by the surrounding glacier.

Before daybreak, the *Canadian* is in Alberta. Medicine Hat is a center for light manufacturing and trade in agricultural products as well as the tapping of an enormous natural gas resource. According to Bill Coo, its name was coined after an altercation between Blackfeet and Cree, during which an ill wind blew the Cree medicine man's hat into the Saskatchewan River.

If you are awake at dawn on the *Canadian*, watch the subtle change in terrain west of Medicine Hat. You are approaching the Third Prairie Plain, higher, drier, and more rolling than the land that lies to the east, and more suited to the traditional Alberta pursuit of cattle ranching than Saskatchewan-style wheat farms—although there is still plenty of wheat grown in Alberta, as the stark elevators marked "Alberta Wheat Pool" will remind you. About 30 miles past Brooks, the CPR tracks begin to form the northern boundary of the Blackfoot Indian Reserve. Crowfoot Creek, which the tracks cross, is named for the great Blackfoot chief who struck a bargain for more land with the CPR after threatening to halt construction across the reserve. Could he have? He might have made a valiant try—but he had already taken into account not only the moderating advice of Father Albert Lacombe, his missionary friend and mentor, but also the question posed to him by North West Mounted Police Commissioner A.G. Irvine: could all the men in the world stop the Bow River from running?

Thirty miles east of Calgary, on a clear day, you can look west to the end of the Third Prairie Plain and the end of all the Canadian plains: the great spine of North America, the Rocky Mountains, finally comes into view. What would occur to you now, if you were on one of those CPR track-laying crews in the spring of 1883? Just from the looks of them, a hundred miles distant, the breaching of those mountains seems impossible to this day.

First, though, there is another vertical improbability to be dealt with, after all these flat expansive miles—the high-rise oil town of Calgary, where the *Canadian* arrives about 8 A.M.

Calgary

If you were to take a map of North America and draw a line from Houston, up through Dallas, over to Denver and north to Calgary, you would have strung together the continent's four pre-eminent oil towns—or, in today's jargon, "centers of the energy industry." All of them share a certain brashness, a rough vivacity that can border on abrasiveness if you take it too seriously. Calgary, the newest and the northernmost of these monuments to our appetite for hydrocarbons, is probably the easiest to like.

Calgary started life as a North West Mounted Police post in 1875. Like Fort Edmonton and Rocky Mountain House farther to the north, Calgary was also an outpost of the Hudson's Bay Company. The fort and trading post were in those days located on the east bank of the Elbow River, near where it joins the broader and swifter Bow. That changed when the tracks of the Canadian Pacific reached Calgary in 1883, and the company located its station on the west bank. Lock, stock, and barrel, the settlers and tradesmen who had gathered near the Mountie post pulled up stakes and moved across the river to be near the depot. Even the fort was relocated to the west bank of the Elbow.

Although the idea of Calgary-as-boomtown may seem to be a recent one, the settlement's growth in those first years following the arrival of the railroad paralleled in swiftness and enthusiasm its development as an oil capital nearly a century later. In the early days, it was Calgary's position as a market town and shipping depot for cattle ranchers that fueled its expansion. The discovery that Alberta rested upon vast underground deposits of petroleum, natural gas, and oil-bearing tar sands, though, is what created the city that we encounter today. Like the metropolises of Texas, Calgary has worked at retaining and enhancing the cowboy mystique it developed during its ranching days, and has applied it to the vastly different but no less glamorous business of mining money from the ground. You can best understand this juxtaposition while looking in a shop window at a pair of $500 lizard-skin boots.

Even if you are not planning an overnight stop in Calgary, the two-and-a-half hour overnight layover scheduled for the *Canadian* after its 8 A.M. westbound arrival will give you plenty of opportunity to look around and see what all this prosperity has wrought. The first thing a lot of train travelers do when they reach Calgary is to head for the top of the Calgary Tower, directly adjacent to the Via station on 9th Avenue, for a 360-degree view of the city and distant Rockies (not so distant, really, after all the mileage the *Canadian* has covered) and breakfast in the 600-foot-high revolving restaurant. Perhaps a better plan would be to take in the view from the Tower, save breakfast for later (or have it earlier on the train), and explore the downtown area on foot.

It may be hard to believe, but before 1967 the tallest building in Calgary was the Pallister Hotel, a CP property that stands next to the station and Tower. Since then, oil has built a slew of skyscrapers, many of them along 5th Avenue S.W. (The N-E-S-W division is focused upon the intersection of the Bow River with Centre Street. The river divides north from south; Centre Street east from west. Numbered streets run north and south and avenues east and west.) The architecture of the big office towers is bold and fanciful, with reflective glass and stark geometry much in evidence. The front-door names are familiar—Shell, Esso, Mobil, B.P., Gulf. The tallest and one of the most dramatic of the new buildings is the Petro Canada Tower, a dark, glass-faced structure scheduled for completion in 1984.

Petro Canada's grand-scale construction venture is illustrative, however, of an unwelcome fact of life in the Calgary of the early 1980s. During the summer of 1983, while interior finish work on the skyscraper proceeded, it was estimated that the vacancy rate upon completion would be as high as 50 percent. The reason for such dire anticipations was the same one behind the momentary arresting of the city's population growth, and the dampening of characteristic ebullience in oil towns from here to Houston. At least temporarily, there was a world petroleum glut, and no one was very enthusiastic about putting new money into exploration and development. Things moved almost too fast in the energy-crisis years of the '70s—and it's a safe bet that more than a few Calgarians would like to see a little of the old verve return to the petroleum market. No doubt it will; don't worry too much about Calgary.

There is more to central Calgary than megabucks architecture. One of the best ways to pass an afternoon here during the warmer months is to walk north on 2nd Street W. to Prince's Island Park. The park, accessible via a foot bridge over a narrow channel of the Bow River, has lovely flower gardens, meandering pathways, summer jazz concerts, and paddleboats for rent. It is a popular spot for sunbathing Calgarians, and one which offers both a fine perspective of the city and a feeling of bucolic isolation from its commotion.

Parks are important to Calgary, and have not been forgotten during the recent building spree. By city ordinance, 1 acre of park land must be set aside for every 3 acres that are developed. This commitment to open space preservation has been a great boon for Calgary's extensive river frontage. For miles, the banks of the Bow and the Elbow are lined with a variety of parks, greenbelts, and bird sanctuaries (the wharf-and-warehouse system never took over here as the Bow is not navigable by larger craft). It's possible to follow a path along the Bow River from Prince's Island Park east to the site of Old Fort Calgary. The outlines of the original fort buildings are indicated here by log posts set in the ground; there is also an interpretive center showing an interesting film on Calgary's history, and a section of the grounds has been replanted with original Third Prairie Plain vegetation. Actually, it's possible to make a beeline to Fort Calgary during the *Canadian*'s layover and see the outdoor portion of the site (the interpretive center doesn't open until 10 A.M., just a half hour before the train's departure). Just turn right on 9th Avenue as you leave the station, and keep an eye on your watch.

The view of the city from the park surrounding the Fort Calgary site is strange and dramatic. The downtown towers are no more than a few hundred yards away, yet the open space in the near and middle distance makes them look as if they spring abruptly from the prairie. Forget that there are suburbs sprawling behind you, and it looks as if you had walked across a wilderness plain to reach a glass mirage.

At the 9th Avenue bridge just past Fort Calgary, you can choose between the Bow and Elbow River paths. If you follow the Bow, you will eventually reach the 12th Street crossover to St. George's Island with its Zoo and Dinosaur Gardens (see "Points of Interest"), a riverside park called the Pearce Estate, and, eventually, the Inglewood Bird Sanctuary. Bring a city map and good walking shoes, and watch for the small blue and green trail signs.

No leave can be taken of Calgary without mention of what happens here for ten days each July. The Calgary Stampede is one of the oldest and probably the most extravagant Western expositions and rodeos in the United States or Canada. It dates back to 1912, and has accrued traditions and inspired annual anticipation of Mardi Gras proportions. It all starts with a Stampede Parade;

in the days to come there are chuckwagon races, bronco and bull riding, steer wrestling and calf roping (there is no oil-drilling event), big-name entertainment, and a midway and Indian village. Meanwhile everybody downtown stays up late and gets hung over, and the tradespeople even take something called a "Stampede Dollar" as legal tender. They cost a dollar.

In 1988, the Stampede will have a counterbalance at the other end of the calendar. Calgary will host the Winter Olympics that year, and the city will see just how much partying it can stand. The smart money says quite a lot—maybe the locals will even field a team against Texas to go out for the gold medal in sheer enthusiasm.

Points of Interest

Glengow Museum and Art Gallery. 9th Avenue and 1st Street S.E. 403-264-8300. The Glenbow is one of the premier repositories of art, artifacts, and written material (the library and archives may be visited) pertaining to the settlement of western Canada. The fur trade, Indian tribes, railroad, RCMP, and oil industry are chronicled, and there is an extensive coin collection. The Glenbow's Western paintings and sculpture are outstanding: included in the collection are works by Remington, Bierstadt, and the great wildlife painter Carl Rungius. Open daily, 10 A.M.–6 P.M. (library and archives 8 A.M.–5 P.M.); Wednesday until 8:30 P.M.

Heritage Park. 1900 Heritage Drive S.W. 403-255-1182. A celebration of prairie life as the first homesteaders knew it, circa 1880–1910. Authentic turn-of-the-century structures—dozens of them—were moved here in a re-creation of the farm and village life of the era. Have lunch or dinner in a 1906 hotel; ride a trolley or a steam train; cruise Glenmore Lake on the sternwheeler S.S. *Moyie*; see a 1949 Selkirk-class 2-10-4 locomotive, largest ever built in the British Commonwealth. Allow at least a half day for a visit to Heritage Park; they've done a nice job here and it would be a shame to rush through. Open daily, May 21 through Sept. 5, 10 A.M.–6 P.M.; weekends and holidays only from Sept. 6 to Oct. 10, same hours.

Fort Calgary. 750 9th Avenue S.E. 403-290-1875. At the site of the old North West Mounted Police Fort (see above) are outlines of fort buildings. Also interpretive displays and films dealing with Indians, Western development, and the growth of Calgary. Open Wednesday through Sunday, 10 A.M.–6 P.M.

Calgary Zoo and Prehistoric Park. 620 12th Street S.E. (St. George's Island). 403-262-8144. Over 1,100 animals in naturalistic settings. Also on the 220-acre site are an enclosed aviairy and tropical plant conservatory, a children's petting zoo, and the "dinosaur gardens," with life-size replicas of the giant lizards. Hours vary with the seasons; phone for information.

Devonian Gardens. Toronto Dominion Square, 8th Avenue S.W. (third level). A 2½-acre indoor park, complete with sculptures and fountains. A refreshing stop during a day's sightseeing.

The Calgary Tourist and Convention Bureau maintains a hospitality center at 1300 6th Avenue S.W. (403-263-8510). The smaller information center at the base of the Calgary Tower is far more convenient to train travelers.

Public Transportation

The Calgary Transit System runs city buses as well as the convenient and expanding new light rail network, which moves right along downtown streets like the trolleys of long ago. Call 403-276-7801 for schedule and route information.

Lodging

As Calgary has grown and spread out, so have its hotels. Fortunately, though, there remains a good selection close by the station and they aren't all expensive (rates vary from about $50 to $110). There's also a youth hostel at 520 7th Avenue S.E. (403-269-8239). The Calgary hostel has 112 beds in a modern, two-story cedar structure located near the Bow River and Fort Calgary.

York Hotel. 636 Centre Street S. (at 7th Avenue). 403-262-5581. The York is a small (108 rooms) hotel in the middle of downtown, just 4 blocks from the Via station. Reasonable rates; air conditioning and cable television; restaurant and laundromat on premises.

The Palliser. 133 9th Avenue. 403-266-8621. The Canadian Pacific's Calgary property was built in 1912, less than 30 years after the tracks came through. It is a stately old place, just renovated but retaining traditional charms. Some of the less expensive rooms are on the small side; if you want to splurge, go for an upper floor with northern exposure. And have some prime rib in the Rimrock Room. Right next to the station; an underground corridor connects the two buildings.

The Westin. 320 4th Avenue S.W. 403-266-1611. Modern and deluxe, like Westins everywhere, this hotel is connected by skywalk and enclosed concourses to downtown business towers. The Westin has a rooftop indoor swimming pool and sauna; also an enclosed shopping arcade and several restaurants and lounges. Rooms in the newer Tower section are priced higher than in the main wing.

Restaurants

Calgary has grown so quickly over the past decade that its restaurants have proliferated virtually at the rate of building permits. The new diversity has little tradition about it, although ambition is often enough accompanied by decent results. One time-honored local specialty that is still quite carefully attended to is Alberta beef, especially prime rib. The recently restored **Rimrock Room**, at the Palliser Hotel, is a favorite steak and prime rib spot. At the **Mad Trapper**, on 11th Avenue S.W., buffalo and other game dishes share the menu with beef. For lighter meals, two downtown choices are **Buzzards**, corner of 10th Avenue and 1st Street, and **Bistro DiVino**, 1st Street near 9th Avenue. Both are popular with a younger clientele.

One warning: Calgary has more than its share of restaurants that close on Sundays. Call ahead to avoid disappointment.

Le Flamboyant. 4018 16th Street S.W. 403-287-0060. Mauritius is an island south of Madagascar in the Indian Ocean. Sybille Melotte, owner-chef of Le Flamboyant, is one of the few North American exponents of its French-African cookery, and surely the only one in Calgary. It's worth the trip to this out-of-the-way neighborhood (call the bus information number for connections) for *bouillabaisse Mauricienne*, beef or shrimp creole, crepes and curries—all distinctly and deliciously different from the more conventional versions. Reservations are a must—this is a very small restaurant.

Pardon My Garden. 435 4th Avenue S.W. 403-265-1116. A cheery spot, big on plants and stained glass as well as Alberta beef. The steaks come with a tasty herb butter; there are also filet of salmon *en croûte*, paella for two, and a fine smoked salmon mousse. A dessert called "Oh Canada" is a crepe that includes Quebec maple syrup, B.C. strawberries, and Alberta cream.

La Chaumiere. 121 17th Avenue S.E. 403-265-1998. A reigning Calgary favorite for the Big Night Out. Rack of lamb glazed with Roquefort cheese; roast pheasant Perigourdine; veal Prince Orloff. La Chaumiere is a bastion of the classic French cooking now so frequently eclipsed by *cuisine nouvelle*. The setting is luxurious.

Calgary to Banff and Lake Louise

Only 81 miles separate Calgary from Banff (and from Banff it is just 35 miles to Lake Louise), but that short distance encompasses the most dramatic change of scenery anywhere along the route of the *Canadian*. From the fringes of the Third Prairie Plain, the train ascends into the foothills and high passes of the Rockies, en route to two storied resorts whose history goes back nearly as far as that of the railroad itself.

(An alternative to staying on the *Canadian* past Calgary is to take one of the rail diesel car trains north to the Alberta Capital of Edmonton, and to continue west from there on the *Skeena* to British Columbia points and the Pacific.)

When you leave Calgary at mid-morning on the *Canadian*, try your best to get a seat on the upper level of the dome car. Each train carries at least two (sometimes three); the last car is always a dome lounge.

As the *Canadian* pulls out of Calgary, you will look out to see soap and water sloshing aginst the windows and men with long-handled scrub brushes cleaning and rinsing the glass. If this seems like a giant car wash, it is—the better to let you see the mountain scenery ahead.

The CPR tracks follow the Bow River as it winds westward out of Calgary towards its glacial sources. There is a scattering of showy new mansions in the foothills west of Calgary, but these soon disappear along with other suburban vistas as the rolling prairie takes over. The tracks cross the Bow River at about 8 and again at about 26 miles out of Calgary, after which the river parallels the route through cattle ranching territory for 28 miles more. The Bow widens into the Ghost Reservoir (on the north, to the right of the tracks) some 34 miles beyond Calgary. Just before you get to the reservoir, between the small settlements of Mitford and Radnor, look to the north side of the tracks to see neatly compressed blocks of sulphur, which is mined nearby.

About 50 miles out of Calgary the tracks cross the Kananaskis River and then again the Bow. Now you are in the Rockies. The mountains begin to loom in the middle distance on both sides of the river and the CPR right-of-way: to the north is Mt. Laurie; to the south, left to right, Heart Mountain, Mt. McGillivray, and Pigeon Mountain. Also to the south and another 10 miles to the west, past Lac des Arcs, is the unmistakeable triple-peaked Three Sisters Mountain. A string of 9,000-foot-plus peaks makes up the Fairholme Range, to the north, while the next major peak to the south is the slab-sided, sharp-crested Mt. Rundle, looking as if it had snapped free of the earth's surface and risen to its nearly 10,000-foot height just this morning. Once you are positioned for a good look at the limestone face of Mt. Rundle, you know that the *Canadian* has entered Banff National Park—Canada's oldest, dating from 1887. It was only a year later that the CPR opened its Banff Springs Hotel. Park, hot springs, and hotel—all combined to make Banff the first of the great Rocky Mountain resorts, and one that has never lost its magic for transcontinental rail travelers.

Banff

One of W. C. Van Horne's more memorable quotes was his bluff observation concerning the opportunities for drumming up passenger business along the newly completed CPR line. "Since we cannot export the scenery," the general manager said during a visit to the Rockies near Banff, "we shall have to import the tourists." That is just what the CPR set out to do, and the Banff Springs Hotel was the keystone of its scheme.

It is impossible to talk about the history of Banff, or of the vast park which surrounds it, without turning again and yet again to the story of the CPR and its grand hotel. Of course we should make no mistake: without the mountains Banff would probably still be known by its original designation of "Siding 29," and not have been named for a distant rocky shire by the practical but nostalgic Scots who built the railway. But the Banff Springs Hotel, made of limestone cut from neighboring Mt. Rundle and by now assuming a little of the weight and stolid permanence of its parent peak, anchors this spot in the minds and affections of even those visitors who haven't slept there. Banff, put simply, is a beautiful place in the mountains where the railway leads to a big Scottish castle.

Banff National Park was created—first as Rocky Mountain National Park in 1887—in fulfillment of Queen Victoria's request that the land surrounding the newly discovered Banff hot springs be preserved in its natural state as a suitable setting for a spa. As we noted above, the hotel followed the spa in short order (the original structure was built of wood; today's "castle" dates from the 1920s) and became the focal point of the CPR's tourist promotions. The park has been expanded considerably since its inception and is quite carefully managed by the federal government. Many visitors are not aware that even the land on which the town of Banff is built is part of the park, and as such is subject to federal controls. Banff is the only town in Canada that has no local municipal government. Parks Canada is the lessor of all property on which all homes and businesses stand, and these leases must be renewed every 42 years. There is one exception, a perpetual lease: that of the Banff Springs Hotel, which is virtually coeval with the park and which stands upon part of the original CPR land grant. Although its lease may be secure, the Banff Springs must submit its rates to approval by Parks Canada, as must all Banff hostelries. Even restaurants must be approved according to types and price ranges. There are yet other controls: the 200 elk that winter on the Banff Springs golf course (rated one of the six best in the world) may not be fenced out, and the course itself must remain open to non-guests as well as guests of the hotel.

The westbound *Canadian* arrives at Banff in the early afternoon. The depot is on the other side of downtown from the Banff Springs Hotel, at the foot of Lynx and Elk streets (nearly all town thoroughfares are named for the local fauna). A little jitney called the "Happy Bus" meets the train and makes a circuit of downtown and the outskirts, stopping at the Springs and other hotels and inns.

The main thoroughfare of downtown Banff is Banff Avenue, 4 blocks from the station by way of Elk Street. It is lined with shops and restaurants, the number and diversity of which reflect not the 4,000 year-round population but the 40,000 visitors who people the streets on a typical day in summer.

Banff Avenue crosses the fast, cold Bow River and terminates at the administrative headquarters of the national park. From here, bear left and follow Spray Avenue to reach the Banff Springs Hotel.

Banff has become quite an arts center. Each summer, the Banff Festival of the Arts brings nearly 1,000 young artists for master classes with professionals, and the public is treated to an ample schedule of plays, opera, recitals, concerts, poetry readings, and art exhibits. The film and television industries have also taken to Banff: the annual film festival has become a sort of Canadian Cannes, and there is a conference each May at which TV executives screen pilots for the coming season. A lot of location shooting goes on as well—the Marilyn Monroe vehicle *River of No Return* was filmed near here, as were parts of all three recent *Superman* films and *Dr. Zhivago*.

If all this implies a bit more bustle than you would prefer at such an otherwise isolated mountain fastness—if it seems as if boosters down through the years have taken Van Horne's idea too closely to heart—just look up and around you. Banff is dwarfed and surrounded by the magnificent Rockies; they alone establish the true perspective of the place and provide the first and best reason for coming here. Anytime is a good time to do so: in the summer, there are warm, dry days, cool nights, and plenty of hiking trails to explore; visit the Parks Canada information center on Banff Avenue for maps and suggestions. In the fall, usually after the first high-altitude snows of late September, the air becomes pellucidly clear and the aspens turn bright yellow. In winter, three fine ski areas offer some of the best slopes on the continent. Package ski holidays can even be arranged to include "heliski" trips to virgin snow beyond the chairlifts and gondolas.

And you can still "take the waters," as Queen Victoria wished. Not take them, exactly, but take to them: the upper hot springs, off Mountain Avenue near the Sulphur Mountain Gondola base, draw their warmth and mineral content from as far down as 15,000 feet beneath the earth's surface, and are piped into an outdoor public bath (lockers, suits, and towels available at modest rental charges) in which the water temperature hovers at about 110 degrees F. (42 C). Try it in the afternoon and then walk the woods trails to the Banff Springs Hotel where the bagpiper is announcing teatime. Are you sufficiently relaxed?

Points of Interest

Luxton Museum. 1 Birch Avenue. 403-762-2388. A look at the lives of the Blackfeet and other Plains Indians, through examples of their tools, weapons, clothing, bead and quill work, and ceremonial artifacts; also dioramas and animal exhibits. This stockade-style building appeared in *Fort Saskatchewan* with Alan Ladd. Open daily, mid-June through September, 9 A.M.–9 P.M.; rest of year, 10 A.M.–5 P.M.

Parks Canada Natural History Museum. 93 Banff Avenue. 403-762-2388. This handsome structure, with its beautiful interior woodwork, was built in 1903 as the park's administration building. Today it houses an extensive mounted collection of local animals and birds (don't miss the 70-lb. beaver), minerals, and a piece of a tree in which are carved the initials of Hudson's Bay Company director Sir George Simpson, first white man in the Bow Valley. Open daily in dummer, 10 A.M.–6 P.M.; in fall and winter, daily except Tuesday and Wednesday, same hours.

Natural History Museum. 112 Banff Avenue. 403-762-4747. (Not to be confused with above museum.) Films, slide shows, and exhibits concentrate upon the geological development and evolution of life in the Rocky Mountains. Dinosaur bones, precious stones, and a speculative model of "Bigfoot"— the legendary apeman of the far west. Open daily at 10 A.M.; closing hours vary with seasons.

Sulphur Mountain Gondola Lift. Mountain Avenue (about 2 miles from downtown). 403-762-2523. Ride an enclosed gondola to the 7,500-foot summit of Sulphur Mountain—the views are spectacular. At the summit there are indoor and outdoor 360-degree observation decks, a restaurant, a herd of Rocky Mountain sheep, and nature trails. Bring a sweater or light jacket, even in summer. Open all year; call ahead for operating times.

Peter Whyte Gallery. 111 Bear Street. 403-762-2291. The Whyte Foundation is an important repository of Rocky Mountain lore; the Archives contain 3,000 volumes, 2,000 maps, and over 100,000 images. The ground-floor art gallery has a permanent collection of the work of major mountain artists. The foundation also manages two nearby historic homes and runs a program of films, lectures, and concerts. Open June 6 through Labor Day, 10 A.M.–6 P.M. (Archives closed Sundays); inquire about house tours.

For information on Banff and environs, stop at the Parks Canada Information Centre on Banff Avenue near Wolf Street: 403-762-3324.

Public Transportation

The "Happy Bus," a service of Brewster Transport, serves downtown Banff and nearby points of interest. Call 403-762-2241 for information.

Lodging

For years, staying in Banff meant staying at the Banff Springs Hotel. Today visitors may choose from the Springs and a score of smaller establishments. At the lower end of the price scale is the **Mountview Youth Hostel**, 760 Banff Avenue (403-762-5774). Rates for double accommodations at other Banff hotels and inns range from $45 to $140; mid to late fall is always the least expensive time to book a room.

Banff Motel. Box 279, 517 Banff Avenue. 403-762-2332/762-4041. Small and inexpensive, but with color television and some two-room kitchenette units. Off-season rates available.

Mount Royal Hotel. Box 550, Banff Avenue. 403-762-3331. Centrally located mid-sized hotel with room service; off season rates. Licensed dining room and cocktail lounge.

Banff Springs Hotel. Spray Avenue. 403-762-2211/800-268-0411. The word "baronial" has been worn thin in describing places like the Banff Springs, but it seems perfectly legitimate here. The present hotel was completed in 1926, and extensive renovations have brought it up to date without infringing on the late Scottish medieval decor. It will take you some time to learn the lay of the building and grounds: there are vast Jacobean halls and lobbies, dozens of quality shops, several lounges (a window seat in the Rundle Lounge is best), three dining rooms as well as several smaller eating places (see below), an indoor pool and health club, and of course the fine 18-hole golf course. Many of the rooms, particularly in the new Honeymoon Tower, have whirlpool baths; spend a few dollars more and specify a large room with a Bow Valley–Mt. Rundle view. Another tip: in July and August, bus tours book heavily at the Springs. In spring and late fall, rates are lower and the place is quieter. In the winter, a younger, skiing-oriented crowd predominates.

The *Canadian* in the Rockies.

Restaurants

The restaurant scene in Banff might be neatly divided between the Banff Springs Hotel and the downtown business district. There are three main dining rooms at the hotel. The **Alberta Room** is the largest, and the one most likely to be busy with tour groups in season. The **Alhambra Room** offers a Spanish-influenced menu and entertainment (usually piano and vocals). Most recommended is the **Rob Roy**, a grill room that treats Alberta beef with respect. The Rundle cut of prime rib is enormous; it's aptly named after the mountain next door. There are also several steak preparations, veal, and British Columbia salmon. The Rob Roy features a dance music combo. The **Conservatory** at the Springs, by the way, serves some of the best croissants west of Montreal.

Among the favored places in town are **Ticino**, on Wolf Street, for fondue and fettucini, and the **Paris**, on Banff Avenue—the latter especially for hearty and inexpensive lunches. But perhaps the best local reputation belongs to **Le Beaujolais**, Banff Avenue and Buffalo Street. 403-762-2712. Exquisite veal dishes; Alberta beef six delicious ways; Rocky Mountain trout. Dinner only; expensive but first rate.

Banff to Lake Louise

The ride from Banff to Lake Louise takes only about 45 minutes. As you leave Banff station, look to the left for a last glimpse of the turreted Banff Springs roof. One mile farther, to the north (right) the Vermilion Lakes offer a preview of the glacially-fed pools tucked higher in the mountains, of which Lake Louise is the sublime example. The Bow River still parallels the tracks to the south; the CPR surveyors logically followed the banks of this stream as the easiest approach to the eastern slopes of the Rockies. Not until a couple of miles past Lake Louise station does the CPR roadbed cross the Bow for the last time, leaving the river to wander north to its sources in the same glacier-shrouded massif that gives birth to the South Saskatchewan.

Past the Vermilion Lakes, the peaks of the Sawback Range—Mt. Norquay, Mt. Cory, Mt. Fifi, Cockscomb Mountain, Mt. Ishbel—crowd down upon the route from the north. Ahead, on the same side, Castle Mountain (until 1979, called Mt. Eisenhower; then rechristened with its original 1857 designation) stands massive and aloof. The erosion of alternate sedimentary layers have undermined once gentler slopes and given the mountain its sheer-sided appearance. To the south is the Bow Range and the Valley of the Ten Peaks. About 4½ miles east of Lake Louise, the highest peak visible to the south is Mt. Temple, 11,636 feet. This is also the loftiest mountain that can be seen anywhere along the *Canadian*'s route.

Lake Louise itself is not visible from the train, but a handsome log station building, constructed in 1909 to the specifications of W. C. Van Horne himself, leaves you with no doubt that you've arrived at this most storied of CPR/Via destinations. The rustic station, with its red roof and tall leaded glass windows, once had a starring role in a famous motion picture: remember the snowy country railway station scene in *Dr. Zhivago*?

Lake Louise

In August of 1883, Tom Wilson was a 23-year old packer working with the CPR survey expeditions in the Rockies. One day he asked an Indian guide about the source of the sounds of avalanches which he could hear in the mountains, and the Indian told him that the avalanches were rolling down the slopes of "snow mountain . . . above the lake of the little fishes." Wilson had never seen nor heard of this lake, and asked the Indian to take him there. A short trip brought the pair to a mile-and-a-half-long oval lake, framed at either shore by steep, symmetrical mountain slopes and set against the backdrop of "snow mountain" itself—soon to be known as Mt. Victoria, with its Victoria Glacier. "I tell you," said Wilson 50 years later, "no man has been able to describe that picture painted for the Indians by the Great Spirit. I felt puny in body but glorified in spirit and soul for I was the first white man to look upon it." Wilson named his find "Emerald Lake," after its translucent green waters, but that appellation lasted only though the printing of the first government survey map. Soon it was renamed, after the wife of Canadian Governor-General Lord Lorne and daughter of Queen Victoria. The new name was Lake Louise.

Like Banff, Lake Louise was too promising a tourist destination for the CPR to pass up. When W. C. Van Horne received reports of its beauty and accessibility from Laggan (the original name for the Lake Louise depot), he proposed that a small chalet be built there for the use of day and overnight travelers from Banff. This was done in 1890. That original log cabin burned in 1893, and was replaced by an eight-room hotel. This structure was expanded in 1900, by which time the railroad had imported Swiss guides to help initiate visitors in the ways of rock and ice climbing. Lake Louise was becoming immensely popular with both alpinists and the more sedentary class of tourist, and even more elaborate facilities would be needed to accommodate them comfortably. The Chateau as it stands today dates to 1913 and 1925, a fire having destroyed the last wooden portion in 1924.

A shuttlebus operated by Brewster-Gray Line meets the *Canadian* on its arrival at Lake Louise station early each afternoon. The steep, paved road to the lake and Chateau is only about 3½ miles long; along the way, the bus stops at several smaller hotels and cabin compounds. These provide quite decent lodgings and are somewhat less expensive than the Chateau itself, but the simple fact is that if you have come this far to Lake Louise you are very likely to want to stay *on* the lake, and the Chateau is the only hostelry that can offer that privilege.

When the bus arrives at Lake Louise, the immediate impulse on the part of most visitors is to get through luggage and check-in formalities as quickly as possible and walk around to the front of the Chateau for that first long, unobstructed look at the mountains, lake, and glacier which make up this endlessly photographed and talked-about prospect. But no photographs and no talk can adequately prepare you for the scene—and, as is suggested by Jon Whyte in the prologue to his book *Lake Louise*, it is well to put the verbal and visual fanfare out of mind and try to see it "as Tom Wilson saw it." Screen out your preconceptions, screen out as much as possible the people and man-made things around you, and you cannot be disappointed.

Lake Louise is a mile and a half in length, three-quarters of a mile in breadth, and 270 feet deep. Its jade-green color is derived from the suspension in its waters of microscopic particles of "rock flour"—a byproduct of the glacial scouring of the mountains that reflects light in such a way as to produce this strange and beautiful hue. The Victoria Glacier that feeds Lake Louise seems to be directly at hand, opposite the Chateau, but its 300- to 500-foot-thick mass is actually 6 miles away. If you rent a canoe at the Chateau dock and paddle to the far end of the lake, you can proceed for a short distance up one of the feeder streams that flows down from the glacier. Put your hand in the water and you'll wonder why any liquid this cold hasn't frozen solid.

Many visitors who come to Lake Louise by other means than the train stay only long enough to take in the view. But there's no need to lament the fact that arrival via Via necessitates an overnight stay—in fact, the knowledge that you are ticketed to depart in a day or two may well end up being grounds for disappointment. This is not a sit-on-the-veranda resort, at least not for anyone with an itch for the outdoors. Hiking trails lead in all directions from the Chateau (maps are available in the lobby). One of the easiest and most level trails follows the north shore of the lake; two others lead to rustic teahouses at Lake Agnes (1,700 feet up, 2½ miles distant) and the Plain of Six Glaciers (4½ miles west). These are a real treat. They're open in summer and serve hot soup, fresh breads, and an assortment of teas, all prepared on the premises by a live-in staff. When you have been caught in a drizzle while coming down from the top of Big Beehive, a bowl of thick pea soup at the Lake Agnes Teahouse will seem like the best meal of your life. Both teahouses are also accessible on horseback via a system of bridle trails; stables and guides are at the main parking lot.

The Chateau Lake Louise is now open in the winter, and handles a brisk ski business. Skiing Louise, Mount Norquay, and Sunshine Village all provide challenging downhill runs, with buses leaving the Chateau each morning for all three areas. The Chateau itself is the center for cross-country skiing, with a resident pro, rentals, and trails that lead around and even across the lake into the surrounding mountains. A two-week Christmas celebration makes the Chateau all the more attractive as a skiers' destination.

Lodging

Post Hotel and Pipestone Lodge. Box 69, Lake Louise. 403-522-3989. The Post Hotel is right on the Trans-Canada Highway, just a stone's throw from the station. 38 rooms; 7 with full private bath. Ski packages available; off-season rates spring and fall. Tavern and dining room (see below).

Deer Lodge. Box 100, Lake Louise. 403-522-3747; winter, 762-2057. On access road from station; five-minute walk to lake. Most rooms with private bath. Horseback riding. Cafeteria-style restaurant; outdoor cafe. Open May 24 to Sept. 30.

Chateau Lake Louise. 403-522-3511. Over $15 million in recent renovations have made the Chateau a year-round hotel and brought all facilities up to date. Indoor pool and health club, shops, several restaurants (see below), entertainment, high tea in the afternoon. Full outdoor recreation facilities. (See main description above). Modified American and full American Plans available. Be sure to reserve at least six months early for June through September accommodations; substantial savings apply mid-April through mid-June and in late October.

Restaurants

The veal, beef, and fresh trout come highly recommended at the **Post Hotel**, near the station; the prices are moderate. Guests at the Chateau Lake Louise will, however, find it convenient to dine at the Chateau as well, and three choices are offered. The **Fairview** is the smallest and most formal of the Chateau's dining rooms; dancing nightly. The **Victoria Dining Room** (table d'hote) is the largest, handling tours on the modified American plan. The newest and most interesting Chateau dining room is the **Tom Wilson Rooftop Restaurant**, named for the discoverer of Lake Louise. The views here are splendid and the ambitious menu is remarkably successful: pâtés and terrines are a specialty; entrees may include Arctic char, sole garnished with oysters and aquavit, pork tenderloin Marsala, and delicate panfried veal. Try to get a window table.

Lake Louise to Vancouver

The westbound *Canadian* leaves Lake Louise early each afternoon. Ahead lies 150 of the most spectacularly scenic railway miles in the world—and the most spectacularly difficult to build. Barely more than 5 miles west of Lake Louise is the Continental Divide, which also forms the border between Alberta and British Columbia; Stephen (named for CPR syndicate kingpin George Stephen) is, at 5,332 feet, the highest point along the *Canadian*'s route or, for that matter, at any point on a Canadian rail line. But the cresting of the Rockies does not mean that the route is all downhill from here. Following its negotiation of the Kicking Horse Pass, the *Canadian* must climb again into the Selkirk Range, and only then begin its long descent through the valleys of British Columbia to tidewater.

The Kicking Horse Pass, and the Kicking Horse River fed by the small streams that flow to the west of the Divide, received their names from an incident which occurred during Capt. John Palliser's 1857–1860 exploration of the Canadian Northwest. James Hector, surgeon and geologist attached to the expedition, was thrown from his horse while fording the river and kicked in the head by the wallowing animal. He recovered after nearly being buried by his Indian guides, who were startled when their "corpse" winked desperately at them from its grave.

In 1881, after years of government surveying which had more or less concluded that the transcontinental railway should cross the Rockies well to the north of this area, CPR director James J. Hill accepted some recently submitted opinions regarding the fertility of the southern Canadian prairies (Palliser, after his expedition, had argued that the land to the north would be more productive) and decided that the road would be built through the Kicking Horse Pass. The whole business was a gamble: in addition to pushing the line through the precipitous Kicking Horse, the CPR would have to trust that its surveyors could find a pass through the Selkirks.

The Kicking Horse problem was tackled in the least subtle way imaginable. The original roadbed through the pass was dubbed the "Big Hill." It extended for 8 miles, over a gradient of 4.4 percent or 232 feet per mile. This was exactly twice the steepness which the CPR had formerly pledged would be its maximum. Eastbound, the Big Hill taxed the most powerful steam locomotives: four of the biggest engines were needed to haul a 700-ton train to the top. Westbound, the Hill was an invitation to runaways, air brakes or no air brakes.

Although it had originally been considered a temporary engineering expedient, the Big Hill survived until 1908. That year, the problem of the Kicking Horse Pass was more elegantly solved by the completion of the famous spiral tunnels. These constitute an enormous, elongated figure eight. Westbound trains enter the upper spiral tunnel, which burrows into the side of Cathedral Mountain and loops around so that its exit actually lies lower and farther east than its entrance. Given a long enough train, this means that the engine and first cars could emerge beneath the last cars and the caboose. The procedure is repeated in the second spiral tunnel which bores through the face of Mount Ogden, after which the westerly descent through the valley of the Kicking Horse can be resumed at a far less perilous grade.

Field, British Columbia, is the first stop after the spiral tunnels and the gateway to Yoho National Park. Beyond Field the Van Horne Range stretches to the north, and the Kicking Horse River continues its course along the north side of the track until Ottertail; then along the south side. The *Canadian* follows the sharp dogleg of the Kicking Horse as it turns to the northwest, where it meets the powerful Columbia River at Golden. The tracks parallel the Columbia for some 30 miles, crossing the river at Donald and leaving it behind at Beavermouth to head south along the valley of the Beaver River. Here begins the ascent into the Selkirks, which posed such an awful challenge to the progress of the CPR.

The pass through the Selkirks was found by a cocky, stoic American, Major A. B. Rogers. Rogers had been an Indian fighter and a surveyor on the prairies before James J. Hill hired him to solve the Selkirk problem early in 1881, promising the Major that the pass, if found, would be named after him. On July 24, 1882, Rogers's perseverence and sheer contrariness paid off: having approached the Selkirks from the east in an area corresponding to his previous western-slope explorations, the Major reached the 4,500-foot floor of a valley that promised to offer a feasible, if difficult, passage through the mountains. To this day, that grudging interruption in the great barrier of the Selkirks is known as Rogers' Pass.

Like the Big Hill, Rogers' Pass was a workable but impermanent solution. In 1910, a snowslide in the pass killed 58 people, and soon after work was begun on the 5-mile Connaught Tunnel, through which trains travel today. The original Rogers' Pass route is used by the Trans–Canada Highway, but only in the summer.

The *Canadian* emerges from the Connaught Tunnel into the valley of the Illecillewaet River. Now you are in Glacier National Park. The majestic Illecillewaet Glacier itself is visible to the south as the train passes through Glacier (not a scheduled stop); the snowsheds and tunnels which punctuate this section of track are reminders that this valley still belongs to the mountains and glaciers around it, and not to anything so insubstantial as a transcontinental railway. (The snowsheds, an absolutely necessary appurtenance along here, were conceived after slides continually obliterated the newly built track in the 1880s.)

Just past Revelstoke, the *Canadian* leaves the Illecillewaet behind and again crosses the Columbia, which has looped far to the north since we last saw it in the vicinity of Beavermouth. At Revelstoke there is a half-hour layover (the time is about 6 P.M.); you can get off the train and see the memorial plaques to Major Rogers and the "Royal Hudson" class of steam locomotives.

After Revelstoke the *Canadian* follows the Eagle River. About 14 miles after you pass a brief series of snowsheds, look to the north (right) side of the track at Craigellachie to see the stone cairn which marks the spot where the final spike of the CPR was driven into place on Nov. 7, 1885. This spike was or iron, not gold. Evening stops beyond Craigellachie are Sicamous (the name means "places cut through") and Salmon Arm, both on the shores of meandering Shushwap Lake. Shushwap Lake is the source of the South Thompson River, along which the *Canadian* travels towards Kamloops through the last hours of summer daylight.

During the night, the *Canadian* follows the shores of Kamloops Lake and the Thompson River to the Thompson's meeting with the mighty Fraser, which drains nearly 90,000 square miles over its 785-mile length and is the greatest of the salmon-spawning rivers of the Northwest. Earlier schedules for the *Canadian* allowed some daylight views of the long, canyonlike valley of the Fraser, but with arrival in Vancouver currently scheduled for 7 A.M., there is no daylight time in which to see the more spectacular portions of the route (the same is unfortunately true of the eastbound *Canadian*, which leaves Vancouver late in the evening.

The CPR line between Savona, on Kamloops Lake, and Port Moody, at the mouth of the Fraser, was actually under construction before the syndicate which took responsibility for the transcontinental line was formed in 1881. As the building of the link with the east was one of the conditions on which British Columbia accepted membership in the Canadian confederation, it behooved the government in Ottawa to get started on the project as soon as possible. The contract for the Fraser Canyon section went to an American named Andrew Onderdonk, who continued as subcontractor after the CPR syndicate took over. Onderdonk employed a great many Chinese laborers on his crews; this was largely responsible for the strong Chinese presence in Vancouver. The situation parallels that of the construction of the Central Pacific west from California as the impetus for Chinese settlement in San Francisco.

The Chinese workers along the Fraser had as hard a time as anyone who helped build the CPR, with the possible exception of the men who labored north of the Great Lakes on the Canadian Shield. Like the Shield laborers, the Chinese had to contend daily with dynamite, as well as with the sheer precipices that rise above the river. From these precipices the right-of-way had to be blasted, chiseled, almost literally clawed. A great many lives were lost in building the road over which the *Canadian* now carries its comfortably sleeping passengers to Vancouver.

The construction of another Fraser Canyon roadbed, by the Canadian Northern Pacific Railway in 1912 and 1913, was responsible for perhaps the greatest single disaster ever to befall the British Columbia salmon fishery. The company had hurled tons of rock debris into the Fraser at Hell's Gate, a narrow place in the river about 20 miles north of Yale. In 1913, the Sockeye salmon migration up the Fraser was the heaviest ever. During the high water of June and July the first few salmon made it through Hell's Gate relatively unimpeded, but when the later migration reached the choked-off point, it was stymied by rock and impossibly fast water. Only 30,000 salmon made it through to Seton Lake that year; in 1909, more than one million had gotten through Hell's Gate. In 1914, a rock slide starting high above the new tracks carried away 50 feet of tunnel and slowed the Fraser to a creek-like trickle. It took two years of work to clear the river, and more than 20 years passed before normal migration patterns recovered from the tremendous attrition caused by the Hell's Gate disaster.

As the sun rises west of Mission City, you will see a markedly different terrain than that which the *Canadian* traveled through during the previous evening. The valley here is broad, agricultural—but with the suburbs of Vancouver not far off. If the early colonists at the mouth of the Fraser had had their way, the terminal metropolis would have been closer still; Port Moody, it was assumed, would be the western railhead of the CPR.

But Port Moody was passed by—Van Horne and the other CPR officials decided that there was far more land for rail yards available at a place called Gastown, at the mouth of Burrard Inlet. The track crews pressed on, to a nascent tidewater settlement that would soon surrender that picturesque but wholly undignified handle and begin to call itself by the name Van Horne had picked out: Vancouver.

Vancouver

The younger the city, the more guileless it is likely to be about its image. Vancouver, the colossus of Canada's west coast, will be only 100 years old in 1986. It is one of the main outlets for the raw materials produced in British Columbia, a province richer in natural resources than most of the nations of the world. Timber, minerals, fish—all of these make for a city alive with relentless, swaggering trade, a city of busy freight yards and docks. Yet it remains one of the most beautiful urban centers in North America.

Vancouver occupies a peninsula bound by English Bay and the Burrard Inlet at the point where the mighty Fraser River empties into the sea. Captain George Vancouver arrived here on the H.M.S. *Discovery* in 1792. Less than a century later, the CPR chose Vancouver as the western terminus of its trans-Canadian railway, thus assuring the young town's future as a trading metropolis. It is no coincidence that the arrival of the first transcontinental train and municipal incorporation both took place in the same year—1886.

Vancouver is still an important railroad city, both as the western terminus for Via's transcontinental trains and as the southern terminus for the British Columbia Railway, which provides service from its North Vancouver station (1311 W. First Avenue) to Prince George, in the province's north-central interior, along a route completed as recently as 1956.

Despite Vancouver's youth and mercantile exuberance, the city's aspect is cosmopolitan and sophisticated. It has already matured to the point that restoration of its oldest quarter has been accomplished. This area is called "Gastown," not after its street lighting but in honor of a talkative early settler named "Gassy Jack" Deighton. One of the most interesting attractions here is the Gastown Steam Clock (corner of Cambie and Water streets), a new and beautifully complex instrument that translates steam from underground heating lines into the time of day. Other downtown districts worth visiting include Chinatown, the second largest (after San Francisco) Oriental settlement in North America, and "Robsonstrasse," a stretch of downtown Robson Street lined with the sort of toy shops, pastry houses, and delicatessens you'd expect in Hamburg, Zurich, or Vienna.

The mild Vancouver climate has made this a garden city, renowned for its parks. Stanley Park (see "Points of Interest") is the largest and most varied, although flowers and greenery turn up in every neighborhood.

When all is said and done, though, much of the excitement of Vancouver can be traced to its proximity to what Canadians call "the bush." When you look from one of the downtown towers toward the encircling peaks of the Coast Range or watch a ferry steam off toward the dark, forested immensity of Vancouver Island, you cannot help but recall that this city is but an outpost of civilization at the margin of one of the world's great wilderness empires.

Points of Interest

Stanley Park. A 1,000-acre preserve that occupies an entire peninsula extending into Burrard Inlet. Created not long after the city's founding, it represents an attempt to preserve the rain forest that originally covered the site of Vancouver. While much of this forest remains wilderness, Stanley Park is the home of several of Vancouver's prime visitor attractions. These include the **Stanley Park Zoo** (604-681-1141), open every day, 9 A.M.–5 P.M.; the **Vancouver Public Aquarium** (604-685-3364), which features killer and beluga whale and harbor seal shows, open every day, 10 A.M.–6 P.M.; the **Lost Lagoon Bird Sanctuary; Lumberman's Arch;** and a number of fine totem poles. The park has many miles of walking trails and lovely views in every direction.

Van Dusen Botanical Gardens. Thirty-seventh Avenue and Oak Street. 604-266-7194. Native and exotic plants; also **MacMillan Bloedel Place,** which focuses on the forest ecology and logging industry of British Columbia. Gardens open every day, 10 A.M.–6 P.M. (to 9 P.M., July and August); MacMillan Bloedel Place (604-263-2688), open same hours; closed Saturday mid-October through March and major winter holidays.

Museum of Anthropology. University of British Columbia, Point Grey. N.W. Marine Drive. 604-228-3825. Comprehensive collection of northwest-coast Indian art and artifacts; also an impressive collection of totem poles, both in a 60-foot-high indoor gallery and an outdoor park. Open Wednesday through Sunday, noon–5 P.M.; Tuesday, noon–9 P.M. Closed Monday. Also on the UBC campus are a fine arts gallery, gardens, and museum of geology. Main information number is 604-228-3131.

The New Vancouver Art Gallery. 750 Hornby Street. 604-682-5621. Especially strong in regional contemporary art. Performing arts; free lunchtime concerts. Hours to be announced; phone for information.

Bloedel Conservatory. Queen Elizabeth Park, Thirty-third Avenue and Cambie Street. 604-872-5513. A huge triodetic dome houses separate desert, rain forest, and tropical zones. 400 varieties of plants; 50 bird species. Open every day, 10 A.M.–9:30 P.M.; closes 5:30 P.M. in late fall and winter.

Royal Hudson Steam Train. B.C. Railway, foot of Pemberton Street. 604-987-5211. A fine old restored steam locomotive pulls observation, bar, and passenger cars along scenic Howe Sound to Squamish. You can combine the trip with either an outgoing or return passage on the modern ferry *Brittania;* the entire train-boat excursion takes about 6½ hours. Advance reservations are necessary. Tickets may be purchased at Woodward's or Eaton's stores, at Vancouver Ticket Centre outlets, or from B.C. Railway (number above) or Harbour Ferries Ltd. (604-687-9558). May through early September.

The Greater Vancouver Convention and Visitors' Bureau is at 650 Burrard Street. Call 604-682-2222 for information.

Public Transportation

Vancouver's buses are run by the Metro Transit System. Call 604-324-3211 for schedule and fare information. This being a water city, ferries are also important. British Columbia Ferries (to Horseshoe Bay, Nanaimo, and Sechelt

Peninsula), 604-669-1211; Burrard Inlet Ferry Service (Seabus across Burrard Inlet), 604-324-3211.

Lodging

Vancouver offers a full range of downtown accommodations, with prices increasing for locations near English Bay and Stanley Park. Rates vary from about $35 to $100. All hotels listed here are located on the downtown peninsula; most are between 1 and 2 miles from the station.

Austin Motor Hotel. 1221 Granville Street. 604-685-7235. Nothing fancy, but recently renovated. Near Granville Mall; 1-mile walk to Stanley Park. Most rooms with bath. Restaurant, lounge.

Blue Horizon. 1225 Robson Street. 604-688-1411. 31-story tower convenient to Robsonstrasse shops. Studio suites with dinette and refrigerator. Balconies with view. Restaurant. Indoor pool, sauna.

Hotel Georgia. 801 W. Georgia Street. 604-682-5566. A deluxe downtown hotel near the Granville Mall. In-room movies. Fine Georgia Sea Garden restaurant; also pub and patio lounge with view.

Hotel Vancouver. 900 W. Georgia Street. 604-684-3131. Stately, refined, and luxurious. Occupies entire block. Upper rooms and suites offer fine views; all are elegantly furnished. All services. Excellent restaurants (see below), several lounges.

Restaurants

Vancouver has more than 1,500 restaurants, representing the cuisine of 20 nationalities. There is plenty of good Chinese food here, and Japanese establishments are becoming popular. Seafood—especially fresh Pacific salmon—is also recommended.

Yick Fung. 137 E. Pender Street. 604-682-1514. A favorite of Chinatown residents. Extensive menu of authentic dishes. Try the steamed buns and egg swirl soup with black mushrooms. Abalone in season.

Eddie's Place for Fish. 1177 W. Hastings Street. 604-684-6544. The seafood basics, fresh, served at tables overlooking Burrard Inlet. Specialties depend upon seasonal catch.

The Timber Club. Hotel Vancouver, 900 W. Georgia Street. 604-684-3131. An old address, but an innovative menu, based upon the "nouvelle cuisine" of French chef Paul Bocuse. Also at the Hotel Vancouver is the Panorama Roof Restaurant, with the views you'd expect from the name.

Appendix B: Amtrak's Telephone Network

The following numbers are for fare and regular schedule information, and for making reservations. (Arrival and departure information numbers are listed below.) For reservations and information at all other points in the United States, call 800-USA-RAIL.

Alabama	800-874-2800
Arizona	
Flagstaff	(602) 526-2710
all other points	800-421-8320
Arkansas	800-874-2775
California	
Bakersfield	(805) 327-7863
Davis	(916) 753-6300
Fresno	(209) 252-8253
Los Angeles	(213) 624-0171
Oakland	(415) 982-8512
Sacramento	(916) 485-8506
San Francisco	(415) 982-8512
San Jose	(408) 280-6992
San Luis Obispo	(805) 541-5028
Santa Barbara	(805) 687-6848
all other points	800-648-3850
Colorado	
Denver	(303) 893-3911
all other points	800-421-8320
Connecticut	
Bridgeport	(203) 367-8002
Hartford	(203) 525-4580
New Haven	(203) 777-4002
New London	(203) 442-5910
Stamford	(203) 964-1345
all other points	800-523-5720
Delaware	
Wilmington	(302) 658-1575
all other points	800-523-5700
District of Columbia	(202) 484-7540
Florida	
Fort Lauderdale	(305) 776-6460
Hollywood	(305) 776-6460
Jacksonville	(904) 731-1600
Miami	(305) 371-7738
Ocala	(904) 629-8626
Orlando	(305) 843-8460
St. Petersburg	(813) 822-0175
Tampa	(813) 225-1020
Winter Haven	(813) 299-7725
all other points	800-342-2520
Georgia	
Atlanta	(404) 688-4417
Savannah	(912) 232-0026
all other points	800-874-2800
Idaho	800-421-8320
Illinois	
Alton	(618) 463-0091
Bloomington	(309) 827-8540
Carbondale	(618) 549-5353
Champaign	(217) 352-5922
Chicago	(312) 558-1075
Galesburg	(309) 342-1191
Glenview	(312) 998-6633

Homewood	(312) 799-2811
Joliet	(815) 723-4425
Kankakee	(815) 935-1188
Springfield	(217) 753-3651
all other points	800-972-9147
Indiana	
Indianapolis	(317) 632-1905
all other points	800-621-0353
Iowa	800-621-0353
Kansas	800-421-8320
Kentucky	800-874-2775
Louisiana	
New Orleans	(504) 525-1179
all other points	800-874-2800
Maine	800-523-5731
Maryland	
Baltimore	(301) 539-2112
all other points	800-523-5700
Massachusetts	
Boston	(617) 482-3660
all other points	800-523-5720
Michigan	
Ann Arbor	(313) 663-6051
Battle Creek	(616) 968-8517
Detroit	(313) 963-7396
Jackson	(517) 787-9600
Kalamazoo	(616) 385-2993
Lansing	(517) 372-7638
Niles	(616) 684-7200
Area Code 906 pts	800-621-0317
all other points	800-621-0353
Minnesota	
Duluth	(218) 727-0477
Minneapolis	(612) 339-2382
St. Paul	(612) 339-2382
all other points	800-621-0317
Mississippi	
Jackson	(601) 969-4052
all other points	800-874-2800
Missouri	
Kansas City	(816) 421-4725
St. Louis	(314) 241-8806
all other points	800-621-0317
Montana	800-421-8320
Nebraska	800-421-8320
Nevada	
Reno	(702) 323-4375
all other points	800-421-8320
New Hampshire	800-523-5720
New Jersey	
Newark	(201) 643-1770
New Brunswick	(201) 246-1970
Princeton	(609) 921-8527
Trenton	(609) 394-2604
all other points	800-523-5700

New Mexico
  Albuquerque . . . . (505) 242-7816
  all other points 800-421-8320
New York
  Albany . . . . (518) 465-9971
  Buffalo . . . . (716) 856-1229
  Long Island points
  (Area Code 516 only)
  . . . . (516) 981-9100
  New York City
  (all 5 boroughs) . . . . (212) 736-4545
  Rochester . . . . (716) 454-5210
  Schenectady . . . . (518) 465-9971
  Syracuse . . . . (315) 422-8055
  Utica . . . . (315) 797-5510
  other Area 716 points
  800-523-5720
  all other points 800-523-5700
North Carolina
  Raleigh . . . . (919) 832-5503
  all other points 800-874-2800
North Dakota 800-421-8320
Ohio
  Cincinnati . . . . (513) 579-8506
  Cleveland . . . . (216) 861-0105
  Toledo . . . . (419) 243-1084
  all other points 800-621-0317
Oklahoma
  Oklahoma City . . . . (405) 943-5337
  all other points 800-421-8320
Oregon
  Eugene . . . . (503) 485-1092
  Portland . . . . (503) 241-4290
  Salem . . . . (503) 378-0041
  all other points 800-421-8320
Pennsylvania
  Harrisburg . . . . (717) 232-3916
  Lancaster . . . . (717) 392-6717
  Philadelphia . . . . (215) 824-1600
  Pittsburgh . . . . (412) 621-4850
  all other points 800-562-5380
Rhode Island
  Providence . . . . (401) 751-5416
  all other points 800-523-5720
South Carolina
  Charleston . . . . (803) 723-6679
  Columbia . . . . (803) 779-7181
  Florence . . . . (803) 665-7120
  all other points 800-874-2800
South Dakota 800-421-8320
Tennessee 800-874-2800
Texas
  Fort Worth . . . . (817) 336-1010
  Houston . . . . (713) 757-1713
  Temple . . . . (817) 773-1040
  all other points 800-421-8320
Utah
  Ogden . . . . (801) 479-0772
  all other points 800-421-8320
Vermont 800-523-5720
Virginia
  Richmond . . . . (804) 358-4936
  all other points 800-523-5720
Washington
  Seattle . . . . (206) 464-1930
  Spokane . . . . (509) 747-1069
  Tacoma . . . . (206) 272-0757
  all other points 800-421-8320
West Virginia 800-523-5720
Wisconsin
  Milwaukee . . . . (414) 933-3081
  all other points 800-421-0353
Wyoming 800-421-8320
Call Amtrak Toll-Free From Canada
From the provinces of Ontario except from

Area Code 807) and Quebec . 800-263-8130
From all other points in Canada
. . . . 800-263-8170
Metrophone—for Metroliner Service reservations and information only.
New York City . . . . (212) 736-3967
Philadelphia . . . . (215) 824-4224
Washington, DC . . . . (202) 484-5580
States of Connecticut, Massachusetts, New Hampshire, Rhode Island, Vermont, Virginia, West Virginia 800-523-8760
States of Delaware, Maryland, New Jersey, New York (except area 716) . 800-523-8720
Pennsylvania only 800-562-6990
Newark, Metropark, and Trenton
. . . . 800-523-8720
Wilmington, Baltimore, and Beltway
Station 800-523-8720

Special Teletypewriter Service For Deaf Persons.
Deaf persons with access to a teletypewriter may call the following toll-free 800-numbers to communicate with Amtrak's special teletypewriter service to receive information and make reservations for travel: Nationwide (except Pennsylvania) 800-523-6590
Pennsylvania only 800-562-6990

Today's Train Arrival and Departure Information
The special telephone numbers listed below have been installed for your convenience to provide Amtrak *train arrival and departure information* at the cities indicated. If you do not find your city in the list below, arrival and departure information may be obtained by dialing the telephone number listed for the city or state in which the station is located in the Reservation and Information Telephone Numbers section above. *Please do not use these numbers for making reservations or requesting fares and train information.*
Albany-Rensselaer, NY
. . . . (518) 462-5763
Buffalo, N.Y. . . . . (716) 683-8440
Carbondale, IL . . . . (618) 457-3388
Dallas, TX . . . . (214) 651-8341
Denver, CO . . . . (303) 534-2371
Detroit, MI . . . . (313) 965-0314
Ft. Lauderdale, FL . . . . . . (305) 463-8251
Ft. Worth, TX . . . . (817) 332-2931
Fresno, CA . . . . (209) 486-7651
Fullerton, CA . . . . (714) 992-0530
Glenview, IL . . . . (312) 724-2530
Houston, TX . . . . (713) 224-1577
Hudson, NY . . . . (518) 828-3379
Jacksonville, FL . . . . (904) 768-1553
Joliet, IL . . . . (815) 727-9279
Kansas City, MO . . . . (816) 421-3622
Miami, FL . . . . (305) 691-0125
New Orleans, LA . . . . (504) 528-1600
Orlando, FL . . . . (305) 843-7611
Richmond, VA . . . . (804) 264-9194
Rochester, NY . . . . (716) 454-2894
St. Louis, MO . . . . (314) 231-0061
St. Petersburg, FL . . . . (813) 522-9475
San Diego, CA . . . . (714) 239-9021
Schenectady, CA . . . . (518) 346-8651
Springfield, IL . . . . (217) 753-2013
Syracuse, NY . . . . (315) 463-1135
Tacoma, WA . . . . (206) 627-8141
Tampa, FL . . . . (813) 229-2473
Utica, NY . . . . (315) 797-8962

Appendix C:
Suggested Reading

Anderson, Craig T. *Amtrak Annual*. San Francisco: Rail Transportation Archives (published in annual editions).

Beebe, Lucius. *High Iron: A Book of Trains*. New York: Bonanza Books, c1938.

Beebe, Lucius. *Highball: A Pageant of Trains*. New York: Appleton, Century, Crofts, c1945.

Beebe, Lucius. *The Overland Limited*. Berkeley: Howell-North Books, 1963.

Berton, Pierre. *The National Dream / The Last Spike*. Toronto: McClelland and Stewart Ltd., 1974.

Botkin, B. A., and Alvin F. Harlow, eds. *A Treasury of Railroad Folklore*. New York: Bonanza Books (reprint of 1953 edition).

Carper, Robert S. *Focus: The Railroad in Transition*. South Brunswick and New York: A. S. Barnes and Company, c1968.

Coo, Bill. *Scenic Rail Guide to Central and Atlantic Canada*. New York: Zeotrope, 1983.

Coo, Bill. *Scenic Rail Guide to Western Canada*. New York: Zeotrope, 1983.

Dubin, Arthur D. *Some Classic Trains*. Milwaukee: Kalmbach Books, 1964.

Hart, E. J. *The Selling of Canada: the CPR and the Beginnings of Canadian Tourism*. Banff, Alberta: Altitude Publishing Company, 1983.

Holbrook, Stewart H. *The Story of American Railroads*. New York: Crown/American Legacy Press, 1981 (reprint of 1947 edition).

Lavellée, Omar. *Van Horne's Road*. Railfare Enterprises, 1974.

Theroux, Paul. *The Great Railway Bazaar*. Boston: Houghton Mifflin, 1975.

Theroux, Paul. *The Old Patagonian Express*. Boston: Houghton Mifflin, 1979.

Whitaker, Rogers E. M. and Anthony Hiss. *All Aboard with E. M. Frimbo*. New York: Penguin Books, 1978.

White, John H. *The American Railroad Passenger Car*. Baltimore; Johns Hopkins University Press, 1978.

Whyte, Jon, and Carole Harmon. *Lake Louise: A Diamond in the Wilderness*. Banff, Alberta: Altitude Publishing Company, 1982.

General Index

Index to Routes and Cities

About the Author

Trains are a part of William G. Scheller's family history. His great-grandfather built locomotives, and his mother worked in the freight offices of the Erie. He was, in fact, very nearly born on an Erie local. Although Scheller's own railroad career was confined to a short stint on a Vermont track-repair crew in 1971, he traveled over 34,000 miles by train to research this guide.

A free-lance writer, William Scheller is the author of several books in the Appalachian Mountain Club's *Country Walks* series, and the Massachusetts correspondent and Boston area editor for Fodor's travel guides. He has published more than 70 magazine articles on a wide variety of subjects.

Enjoy bed & breakfast on the East Coast with . . .

The New England Guest House Book, 1984 Edition, Corinne Madden Ross, $7.95 paper. 207 lodgings in Maine, Connecticut, Massachusetts, New Hampshire, Rhode Island and Vermont.

The Mid-Atlantic Guest House Book, Corinne Madden Ross, $7.95 paper. 118 lodgings in New York, New Jersey, Pennsylvania, Delaware, Maryland and West Virginia.

The Southern Guest House Book, 1984 Edition, Corinne Madden Ross, $7.95 paper. 107 lodgings in Alabama, Florida, Georgia, Louisiana, Mississippi, North Carolina, South Carolina, Tennessee, Virginia and the District of Columbia.

The Best Bed & Breakfast in the World, 1984 Edition, Sigourney Welles & Jill Darbey, $10.95 paper. More than 800 personally recommended establishments in Great Britain and Ireland with a special section on London and tear-out booking forms.

Copies of these and other East Woods Press books are available from your bookseller or directly from The East Woods Press, 429 East Boulevard, Charlotte, N.C. 28203. (704) 334-0897. For orders **only,** call toll-free (800) 438-1242, ext. 102. In N.C. (800) 532-0476.

Please send me the following book(s)_____ _____

_____

_____

_____

I am including $1.50 shipping and handling per book.
Enclosed is my check, Visa or MasterCard information

_____

Please send a complete catalog of East Woods Press
books_____
Send to:

_____

_____

_____

East Woods Press Books

Order from:

The East Woods Press
429 East Boulevard
Charlotte, NC 28203